FROM CASE TO LAW

A STUDY ON HOW CASES FULFIL THE ROLE OF A SOURCE OF LAW IN THE NETHERLANDS AND ITS IMPLICATIONS FOR CHINA AND COMPARATIVE LAW

William Jing Guo

AF763741

Routledge
Taylor & Francis Group
LONDON AND NEW YORK

The publication of this book is made possible by a grant from the Netherlands Organization for Scientific Research (NWO) under project number 017.007.085.

First published in 2015 by Amsterdam University Press Ltd.

Published 2025 by Routledge
4 Park Square, Milton Park, Abingdon, Oxon OX14 4RN
605 Third Avenue, New York, NY 10158

Routledge is an imprint of the Taylor & Francis Group, an informa business

© William Jing Guo / Taylor & Francis Group 2015

All rights reserved. No part of this book may be reprinted or reproduced or utilised in any form or by any electronic, mechanical, or other means, now known or hereafter invented, including photocopying and recording, or in any information storage or retrieval system, without permission in writing from the publishers.

Trademark notice: Product or corporate names may be trademarks or registered trademarks, and are used only for identification and explanation without intent to infringe.

ISBN: 9789056297596 (pbk)
ISBN: 9781003696100 (ebk)

Cover design: Coördesign, Leiden

For Product Safety Concerns and Information please contact our EU representative: GPSR@taylorandfrancis.com
Taylor & Francis Verlag GmbH, Kaufingerstraße 24, 80331 München, Germany

Table of Contents

INTRODUCTION

1. Background and research questions

Since the beginning of the 20th century, a considerable body of English-language comparative law literature has emerged that studies the role of cases in civil law jurisdictions.[1] One of the reasons why this topic has attracted and still attracts so much academic attention is that the question whether cases are recognized as a source of law used to be regarded as a key criterion for the distinction between the common law and the civil law.[2] Originally, it was accepted that the doctrine of precedent is a unique feature of the common law legal family, i.e. a crucial distinction between the common law and the civil law is that judges in common law jurisdictions are bound by precedents whereas cases in civil law jurisdictions have no particular normative force beyond the litigating parties, so that judges are free to deviate from previous decisions.[3] Subsequently, many scholarly writings emerged that refute or qualify this view.[4] These studies demonstrate that in many continental European civil law jurisdictions cases have acquired such a highly influential status in adjudication practice that judges are in fact bound by certain types of previous court decisions.[5] These findings triggered some scholars to argue that the common

[1] See e.g. Deák 1934, Goodhart 1934, Lipstein 1946, Meijers 1951, Dainow 1966, Silving 1966, Dawson 1970, Dainow 1974, Rudden 1974, Lawson 1977, Cappelletti 1981, Van Caenegem 1987, MacCormick & Summers 1997b, Zweigert & Kötz 1998, p. 256-275, Adams 1999, Eng 2000, Butler 2002, Baade 2002a, Baade 2002b, Hondius 2003, Lundmark 2003, Hondius 2004, Hondius 2007b and Komárek 2013.

[2] See e.g. Deák 1934, p. 340 and Vogenauer 2006, p. 873.

[3] See e.g. Goodhart 1934.

[4] See e.g. Lipstein 1946, p. 34-35, Loussouarn 1958, p. 255, Dainow 1966, p. 426, Baudouin 1974, p. 12, Van Caenegem 1987, p. 40 and MacCormick & Summers 1997c, p. 2.

[5] See e.g. Siving 1966, p. 200, Yiannopoulos 1974, p. 76, Merryman 1974, p. 194-196, Kiel & Göttingen 1997, p. 24-25 and Zweigert & Kötz 1998, p. 263.

law and the civil law legal families are converging.[6] Moreover, since the 1980s, these findings have been used in China, where cases are not officially recognized as a source of law, to justify experiments that seek to increase the use of cases in adjudication practice.[7]

Thanks to the scholarly works in this field, we have gained a much richer and more nuanced understanding of the role of cases in civil law jurisdictions than a century ago. However, despite the progress that has been made, it is still too early to conclude that all important issues and aspects in this field have been thoroughly explored. In fact, the existing literature in this field focuses largely on the question whether cases have force in court practice in civil law jurisdictions and if so, what kind of force they have and how this force resembles or differs from the binding force of precedents in common law legal systems under the doctrine of *stare decisis*.[8] The dominant conclusion is that in practice cases function as a source of law in many European civil law jurisdictions, and that the actual force that certain types of cases have in these civil law jurisdictions is quite similar to the binding force that precedents carry in common law jurisdictions.[9] However, the question *how* cases actually fulfil the role of a source of law in a civil law jurisdiction has not yet been thoroughly explored. Some scholarly writings did touch upon this how-question, but they tend to focus chiefly on the role of judges and court-related institutions in the functioning of case law in civil law jurisdictions, whereas the contribution by other relevant actors, institutions and practices such as legal scholars, case publication and legal education to the operation of case law in civil law jurisdictions rarely attracts equal

---

[6] See e.g. Zweigert & Kötz 1998, p. 271 and MacCormick & Summers 1997a, p. 531-535. For different views see e.g. Cappelletti 1981, p. 66, Adams 1999, p. 465-466, Haazen 2007, p. 228 and Komárek 2012, p. 67.
[7] See e.g. Zeng 2004, p. 63-64 and Zhang 2004, p. 99, 100, 105.
[8] See e.g. Silving 1966, Lund 1997, Zweigert & Kötz 1998, p. 256-275, Eng 2000 and Taruffo 2007.
[9] See e.g. Lawson 1977, p. 82-83, David 1984, p. 116 and p. 136, Van Caenegem 1987, p. 40, MacCormick & Summers 1997a, p. 531-533 and Zweigert & Kötz 1998, p. 263.

scholarly attention.[10] This emphasis on the role of judges and court-related institutions is not entirely surprising, once one realizes that the current studies on the role of cases in civil law jurisdictions are dominated by the paradigm of the common law doctrine of *stare decisis*.[11] It seems to have become a common practice among scholars who study the role of cases in civil law jurisdictions to analyse the functioning of case law in civil law jurisdictions by adopting common law concepts such as *stare decisis*, *ratio decidendi*, *obiter dictum*, binding authority, persuasive authority, distinguishing, overruling and so on.[12] In other words, existing studies on the role of cases in civil law jurisdictions tend to examine case law in civil law jurisdictions from the perspective of the common law doctrine of precedent. As judges play a prominent and decisive role in the functioning of case law in common law jurisdictions, it is not surprising that scholarly writings that rely heavily on the common law paradigm concentrate largely on judges and court-related institutions while studying the role of cases in civil law jurisdictions.

This study proposes that the question how cases actually fulfil the role of a source of law in a civil law jurisdiction is worth careful investigation, as the answer to this question can yield insights that may further enrich our understanding of the role of cases in civil law jurisdictions. Answering this how-question can,

---

[10] See e.g. MacCormick & Summers 1997b and Hondius 2007b. This is of course not to say that aspects such as the role of legal scholars in the functioning of case law, the use of cases in legal education in civil law jurisdictions and the way cases are published have never been discussed in the existing literature, but it should be observed that references to these aspects in the existing literature tend to be rather brief and scattered. For scholarly writings that mention the role of legal scholars in the functioning of case law in civil law jurisdictions see e.g. Yiannopoulos 1974, p. 77, Taruffo 1997, p. 457 and Hondius 2007a, p. 21. For publications that have touched upon the case publication in civil law jurisdictions see e.g. Deák 1934, p 341 footnote 8 and p. 342 footnote 9, Lawson 1977, p. 84 and Taruffo 1997, p. 451. For writings that have paid attention to the use of cases in legal education in civil law jurisdictions see e.g. Deák 1934, p. 354 and Dainow 1966, p. 428-430.

[11] See the analysis in Komárek 2013.

[12] See e.g. Lipstein 1946, p. 35-36, Merryman 1974, p. 194, Eng 2000, p. 278-279, Hondius 2003, p. 417, Haazen 2007, p. 237-238 and p. 244.

for example, reveal fresh insights for the debate on the question whether the common law and the civil law legal families are converging.[13] If it turns out that the result that cases function as a source of law in civil law jurisdictions is achieved through a different way from what leads to the prominent status of precedents in common law jurisdictions, doubt can be cast on the observation that the civil law and the common law are converging.[14]

Moreover, it is worth noting that not in all codified legal systems cases have become a source of law in practice. In some former socialist countries in Eastern Europe as well as in some developing countries with a codified legal system elsewhere in the world, cases have not (yet) been able to acquire as significant a role as that in many civil law jurisdictions in Western Europe.[15] China is a good example of such countries.

Since the communists seized power in China in 1949, cases have been excluded as a source of law, as the socialist political and legal theory denies courts lawmaking power.[16] Since the 1980s, however, there is a growing interest among judges and legal scholars in China to enhance the use of cases in court practice.[17] Whether a case law system can be developed within the codified legal system in China and if so, how cases can be used in court practice to enhance legal unity and legal certainty is a question that has triggered a huge debate in China.[18] Many participants in this debate adopted the method of comparative legal research to seek

---

[13] For scholarly writings that discuss a possible trend of convergence between the civil law and the common law see e.g. Deák 1934, p. 341, David 1984, p. 10-11 and P. 137, Markesinis 1994, p. 30-32, MacCormick & Summers 1997c, p. 2, MacCormick & Summers 1997a, p. 531-535, Zweigert & Kötz 1998, p. 71 and p. 259-265, Baade 2002, Hondius 2003, De Cruz 2007, p. 98 and p. 499 and Bogdan 2013, p. 75. Compare these writings with e.g. Dainow 1966, p. 427, Cappelletti 1981, Adams 1999, p. 465-466, Haazen 2007, p. 228 and Komárek 2012, p. 67.

[14] For a detailed analysis of the relevance of this research for the convergence debate see chapter four.

[15] See e.g. Hondius 2007a, p. 21-23, Tran 2009, p. 8, Griffiths 2011 and Innis & Jaihutan 2014, paragraph 1.2.

[16] See the sources cited in the introduction of chapter five of this study.

[17] For details see the paragraph that examines the evolution of China's Case Guidance System in chapter five.

[18] Ibid.

inspiration from the functioning of case law in other countries.[19] The focus of such comparative legal research in the case law debate in China has thus far been primarily on common law jurisdictions.[20]

Exploring how cases fulfil the role of a source of law in a European civil law jurisdiction can be relevant for China's efforts to enhance the use of cases. Of course, the political and social settings in China differ considerably from those in European jurisdictions where in practice cases have developed into a source of law. Accordingly, it would most probably not be a wise move to transplant the case law practices from a European civil law jurisdiction to China. On the other hand, such differences do not mean that there is nothing useful in the experiences with case law in a European civil law jurisdiction for Chinese judges and legal scholars that seek to develop a case law system in China. Understanding how case law actually works in a civil law jurisdiction in continental Europe may, for example, help to clarify some of the misconceptions that underlie the efforts in China to stimulate the use of cases in court practice.[21] Doing so may also help to draw the attention of judges and legal scholars in China to some of the aspects[22] that have been largely overlooked so far in their quest for a workable case law system.

In an effort to make a contribution to the existing English-language comparative law literature on the role of cases in civil law jurisdictions, this study seeks to answer the following first research question:

How do cases fulfil the role of a source of law in the Netherlands?

---

[19] See the subparagraph on methodological observations in chapter six of this study.

[20] Ibid.

[21] One such misconception is that it is due to the influence of the common law that cases become influential in civil law jurisdictions. For details see the subparagraph in chapter six of this study that clarifies this misconception.

[22] One such overlooked aspect is the possible contribution of legal scholars to the forming and development of case law, see the paragraph in chapter six that discusses the contribution that legal scholars can make to the functioning of case law in China.

The Netherlands is an understudied yet interesting European civil law jurisdiction where cases, despite the original intention of the legislature in the mid-19th century to uphold legislation as the only source of law,[23] developed into a source of law in practice around the beginning of the 20th century.[24] Why the Netherlands was selected for this study will be further explained in the paragraph on methodology in this introduction.

The answer to the first question will be placed in two different contexts in order to explore the broader implications of this study. In the first place, the findings of this study will be linked with the existing English-language literature related to the role of cases in civil law jurisdictions. In this context, this study will raise and seek to answer the second research question:

What insights can the answer to the first question contribute to the existing English-language literature related to the role of cases in civil law jurisdictions?

Moreover, the findings of this study with regard to the first main research question will be linked with China's efforts to improve the use of cases in court practice. This leads to the last research question:

What implications can be drawn from the answer to the first question that may be useful for China to further enhance its case law practice?

This last research question has two preliminary questions, i.e. what exactly does China need case law for and what has China done so far to develop case law? These preliminary questions will be explored in chapter five of this study, which will set the stage for the final chapter, where the last research question, i.e. the relevance of the experiences with case law in the Netherlands for China, will be investigated.

The nature of this study is explorative. One of the key points that this study wishes to stress is that it is through a process that involves multiple actors, institutions and practices that cases fulfil the function of a source of law in the Netherlands and, by cautious

---

[23] For details see the paragraph in chapter three of this study that analyses the relevant legislative provisions in the Netherlands, in particular the *Kingdom Legislation Act (Wet houdende algemeene bepalingen der wetgeving van het koninkrijk)*.

[24] See e.g. Scholten 1931, p. 114-124 and Telders 1938.

analogy, other civil law jurisdictions. Although judges and court-related institutions undoubtedly play an important role in this process, this study wishes to emphasize that their contribution should be put into perspective.

2. The concept of case law mechanism

One of the difficulties that I encountered was that the existing literature does not provide a proper concept that adequately captures the way case law functions in a civil law jurisdiction. Some existing studies use concepts adopted from the common law doctrine of precedent to capture the functioning of case law in civil law jurisdictions such as "a light variant of precedent"[25] or "soft *stare decisis*".[26] Although drawing an analogy is a commonly adopted approach in comparative law, this study wishes to avoid using concepts adopted from the common law doctrine of precedent to capture the way cases fulfil the role of a source of law in civil law jurisdictions. This is not only because such concepts are not sufficiently accurate, but also because the use of these concepts may have an unintended consequence of causing readers to, consciously or unconsciously, project a common law understanding of precedent to the functioning of cases as a source of law in civil law jurisdictions.[27]

By reviewing and reflecting upon literature on case law in civil law jurisdictions and by exchanging ideas with a number of legal scholars on this topic, I developed the concept of "case law mechanism" to capture the way case law functions in civil law jurisdictions. Important to the forming of this concept is one of the initial findings of the literature review, i.e. it is not one single actor or one single legal institution that enables cases to fulfil the role of a source of law in the Netherlands. For example, it is not true that cases have become a source of law in the Netherlands because the legislature or the judiciary has at a certain moment created a formal legal institution modelled after the common law doctrine of precedent that attributes binding force to certain types of cases, as existing research demonstrates that there is no such formal legal

---

[25] Hondius 2003, p. 417.
[26] Lundmark 2003.
[27] Komárek 2012, p 54.

institution in the Netherlands.[28] Nor is it true that the institution of appeal and cassation sufficiently accounts for the fact that cases are treated as a source of law in practice. After all, the institution of appeal and cassation already existed when the Dutch Civil Code was introduced in 1838, but the existing literature shows that cases were not treated as a source of law in the 19th century.[29]

The initial findings of my literature review pointed to the direction that multiple institutions and practices involving various actors are engaged in the operation of case law in the Netherlands. Research by Kottenhagen, for example, shows that case publication is of great importance for cases to fulfil the role of a source of law and that both judges and legal scholars play a significant role in determining which cases will be published.[30] The publications of Bruinsma and Draaisma & Duynstee illustrate that not only judges, but also legal scholars influence which judgments eventually become leading cases.[31] The work of Vranken indicates that widespread use of cases in legal education also has a certain effect on the status of cases as a source of law in practice.[32] By reflecting upon such scholarly writings I developed the concept of case law mechanism, which is defined as a set of institutions and practices in a codified legal system that jointly enable legal norms to be derived from cases through a process of publishing, organizing, interpreting, evaluating and applying court judgments.

3. Analytic framework

Another limitation of the existing literature is that it does not provide a readily usable analytic framework to study how cases fulfil the function of a source of law in a civil law jurisdiction. As revealed in the previous paragraph, some existing studies do touch upon various elements that are related to the functioning of case law in civil law jurisdictions, but these elements have not been put together in an organized structure. This study developed a

---

[28] For details see chapter three of this study.

[29] See e.g. Opzoomer 1865, p. VII, Diephuis 1869, p. 25 and Land 1899, p. 12.

[30] Kottenhagen & Kaptein 1989 and Kottenhagen 1994.

[31] Bruinsma 1988a, p. 105-121 and Draaisma & Duynstee 1988.

[32] Vranken 1995, p. 116.

framework that can help to illustrate how the various elements that have been fragmentally described in the existing literature relate to each other and form a whole. This framework combines two possible approaches, i.e. a structural and a processual approach, that can be adopted to analyse the case law mechanism in a given jurisdiction. The details of this framework will be presented in the following subparagraphs.

3.1 Structural approach

One possible way to analyse the case law mechanism in a certain jurisdiction is to adopt a structural approach. Such an approach sees the case law mechanism of a given jurisdiction as a machine consisting of a number of parts including various formal or informal institutions and practices (see Figure 1). The key task of a researcher would then be to identify what these parts are and how the functioning of each part and the interaction between the different parts contribute to the functioning of the machine as a whole.

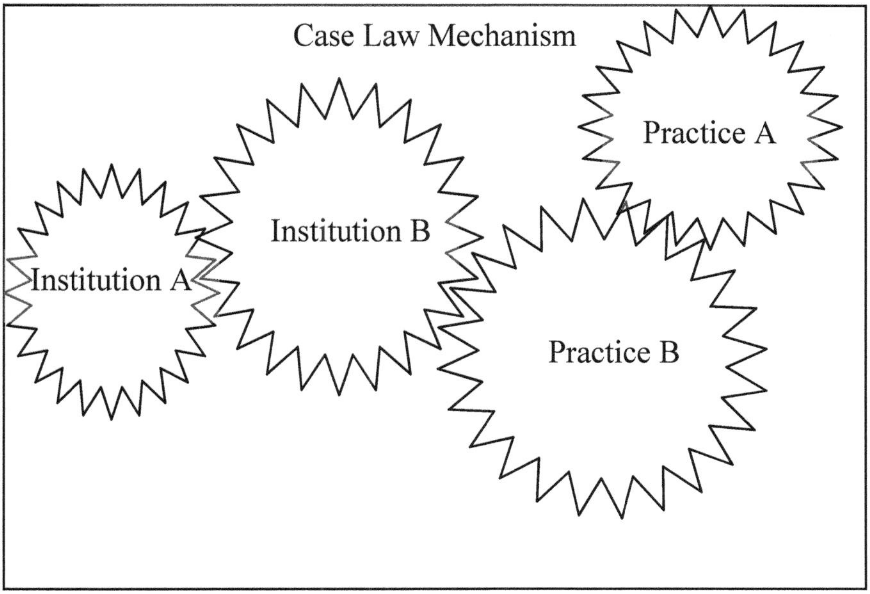

Figure 1 Example of the structural approach

3.2 Processual approach

Another possible approach is to view the case law mechanism as a process consisting of a number of phases or steps, such as the phase of selecting binding cases from a pool of candidate cases followed by the phases of publishing and applying the selected binding cases in later court decisions (see Figure 2). Some Chinese scholars have implicitly adopted this approach in their writings on possible designs of a case law system for China.[33] The key task of a researcher adopting such an approach would be to identify which steps the case law mechanism of a given jurisdiction consists of and to find out the operating procedure in each step.

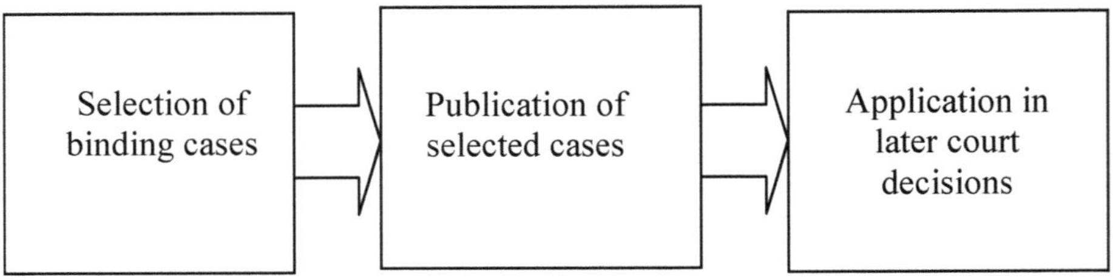

Figure 2 Example of the processual approach

3.3 Combined approach

The analytic framework developed in this study combines the structural and the processual approach. The first step is to identify the operation of a case law mechanism as a process that consists of two major phases, i.e. the publication and utilization of cases (see Figure 3). The second step is to identify which actors, institutions and practices are involved in each phase and to find out how these actors, institutions and practices contribute to the function of the case law mechanism as a whole.

[33] See. e.g. Ding 2008a and Hu & Yu 2009.

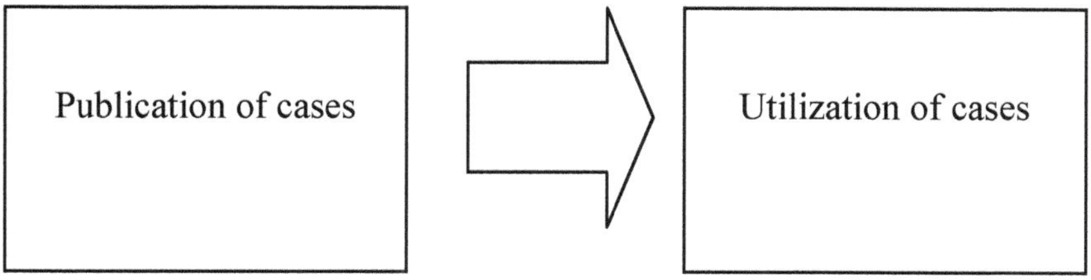

Figure 3 Case law mechanism as a process of publication and utilization of cases

This analytic framework is inspired by, among other scholarly writings, the work of Nederpel, which makes a distinction between judge-made norms contained in judicial decisions on the one hand and legal norms on the other.[34] According to Nederpel, judicial decisions are based on explicitly or implicitly formulated rules, many of which are created by judges.[35] Such judge-made norms, as Nederpel observes, do not automatically become the law.[36] Whether judge-made norms contained in a case become the law depends on, in Nederpel's view, how judges use these norms in court practice, i.e. only norms that judges constantly follow in later adjudication practice become the law.[37]

I agree with Nederpel's observation that whether norms contained in a case become the law depends eventually on how they are used. Accordingly, the analytic framework developed in this study identifies the utilization of cases as a key phase in a case law mechanism. However, it is doubtful whether norms contained in cases become the law *only* depends on how they are used in court practice. First of all, Nederpel's analysis does not address the importance of case publication. As Loussouarn rightly observes, it is hard to imagine how a case can become a legal authority if it has not been published.[38] Perhaps publication is such an obvious requirement that Nederpel did not deem it necessary to mention. However, an obvious requirement is not necessarily a trivial or

[34] Nederpel 1985.
[35] Nederpel 1985, p. 110.
[36] Nederpel 1985, p. 111.
[37] Nederpel 1985, p. 111-112.
[38] Loussouarn 1958, p. 529.

simple one. Which cases are published, as Snijders demonstrates in his research, can have a serious impact on what eventually becomes the law.[39] Moreover, Van Opijnen's research demonstrates that the mode of case publication varies greatly among different jurisdictions.[40] These findings led to the incorporation of case publication into the analytic framework as a crucial phase in the operation of a case law mechanism.

Furthermore, Nederpel's analysis focuses solely on how judges use cases in court practice. The initial findings of my literature review, however, suggest that there are other actors such as legal scholars, practising lawyers, law teachers and students that make use of cases and that how a case is used in court practice is but one of the many factors that jointly influence its status.[41] Accordingly, the analytic framework broadens the scope of investigation in the utilization phase from the use of cases in adjudication to include the use of cases in scholarly legal research as well as in legal education.[42]

4. Methodological choices and limitations of the study

An in-depth research into the way cases fulfil the role of a source of law in a European civil law jurisdiction involves many methodological choices. This paragraph will discuss some of the choices that are of influence on the entire study. Methodological choices that are specific to a particular chapter will be discussed in the relevant chapter.

---

[39] Snijders 1977.

[40] Van Opijnen 2011b and Van Opijnen 2014, p. 134-147.

[41] See Glastra van Loon e.a. 1968, p. 145, Groenendijk 1981, p. 78-79, Draaisma & Duynstee 1988, Vranken 1995, p. 69 and p. 116, Haazen 2007, p. 246-251 and Haas 2010, p. 162.

[42] See the following paragraph for an explanation on this methodological choice.

4.1 Why the Netherlands?

In many continental European jurisdictions cases have developed into a source of law in practice.[43] Instead of studying how cases fulfil the function of a source of law in some larger jurisdictions such as Germany and France, this research studies the case law mechanism in the Netherlands, a relatively small and less well-known jurisdiction. This methodological choice has been made on the basis of a number of considerations.

An important consideration is related to the requirement of a study of this type, the expertise of the researcher and the limited time available. An in-depth study as to how cases actually fulfil the role of a source of law in a particular jurisdiction, as set out in the analytic framework in the previous paragraph, requires the researcher to be very familiar with the studied jurisdiction. In a study of this kind, mere knowledge of the law in books is far from sufficient, as there is often a considerable gap between the role of cases as defined in statutes and theoretic writings and the actual force that cases carry in practice in a continental European civil law jurisdiction.[44] In order to successfully carry out a study of this type, the researcher must be able to understand the operation of a range of institutions and practices that involve various actors. How these institutions, practices and actors operate is not always neatly recorded in written materials. Even where some rules of operation are recorded in written materials, they may be scattered among various sources and how they actually function in practice may be different from what the written materials suggest. These challenges require the researcher to access a huge body of written and unwritten sources and to be able to appreciate the subtleties of the practice. Given these challenges and the limited time available, I have chosen to study the Netherlands, the jurisdiction where I have received my legal education and where I have easier access to various sources than in other continental European jurisdictions.

---

[43] These jurisdictions include, among others, Germany, France, Belgium and Italy, see e.g. Kiel & Göttingen 1997, Yiannopoulos 1974, Adams 2007 and Merryman 1974.

[44] See e.g. Lipstein 1946, p. 34-35, Loussouarn 1958, p. 255, David 1984, p. 10 and p. 112 and Adams 2007, p. 149.

Another reason for studying the case law mechanism in the Netherlands is that the Netherlands is the only Western European civil law jurisdiction that has introduced a new Civil Code in the second half of the 20th century.[45] As such, the Netherlands offers a precious opportunity to study the possible influence of recodification on the role of cases as a source of law. It would, for example, be interesting to verify whether recodification induces a return to legalism, thus weakening the status of cases as a source of law. [46]

Yet another reason for choosing the Netherlands as the object of study is that, contrary to some larger jurisdictions such as Germany and France, relatively little has been written about the Netherlands in the existing English-language comparative law literature.[47] An in-depth study of the case law mechanism in the Netherlands can be a valuable addition to the limited English-language literature on this understudied jurisdiction.

The choice to limit the scope of investigation to the Netherlands does trigger an important question, i.e. whether the findings of this study can be generalized to other continental European civil law jurisdictions. Due to the lack of in-depth and systematic studies on how cases actually fulfil the role of a source of law in other continental European civil law jurisdictions, it is very difficult to ascertain whether the case law mechanism in the Netherlands is representative of the way case law functions in continental European civil law jurisdictions. Scholarly writings on the role of cases in France and Germany in the existing literature, for example, do suggest that the case law mechanism in the Netherlands bears many similarities to the way cases fulfil the role

[45] Although many civil law jurisdictions have revised their civil codes, the Netherlands is the only Western European civil law jurisdiction that has replaced its old Civil Code with a new one, which has an entirely new structure. See e.g. Dainow 1956 and Hondius 1988a. For revisions in some other civil law jurisdictions see e.g. Fauvarque-Cosson & Fournier 2012, p. 346 and Dedek & Schermaier 2012, p. 356.

[46] For details see the relevant passages in chapter three of this study that discuss this question.

[47] For some examples see Glastra van Loon e.a. 1968, Drion 1968a, Hartkamp 1992 and Haazen 2007.

of a source of law in these two prominent civil law jurisdictions.[48] Official case publication, i.e. publication of cases by the judiciary, for example, has been institutionalised not only in the Netherlands, but also in Germany and France.[49] Moreover, existing literature suggests that scholarly case law research plays a similarly important role in the functioning of case law in Germany and France as in the Netherlands.[50]

Obviously, such similarities reflected in scattered writings are incapable of firmly establishing that the Netherlands is a representative example of continental European civil law jurisdictions in terms of the actual operation of case law. On the other hand, the similarities between the Netherlands and other European civil law jurisdictions suggest that it cannot be said that the way cases fulfil the role of a source of law in the Netherlands deviates drastically from the way case law functions in major European civil law jurisdictions. Accordingly, it is neither justified to blindly generalize the findings of this study to other European civil law jurisdictions, nor is it appropriate to dismiss the relevance of this study by asserting that the Netherlands is a trivial and deviant European civil law jurisdiction.

I am aware of the limitations imposed by the choice to study only one small European civil law jurisdiction. Accordingly, this study does not assert that its findings reveal how cases fulfil the role of a source of law in all European civil law jurisdictions. Instead, it wishes to use its findings to trigger the readers to reflect on some of the assumptions underlying many of the existing writings on the role of cases in civil law jurisdictions as well as on some debated issues that are related to this topic. More importantly, this study wishes to trigger the interest among legal scholars to conduct in-depth and systematic studies on how cases actually fulfil the role of a source of law in other civil law jurisdictions and to compare their results with each other as well as with the findings of this study.

---

48 See e.g. Loussouarn 1958, Yiannopoulos 1974, Kiel & Göttingen 1997, Troper & Grzegorczyk 1997, Dedek & Schermaier 2012 and Fauvarque-Cosson & Fournier 2012,

49 See e.g. Troper & Grzegorczyk 1997, Kiel & Göttingen 1997 and Van Opijnen 2011b.

50 See e.g. Troper & Grzegorczyk 1997, Kiel & Göttingen 1997 and Fauvarque-Cosson & Fournier 2012.

4.2 Timespan

Although the Netherlands is a small jurisdiction, as soon as one embarks on a quest to closely examine the operation of its case law mechanism, one realizes that there are so many potentially relevant things to examine that, given the limited time available, it would be impossible to investigate all of them. Consequently, further methodological choices have to be made.

One of the choices to make is to define the timespan that this study covers. After all, it has taken a long time for the case law mechanism in the Netherlands to evolve into its current shape.[51] Due to the limited time and historical sources available, it is impossible to elaborately explore how cases evolved into a source of law throughout time in the Netherlands in this study. Consequently, I have chosen to focus on the current situation: i.e. how cases *nowadays* actually fulfil the role of a source of law in practice. It should be noted that although the focus is on the present, this study does refer to situations in the past where such references can help us better understand the present-day situation by putting it in a proper historical context.[52] When researching relevant historical background information, the year 1838 has been taken as the starting point. This choice has been made, as it was in 1838 that the Netherlands introduced its first Civil Code and the Kingdom Legislation Act,[53] which can be seen as demonstrating a fairly clear intention of the legislature to uphold legislation to be the only source of law and to limit the authority of cases to bind only the litigating parties.[54]

---

[51] Commercial case publication, for example, already existed in the Netherlands long before the first Civil Code was introduced in 1848, see Jansen & Zwalve 2013, p. 133-185.

[52] Especially when exploring case publication in the Netherlands and the recognition of cases as a source of law, this study consulted many historical sources. For details see chapter one and chapter three.

[53] Diephuis 1869, p. 2.

[54] See e.g. Opzoomer 1865, p. 25, Diephuis 1869, p. 86-87, Land 1899, p. 6 and Van Apeldoorn 1939, p. 71.

4.3 The scope of the studied cases

The Netherlands is a member state of the European Union and a member state of the European Convention on Human Rights. Cases decided by the Court of Justice of the European Union and the European Human Rights Court are used in scholarly writings, legal education and court practice in the Netherlands as authoritative materials. [55] In this study, however, I have chosen to limit the research to the publication and the utilization of cases decided by national courts of the Netherlands.

One of the considerations underlying this choice is of a practical nature, i.e. the limited time and resources. Another reason for making this choice is that the authoritative status of cases decided by the Court of Justice of the European Union and the European Human Rights Court can be said to rely ultimately on obligations imposed upon the Netherlands by treaties that the country signed and ratified, but the status of cases decided by national courts as a *de facto* source of law is not related to similar duties imposed by treaties or legislation.[56] Still anther reason to limit the research to cases decided by national courts is related to one of the purposes of this study, i.e. seeking insights that may be helpful for China to enhance its case law practice. The case law debate in China and the efforts to enhance the use of case law in China are focused on national cases instead of cases decided by international or supranational courts. How cases decided by the Court of Justice of the European Union and the European Human Rights Court are treated in the Netherlands is accordingly less relevant for the purpose of seeking practical insights than the way cases decided by national courts are published and used in the Netherlands.

4.4 Why China?

As has been pointed out in the first paragraph of this introduction, cases have not developed into a source of law in all codified legal

[55] See e.g. Hondius 2007a, p. 19, Lindenbergh & Van Maanen 2011 and Gerards & Fleuren 2013.

[56] For details, see the paragraph in chapter three of this study that examines the relevant legislation in the Netherlands.

systems. In some former socialist countries in Eastern Europe as well as in some developing countries with a codified legal system elsewhere in the world such as Indonesia and Vietnam, cases have not (yet) been able to fulfil the role of a source of law.[57] This raises the question why this study focuses on China instead of any other country with a codified legal system where cases have not (yet) acquired as significant a role as that in many civil law jurisdictions in Western Europe. To this question, there is a subjective as well as an objective answer, which will be clarified in the following passages.

A subjective answer is that I am capable of reading and speaking Chinese, but do not master the official languages in other countries with a codified legal system where cases have not (yet) been able to fulfil the role of a source of law. Accordingly, it is much easier for me to access written and un-unwritten sources in China than in other codified legal systems where cases have not (yet) developed into a source of law in practice.

An objective answer is that China introduced a new legal institution called the "Case Guidance System" in November 2010, which seeks to enhance the use of cases in court practice throughout China by authorizing the Supreme People's Court to select so-called "guiding cases" from candidate cases recommended by lower courts across China.[58] This new legal institution has a peculiar design.[59] To my best knowledge, a similar legal institution has not been introduced in Indonesia, Vietnam or former socialist countries in Eastern Europe.[60] Against this background, China seems particularly worth studying as it has a unique formal legal

[57] See e.g. Hondius 2007a, p. 21-23, Tran 2009, p. 8, Griffiths 2011 and Innis & Jaihutan 2014, paragraph 1.2.

[58] See e.g. Supreme People's Court of the People's Republic of China 2010b and Jiang 2011a.

[59] For details see the paragraph in chapter five of this study that explores the design of this new legal institution.

[60] I presented my findings with regard to China's Case Guidance System to legal scholars that are familiar with and law students that come from Indonesia, Vietnam as well as some former socialist countries in Eastern Europe. The feedback that I obtained indicates that none of these jurisdictions has introduced a formal legal institution similar to China's Case Guidance System.

institution that is specially designed for the purpose of stimulating the development and use of case law.

I am aware that I cannot establish that China is representative of codified legal systems where cases have not (yet) developed into a source of law, as I have not been able to consult extensive literature concerning the use of cases in other codified legal systems where cases have not (yet) been able to fulfil the role of a source of law in practice. Accordingly, this study does not claim that the insights that were carefully drawn from the experiences with case law in the Netherlands for China to further enhance the use of cases can be generalized to other codified legal systems where cases are still not being used as a source of law in practice. Readers from such legal systems are urged to carefully verify the relevance of the thoughts presented in chapter six of this study for their home jurisdictions.

4.5 Quoting Dutch and Chinese sources

This study examines a fairly large amount of Dutch and Chinese sources such as legislation, scholarly writings, court judgments and policy documents. When such materials are quoted, this study provides an English translation, but has chosen not to provide the original Dutch or Chinese texts in addition to the English translation. A key reason for doing so is to facilitate readers that do not master Dutch or Chinese and at the same time to save space in this book. Readers that prefer to consult the original materials can find these materials by using the references provided. All translations are mine unless otherwise indicated.

5. Structure of the book

The main body of this book consists of two major parts. The first part (chapter one, two and three) focuses on the Netherlands. The second part (chapter four, five and six) puts the findings of the first part in a broader context and seeks to explore the implications of the first part for the discussion in comparative law on the role of cases in civil law jurisdictions (chapter four) and for China's quest for a case law system (chapter five and six).

The first chapter investigates the first phase in the case law mechanism and seeks to ascertain how cases are published in the Netherlands. This chapter examines two major case publication channels, i.e. commercial case publication by profit-oriented publishers and official case publication by the judiciary. It investigates a series of questions such as which actors are involved in the publication of judgments, what proportion of decided cases is published, what the selection criteria are for publication, through which mechanisms published cases can be found and how practising and academic lawyers reflect on the way cases are published in the Netherlands. This chapter also reflects on the role that case publication fulfils in the case law mechanism.

The second chapter investigates the next phase in the case law mechanism and explores how cases are used in the Netherlands. Not only does it examine how cases are used in adjudication, it also examines how cases are used in scholarly research and in legal education. Furthermore, this chapter explores the contribution made by the different users to the functioning of cases as a source of law.

The third chapter examines the recognition of cases as a source of law in the Netherlands. It investigates whether the legislature, judges and legal scholars in the Netherlands explicitly or implicitly recognize cases as a source of law. This chapter also reflects on the dynamics between the actual functioning of cases as a source of law in practice on the one hand and the explicit or implicit recognition of cases as a source of law on the other.

The fourth chapter links the first part of this study with the existing body of English-language comparative law literature related to the role of cases in civil law jurisdictions. In particular, this chapter will explore the implications of the findings of the first part of this study for three debates in this body of literature, i.e. (1) whether the common law and the civil law legal families are converging, (2) whether civil law jurisdictions have a workable case law method and (3) whether it would be wise for civil law jurisdictions to adopt the doctrine of precedent.

The fifth chapter concentrates on China's efforts to develop a case law system since the 1980s. This chapter sets the stage for the final chapter by answering an important preliminary question, i.e. what does China need case law for and what has China done so far to develop case law. The main focus of this chapter is on a new legal institution in China called “Case Guidance System”, which was introduced by the Supreme People’s Court of China in November 2010. This chapter first examines the reasons that have triggered the Supreme People’s Court to introduce this new legal institution. Then it examines the evolution, design and functioning of the Case Guidance System. The final paragraph of this chapter will reflect on some of the limitations of the Case Guidance System.

The last chapter builds upon the first three chapters as well as the data and analysis presented in chapter five. It will carefully draw some insights from the experiences with case law in the Netherlands that may be useful for China to further enhance the use of cases. In particular, this chapter will discuss the possible contribution that legal scholars and legal education can make to the development of a well-functioning case law system in China.

The final conclusion will summarize the key findings of this study, put them in an interrelated context, reflect upon them and seek insights at an overarching level.

Chapter 1

Publication of cases in the Netherlands

Chapter 1 Publication of cases in the Netherlands

1. Introduction

The introduction of this study presented the concept of case law mechanism and defined it as a set of institutions and practices in a codified legal system that jointly enable legal norms to be derived from cases through a process of publishing, organizing, interpreting, evaluating and applying court judgments. Subsequently, an analytic framework was presented that identifies the operation of a case law mechanism as a process consisting of two major phases: the publication and the utilization of cases. Publication is identified as the first phase, because before any court judgment can become a leading case, it must be, in the first place, be brought out of the sphere of the court that has made the judicial decision and be made accessible to the public, otherwise it would be very difficult, if not impossible for various users to get to know the content of the case and to use it.[61] Moreover, as long as not all court judgments are published, it is important to ascertain how cases are selected for publication, because this selection determines which cases will be given a chance to be detected and used by various players in law and hence stand a chance of ultimately becoming a leading case that shapes the law.

In accordance with the analytic framework presented in the introduction, this study begins its enquiry into the way cases fulfil the role of a source of law in the Netherlands by examining how cases are published. This chapter will investigate a series of questions concerning case publication, such as which actors are involved in the publication of judgments, what proportion of decided cases is published, what the selection criteria are for publication, through which mechanisms published cases can be found and how practising and academic lawyers reflect on the way cases are published in the Netherlands. This chapter will also reflect on the role that case publication fulfils in the case law mechanism.

The main body of this chapter consists of two parts. Paragraph two examines commercial case publication, and paragraph three focuses on official case publication. Case

[61] See e.g. Loussouarn 1958, p. 259, Kavass 1977, p. 107, Lawson 1977, p. 84, Adams 1999, p. 466 and Kottenhagen & Kaptein 1989, p. 1.

publication is defined as making court judgments accessible to the public through various media such as periodicals and online databases.[62] Commercial case publication refers to the practice that profit-oriented publishers make court judgments accessible to the public through paper or digital periodicals and online databases. Official case publication refers to the practice that the judiciary makes court judgments accessible to the public through paper or digital media. The distinction between commercial and official case publication[63] is meaningful and important for the purpose of this study, because the actors involved as well as some other relevant aspects of these two modes of case publication are different. The key findings will be summarized in the conclusion.

The main method used in this chapter is literature and archive research. A supplementary method is the expert interview. The studied materials include, in the first place, scholarly writings on case publication in the Netherlands from different periods of time since 1838. These materials have been found chiefly by searching in two online databases: Picarta[64] and Rechtsorde[65]. In addition, first-hand data have been collected through archive research in the law library as well as the main library of the University of Amsterdam. In particular, various case report periodicals since the 1830's have been consulted in order to find out various aspects of commercial case publication, such as publication format, search mechanisms and case annotation styles. Moreover, interviews with 13 judges,[66] two court staff members[67], three editors of case reporting periodicals[68] and one interview with a researcher

---

[62] This definition is inspired by Article 1 paragraph a of the new case publication selection criteria published on the official portal website of the judiciary of the Netherlands, see Appendix 3.

[63] This distinction is also commonly adopted in the existing literature, see e.g. Taruffo 1997, p. 451-454 and Van Opijnen 2011b.

[64] www.picarta.nl.

[65] www.rechtsorde.nl.

[66] Interviews NL20130923, NL20131008-1, NL20131008-2, NL20131017, NL20131021, NL20130122, NL20131028, NL20131029, NL20131031, NL20131107-1, NL20131107-2, NL20131107-3 and NL20131114. The interview notes are all on file.

[67] Interviews NL20131021-2 and NL20131024.

[68] Interviews NL20130603, NL20131021 and NL20131031.

who has conducted an in-depth PhD research into the way cases are published in the Netherlands[69] were conducted.[70] These interviews have been used as a supplementary method to verify the data obtained and to collect data that are missing in the above-mentioned sources, in particular with regard to the selection procedure for official case publication and selection criteria used in commercial case publication.

2. Commercial case publication

Despite the fact that the dominant legal theory in the 19th century held that cases were not a source of law,[71] commercial case publication began to emerge immediately after the Netherlands introduced its Civil Code in 1838.[72] As many as five periodicals started to publish court judgments soon after the Dutch Civil Code went into force.[73] Since then the number of periodicals containing case reports continued to grow.[74] Historical research suggests that, by the middle of the 1870s, case reporting by way of commercial periodicals had become an established practice in the Netherlands.[75] Nowadays there are over 100 periodicals that publish court

---

[69] Interview NL20121017.

[70] The method used is a semi-structured interview. The respondents were found through my personal network. I am aware that, due to this selection method and the relatively small number of respondents, doubt can be cast on the representativeness of the data obtained through these interviews. It should, however, be pointed out that the vast bulk of the data have been obtained through published written sources. This study welcomes other researchers to conduct more extensive interviews with systematically selected respondents to verify the findings of this chapter.

[71] See e.g. Opzoomer 1865, p. VII, Diephuis 1869, p. 25, Teixeira de Mattos 1885, p. 31 and Land 1899, p. 12.

[72] It should be noted that case publications existed before the introduction of the Civil Code in the Netherlands. *Periodical Dictionary of Administrative and Judicial Decisions*, for example, began to publish cases as early as 1829, see Appendix 1.

[73] See Appendix 1.

[74] See Appendix 1.

[75] Jansen & Zwalve 2013, p. 196.

judgments, many of which are specialized journals that focus on very specific areas of the law.[76]

Although commercial case publication has been an established practice in the Netherlands for almost two centuries, quantitative data suggest that, despite the large number of periodicals, only a tiny proportion of decided cases is published through this channel. A research commissioned by the Ministry of Justice in the 1970s revealed that out of the 603500 judgments handed down in 1976 only 0.48% was published.[77] This low publication rate seems to remain fairly stable. As Table 1 shows, the rate of cases published in commercial periodicals never exceeded half a per cent out of the total of decided cases in the first decade of the 21st century.

Year	Total decided cases	Cases published in commercial periodicals[78]	Percentage
2001	1,450,000[79]	6369	0.44%
2002	1,555,880[80]	7250	0.47%
2003	1,561,960[81]	7384	0.47%
2004	1,767,810[82]	7130	0.40%
2005	1,801,000[83]	7230	0.40%
2006	1,752,420[84]	8147	0.46%

---

[76] See Appendix 1.

[77] De Jong 1981, p. 5.

[78] Data in this column are based on Van Opijnen 2011a, p. 2143, Table 1. It should be noted that Van Opijnen's research data do not cover cases published in *all* commercial periodicals in the Netherlands, but rather cases published in commercial periodicals that have been included in the electronic database of the LJN-index. As the LJN-index includes the most commonly used legal periodicals, the data can be very close to the entire number of cases published in all commercial periodicals in the Netherlands. See interview NL20121017 as well as the methodological notes in Van Opijnen 2011a, p. 2150.

[79] Raad voor de Rechtspraak (Council for the Judiciary) 2003, p. 49.

[80] Raad voor de Rechtspraak (Council for the Judiciary) 2004, p. 57.

[81] Raad voor de Rechtspraak (Council for the Judiciary) 2006, p. 79.

[82] Ibid.

[83] Ibid.

2007	1,726,400[85]	8249	0.48%
2008	1,827,620[86]	8430	0.46%
2009	1,935,260[87]	8695	0.45%
2010	1,960,900[88]	8577	0.44%

Table 1 Case publication rate[89] in commercial periodicals 2001-2010

Moreover, quantitative data suggest that the case publication rate varies significantly among different levels of courts. In the first half of the 1970s, for example, 83.7% of all the civil cases decided by the Supreme Court was published, whereas only 10% of the civil cases decided by all five courts of appeal was published in 1973. [90] Another study suggests that about 55 to 60% of all cases decided by the Supreme Court in 1994 was published.[91] The publication rate of cases decided by courts of appeal in that year was 10%, whereas the publication rate of cases decided by district courts was only 0.5%.[92]

The low overall case publication rate as well as the significant variation in case publication rates among different levels of courts raises a crucial question, i.e. how cases are selected for commercial publication. The next subparagraph will therefore investigate which actors play a key role in determining which cases will be published in commercial periodicals and which criteria are used in the selection process. In addition, the next subparagraph will examine some other aspects of commercial case publication such as the publication format, the practice of case annotation, search mechanisms and reflections on commercial case publication by academic and practising lawyers in the Netherlands.

---

[84] Raad voor de Rechtspraak (Council for the Judiciary) 2009, p. 65.

[85] Ibid.

[86] Raad voor de Rechtspraak (Council for the Judiciary) 2011, p. 54.

[87] Ibid.

[88] Ibid.

[89] The case publication rate indicates what percentage of judgments handed down in a certain year has been published.

[90] Snijders 1978, p. 203.

[91] Van Dunné 1994, p. 1.

[92] Ibid.

2.1 Selection of cases for commercial publication

2.1.1 Actors involved in the selection

Each periodical that reports cases has an editorial board that decides which cases will be published.[93] It is usually a team of prominent legal scholars and experienced practising lawyers that form an editorial board.[94] Although editors are the final selectors in commercial case publication, they are not the only actors that determine which cases will be published in commercial periodicals. After all, editors do not have direct access to the archives of various courts where decided cases are filed, so that they have to depend on other actors to supply them with cases. This practice means that the suppliers of cases play an important role in the selection process, as they determine which cases will be available to the editors.

Traditionally, editors relied primarily[95] on the so-called "correspondents" in courts to send them cases.[96] Throughout the years, publishers have developed a network of "correspondents" in various courts.[97] The correspondents are judges and court staff that have agreed to regularly send certain types of cases decided in the courts where they work to the editorial boards of various periodicals.[98] It used to be through these correspondents that editors obtained a regular supply of cases for publication.

The importance of the role of court correspondents as case suppliers, however, has been declining significantly since the judiciary launched its online judgments database in 1999, which is

---

[93] Van Arkel 1994, p. 82-83. See also interviews NL20131024 and NL20131031.

[94] See e.g. Van Arkel 1994, p. 83 and Jansen & Zwalve 2013, p. 220.

[95] Another possible channel through which editors obtain cases is to request a specific court to send copies of specific cases to them, see Schuijt 2004, p. 18.

[96] Kottenhagen & Kaptein 1989, p. 27.

[97] See e.g. Crommelin 1988, p. 752 and De Meij e.a. 2006, p. 18.

[98] See Voskuil 1980, p. 38-61. The correspondents rarely receive monetary rewards. Often they get a free subscription to the periodicals to which they send cases as reward for their contribution. See De Meij e.a. 2006, p. 18.

commonly referred to as *Rechtspraak.nl.* [99] Interviews with periodical editors, judges and court staff indicate that nowadays editors obtain the vast bulk of cases by searching directly in the official online judgments database of the judiciary instead of through court correspondents.[100] Although in many courts there are still correspondents, the accent of their work has shifted from selecting and sending cases to editorial offices of various periodicals to primarily responding to periodical editors' requests for copies of specific cases.[101]

Another source of case supply that periodical editors rely on, both before and after the launch of the online judgments database of the judiciary, is litigating parties and/or their counsels. [102] For various reasons, litigating parties and/or their counsels may wish to see the judgments in their cases be published and may send them to the editorial boards of relevant periodicals. [103] This happens, however, on an ad hoc basis and does not constitute the major source of supply.[104]

In sum, the selection process of commercial case publication has two rounds. The first round takes place primarily in various courts where judges play a decisive role in determining which cases will be published in the online judgments database of the judiciary.[105] During the second round, periodical editors (i.e. expert academic and practising lawyers) make a final decision.

2.1.2 Selection criteria

Given the low publication rate and the large number of actors involved in the selection process, one may expect that well-defined selection criteria have been developed in commercial case publication, because otherwise it would be difficult to ensure a

---

[99] For more details of the online judgments database see the next paragraph of this chapter.

[100] See e.g. interviews NL20131021, NL20131024 and NL20131031.

[101] Interviews NL20131021 and NL 20131024.

[102] Van Opijnen 2006b, p. 18.

[103] De Meij e.a. 2006, p. 34.

[104] Crommelin 1988, p. 752.

[105] For a detailed account of the institution of official case publication see the next paragraph.

consistent selection policy. In practice, however, commercial periodicals rarely disclose their selection criteria.[106] A closer look at some of the published selection criteria reveals that they usually contain fairly abstract standards, which give the selectors a large margin of appreciation.[107] The six selection criteria used by the *Nederlandse Jurisprudentie (Netherlands Cases)*, for example, can be summarized as:[108]

- legal importance[109]
- topical value[110]
- value for the forming of new law[111]
- concretization of open norms[112]
- remarkable facts[113]
- importance that reaches beyond the specific decided case[114]

The selection criteria of another periodical, *Tijdschrift voor Consumentenrecht en handelspraktijken* (*Consumer Law and Trade Practice Journal*), are similarly formulated in a non-detailed fashion:[115]

- balanced case reporting on various aspects of consumer law[116]
- representativeness[117]

---

[106] Kottenhagen & Kaptein 1989, p. 18.

[107] Van den Berg 1994, p. 961.

[108] These criteria have been published in a newsletter of the *Nederlandse Jurisprudentie* in 1986, see Kottenhagen & Kaptein 1989, p. 33.

[109] The original Dutch text is "juridisch belang van een zaak".

[110] The original Dutch text is "zit er actualiteitswaarde aan een uitspraak".

[111] The original Dutch text is "vindt rechtsvorming plaats".

[112] The original Dutch text is "worden open rechtsnormen ingevuld".

[113] The original Dutch text is "het bieden van een 'zeker kleurengamma ten aanzien van feitelijke oordelen".

[114] The original Dutch text is "in hoeverre de beslissing van de rechter die op dat moment oordeelt ook buiten de gegeven casuspositie van belang is".

[115] Hondius 2005, p. 37-38.

[116] The original Dutch text is "evenwichtige verspreiding over de verschillende onderdelen van het consumentenrecht".

[117] The original Dutch text is "gepubliceerde uitspraken zijn representatief voor de betrokken instantie".

- nature of the magazine[118], i.e. only consumer law cases will be published
- value for the forming of new law[119]

Interviews with court correspondents suggest that unpublished selection criteria also tend to be vague and flexible.[120] Cases may be selected for publication because they deviate from previous judgments, because they involve an issue on which few judgments have been published or because they attract a lot of public attention.[121] Wide use of such broad selection criteria prompted, as will be revealed further in this chapter, doubts among some academic lawyers on the consistency of the selection policy as well as on the representativeness of the selected cases.[122]

2.2 Publication format and case annotation

Although there is no uniform case publication format among the large number of periodicals that report cases, a typical case report usually contains three elements:

(1) technical details, such as the name of the court, the date on which the judgment was handed down, the case number etc.;
(2) information added by editors to facilitate reading and searching, such as key words and summaries;
(3) the judgment in full text or part(s) of the judgment.[123]

Some cases decided by the Supreme Court are published together with an advisory opinion of an Advocate General.[124]

---

[118] The original Dutch text is "aard van het tijdschrift".
[119] The original Dutch text is "of de betrokken uitspraak een bijdrage kan leveren aan de rechtsvorming".
[120] Voskuil 1980, p. 61. See interviews NL20131008, NL20131021 and NL20131031.
[121] See sources cited in the previous note.
[122] See the subparagraph in this chapter on the reflections of academic and practising lawyers on commercial case publication.
[123] Whether a judgment will be published in full or in part, and if in part, which part(s) will be published is determined by the editors of periodicals, see interview NL20131031.

Moreover, some important cases are published together with an annotation, which can be very helpful for understanding and applying the published cases. Since case annotation has become a very important practice in commercial case publication in the Netherlands, the following passages will look at this practice in greater detail, examining the origin of this practice as well as the authors, the form, the substance and the impact of case annotations.

Historical research reveals that the practice of case annotation originated in France.[125] There is some debate on the question when case annotation first emerged in the Netherlands. According to Bloembergen, it was Meijers (1880-1954), a prominent law professor at Leiden University, who first started to annotate cases published in the journal *Weekblad van het recht*[126] in 1910.[127] Jansen, however, argues that the first case annotator in the Netherlands was most probably Van Boneval Faure (1826-1909), who wrote comments on cases published in the *Regtsgeleerd bijblad behoorende tot de Nieuwe bijdragen voor regtsgeleerdheid en wetgeving*[128] in the mid-19th century.[129] Despite such controversies on the exact time when case annotations began to emerge in the Netherlands, it can reasonably be said that case annotation became an established practice in the early decades of the 20th century.[130]

Editors of periodicals tend to invite prominent legal scholars to annotate published cases.[131] In addition to legal scholars' annotations, some periodicals also publish annotations written by practising lawyers. Exceptionally, even judges of the Supreme

---

[124] Advocates General are officials of the Public Prosecution service that are based in the Supreme Court. One of their primary tasks is to deliver advisory opinions to the Supreme Court in criminal, civil and tax cases. Such opinions are not binding for the Supreme Court, but in practice Supreme Court judges do take these opinions seriously, see Bruinsma 1988a, p. 59-78.

[125] Jansen 2003, p. 1757-1759.

[126] The title of this periodical can be translated as *Law Weekly*.

[127] Bloembergen 2002, p. 88.

[128] The title of this journal can be translated as *Supplement to the Contribution to the Study of Law and Legislation*.

[129] Jansen & Zwalve 2013, p. 200-201.

[130] See e.g. Fockema Andreae 1938, p. 90 and Remmelink e.a. 1988, p. 9.

[131] Remmelink e.a. 1988, p. 6 and Lindo 1993, p. 1301.

Court wrote annotations to comment on, among other things, cases that they themselves have decided.[132]

Which cases will be annotated is often a choice jointly made by editors of the various commercial periodicals and annotators that have agreed to cooperate with them.[133] The criteria that editors and annotators use to select cases that will be annotated are not well articulated.[134] A common perception is that it is important[135] cases that are selected for annotation.[136] Quantitative empirical data reveal that it is mainly cases decided by the highest courts that are annotated.[137]

A case annotation takes the form of a short commentary on a published case. As Figure 4 demonstrates, the average length of annotations rarely exceeds 1,000 words.

---

[132] See e.g. Remmelink e.a. 1988, p. 10. It should be emphasized that nowadays commercial periodicals no longer invite Supreme Court judges to write annotations, although occasionally they do invite some former Supreme Court judges to write annotations. See e.g. Bloembergen 2002, p. 88.

[133] See e.g. Crommelin 1988, p. 753 and Lindo 1993, p. 1301.

[134] According to Crommelin, for example, the criterion is whether readers need clarification of a case. This is obviously a very general and flexible criterion. See Crommelin 1988, p. 753.

[135] Obviously, "importance" is by no means a precise selection criterion, as it merely shifts the question to what constitutes an important case. It seems that editors and annotators primarily rely on their professional experiences and subjective evaluation to determine which cases will be annotated.

[136] Kottenhagen & Kaptein 1989, p. 43. Interviews with judges indicate that whether a case has been annotated and if so, how many annotations have appeared is often perceived as a sign of the legal importance of a case, and that judges are more likely to, all else being equal, pay attention to an annotated case than one that has not been annotated. See e.g. interviews NL20131008-1, NL20131022, NL20131107-3 and NL20131114.

[137] Van Opijnen 2011a, p. 2145-2146.

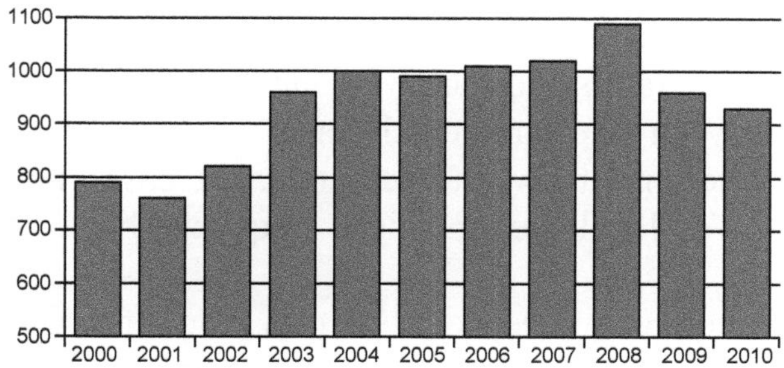

Figure 4 Average length of case annotations (number of words) 2000-2010[138]

The content of case annotations can vary from annotator to annotator.[139] In general, however, it can be said that case annotations usually contain the following elements:

(1) A very brief summary of the facts and how the case has been decided in previous instances.[140]
(2) An analysis of the key legal questions involved in the annotated case and an explanation of the court's answers to these questions.[141]
(3) An analysis of the position of the case in the legal system. Annotators often make great efforts to ascertain and explain whether, and if so, how an annotated case fits in the legal

[138] Van Opijnen 2011a, p. 2145.

[139] For a summary of different annotation styles see Bruinsma 1988a, p. 111.

[140] It should be noted that some annotators have a very concise writing style, tending to skip the facts and the decisions of the previous instances in their comments, see e.g. the annotations by G.J. Scholten to the *Cellar Trapdoor* (HR 5 November 1965, NJ 1966, 136) and the *Pos/Van den Bosch* case (HR 17 November 1967, NJ 1968, 42). Whether the advisory opinion of an Advocate General is published together with the judgment may also affect an annotator's decision whether or not to mention the facts and decisions of previous instances in the annotation, as it is common for an Advocate General to include such materials in his or her opinions.

[141] A case may involve a number of disputed questions of law. Which of these disputed questions will be analyzed in an annotation depends on the choice of the annotator. Different annotators may choose to comment on different aspects of a case. The choice can be related to the expertise of the annotators. See Bloembergen 2002, p. 90.

system and what it adds to the existing system.[142] It is very common for annotators to analyse and explain the relationship between the annotated cases and previous cases.[143] Also the link between the annotated cases and legislation[144] and/or legal theory[145] is a frequent object of analysis.

(4) Evaluation of the court decision.[146] It is common that annotators express their opinions on the soundness, the desirability or some other aspects of the court decision that they comment on.[147] Such opinions can be positive[148] or critical.[149]

(5) Implications for future practice.[150] Another key question that case annotations often discuss is the possible impact of the annotated court decisions on future cases. It is, for example,

---

[142] See Bloembergen 2002, p. 90.

[143] See e.g. paragraph 2 of G.J. Scholten's annotation to the *Bull Calf* case (HR 7 March 1980, NJ 1980, 353) as well as Paragraph 1 of N.J. Nieuwenhuis' annotation to the *Potassium Mine* case (HR 23 September 1988, NJ 1989, 743).

[144] See e.g. paragraph 1 of C.J.H. van der Brunner's annotation to the *Shell/State* case (HR 30 September 1994, NJ 1996, 196) as well as paragraph 2 of the same author's annotation to the *DES Daughters* case (HR 9 October 1992, NJ 1994, 535).

[145] See e.g. the first and the second paragraph of Molengraaff's annotation to the *Lindenbaum/Cohen* case (HR 31 January 1919, NJ 1919, 161) as well as paragraph 2 of C.J.H. van der Brunner's annotation to the *DES Daughters* case (HR 9 October 1992, NJ 1994, 535).

[146] Bloembergen 2002, p. 97-98.

[147] Snijders 2003.

[148] Molengraaff, for example, was very positive about the *Lindenbaum/Cohen* case decided by the Supreme Court (HR 31 January 1919, NJ 1919, 161). In the last paragraph of his annotation to this case, Molengraaff wrote "(s)eldom has the Supreme Court decided a case that can be expected to have such a salutary influence on our legal life".

[149] J.B.M. Vranken, for example, pointed out a flaw of circular argumentation by the Supreme Court in the *Baby Kelly* case (HR 18 March 2005, NJ 2006, 606) in paragraph 17 of his annotation to this case. Another example is that, in his annotation to the *Cellar Trapdoor* case (HR 5 November 1965, NJ 1966, 136), G.J. Scholten criticized the criteria formulated by the Supreme Court in that decision as being incomplete.

[150] Snijders 2003.

very common that annotators analyse how broad or narrow a norm formulated in the annotated case is likely to be interpreted and what kind of cases in the future are likely to be affected by the annotated court decision. [151]

The practice of case annotation fulfils a number of important functions. First of all, case annotations are of great value to judges and practising lawyers, as they are usually concise and offer useful insights for future practice.[152] In this sense, case annotations form an important bridge between legal scholarship and legal practice.[153] In addition, case annotations form a valuable source of feedback to judges.[154] There are, for example, cases where the judicial decision is clearly inspired by ideas that have been expressed in previous case annotations. [155] Moreover, case annotations serve a useful educational function, as they can help law students to better understand the essence and the relevance of a case by putting it in a proper context of legislation, doctrinal writings and previous cases.[156]

Although the value and influence of specific case annotations can vary depending on the authority of the annotators and the soundness of the analysis in the annotations, the value of the practice of case annotation as a whole is commonly deemed very high in the Netherlands.[157] In a time when more and more court decisions are freely available on the Internet (details of which will be examined in the following paragraph of this chapter), case annotations are considered as a core added value of commercial

---

[151] See e.g. the conclusion of N. J. Nieuwenhuis' annotation to the *Potassium Mine* case (HR 23 September 1988, NJ 1989, 743) and paragraph 7 of C.J.H. van der Brunner's annotation to the *DES Daughters* case (HR 9 October 1992, NJ 1994, 535).

[152] See e.g. interviews NL20131008-1, NL20131022, NL20131107-3 and NL20131114.

[153] Snijders 2003.

[154] Draaisma & Duynstee 1988, p. 25.

[155] Lindo 1993, p. 1301.

[156] At Leiden University Law School, for example, annotations to some cases are compulsory study materials for law students, see e.g. Leiden Law School 2012b, p. 3 and Leiden Law School 2012f, p. 1.

[157] See e.g. Snijders 2003 and Hondius 2007a, p. 21.

case publication.[158] A noteworthy recent development in this context is that many universities in the Netherlands nowadays no longer recognize case annotations as academic publications.[159] At present this downgrade of the status of case annotation has not led to a dramatic decrease in the number of annotated commercial case publication periodicals,[160] but some legal scholars have expressed concerns that in the long term this downgrade may hurt the operation of case law in general as it suppresses legal scholars' willingness to write case annotations.[161]

2.3 Search mechanisms

As the volume of published cases grows year by year, publishers have developed increasingly powerful mechanisms to improve the findability of published cases. The following passages will examine how the search mechanisms evolved in commercial case publication since 1838.

In the earliest decades after the introduction of the Dutch Civil Code in 1838, periodicals that published court judgments depended largely on some simple search tools such as chronological tables of cases[162] and indexes based on key words[163] and/or article numbers of legislative provisions.[164] The tables and indexes in a number of case publication volumes were sometimes integrated into an index volume[165] so that readers could search across cases published in different years.[166] A disadvantage of these earlier search tools is that it was difficult to search across different

---

[158] See e.g. Bergwerf & Houweling 2008, p. 9 and Van Opijnen 2011a, p. 2145.
[159] For an analysis of the reasons that have led to this recent development see Schlossels 2012, p. 230-231.
[160] Van Opijnen 2011a.
[161] See e.g. Snijders 2003 and Schlossels 2012.
[162] See e.g. Van Den Honert 1942, p. I-IV.
[163] See e.g. Brocx & Stuart 1839, p. 417-464 and Van Vleuten & Perk 1839, p. 1-10.
[164] See e.g. Van Den Honert 1942, p. VII-XXVI.
[165] See e.g. Brocx & Stuart 1855.
[166] Even today many periodicals are still offering indexes as a basic search tool, see e.g. the last editions of *Nederlandse jurisprudentie* (*Netherlands Cases*)

periodicals, as the indexes of various periodicals were not integrated into one search platform.

An improved search tool emerged in 1850 when a book with the nickname *Leons Regtspraak* (*Leon's Cases*) was first published.[167] A swift look at the table of contents may give the impression that this book is merely a collection of legislation, as the title of each chapter corresponds with the name of a statute[168] or law code [169]. However, what makes this book unique is that it incorporated references to published cases[170] and scholarly writings into the legislative provisions. For example, under article 1401 of the Civil Code (the general tort clause), the author integrated references to and short summaries of more than 40 cases published in various periodicals in the period between October 1838 and September 1850. [171] Moreover, the author integrated scholarly writings related to this legislative provision as well.[172] In this way, readers are not only able to find cases and literature across different years, but also across different periodicals.

Another integrated search tool was a periodical called *Repertorium van de Nederlandse jurisprudentie en rechtsliteratuur* (*Index of Dutch Cases and Legal Literature*). This magazine emerged in 1878 and ended in 1944. As the title suggests, this periodical contains an alphabetic keyword index that incorporates published cases and legal literature, which enables the users to search cases and academic legal writings across various years and across various periodicals.

A common limitation of *Leons Regtspraak* and the *Repertorium* was that "real time" search was not possible, because

---

[167] Leon was the author of the book, see Leon 1850a and Leon 1850b.

[168] For example, chapter three of the first volume of this books is "Grondwet van 1840" (Constitution of 1840).

[169] For example, chapter four of the second volume of this book is "Burgerlijk Wetboek" (Civil Code).

[170] Contrary to what the title of this book suggests, it does not only contain references to published cases decided by the Supreme Court, but also references to published judgments of lower courts, see e.g. p 358, 361 and 362 of the second volume.

[171] See Leon 1850b, p. 356-362.

[172] References to writings of prominent legal scholars such as Diephuis and Asser can be found, for example, on page 362 of the second volume.

there was a gap between the time when a case was published in a periodical and when the search instruments were published. *Leons Regtspraak*, for example, was published yearly,[173] so each edition enabled the users to search for cases published in the past year, but not in the current year.

The problem of delay was solved by a better search tool called the card system. Publisher Tjeenk Willink introduced this search instrument in 1913, when it began to publish the well-known case law report *Nederlandse Jurisprudentie* (*Netherlands Cases*). A key feature of this case report periodical was that case publications were accompanied by a card system.[174] The card system took the physical shape of boxes with cards that were divided into six legal areas.[175] Cards were organized in the order of article numbers of statutory provisions and contained references to cases published in the *Nederlandse Jurisprudentie* and many other periodicals.[176] A major innovation of this system was that the cards were updated as soon as new cases were published, so that users could easily find recently published cases without a significant delay.[177] The card system became so popular in the Netherlands that its use soon spread to many other areas.[178]

Although the inventor of the card system asserted that this system was future proof, it has not been able to escape the fate of being replaced by more advanced and powerful search mechanisms: computerized search tools, first in the form of CD-roms and DVDs with an incorporated search function between the 1980s and mid-1990s, and later in the form of online databases with powerful search engines.[179] Nowadays users of commercial online legal databases can find published cases by the date of decision, key

---

[173] Henssen 1998, p. 77.

[174] The inventor of the card system drew inspiration from a similar German system, see Remmelink e.a. 1988, p. 9.

[175] Editors' Board Rechtsgeleerde Magazijn 1913.

[176] Crommelin 1988, p. 745.

[177] The card system introduced by the *Nederlandse Jurisprudentie* was a great success, see e.g. Van Holk 1963, p. 648, Remmelink e.a. 1988, 8-9 and Hoefer-van Dongen 1988.

[178] Henssen 1998, p. 77.

[179] Important examples are Kluwer Navigator (www.kluwernavigator.nl) and Opmaat (http://opmaatnieuw.sdu.nl).

words, party names, article numbers of statutory provisions, as well as many combinations of these elements. Information provided by commercial legal databases is often highly integrated, so that users can easily find cases and legal literature published in different years and different periodicals. Also the issue of delay has been successfully addressed by online databases, since the databases are updated so frequently that cases can be found in these databases soon after they are published.

The evolution of commercial case search mechanisms reveals that case publication is not merely a question of making cases available by simply putting the texts of judgments in paper periodicals or computerized databases, but is also about making published cases findable. Moreover, the evolution process suggests a trend towards more and more integrated case search tools, as well as striving towards a minimum delay between the moment of case publication and that of integrating the published case into search tools.

2.4 Academic and practising lawyers' reflections on commercial case publication

When commercial case reports emerged after 1838, the overall reaction was quite positive.[180] In 1840, for example, De Pinto, a prominent practising lawyer, wrote the following comments on the emergence of a case report periodical commonly referred to as *Van den Honert's Collection of Cases*:[181]

> I have repeatedly pointed out that a good collection of cases decided by the Supreme Court is indispensible for the use of a generally written code. That is, I would say, something that no one can doubt about and therefore does not need to be argued. Nevertheless, nobody has fulfilled this need. Things that already existed were totally insufficient or unusable. It is therefore no wonder that nearly everyone warmly welcomes this new case report periodical.

---

[180] See e.g. De Pinto 1840 and De Vries & Molster 1860.
[181] De Pinto 1840, p. 357-358.

For more than one century, the way cases were published through commercial periodicals did not provoke significant debates among academic or practising lawyers and systematic research into this matter seemed to be absent.[182] This situation changed in the 1970s and 1980s, when the Ministry of Justice commissioned a systematic research into the way cases were published[183] and a number of scholars began to critically reflect on the long-established practice of commercial case publication.[184] Research and debates on this topic since the 1970s reveal a number of significant shortcomings of commercial case publication, which will be briefly examined in the following passages.[185]

1. Too few cases are published.[186] As table 1 illustrates, not even a half per cent of all decided cases is published each year. Kottenhagen argues that such a low publication rate can lead to

---

[182] Kottenhagen & Kaptein 1989, p. 18-26 gives an overview of systematic research into this matter. The study by Kottenhagen and Kaptein shows that systematic research into this matter started rather late, namely in the 1970's.

[183] Kottenhagen & Kaptein 1989, p. 19-24.

[184] See e.g. Kottenhagen & Kaptein 1989, Van Dunné 1994 and Kottenhagen 1994.

[185] Writings that critically reflect on commercial case publication were primarily published in the period between the 1970s and the mid-1990s. It seems that after this brief period the topic of commercial case publication lay dormant again. The readers are reminded of the fact that the sources cited in the following passages come largely from the 1970s and 1980s and that a part of the cited research was restricted to some areas of the law. It would require too much time for the current study to verify whether every shortcoming identified in the cited literature is still present today and whether certain limitations identified in certain areas of the law were or are still present in other areas of the law. It should be noted that the purpose of this subparagraph is not to get substantively involved in the debates on commercial case publication in the Netherlands, but to inform the reader of the way Dutch academic and practising lawyers perceived the merits and limitations of commercial case publication before the birth of official case publication, and to create a context for the reader to better appreciate what has made the judiciary in the Netherlands introduce an official online judgments database in 1999.

[186] Van Dunné 1994, p. 1.

inequality between litigating parties, because some large organizations that frequently litigate, such as big law firms and insurance companies, have their own collections of non-published cases, which may put their opponents who do not have such collections in a disadvantaged position.[187]

2. Lack of transparent and well-defined selection criteria for publication.[188] Kottenhagen's research points out that almost no commercial periodical has a set of explicit selection criteria for case publication.[189] Moreover, his research suggests that personal preferences of editors can have a significant influence on the types of cases that are selected for publication.[190]

3. Published cases are not representative of all court decisions.[191] Snijders' research, for example, shows that the visitation (*omgangsregeling*) cases published in the *Nederlandse Jurisprudentie* (*Netherlands Cases*) are exceptional court decisions that do not represent the court practice in general.[192] Hartkamp's research suggests that published tenancy cases lack representativeness in terms of regions, since it is primarily cases decided by courts in the economically more developed regions that are published.[193]

4. There is a significant delay in case publication.[194] A research among users of the *Nederlandse Jurisprudentie* (*Netherlands Cases*) shows that 53% of the respondents is of the view that it takes too long before cases are published.[195] Quantitative data suggest that on average it takes 103 days before a case is published in an annotated commercial case report periodical.[196]

---

187 Kottenhagen 1994, p. 42.
188 See e.g. Hondius 1973, p. 746 and De Jong 1980.
189 Kottenhagen 1994, p. 42.
190 Kottenhagen & Kaptein 1989, p. 38-43.
191 See e.g. Kottenhagen & Kaptein 1989, p. 99 and Matthijssen 2000, p. 13.
192 Snijders 1977.
193 Hartkamp 1981, p. 356.
194 See e.g. Franken 1981, p. 393 and Kottenhagen 1994, p. 42.
195 Crommelin 1988, p. 755.
196 Van Opijnen 2011a, p. 2144-2145.

5. Too expensive. Some commentators are concerned that subscription fees to commercial case publication periodicals are usually so high that non-professional users may not be able to afford them.[197] This is deemed problematic because such a price barrier may hinder the public from knowing the law and it may also weaken the public's ability to exercise a certain degree of supervision on the work of the courts.[198]

2.5 Sub-conclusion on commercial case publication

Data collected in this paragraph suggest that commercial case publication has a highly practice-oriented nature. It has been developed largely to facilitate the practice of law, i.e. the work of judges and lawyers.[199] Case selection and annotations tend to focus on legally significant cases that are likely to affect the practice of law, rather than providing a representative picture of the functioning of the courts. Also the relatively high prices suggest that commercial case publication has been developed primarily to satisfy the needs of professional users, rather than to keep the public informed of case law development or to enhance the transparency of the work of the courts.

The practice-oriented and profit-driven nature of commercial case publication led to the question whether it is desirable to leave such an important task as case publication nearly entirely to commercial entities. Since the 1970s and in particular in the 1980s, there has been a growing awareness that it is a responsibility of the government to make cases accessible to the public.[200] The cornerstone of the reasoning underlying such a conviction is that in a democratic constitutional state, the government has the responsibility to make the law accessible to the public.[201] As over the years cases have developed into an essential source of law in

---

[197] Van Holk 1963, p. 644 and Matthijssen 2000, p. 17.
[198] Matthijssen 2000, p. 16-17.
[199] See e.g. De Pinto 1840 and De Vries & Molster 1860.
[200] See e.g. De Jong 1980, p. 2, Editors' Board 1982, p. 3-4 and Commissie Jurisprudentiedocumentatie (Case Law Documentation Committee) 1994.
[201] See e.g. Hondius 1973, p. 746 and Kottenhagen & Kaptein 1989, p. 99.

practice in the Netherlands,[202] the government should, in addition to legislation, make cases accessible to the public.[203] Also the idea of public oversight on the work of the courts has contributed to this awareness.[204] This growing conviction has eventually led to the emergence of online official case publication in the late 1990s, which will be examined in greater details in the following paragraph.

3. Official case publication

For well over one and a half century, cases used to be nearly exclusively[205] published through commercial paper and digital periodicals in the Netherlands. The close to monopoly position of commercial publishers in case publication ended in December 1999, when the official portal website of the judiciary (www.rechtspraak.nl) was launched.[206] The launching of this official website was part of a broader government initiative to make government information better accessible to the public.[207] A crucial component of the website is an online database through which a selection of judgments of all courts is published.

In the first decade of its existence, the official portal website published more than 200,000 cases.[208] The publication rate grew from 0.48% to 1.4% during the first decade of the 21st century (see Table 2). In a little more than ten years time, the official website of the judiciary has become an important source of case law information in the Netherlands.[209]

---

[202] See e.g. Telders 1938, p. 202, Van Apeldoorn 1939, p. 86, Polak 1953, p. 38, Glastra van Loon e.a. 1968, p. 139 and Brunner 1994, p. 32.
[203] Hondius 1973, p. 746 and Kottenhagen & Kaptein 1989, p. 99.
[204] Matthijssen 2000, p. 10.
[205] For some rare examples of cases published by the government in the *Staatsblad* (*Bulletin of Acts and Decrees of the Kingdom of the Netherlands*) and the *Staatscourant* (*Netherlands Government Gazette*), see De Jong 1981, p. 2.
[206] Mommers & Zwenne & Schermer 2010, p. 2073.
[207] See Ministerie van Binnenlandse Zaken (Ministry of Internal Affairs) 1997.
[208] Van Opijnen 2011a, p. 2142.
[209] Van Opijnen 2011a, p. 2147.

Year	Total Decided Cases	Published[210]	Percentage
2001	1,450,000[211]	6967	0.48%
2002	1,555,880[212]	10308	0.66%
2003	1,561,960[213]	11905	0.76%
2004	1,767,810[214]	14424	0.82%
2005	1,801,000[215]	16361	0.91%
2006	1,752,420[216]	19539	1.1%
2007	1,726,400[217]	22112	1.3%
2008	1,827,620[218]	24588	1.3%
2009	1,935,260[219]	26417	1.4%
2010	1,960,900[220]	27735	1.4%

Table 2 Case publication rate through the official website of the Judiciary 2001-2010

3.1 Selection of cases for official publication

3.1.1 Actors involved in the selection

Although the official website of the judiciary offers an integrated platform to publish cases decided by all courts in the Netherlands, there is no centralized editing office that decides which cases will be published. Each court selects its own cases for publication.[221] It is also the individual courts that take care of the technical tasks of editing and uploading the selected cases into the online database, so

[210] Data in this column are based on Van Opijnen 2011a, p. 2143, Table 1.
[211] Raad voor de Rechtspraak (Council for the Judiciary) 2003, p. 49.
[212] Raad voor de Rechtspraak (Council for the Judiciary) 2004, p. 57.
[213] Raad voor de Rechtspraak (Council for the Judiciary) 2006, p. 79.
[214] Ibid.
[215] Ibid.
[216] Raad voor de Rechtspraak (Council for the Judiciary) 2009, p. 65.
[217] Ibid.
[218] Raad voor de Rechtspraak (Council for the Judiciary) 2011, p. 54.
[219] Ibid.
[220] Ibid.
[221] Mommers & Zwenne & Schermer 2010, p. 2074.

that the public can access them through the official portal website of the judiciary.[222]

Each court is supposed to set up a team to take care of the selection and publication of its own cases.[223] In practice, it is usually the judges in various sections of a court that select cases for publication.[224] On the whole, it can be said that the selection process is decentralized and closed, as in practice it is normally the individual judges in various courts that determine which cases that they themselves have decided will be published and it is nearly impossible for actors outside the judiciary to directly influence the selection process.[225]

3.1.2 Selection criteria

Since its launch in 1999, the official website has published two sets of selection criteria.[226] The first set of criteria was in use from December 1999 until March 2012, when it was replaced by a new set.[227]

The old selection criteria were drafted in very general language. In total there were ten criteria. The first criterion was, for example, "public attention".[228] The second criterion was also very vague: "importance for the public life".[229] Other criteria were drafted in similarly broad terms,[230] except the last four negative criteria that clearly defined which cases would not be published, such as personal and family law cases that have been concluded in

[222] Matthijssen 2000, p. 41.
[223] De Meij e.a. 2006, p. 14.
[224] See e.g. Van der Hoek 2010 and Van Opijnen 2014, p. 220-221. See also interviews NL20131008-1, NL20131021, NL20131022, NL20131024, NL20131028, NL20131031, NL20131107-1 and NL20111114.
[225] In theory, the public can request a court to publish a specific case that the court has decided through the official website. This rarely happens in practice. See Jongeneel 2010, p. 2415 footnote 9.
[226] See Appendix 2 and 3.
[227] Editors' Board 2012.
[228] See Appendix 2.
[229] See Appendix 2.
[230] See Appendix 2.

first instance without an appeal being lodged and civil cases that have been concluded in absentia.

A source of inspiration for the drafters of the selection criteria was a recommendation adopted by the Committee of Ministers of the Council of Europe in 1995 [hereafter Recommendation R (95) 11][231], which encourages member states to set up automated case law retrieval systems (i.e. case law databanks) that would facilitate better public access to court judgments.[232] One of the basic principles of Recommendation R (95) 11 is that member states are allowed to select cases for publication, as long as the selection is *objective* and the selected court decisions are *representative* of the case law in the sector of law where the selection is made.[233] Furthermore, the Recommendation proposed two types of selection criteria: positive criteria and negative ones.[234] The essence of the negative selection criteria is that in principle all cases will be published except judgments that are evidently of little value because, for example, the grounds on which the court decisions are based are stated according to a standard formula.[235] Positive selection criteria, on the other hand, suggest that cases will not be published unless they possess certain merits that justify publication.[236] Furthermore, the Recommendation explicitly encourages member states to apply the negative selection method to cases decided by the highest courts in all fields of law.[237] In other words, the Recommendation suggests that all cases decided by the highest courts in all legal areas should be published, unless they are evidently of little value.

A comparison between the old selection criteria and Recommendation R (95)11 reveals that, formally, the old criteria were not entirely in conformity with the Recommendation. It is, for example, striking that the Recommendation puts great emphasis on

---

[231] Committee of Ministers of the Council of Europe 1995.
[232] Van Opijnen 2006b, p. 14 and Phillippart 2010.
[233] Paragraph III, sub-paragraph 2, Appendix I of Recommendation R (95) 11, see Committee of Ministers of the Council of Europe 1995.
[234] Paragraph II, sub-paragraph 5, Appendix II of Recommendation R (95) 11, see Committee of Ministers of the Council of Europe 1995
[235] Ibid.
[236] Ibid.
[237] Ibid.

the objectivity of case selection for publication,[238] whereas it is highly doubtful how objective the broadly drafted old selection criteria adopted by the judiciary were. Moreover, the old selection criteria did not explicitly state that the method of negative selection would be applied to cases decided by the highest courts. Implicitly, however, the old selection criteria did adopt the method of combining positive criteria with negative ones.[239] Moreover, in practice the highest courts did apply the negative selection method by publishing all their judgments through the official website except those without substantive content.[240]

The abstract and vague selection criteria incurred frequent criticism from both within and outside the judiciary.[241] In order to better facilitate the selection process and to increase the transparency of the selection policy, the judiciary published a new set of selection criteria in March 2012. The new criteria contain a number of improvements.

First of all, the new criteria are more elaborate. The old criteria were rather sketchy, containing only 261 words, whereas the new criteria (948 words) are almost four times as lengthy as the old. Moreover, the new criteria are published together with elaborate explanations (1689 words) that provide useful clarifications to each selection criterion as well as to the new criteria in general. The clarifications can be very useful for understanding and applying the criteria.

A second improvement is that the new criteria explicitly adopt the negative method in the selection of cases decided by the highest courts as well as three special court sections.[242] This change makes the previous *implicit* practice of publishing all highest courts' judgments with substantive content *explicit*.

---

[238] See e.g. paragraph III, sub-paragraph 2, Appendix I of Recommendation R 95 (11) and paragraph II first sentence, Appendix II of Recommendation R (95) 11.

[239] The last four criteria can be seen as negative ones, whereas the rest were positive. See Appendix 2.

[240] Van Opijnen 2011b. p. 177.

[241] Editors' Board 2012, p. 1436.

[242] See Article 3 of the new selection criteria and the explanation to this criterion in Raad voor de Rechtspraak (Council for the Judiciary) e.a. 2012.

A third improvement is that the new criteria use much more objective selection standards than the old. An objective selection standard is a criterion that is, in principle, susceptible to only one interpretation.[243] In other words, a selector has, in principle, no margin of interpretation when applying an objective selection criterion. The old selection criteria contained only four objective standards.[244] Moreover, the objective standards of the old criteria were only used to identify which cases were *not* supposed to be published. The new selection criteria use 19 objective standards to indicate which cases should be published.[245] Broader use of objective selection standards provides more concrete guidance to the selectors than the old criteria. Another advantage of using objective standards is that it makes the selection decision more verifiable than using primarily subjective criteria.

A fourth improvement is that the new selection criteria and the explanations articulate an active case publication principle, i.e. courts should try to publish as many cases as possible, whereas the old criteria did not convey such a message. Article 5 paragraph a of the new selection criteria, for example, states that a judgment will always be published if before, during or after the court session the case has attracted attention of the public media in the broadest sense. Terms such as "always", "before", "during", "after" and "in the broadest sense" indicate that courts are supposed to apply a broad, rather than restricted publication policy in cases that have attracted public attention. Another example is Article 6 paragraph 1, which explicitly states that certain types of cases should be published "as much as possible". Still another example is the explanation to Article 5 paragraph e, which says:[246]

> A broad interpretation of this subparagraph is appropriate, since the selector is not always able to ascertain to what extent a judgment indeed has a precedent forming character: in fact, doubt about the legal importance of a

---

243 Kottenhagen & Kaptein 1989, p. 28.

244 See the last four standards of the old criteria in De Meij e.a. 2006, p. 15.

245 See Article 3, Article 4 and Article 5 paragraph b of the new selection criteria.

246 See Appendix 3.

judgment is by itself already sufficient for deciding to publish it.

3.2 Publication format

Since its launch in 1999, the official website of the judiciary has been using the Internet as the sole medium for case publication. Cases are published online in a uniform format, which contains three parts:

1. Technical details of a case such as the European Case Law Identifier (ECLI) number[247] (prior to June 2013 the LJN number was published),[248] case number,[249] name of the court, date of the judgment, date of publication, field of law etc. A noteworthy and useful feature of the official case publication is that if a case published in the official online database has also been published and/or annotated in one or more commercial case report periodicals, the details of commercial publication such as the name(s) of the periodical(s), the publication year and sequence number as well as the name(s) of the annotator(s) are integrated into the technical details of the official case publication.[250]

---

[247] The European Case Law Identifier (ECLI) number is a case law citation standard developed by the European Union to facilitate the correct and unequivocal citation of judgments of the European and national courts, see https://e-justice.europa.eu/content_european_case_law_identifier_ecli-175-en.do.

[248] LJN is an abbreviation of *Landelijk Jurisprudentienummer* (national case law number). One of the core functions of LJN was to facilitate the searching and citing of cases by giving each case a unique identification code. The LJN was a national case law identification system in the Netherlands. It was replaced by a European case law citation standard (ECLI) in June 2013. For details see the following subparagraph.

[249] The case number should not be confused with the European Case Law Identifier (ECLI), as the former is a code assigned to a case by the court that has decided it for chiefly administrative purposes, whereas the latter is a code that follows a European standard that chiefly serves the purpose of facilitating the identification and unequivocal citation of judgments across Europe.

[250] The Dutch term for such publication details is "vindplaats", which literally means "place where something can be found".

2. Content indication.[251] This part is usually very brief, containing a number of key words or short sentences that give an indication of the substance of the case.
3. The judgment in full text. Judgments are published in unedited form, except that information that could reveal the identity of natural persons is erased.[252]

A major difference between official case publication and commercial publication is that cases published on the official website of the judiciary are not annotated. Another difference is that the content indication of officially published cases tends to be rather short, whereas some commercial periodicals provide quite elaborate summaries of some of the published cases.[253]

3.3 Search mechanisms

The official website of the judiciary has a built-in case search engine.[254] The search engine offers its users a number of search possibilities to find cases published on the website. Users can search by technical details of a case, such as the case number or the European Case Law Identifier (ECLI). It is also possible to search by the area of law, by court name or by date of judgment. Still another possibility is to search by key words. Furthermore, users can combine search approaches, such as searching by court name and key words.

In this context it is worth noting that the judiciary introduced an innovative and useful case search tool called the LJN-index in

[251] The Dutch term is "inhoudsindicatie".

[252] Names of natural persons who are involved in the case in professional capacities such as judges, lawyers and interpreters do not have to be anonymized, for more details see Raad voor de Rechtspraak (Council for the Judiciary) 2007.

[253] For example, the content indication of the case ECLI:NL:HR:2011: BO5803 decided by the Supreme Court published on the official website has only 55 words, whereas the commercial periodical *Nederlandse Jurisprudentie (Netherlands Cases)* provides a summary of 561 words. For more examples compare the content indication of the officially published version of the following cases with the summaries of the commercially published versions: ECLI:NL:HR:2011:BP0567, ECLI:NL:HR:2010:BN6236 and ECLI:NL:HR:2011:BP6996.

[254] http://uitspraken.rechtspraak.nl/.

February 2006, which existed as a separate search tool in addition to the comprehensive built-in case search engine on the official website of the judiciary until June 2013 when the LJN-index search functionality was integrated into the built-in case search engine.[255] A key feature of the LJN-index was the possibility for users to find out in which commercial periodicals a case had been published and/or annotated. The index achieved this feature by assigning a unique identification code called the *Landelijk Jurisprudentienummer* (national case law number) to each case published on the official website of the judiciary as well as to each case published in commercial periodicals that had been integrated into the Judiciary's internal legal information portal website *Porta Iuris.*[256] By creating this national case law identification system, the LJN-index successfully built a bridge between officially and commercially published cases. When the national case law number of a judgment was entered into the search field, the LJN-index would reveal whether, and if so, in which commercial periodical(s) the case had been published. Moreover, the search result would show whether, and if so, in which periodical(s) the case had been annotated. This feature can be very useful for users who find a case through the built-in case search engine on the official website and wish to find possible annotations to the case in commercial periodicals.

As in June 2013 the LJN-index ceased to exist and was replaced by ECLI, the search functionality of the LJN-index was integrated into the comprehensive built-in case search engine on the official website of the judiciary.[257] In this way, the technical move to switch from LJN to ECLI did not affect the innovative search functionality introduced by the LJN-index, as after the switch users are still able to find the commercial periodicals in which a case has been published and annotated by entering the unique identification

---

[255] http://www.rechtspraak.nl/Uitspraken-en-Registers/Uitspraken/Hulp-bij-zoeken/Pages/default.aspx#TOCHeadingRichHtmlField14.

[256] It should be noted that a case acquires only one LJN identification code if it is published both on the official website of the judiciary and in commercial periodicals. For more details of the LJN-index see Van Opijnen 2006a.

[257] See http://www.rechtspraak.nl/Uitspraken-en-Registers/Uitspraken/Pages/ECLI.aspx.

code of a case into the appropriate search field of the built-in case search engine on the official website of the judiciary.[258]

3.4 Academic and practising lawyers' reflections on official case publication

Since going online in December 1999, the official portal website of the judiciary has made considerable contributions to the accessibility of cases in the Netherlands, which has earned positive reactions from commentators. An obvious contribution is that official case publication eliminated the price barrier of commercial case publication, as cases are nowadays available on the official website of the judiciary free of charge.[259] Moreover, thanks to official case publication, the overall case publication rate and the total number of published cases in the Netherlands have more than doubled in ten years time (see Table 3 and compare it with table 1 and 2).[260] Even critics of the selection mechanism of official case publication admit that the official website of the judiciary has become one of the most important sources of legal information in the Netherlands.[261]

Year	Total decided cases	Cases published in commercial periodicals and on the official website of the	Percentage

[258] Raad voor de Rechtspraak (Council for the Judiciary) 2012.
[259] Bergwerf & Houweling 2008, p. 9.
[260] Van Opijnen 2011a, p. 2149.
[261] Mommers & Zwenne & Schermer 2010.
[262] Data in this column are based on Van Opijnen 2011a, p. 2143, Table 1. It should be noted that Van Opijnen's research data do not cover cases published in *all* commercial periodicals in the Netherlands, but rather cases published in commercial periodicals that have been included in the electronic database of the LJN-index. As the LJN-index includes the most commonly used legal periodicals, the data can be very close to the entire number of cases published in all commercial periodicals and through the official website of the judiciary in the Netherlands. It should further be

		judiciary[262]	
2001	1,450,000[263]	10579	0.73%
2002	1,555,880[264]	13826	0.89%
2003	1,561,960[265]	15159	0.97%
2004	1,767,810[266]	17019	0.96%
2005	1,801,000[267]	18560	1,03%
2006	1,752,420[268]	21408	1,22%
2007	1,726,400[269]	23684	1,37%
2008	1,827,620[270]	26163	1,43%
2009	1,935,260[271]	27898	1,44%
2010	1,960,900[272]	28800	1,47%

Table 3 Overall case publication rate (both commercial and official case publication) 2001-2010

Still another contribution welcomed by commentators is that, thanks to official case publication, the delay in case publication has been shortened. A study on the publication of labour law cases reveals that, on average, labour cases are published 35 days earlier on the official website than in a specialized case report periodical *Jurisprudentie arbeidsrecht (Labour Law Cases)*.[273] Another study reveals that in 2010, more than half of all cases available on the official website were published within seven days, and that nearly all cases decided by the Supreme Court were published on the same

---

noted that in his paper Van Opijnen has taken proper technical measures to prevent double counting of cases that have been published both on the official website of the judiciary and in commercial periodicals. See interview NL20121017 and the methodological notes to Van Opijnen's paper in 2011, see Van Opijnen 2011a, p. 2150.

263 Raad voor de Rechtspraak (Council for the Judiciary) 2003, p. 49.

264 Raad voor de Rechtspraak (Council for the Judiciary) 2004, p. 57.

265 Raad voor de Rechtspraak (Council for the Judiciary) 2006, p. 79.

266 Ibid.

267 Ibid.

268 Raad voor de Rechtspraak (Council for the Judiciary) 2009, p 65.

269 Ibid.

270 Raad voor de Rechtspraak (Council for the Judiciary) 2011, p. 54.

271 Ibid.

272 Ibid.

273 Bergwerf & Houweling 2008.

day the judgment was handed down.[274] The delay in commercial case publication in 2010 was considerably longer, as the median publication delay was 81 days.[275] Timely publication is therefore deemed as one of the key strengths of official case publication.[276]

Despite these contributions, official case publication incurred criticism, mainly due to its case selection practice.[277] As mentioned earlier in this paper, the old selection criteria attracted criticism both from within and from outside the judiciary due to their vagueness.[278] Also the fact that case selection is controlled entirely by judges incurs criticism, as some commentators argue that such a practice may raise the impression of censorship.[279] Accordingly, these commentators suggest that, as one of the alternatives to the current selection mechanism, the selection should be made by an organization entirely independent from the judiciary.[280]

It is worth noting that particularly in recent years some commentators have been calling for the judiciary to abandon the practice of selecting cases for publication all together and to publish all judgments online.[281] Some of these commentators base their argument on legal provisions such as Article 6 of the European

---

[274] Van Opijnen 2011a, p. 2144.

[275] Ibid.

[276] Bergwerf & Houweling 2008, p. 9 and Van Opijnen 2011a, p. 2149. It should be noted that the high speed with which cases are published on the official website of the judiciary is achieved not only by using the internet as the publication medium, but also by eliminating time-consuming elements such as adding summaries and annotations to the published cases.

[277] Another aspect of official case publication that has been frequently criticized is the anonymization policy and practice, see e.g. Schuijt 2004 and De Meij e.a. 2006.

[278] Editors' Board 2012, p. 1436.

[279] See e.g. Mommers & Zwenne & Schermer 2010, p. 2077.

[280] See e.g. Mommers & Zwenne & Schermer 2010, p. 2077. This proposal is not entirely new. A decade before the launch of the official website, some scholars already suggested that case selection should be done by actors independent of the judiciary, see Kottenhagen & Kaptein 1989, p. 112-113.

[281] Even before the launching of the official website, some commentators were already arguing that all cases should be published on the internet, see e.g. De Mulder 1996.

Convention on Human Rights and Article 121 of the Dutch Constitution.[282] Others argue that the current case selection practice should be abolished, because it results in a small and unrepresentative sample of cases being published, which makes legal and social scientific research nearly impossible.[283]

Criticism on the selection criteria led the judiciary to adopt more detailed and more objective selection standards.[284] The suggestion to entrust the task of case selection to an organization independent of the judiciary, however, has not yet caused the judiciary to change its current case selection practice.[285] Nor has the recommendation to publish all cases been adopted. An argument against publishing all cases is that it is useless to publish the vast body of judgments that contain merely standardized formulas.[286] Another argument that rejects publishing all cases is that doing so would make it difficult to search among the vast body of published judgments.[287] Still another argument against publishing all cases is that doing so would cost too much money, especially given the fact that anonymization of judgments still has to be done manually.[288] Given these arguments it seems very unlikely that the judiciary would soon switch from the practice of selecting cases for publication to publishing all cases. Whether in the long run the judiciary will eventually publish all court judgments still remains to be seen.

4. Concluding remarks

The data collected in this chapter reveal that case publication has been an established practice in the Netherlands for well over a century.[289] Nowadays, there are two channels through which cases

---

[282] De Meij e.a. 2006, p. 3-8.
[283] Mommers & Zwenne & Schermer 2010, p. 2072.
[284] Raad voor de Rechtspraak (Council for the Judiciary) e.a. 2012.
[285] The argument that case selection by judges may raise the impression of censorship has been dismissed as lacking substantive evidence, see Van der Hoek 2010.
[286] See e.g. Van der Hoek 2010.
[287] See e.g. Jongeneel 2010, p. 2145.
[288] See e.g. Phillippart 2010.
[289] See Jansen & Zwalve 2013, p. 196 and Appendix 1.

are made accessible to the public, i.e. the official website of the judiciary and various commercial case reporting periodicals. Case publication fulfils an important role in the case law mechanism in the Netherlands, as it builds a bridge between the vast body of decided cases and the various users of cases. At the same time, case publication can be said to fulfil a selection function in the case law mechanism in the Netherlands, as case publication is an important step in a chain that determines which judgments eventually become the leading cases that shape the law.

4.1 Bridge function

A basic yet important contribution that case publication makes to the case law mechanism is that it makes a body of selected court judgments available to users beyond the courts that have decided the cases. Without case publication, it would be very difficult for judges, practising lawyers and legal scholars to use previous cases to solve problems in legal practice and to further develop the law, because they would have considerable difficulty in accessing court judgments.[290]
The task of making court judgments available to the public used to be nearly solely fulfilled by commercial case publication.[291] Since

---

[290] This study does not argue that without case publication it would be totally impossible for judges, practising lawyers and legal scholars to use cases. The judiciary in the Netherlands, for example, has an internal digital database named the E-archief where all court judgments are stored, see Van Opijnen 2006b, p. 18 and interview NL 20131008-2. This means that at least in theory, judges nowadays do not have to rely on official or commercial case publication to access judgments made by their colleagues. However, before this digital database was created, judges had to rely primarily on published cases in order to know how their colleagues had decided certain issues in previous judgments. In fact, even after the creation of this digital database, judges still use the official online judgments database of the judiciary and commercial case reporting periodicals to find cases. See e.g. interview NL20130923, NL20131008-1, NL20131008-2, NL20131021, NL20131022 and NL20131024.
[291] For some rare examples of cases published by the government in the *Staatsblad* (*Bulletin of Acts and Decrees of the Kingdom of the Netherlands*) and the *Staatscourant* (*Netherlands Government Gazette*), see De Jong 1981, p. 2.

the launch of the online judgments database by the judiciary in 1999, however, this task has been gradually taken over by official case publication.[292] Nowadays commercial publishers are largely publishing cases that have already been made available in the online judgments database by the judiciary. This, however, does not mean that commercial case publication has become redundant. The reasons why commercial case publication has not disappeared, even though the cases that commercial publishers nowadays publish have already been made available by the judiciary free of charge on its official website, are related to two other ways through which case publication makes a contribution to the case law mechanism, i.e. making cases findable and better understandable. These two aspects will be further discussed in the following passages.

One of the difficulties in using cases as a source of law is that when a relatively large volume of cases has been made available to the public, it could be time-consuming and troublesome for users to, without the assistance of a good search tool, manually comb through the large body of published judgments in order to find the cases that are relevant for them. Developing good systems to classify and organize published cases so that users can quickly find the cases they need is therefore of great importance. As this chapter has revealed, both commercial publishers and the judiciary have made a considerable contribution to the enhancement of the findability of published cases by improving the search tools that they provide. There is a trend towards more and more integrated search tools as well as striving towards a minimum delay between the moment of case publication and that of integrating the published case into search tools. In this respect, commercial case publication seems to offer more powerful solutions, as the online databases of some publishers provide highly integrated search tools that can help users to find not only cases, but also related legislation and scholarly works easily and quickly, whereas the search tools in the official online judgments database of the judiciary do not offer a similar functionality.[293]

Not only does case publication in the Netherlands make cases available and findable, it also adds relevant information to published cases that can help the user to quickly grasp the essence

[292] See e.g. Van Opijnen 2006b and Van Opijnen 2011a, p. 2143.
[293] See e.g. http://www.kluwernavigator.nl/ and http://opmaat.sdu.nl/.

of published judgments. In official case publication, a number of key words or sentences is added to each published case to indicate the essence of the judgment.[294] Commercial publishers usually add a summary to published cases. [295] Moreover, commercially published cases are sometimes accompanied by an annotation, i.e. a brief commentary by a (prominent) legal scholar or practising lawyer that usually summarizes the essence of the judgment, ascertains the place of the case in the legal system, evaluates the soundness of the decision and explores possible implications of the case for future practice. The value of the practice of case annotation as a whole is commonly deemed very high in the Netherlands, as case annotations can not only benefit judges and practising lawyers by saving them time and offering them insights for future practice, but can also serve an educational function by helping law students to better understand the essence and the relevance of an annotated case.[296]

4.2 Selection function

This chapter revealed that far from all decided cases are published in the Netherlands.[297] Even in today's Internet age, the overall case publication rate in the Netherlands is still barely 1.5%.[298] The fact that only a very small proportion of all decided cases is published has implications for the way case law develops and functions in the Netherlands.

One effect of publishing only a small proportion of decided cases is that it can help prevent the body of published cases from growing so huge that it would become extremely difficult and time-consuming for users to find the cases that they need.[299] This, as has been revealed in this chapter, has been used as an argument to reject

---

[294] This is called "inhoudsindicatie" in Dutch, which can be translated as content indication.
[295] See e.g. HR 25 May 2012, NJ 2012, 340 and HR 11 April 2014, NJ 2014, 309.
[296] See e.g. Snijders 2003, Hondius 2007a, p. 21, Leiden Law School 2012b, p. 3 and Leiden Law School 2012f, p. 1.
[297] See table 1, 2 and 3.
[298] See table 3.
[299] See e.g. Jongeneel 2010, p. 2145 and Van der Hoek 2010.

the proposal by some legal scholars for the judiciary to abandon the practice of selecting cases for publication and to switch to publishing all cases online.[300]

Another, and arguably much more significant effect of publishing only a small proportion of all decided cases is that, instead of being a mere neutral tool through which users gain access to decided cases, case publication has become a step in the case law mechanism in the Netherlands that fulfils a substantive role, i.e. it has become a link in a chain that determines which court judgments eventually become leading cases that shape the law. After all, it is usually published cases that will be used to decide future cases and to further develop the law.[301] Accordingly, by determining which cases are made accessible to the public and which are not, case publication can have a significant impact on the substance of the law. If many exceptional cases are published that do not represent the majority approach adopted by courts on a certain issue whereas cases that do represent the majority approach are not published because they are conventional and thus less sensational, case publication may create a distorted image of the court practice. Doing so would create a risk that users of cases could be misled into perceiving the exceptional cases as the common approach in court practice.[302]

One possible solution to prevent the risk of case publication being intentionally or unintentionally abused to manipulate the

---

[300] See the subparagraph in this chapter that reviews academic and practising lawyers' reflections on official case publication in the Netherlands.

[301] As has been mentioned earlier in this chapter, the judiciary in the Netherlands has an internal digital database named the E-archief where all court judgments are stored, see Van Opijnen 2006b, p. 18 and interview NL 20131008. Some judges indicated during interviews that they do make use of this internal database to find unpublished cases that bear relevance to the cases that they decide, see interviews NL 20131008 and NL 20131107-3. It is therefore not true that only published cases influence judicial decision-making. This, of course, does not change the fact that it is usually published cases rather than the unpublished ones that influence the development of the law. After all, it is published cases that are cited in judgments and practising lawyers, legal scholars as well as other actors outside the judiciary normally only have access to published cases.

[302] See Snijders 1977 and interview NL20131021.

development of case law is to abandon the practice of selection and to publish all decided cases.[303] This chapter showed that the judiciary in the Netherlands did not adopt this solution, even though some legal scholars have been arguing for this in recent years.[304] Instead, the judiciary seeks to limit this risk by, among other things, making the selection criteria more elaborate and objective.[305] One of the purposes for doing so could be to enhance the transparency and verifiability of case selection for publication, thus counterbalancing the fact that published cases are not selected by a neutral and independent third party, but by judges that have decided the cases, who can be perceived to have a personal interest in "hiding" certain (types of) cases.[306] Another strategy of the judiciary to limit this risk is to follow the recommendation of the Committee of Ministers of the Council of Europe by adopting a negative method in the selection of cases decided by the highest courts and three special court sections, i.e. these cases should in principle all be published unless they are evidently of little value.[307] With regard to the publication of cases decided by other courts, the attitude of the judiciary seems to be increasingly active, as judges are nowadays encouraged to publish as many cases as possible.[308] It seems that the judiciary is trying to seek a balance among competing considerations, such as managing the volume of published cases to prevent difficulties in searching and using cases, protecting the privacy of litigants by deleting information in published judgments that could reveal the identity of litigants and limiting the risk of case publication being abused to manipulate the

---

[303] See e.g. De Mulder 1996, De Meij e.a. 2006 and Mommers & Zwenne & Schermer 2010.

[304] See the subparagraph in this chapter that reviews academic and practising lawyers' reflections on official case publication in the Netherlands.

[305] Raad voor de Rechtspraak (Council for the Judiciary) e.a. 2012.

[306] See Mommers & Zwenne & Schermer 2010, p. 2077.

[307] See e.g. Article 5 Paragraph a and Article 6 Paragraph 1 of the new selection criteria and the explanation to this criterion in Raad voor de Rechtspraak (Council for the Judiciary) e.a. 2012.

[308] See e.g. Article 3 of the new selection criteria and the explanation to this criterion in Raad voor de Rechtspraak (Council for the Judiciary) e.a. 2012.

development of case law. How well the judiciary succeeds in finding a proper balance and whether the judiciary will or should eventually publish all cases or at least adopt a negative method in the selection of cases decided by all courts can be interesting topics for future research.

Chapter 2

Utilization of cases in the Netherlands

Chapter 2 Utilization of cases in the Netherlands

1. Introduction

The previous chapter examined the first phase in the operation of the case law mechanism in the Netherlands, namely how cases are published. Getting published is a necessary, but obviously not sufficient condition for a court judgment to become a leading case that shapes the law. If, for example, a published case never catches the attention of legal scholars, practising lawyers and judges, it will not be cited in court judgments or scholarly writings and hence will be forgotten instead of becoming a leading case. Consequently, it is logical for this chapter to, following the previous chapter that has investigated how cases are published, examine how cases are used in the Netherlands.

The utilization of cases has long been the focus in the existing literature on the role of cases in civil law jurisdictions.[309] In particular, scholars tend to concentrate on how a particular type of actors, namely judges, makes use of cases in court practice.[310] This research wishes to, as already explained in the introduction of this study, broaden the scope of investigation on the use of cases.[311] The following three paragraphs will successively investigate how cases are used in scholarly legal research, legal education and adjudication in the Netherlands. This chapter will demonstrate that in the Netherlands there are multiple actors that make use of cases and that the way each type of actor uses cases makes a certain contribution to the functioning of cases as a source of law.

---

[309] See e.g. Lipstein 1946, Silving 1966, Dawson 1970, Rudden 1974, Zweigert & Kötz 1998, p. 256-275, Eng 2000, Komárek 2013.

[310] This is of course not to say that the way other actors make use of cases has never been discussed in the existing literature. Deák 1934, p. 354 and Dainow 1966, p. 428-430, for example, mentioned the use of cases in legal education in civil law jurisdictions. Yiannopoulos 1974, p. 77 and Taruffo 1997, p. 457, for example, touched upon the use of cases by legal scholars in civil law jurisdictions. However, references to the way cases are used by other actors than judges are rather brief and lack in-depth analysis.

[311] See the paragraph in the introduction to this book that explains the analytic framework developed by and used in this study.

Nowadays cases are widely used in different settings by various users in the Netherlands. Not only do judges, legal scholars and law students, but also practising lawyers and even the legislature make use of cases.[312] This chapter focuses on the use of cases in adjudication, in scholarly legal research and in legal education, but does not examine how the legislature makes use of cases. This choice is made, on the one hand, due to the limited time and resources, but also because the next chapter will briefly cover the way cases are used in legislation.[313] How practising lawyers make use of cases is also an interesting topic to investigate. However, this chapter will not elaborate on this point, but the investigation into the way judges make use of cases does touch upon the role of practising lawyers.[314] This choice is made again due to the limited time and resources available. This study welcomes other researchers to conduct in-depth studies into the way practising lawyers make use of cases and their contribution to the case law mechanism.

Furthermore, it should be noted that nowadays cases are widely used in all major legal areas in the Netherlands, including civil, criminal, constitutional and administrative law.[315] This chapter focuses on the use of cases in civil law, in particular tort law. Two major considerations have led to this choice. First, civil law, in particular tort law, is an area where the use of cases as a source of law is particularly active and visible, as this is an area where the legislation contains many flexible or broadly drafted norms that need to be further specified in adjudication practice.[316] Secondly, I graduated in Dutch civil law, and am hence more capable of

---

[312] See e.g. Scholten 1931, p. 115, Schoordijk 1988, p. 52 and Giesen & Schelhaas 2008, p. 136.

[313] See the relevant passages in chapter three that examine some of the legislation techniques that the legislature in the Netherlands uses.

[314] See the paragraph in this chapter that examines the way cases are used in adjudication practice.

[315] See e.g. Schlossels & Zijlstra 2010, Kelk & De Jong 2013 and Konijnenbelt & Van Male 2014.

[316] Hartkamp and Sieburgh, for example, observe that no other provision of the old Civil Code has led to so many cases and scholarly writings as Art. 1401 (current Art. 6:162 BW, the general clause of tort law), see Hartkamp & Sieburgh 2011b, § 2.

appreciating the use of cases in this area than in criminal or administrative law. I am aware of the limitations imposed by this methodological choice, and hence do not assert that the findings can be generalized without qualification of the way cases are used in other legal areas in the Netherlands. This is, of course, not to say that the way cases are used in civil law deviates fundamentally from the way they are used in other legal areas. In fact, discussions with legal scholars[317] and judges[318] who are familiar with other areas of the law indicate that the way cases are used in, for example, criminal and administrative law does bear similarities to the way cases are used in civil law in the Netherlands. Scholars who are familiar with other legal areas are welcome to conduct similar research into the way cases are used in those areas and to compare their findings with this study, so that we will be able to gain more comprehensive insights into the way cases are used in the Netherlands.

2. Use of cases in scholarly legal research

2.1 Method

One of the challenges for this part of the study is that there is an enormous amount of data (i.e. cases are used in a vast array of scholarly writings), whereas the existing literature does not offer a readily usable analytic framework. In order to obtain a general impression of the use of cases in academic legal research and to develop an analytic framework, I conducted a pilot study. The primary method was text analysis. The studied sources included relevant literature on the role of legal scholars in general[319] and randomly selected writings of legal scholars where cases are

[317] I presented the findings of this research at four universities in the Netherlands to legal scholars who are specialized in different legal areas. The feedback that the audience gave during the discussion sessions indicates that the way cases are used in other areas of the law bears similarities with the findings of this chapter.
[318] See e.g. interviews NL20131008-1, NL20131029 and NL20131107-3.
[319] E.g. Bruinsma 1988a, p. 105-121, Vranken 1995, p. 110-190 and Van Maanen 2007.

used.[320] In addition, semi-structured interviews have been conducted with two law professors to obtain data that are missing in the studied written sources, in particular with regard to the ways legal scholars systemize and interpret cases.[321]

The main research used the method of text analysis. For obvious reasons, it is impossible to study all available academic legal writings on every area of the law. The research was limited to the area of tort law for reasons already mentioned in the introduction to this chapter.

The studied sources include two types of scholarly writings: books and journal articles. In total, five books were selected: the *Asser Series*,[322] *Monographs on the Civil Code: Tort*,[323] *Text and Comments on the Civil Code*,[324] the *Green Series*[325] and a textbook on tort law[326]. The selection was inspired by the method of stratified sampling. I first identified three types of books written by legal scholars: handbooks, textbooks and practice-oriented books. The *Asser Series* and *Monographs on the Civil Code: Tort* are well-known and influential handbooks. The textbook written by Spier e.a. was chosen as an example of textbooks, as it is used in the legal education at, among others, Leiden University,[327] Tilburg University[328] and Maastricht University.[329] The *Green Series* and

---

[320] E.g. Jansen 1967, Rutten-Roos 1970, Tjong Tjin Tai 2005, Brunner 2011 and Nieuwenhuis 2013.

[321] Interviews NL20130304 and NL20130305.

[322] The Dutch title is *Mr. C. Assers Handleiding tot de beoefening van het Nederlands Burgerlijk Recht, Verbintenissenrecht, Deel 6-IV Verbintenis uit de wet*, see Hartkamp & Sieburgh 2011a.

[323] The Dutch title is *Monografieën BW, B 45 Onrechtmatige daad: algemene bepalingen*, see Jansen 2009.

[324] The Dutch title is *Burgerlijk Wetboek: de tekst van de boeken 1, 2, 3, 4, 5, 6, 7, 8, 10 van het BW en International Convention for the unification of certain rules of law relating to bills of lading, voorzien van commentaar,* see Nieuwenhuis & Stolker & Valk 2011.

[325] The Dutch title is *De Groene Serie*, see Jansen 2012.

[326] Spier e.a. 2012.

[327] See https://studiegids.leidenuniv.nl/courses/show/35418/ verbintenissenrecht.

[328] See http://mystudy.uvt.nl/it10.vakzicht?taal=n&pfac=&vakcode =650262.

[329] See http://www.maastrichtuniversity.nl/web/Main1/SiteWide/

Text and Comments on Civil Code are books chosen as examples of practice-oriented books, as these two books are widely used by judges and practising lawyers.[330]

In addition, articles on tort law in four law journals (*NJB*,[331] *AA*[332] *NTBR*,[333] and *MvV*[334]) from 2008 till 2012 have been studied. The selection was made primarily on the basis of the target audience and the general style of the journals. The *NJB* was chosen because it is a highly prestigious and widely used general[335] law journal that has a widely defined audience including practically all legal scholars and practitioners. *Ars Aequi* is also a general law journal, but it has a more specific target audience, namely law students. The *NTBR* is a journal specialized in private law with a slightly scholarly style, whereas the *MvV* is essentially specialized in the same area as the *NTBR* but has a slightly more practical flavour. The timespan of five years was chosen for the practical reason that the limited time available for this research does not allow a larger sample of journal articles to be studied. The starting point was set to 2008 because the five-year timespan from 2008 till 2012 is the most recent to the time when the research was conducted.

2.2 Findings

In the decades immediately following the introduction of the Old Dutch Civil Code in 1838, cases did not play a particularly prominent role in academic legal research.[336] It used to be common that handbooks clarified the law from the perspective of law professors, with occasionally a casual footnote that referred to one

---

courseDetailpagina/OnrechtmatigeDaadEnSchadevergoeding500199362012NlPRI4008.htm.

[330] See e.g. interviews NL20131008, NL20131017, NL20131021, NL20131022 and NL20131114.

[331] The Dutch title is *Nederlands Juristenblad.*

[332] The Dutch title is *Ars Aequi.*

[333] The Dutch title is *Nederlands Tijdschrift voor Burgerlijk Recht.*

[334] The Dutch title is *Maandblad voor Vermogensrecht.*

[335] The journal covers all major areas of the law, such as civil law, criminal law, administrative law and international law.

[336] Brunner 1994, p. 32.

or two Supreme Court decisions where the Court had, in the eyes of the law professors, expressed a different opinion.[337] This situation began to change in the early decades of the 20th century, when prominent law professors such as Meijers and Scholten began to annotate cases.[338] Nowadays, legal scholars pay close attention to cases in their research. Nearly every type of academic legal writing involves judicial cases. Almost every law journal deems it a crucial task to keep its readers informed of the latest cases.[339] Handbooks and textbooks are frequently updated to incorporate the relevant cases that have emerged since the last version.[340]

Writings of legal scholars where cases are used can be roughly divided into two categories: case-focused and system-oriented. A key feature of case-focused writings is that they intensively discuss the substance and implications of one or a couple of (related) cases.[341] System-oriented writings, on the other hand, provide an overview of a certain field of the law[342] or discuss a specific legal device.[343] Within each category, a further distinction can be made between descriptive and evaluative writings, the difference being that descriptive writings do not[344] contain explicit opinions of legal scholars on the soundness and desirability of the discussed judicial decisions, whereas evaluative ones do.[345] This typology can be visualized as in Table 4. The following two subparagraphs will take a closer look at the different types of scholarly legal writings.

	Case-focused	System-oriented
Descriptive		
Evaluative		

Table 4 Typology of scholarly legal writings that involve cases

[337] Bruinsma 1988a, p. 115
[338] Ibid.
[339] Vranken 1995, p. 114.
[340] Vranken 1995, p. 114.
[341] See e.g. Tjong Tjin Tai 2005 and Jansen 1967.
[342] Handbooks and textbooks belong to this category.
[343] See e.g. Klaassen 2012 and Hartlief 2013.
[344] See e.g. Wessels 2006 and Enneking 2013.
[345] See e.g. Roelofs 2008 and Giesen 2008.

2.2.1 Descriptive scholarly writings involving cases

As the above-presented typology suggests, descriptive scholarly writings include two subtypes, i.e. case-focused and system-oriented writings. Contrary to what the term "case-focused" might suggest, it is not true that case-focused scholarly writings only discuss the content of a particular case without any effort to embed the discussed case in a broader system. Nor is it true that system-oriented writings solely seek to systemize judicial decisions without properly assessing the content of individual cases. In fact, both case-focused and system-oriented descriptive writings essentially do two things:

(1) interpretation, i.e. identifying and explaining what has been decided in a case, and
(2) systemization, i.e. verifying and explaining whether, and if so how a judicial decision fits in the system of the law.

The following passages will examine these two aspects in details.

2.2.1.1 Interpretation

Although both case-focused and system-oriented descriptive scholarly writings seek to identify and explain what has actually been decided in a case, they differ in the intensity and details with which they treat this aspect. System-oriented writings usually give a much briefer account of the content of a case than case-focused scholarly works. Very often, system-oriented writings summarize the essence of a case in no more than one or two sentences by distilling a norm from the judicial decision.[346] Most case-focused writings, on the other hand, do not only distil a norm or norms from a judicial decision, but also summarize the key facts, analyse the legal reasoning that the court employs to reach the decision and explore possible implications of the discussed case for similar or related cases in the future.[347] Some case-focused writings even provide a brief explanation of the background of the lawsuit and give a summary of the judgments in lower instances before the case

[346] See e.g. the cases and the comments to them in Nieuwenhuis & Stolker & Valk 2011, Article 6:162, Commentary 5, paragraph a.
[347] See e.g. Haas 2010 and Fernhout 2010.

reached the Supreme Court.[348] These findings can be summarized in a table (see Table 5).

	Case-focused	System-oriented
Background of the case	Sometimes included	Seldom included
Facts	Usually included	Seldom included or very brief
Norms that can be distilled from the case	Usually included	Usually included
Analysis of the legal reasoning of the court	Usually included	Seldom included or very brief
Implications for future cases	Usually included	Seldom included or very brief

Table 5 Comparison of interpretive aspects of case-focused and system-oriented descriptive scholarly writings

2.2.1.2 Systemization

Although most case-focused writings intensively discuss only one case, they do not analyse the case as an isolated island. Instead, scholars frequently refer to relevant legislation, doctrines and previous cases, thus putting the discussed case in a broader perspective.[349] Such systemization efforts help to clarify the significance of the discussed case for the development of the law and for future practice.

The systemization aspect is particularly prominent in system-oriented writings. After all, a key feature of system-oriented writings is that they process a large amount of judicial cases by allocating them to proper places within a certain framework and by organizing them in a certain order. Throughout the years scholars have developed a number of ways to accomplish this task. This

[348] See e.g. Lindenbergh 2008c and Wegerif 2011.
[349] See e.g. Fernhout 2010 and Haas 2010.

study has been able to identify two basic systemization models and three frequently used grouping patterns.[350]

One basic case systemization model is to adopt the structure of a piece of legislation and to allocate cases to the legislative provisions to which they are related. This study defines it as the legislative case systemization model. Both the *Green Series*[351] and the *Text and Comments on the Civil Code*[352] follow this model. These books adopt the structure of the Civil Code. Scholars comment on each article of the Code. Cases that are related to a particular article of the Code are integrated into the scholarly comments.[353]

Another basic model is to systemize cases according to a doctrinal structure. This study defines it as the doctrinal case systemization model. Many handbooks,[354] textbooks[355] and system-oriented journal articles[356] adopt this model. These academic writings do not contain scholarly comments to a piece of legislation on an article-by-article basis. Instead, they follow a structure developed by scholars that reveal the interrelationship between various components of a certain field of the law or a legal doctrine. Cases are allocated to the doctrinal components with which they are associated.[357]

It sometimes occurs that many cases are related to the same legislative provision or the same doctrinal point. Scholars have developed various ways to organize such related cases. A frequently used method to group related cases is, what this study calls, the "norm application" pattern. An author who uses this pattern to group cases first identifies a case that has established a certain

---

[350] This study does not claim the discovered models and patterns to be exhaustive, but they do seem to be the common ones.

[351] See Jansen 2012.

[352] See Nieuwenhuis & Stolker & Valk 2011.

[353] See e.g. Nieuwenhuis & Stolker & Valk 2011, Article 6:163, commentary 1-4 and Jansen 2012, Article 6:162, commentary 1-7.

[354] See e.g. Jansen 2009 and Hartkamp & Sieburgh 2011b.

[355] See e.g. Spier e.a. 2012.

[356] See e.g. Noorlander & Paijmans 2011 and Tjong Tjin Tai 2011.

[357] See e.g. Jansen 2009, p. 50-57 and Hartkamp & Sieburgh 2011b, commentary no. 35 on the five elements of an action based on tort.

norm.[358] Then the author lists a group of cases where the norm has been applied in different situations in order to illustrate the content of the norm.[359]

"Norm modification" is another frequently used case grouping pattern. This pattern usually serves to illustrate how a certain point in law has been developed in a series of cases. The grouping begins with a case that has established a general starting point or a general rule. This leading case is then followed by a group of cases that have modified the starting point or general rule by making subtle distinctions, limiting or broadening the scope of the general rule, specifying sub-norms or creating exceptions.[360]

Still another grouping pattern is, what this study calls, the "diversity" pattern. It sometimes occurs that different courts adopt different solutions to a particular legal problem. Under such circumstances, legal scholars may point out that courts have adopted different approaches on the issue and group the cases related to the issue by sorting them to each of the competing solutions.[361]

2.2.2 Evaluative scholarly writings involving cases

In case-focused and system-oriented evaluative academic writings, legal scholars not only interpret what a court has decided in a case, but also explicitly comment on how good or how bad the decision

---

[358] See e.g. Lindenbergh 2008b, p. 598, footnote 9. See also the case HR 22 November 1974, *NJ* 1975, 149 cited in Jansen 2012, Art. 6:162, Commentary 89.2.

[359] See e.g. Lindenbergh 2008b, p. 599, footnotes 10. See also the cases Rb. Arnhem 2 April 2002, *NJKort* 2003, 6, Rb. Roermond 11 June 2003, *VR* 2005, 24 and Rb. Breda 12 November 2008, *NJF* 2008, 512 cited in Jansen 2012, Art. 6:162, Commentary 89.2.

[360] See e.g. Hartkamp & Sieburgh 2011b, commentary 45, where the case HR 17 September 1982, *NJ* 1983, 278 (*Zegwaard/Knijnenburg*) is cited as a case that established a rule, whereas the case HR 3 November 2000, *NJ* 2001, 108 (*ABS/Groenewegen*) is cited as an exception to the rule. See also Nieuwenhuis & Stolker & Valk 2011, Article 6:162, Commentary 7 and 8b.

[361] See e.g. Noorlander & Paijmans 2011, paragraph 4.1-4.3 and Jansen 2012, Article 6:162, Commentary 91.1.

is.[362] Some scholars go even further to argue what a better decision or solution would have been.[363]

Evaluative scholarly comments on judicial decisions can be positive[364] or critical.[365] A closer look at evaluative scholarly comments on cases suggests that both in case-focused and in system-oriented evaluative writings legal scholars seem to perform the role of "quality control" inspectors[366] by examining and evaluating various aspects of a judicial decision. An important aspect that scholars examine closely is how the court arrives at its decision. In particular, scholars are keen to point out mistakes in the court's legal reasoning.[367] Criticism on courts' legal reasoning may involve legal technical deficiencies such as wrongly applied techniques to interpret statutory provisions[368] as well as distorted interpretation and improper application of norms established in earlier cases.[369] Also logic errors such as circular or self-contradictory reasoning frequently attract scholarly criticism.[370] Furthermore, it is worth noting that scholars check whether the court has violated procedural norms while arriving at its decision. Where a judicial decision has a norm-creating element, for example, legal scholars may verify whether the court has exceeded the boundaries of its lawmaking power.[371]

---

[362] See e.g. Kottenhagen 2010a and Oldenhuis 2010.

[363] See e.g. Lindenbergh 2008a, p. 239 and Hartlief 2011.

[364] See e.g. Lindenbergh 2008d, p. 120 and Oldenhuis 2011.

[365] See e.g. Hartlief 2010 and Oldenhuis 2010.

[366] This term is inspired by Bruinsma, who draws an analogy between the Supreme Court and the quality control department of a company, see Bruinsma 1988b. If the Supreme Court can be seen as to perform the task of quality control within the judiciary, it seems fair to say that legal scholars perform the task of quality control vis-á-vis the courts, including the Supreme Court.

[367] See e.g. Lindenbergh & Van der Zalm 2009, p. 148 and Schutgens 2009, p. 854. Schutgens 2009; Lindenbergh & Van der Zalm 2009.

[368] See e.g. Kolder 2010, paragraph 5 and Van Dam 2010, footnotes 93 and 94.

[369] See e.g. Arons 2012, footnote 31, where the author criticized the District Court Utrecht for neglecting a key norm established in an earlier relevant case decided by the Supreme Court.

[370] See e.g. Kottenhagen 2010b and Oldenhuis 2010.

[371] See e.g. Kottenhagen 2011.

Another aspect that frequently provokes evaluative scholarly comments is how the court justifies and explains its decision. A judgment where the court jumps to its conclusion without sufficiently explaining the reasons for doing so is often a target of scholarly criticism.[372] Scholars are also keen to point out some crucial aspects that the court has ignored in the justification of its decision.[373]

Still another aspect that scholars pay close attention to is the quality of the court's solution to the disputed issue. Where the disputed issue is a question of law and the court (implicitly or explicitly) creates a rule in its judgment, scholars may criticize the decision if the rule produced by the court is vague or uncertain.[374] Where the court imposes a sanction on a litigating party, scholars may verify whether the sanction is disproportional.[375] Furthermore, scholars often evaluate the quality of a court decision by exploring its possible consequences. Nieuwenhuis, for example, praised the controversial *DES Daughter* case for it has reached very positive results beyond the litigated case itself, i.e. preventing hundreds of similar lawsuits and promoting a piece of good legislation later on.[376] Hartlief, on the other hand, criticized the Supreme Court's decision in the *Hammock* case, because it creates uncertainty about the application of Article 6:179 and Article 6:173 of the Civil Code.[377]

These findings can be summarized in a "check list" (see Table 6). This list is not exhaustive. Nor does this study suggest that legal scholars explicitly go through the list while examining every court decision. Nonetheless, the list does provide an overview of the key points which legal scholars are likely to examine when evaluating judicial decisions.

A. How does the court arrive at its decision?		
	1. Has the court made mistakes in its legal reasoning?	
		(1) Has the court correctly identified, interpreted and

[372] See e.g. De Groot 2011 and Arons 2012.
[373] See e.g. Arons 2012.
[374] See e.g. Hartlief 2008, p. 900 and Kottenhagen 2010b.
[375] See e.g. Bartman 2011, p. 130.
[376] Nieuwenhuis 2010, p. 418.
[377] Hartlief 2011.

			applied relevant legislative provisions?
			(2) Has the court correctly identified, interpreted and applied norms established in earlier cases?
			(3) Has the court made logic errors such as circular or self-contradictory reasoning?
	2. Has the court violated procedural norms while arriving at its decision?		
B. How has the court justified and explained its decision?			
	1. Has the court provided justification for its decision?		
	2. Has the court ignored certain crucial elements in the justification that it provided?		
C. Quality of the court's answer to the disputed issue			
	1. If the court explicitly or implicitly devises a rule in its answer to a disputed point of law, is the rule vague?		
	2. If the court imposes a sanction on one or more of the litigating parties, is the sanction disproportional?		
	3. Is the decision likely to trigger undesirable consequences?		

Table 6 "Check list" for scholarly evaluation of court decisions

2.2.3 Contribution to the case law mechanism

The findings presented in the above subparagraphs indicate that legal scholars do not treat cases randomly. Instead, they have developed certain patterns to systematically process cases and to incorporate them in scholarly writings. The relevance of scholarly writings for the operation of case law in civil law jurisdictions may not seem particularly noteworthy to researchers adopting a judge/court-centred approach that seeks to study the role of cases by focusing on the analysis of published court judgments. After all, it is uncommon in the Netherlands and some other civil law jurisdictions for judges to cite or discuss scholarly writings in their judgments.[378] Accordingly, researchers may, if they concentrate on studying court judgments, overlook the importance of scholarly writings for the operation of case law.

This study argues that scholarly research that processes cases makes a significant contribution to the operation of case law in the Netherlands, even though the ways through which legal

[378] Vranken 1995, p. 110 and Hesselink 2001, p. 14, footnote 20.

scholars influence the operation of case law may not always be direct or explicit. A relatively tangible way through which legal scholars contribute to the operation of case law is that normative proposals advanced by legal scholars in evaluative scholarly writings as to how a certain issue should be addressed may eventually be adopted by courts and thus exercise a strong influence on the development of the law. A good example is that the proposal by Molengraff, a prominent Dutch legal scholar in the 19th century, to expand the scope of "unlawful acts" in tort law to include acts that violate what according to unwritten law has to be regarded as proper social conduct was eventually adopted by the Supreme Court in the *Lindenbaum/Cohen* case in 1919, which significantly changed the landscape of tort law in the Netherlands.[379]

A less explicit way through which legal scholars influence the operation of case law is that normative comments expressed by legal scholars in evaluative writings may affect the likelihood that the commented cases are followed in court practice. In the *Epskamp/Brand* case,[380] for example, the Court of Appeal in Amsterdam refused to follow an interpretation adopted by the Supreme Court in a set of previous cases, due to, among other things, severe criticism expressed in scholarly writings on the Supreme Court's interpretation.[381] Also interviews with judges conducted by this study indicate that judges do take scholarly evaluative comments on cases into careful consideration and that (persistent) scholarly criticism on a case may reduce the likelihood that judges follow the criticized decision, whereas positive scholarly reaction to a case may add to the weight that the case carries in judicial deliberation.[382]

Another indirect yet relevant way through which normative scholarly writings contribute to the operation of case law is that scholarly efforts to critically review published cases stimulate judges to enhance the quality of their work. Writings in the existing

---

[379] Van Maanen 2009.

[380] Hof Amsterdam 19 December 1991, *NJ* 1993, 36 (*Epskamp/Brand*), cited in, among other scholarly writings, Haazen 2007. p. 234.

[381] Ibid.

[382] See e.g. NL20130912, NL20131008-1, NL20131017, NL20131022, NL201310031 and NL20131114.

literature[383] and interviews conducted by this study suggest that judges are aware that legal scholars closely monitor their work and that many of them perceive it as undesirable to attract severe criticism from the legal academic forum by producing flawed judgments.[384] If the Supreme Court can be said to fulfil the role of a "quality inspector" inside the judiciary,[385] it seems fair to say that legal scholars perform the role of an external "quality inspector" that helps maintain a decent level of overall quality of court judgments, which in its turn is conducive for a well-functioning case law mechanism.

Even descriptive scholarly writings, where the role of legal scholars is commonly presumed to be that of a detached spectator giving a neutral account of the state of the law, are capable of influencing the functioning and the development of case law. The very fact that legal scholars choose to closely analyse a particular judicial decision in case-focused descriptive writings may be perceived as a sign that the analysed case is of particular noteworthy interest, which may accordingly have the effect of, however slightly, increasing the likelihood that the analysed case catches the attention of judges, practising lawyers or other players in law, and subsequently exercises a certain influence on judicial deliberation, scholarly doctrinal forming or legal teaching.[386]

System-oriented descriptive scholarly writings can also affect the development of case law due to, among other things, the many choices that legal scholars make in the way they select, interpret and systemize cases. Which cases do legal scholars select to involve in their research and to incorporate into their system-oriented descriptive publications? If the court's holding in a judicial decision is susceptible to different understandings, how do legal scholars interpret the case and what do they present as the essence of the case in their descriptive writings? If various courts have adopted divergent positions towards an issue, do legal scholars ascertain whether there is a prevailing approach among the courts and if so, which cases do they present in their descriptive

---

383 Draaisma & Duynstee 1988, p. 25.

384 See e.g. NL20131017, NL20131022, NL20131029 and NL20131031.

385 Bruinsma 1988b, p. 4.

386 See e.g. Jansen 1967 and interviews NL20130304, NL20131107 and NL20131031.

publications as reflecting the dominant view? Obviously, the way legal scholars deal with these questions may not be able to single-handedly dictate which judicial decisions become the leading cases that shape the law, but the choices made by legal scholars are capable of, however subtly, affecting which cases are likely to be consulted and applied by other users such as judges and practising lawyers as well as how such cases are likely to be understood and applied by those users. One may infer that this influence pattern is subtle and indirect, but it would be a mistake to assume that the effect of descriptive scholarly writings on the development of case law is trivial. By choosing a group of cases to be included in system-oriented descriptive scholarly writings, legal scholars give these cases a status that many published cases never get, thus fulfilling an important selective role in influencing which cases eventually become the law.

An even more indirect but perhaps the most important contribution by legal scholars to the case law mechanism is that the results of their work make it easier for other users to make use of cases and hence facilitate cases to fulfil the role of a source of law in practice.[387] Without the efforts by legal scholars to carefully select, interpret and systemize cases, judges and lawyers would have to comb through the vast body of published judicial decisions to find the relevant cases, to make sense of the holdings in those cases, to map out the relationship among the published cases and to ascertain how those cases relate to legislation. Such work by judges and lawyers would be so time-consuming and costly that one may rightly doubt whether cases could be efficiently used as a source of law in practice, if individual judges and lawyers would have to conduct the work of legal scholars in all the cases they handle. Of course, this study does not suggest that, as long as there are legal scholars that study and systemize cases, judges and lawyers no longer need to conduct any case research in their work. However, this study does wish to stress that judges and lawyers do derive great benefit from scholarly efforts to study and systemize cases, as they no longer have to repeat certain case research and, when they do need to carry out their own case research, they can use the

[387] All interviewed judges agree that the scholarly works facilitate their adjudication practice, see their responses to question 20 of Appendix 4.

existing scholarly works as a helpful starting point.[388] One may, of course, downplay the significance of legal scholars by qualifying the role of legal scholars as "assisting" or "supporting" the legal practice. However, this study prefers to see legal scholars as bridge-builders between the vast body of published court judgments and other users of cases. Without the scholarly efforts to select, interpret and systemize cases, published court judgments would remain like loose sand. It is legal scholars who play an important role in transforming such loose sand into building materials that can be conveniently used by other actors such as judges, lawyers and law students. Through this transformation legal scholars create great added value and make a considerable contribution to the operation of the case law mechanism.

3. Use of cases in legal education

3.1 Method

There are in total ten universities in the Netherlands that offer legal education.[389] This research focuses on Leiden University as an example. This choice is made because a small pilot study I conducted suggests that the way cases are used in legal education at Dutch universities is fairly similar.[390] In order to verify the representativeness of the findings of this study, six respondents that have received legal education or have had teaching experience at five universities[391] have been requested to read a draft version of the

---

[388] See e.g. NL20131008-1, NL20131022, NL20131107 and NL20131114.

[389] The ten universities are University of Amsterdam, VU University Amsterdam, University of Groningen, Leiden University, Maastricht University, Radboud University Nijmegen, Erasmus University Rotterdam, Tilburg University, Utrecht University and Open University. See Smits 2012, p. 624.

[390] The pilot study consists primarily of discussions with teachers, students and graduates of universities that offer legal education. I also vistied the websites of the law faculties of the ten universities to obtain information on their legal education.

[391] The universities include Utrecht University, Radboud University in Nijmegen, University of Amsterdam, VU University Amsterdam and Erasmus University in Rotterdam.

main findings and to give feedback. The feedback confirmed that the way cases are used at these universities is indeed very similar to the descriptions provided by this study. Differences indicated by the respondents have been incorporated into the final version of this study.

The examined materials include primarily syllabi, exercise books, textbooks and exams of private law courses taught at Leiden University Law School. In addition, semi-structured interviews with two law professors who teach private law courses have been conducted in order to obtain data that are missing in written materials, in particular with regard to the reasons why cases are used in legal education and factors that law professors take into account when considering which cases should be assigned as compulsory learning materials.[392]

3.2 Findings

It is difficult to trace when exactly cases began to be incorporated in university legal education in the Netherlands. I have found two pieces of scholarly writings that point to the early decades of the 20th century as the starting point of using cases in university legal education in the Netherlands.[393] Despite some uncertainty about the exact starting point, it is plain that in the 19th century cases were not, or at least not widely used in legal education, but nowadays using cases in legal education has become a common practice at Dutch universities.[394] The prominence of cases in legal education has reached such a degree that Vranken wrote the following passage in 1995:[395]

> Not only has he (a law student) been required to study legislation and legal literature, at least an equal amount of attention, if not more, has been paid to cases. He has to study hundreds of them.

---

[392] Interviews NL20120327-1 and NL20120327-2.

[393] Brunner 1994, p. 34 and Fockema Andrea 1938, p. 73.

[394] As already mentioned earlier in this subparagraph, there are ten universities in the Netherlands that offer legal education. Cases are widely used in the legal education at all of these universities, see Vranken 1995, p. 116.

[395] Vranken 1995, p. 116.

Cases used in legal education can be divided into two types (see Figure 5). The cases that students are assigned to study belong to the first type.[396] The second type includes cases that students must find using search tools. The distinction between these two types is not related to the content of the cases, but rather whether students are required to actively search for the cases. The first type of cases will be referred to as "assigned cases" further in this study and the second type as "non-assigned cases".

Among the assigned cases, two subtypes can be identified. The first subtype are cases that are selected as teaching materials for the purpose of illustrating how certain legal norms are applied in practice.[397] In other words, these cases are used as examples and the emphasis is not on the legal norms, but on the application of those norms. The second subtype includes cases that have contributed to the development of the law by, among other things, giving new interpretations to existing legal concepts or rules. These cases are selected as teaching materials due to their normative impact rather than their illustrative value. The following subparagraphs will take a closer look at the use of the various types of cases in legal education.

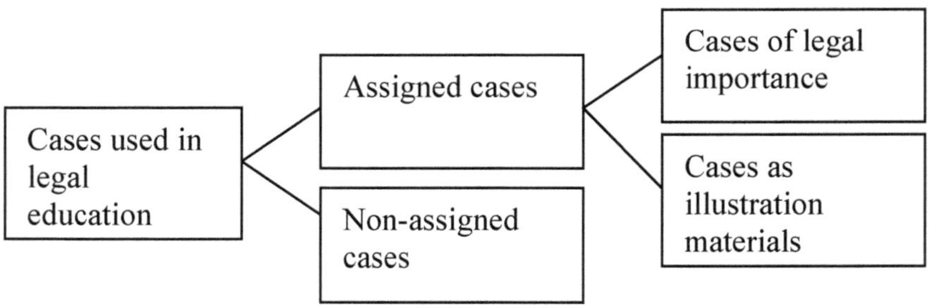

Figure 5 Typology of cases used in legal education

[396] The text of the assigned cases is sometimes incorporated into the syllabi or exercise books, see e.g. Leiden Law School 2012f, p. 24-28 and Leiden Law School 2012e, p. 2. Usually, however, case citations or links to online case publications are provided in syllabi or exercise books so that students can easily find the text of the assigned cases, see e.g. Leiden Law School 2012g, p. 7.

[397] Interviews NL20120327-1 and NL20120327-2.

3.2.1 Assigned cases

University legal education in the Netherlands normally consists of two phases: a three-years' bachelor programme and a one-year master programme.[398] At Leiden University, for example, a student who intends to obtain a master's degree in law normally needs to complete about 33 courses (25 bachelor courses[399] and 8 master courses[400]). The syllabus of almost every law course[401] requires the student to study, and in some events even to memorize, a certain amount of judicial cases.[402] Also the textbooks used in various law courses usually contain references to a large amount of cases.[403] These cases constitute the type one cases, as set out earlier in the typology. A common feature of this type of cases is that students are clearly instructed *which* particular cases they are required to study, so that they do not need to undertake complicated search activities. Even though the syllabi of some law courses only provide case citations instead of the full text of the required cases, the search activity that a student needs to undertake is usually simple and straightforward. Typing the citation in an online case database is usually sufficient.

Some of the type one cases are selected due to their illustrative value.[404] These cases are primarily meant to show the students how an abstract legal norm is applied in practice. Students are usually not required to carefully analyse these cases. Normally they would not need to use these cases in exams.

---

[398] See websites of the law schools of the ten universities that offer legal education.

[399] Bachelor thesis is counted as one course.

[400] Master thesis is also counted as one course.

[401] Although I have only examined teaching materials used in private law courses, cases are also widely used in the teaching of other areas of the law such as criminal, constitutional and administrative law, see interviews NL20120327-1 and NL20120327-2.

[402] See e.g. Leiden Law School 2012f, p. 1-2 and Leiden Law School 2012g, p. 7.

[403] See the extensive table of cases in e.g. Hijma e.a. 2010 and Spier e.a. 2012.

[404] Interviews NL20120327-1 and NL20120327-2.

A more important subcategory of type one cases is formed by judgments that are of great legal importance.[405] Students are required to study these cases because these judgments have added something new to the previously existing body of legal norms. A very small number of these legally important cases are selected due to their historic value.[406] These cases are usually no longer used in legal practice because they have been incorporated into legislation or replaced by new cases, but historically they have made such a prominent contribution to the development of the law that professors would still require students to study them.[407] The vast majority of the legally important cases, on the other hand, are of significant practical value. Without knowledge of these prominent cases, the student's knowledge of the law would be incomplete, as the norms contained in them are treated in practice as the existing law.[408]

Students are required to study the legally important cases carefully. The syllabi of many courses instruct students to read not only the original judgments, but also the available scholarly annotations to the legally important cases.[409] Students may often need to use the legally important cases to answer questions or to apply them to solve legal problems in homework assignments.[410] Also exam questions require students to cite and apply the legally important cases that they have been required to study.[411] Since some exams do not allow students to consult case law collections,[412]

---

405 Interviews NL20120327-1 and NL20120327-2.

406 A good example is HR 31 January 1919, *NJ* 1919, 161 (*Lindenbaum/Cohen*), which significantly changed the landscape of tort law in the Netherlands. The holding of this case was later codified in Article 6:162 of the new Dutch Civil Code.

407 Interview NL20120327-1.

408 Interviews NL20120327-1 and NL20120327-2.

409 See Leiden Law School 2012i, p. 3 and Leiden Law School 2012f, p. 1-2.

410 E.g. Leiden Law School 2012g, p. 18 Question II-2 and p. 25 question IV-1, Leiden Law School 2012i, p. 14 Question 1.2 and Leiden Law School 2012e, p. 8 Question 6.

411 E.g. Leiden Law School 2011 Question 8, Leiden Law School 2012d Question 5 and Leiden Law School 2012c Question 1.

412 The number of exams that do not allow students to consult case law collections varies from university to university. Leiden University seems

students must memorize the key points of a certain amount of legally important cases.

By studying assigned illustrative and legally important cases, students gradually develop the skills and techniques to read and analyse cases.[413] The skills required to answer homework or exam questions by using the legally important cases, however, are usually not complicated. Very often, students only need to apply the norm contained in a case that they have been required to study as if it were a legislative norm while citing the name of the case as the basis for a legal proposition.[414]

3.2.2 Non-assigned cases

In addition to cases that students are explicitly required to study, legal education in the Netherlands also involves cases that students must actively find and use. Students usually learn to deal with this type of cases at a relatively advanced stage of their study in courses such as moot court and some master courses.[415] Writing a bachelor or master's thesis may also require students to actively search for, evaluate and use cases.[416]

---

to be relatively strict in this respect. A rare example of an exam that allows students to consult case law collections in Leiden is the exam civil procedure for master students, see Leiden Law School 2012h, p. 4. At the Radboud University, however, students are usually allowed to consult case law collections during exams, see interview NL20140627.

[413] At the beginning of their legal education, first year's law students usually get some instructions on how to read cases, see Syllabus Introduction to Civil Law (*Inleiding burgerlijk recht*), p 47. These instructions, however, tend to be relatively abstract. The assigned cases give the students an excellent opportunity to apply the instructions that they have learned. First year's law students at the VU University Amsterdam and the University of Amsterdam also receive similar instructions and training, see interviews NL20131212 and NL20140721.

[414] See Hesselink 2001, p. 18-19.

[415] See Leiden Law School 2012a, p. 11-14 and Leiden Law School 2012h, p. 3-5. Students at the VU University Amsterdam begin relatively early to train such skills in courses such as Arresten lezen (Reading Cases), Juridische vaardigheden (Legal Skills) and Rechtzoeken (Searching for the Law), see interview NL20140721.

[416] See Leiden Law School 2012a, p. 15.

Moot court and some practice-oriented master courses often contain assignments that require students to solve a legal problem with (imaginary) facts and legal claims, which resemble to a certain extent legal disputes in practice.[417] Teachers do not tell students which cases may be relevant for them to complete their assignments. Instead, the student must analyse the problems by him/herself and determine whether, and if so, what kind of cases may be needed. Then the student needs to develop a search strategy, using various search tools and techniques to find the possibly relevant cases.[418] Once these cases have been found, the student must read and analyse them to determine their relevance. Finally, if he or she deems a found case relevant and usable, the student must apply the case to solve the problem at hand. Such an exercise trains the student to acquire a series of skills and techniques, such as using case law search tools, analysing, evaluating and applying cases. Similarly, writing a thesis may also help students enhance these skills and techniques.

3.2.3 Contribution to the case law mechanism

When it comes to the relationship between using cases in legal education and the status of cases as a source of law in legal practice, there is a traditional view that adopts a "one-way street" thinking.[419] According to this view, it is due to the fact that in legal practice cases have acquired a highly important status that legal education began to use cases.[420] In other words, this view tends to assume that legal education merely follows and reflects the trends in legal practice.

This study, however, prefers a "two-way street" model to analyse this relationship. In the comparative law literature, the "two-way street" model has already been presented in a paper by Dainow in 1966:[421]

---

[417] See Leiden Law School 2012a, p. 16-18.

[418] Teachers do provide students with general instructions on search methods and case citing rules, see Leiden Law School 2012a, p. 18-26.

[419] See e.g. Fockema Andreae 1938, p. 73.

[420] Ibid.

[421] Dainow 1966, p. 428.

> There is naturally a direct reciprocal influence between the nature of a legal system and the pattern of legal education. The nature of the former promotes the method of the latter, which in turn perpetuates the original character of the system. The program of law studies and the method of legal education establish and fix the fundamental understanding and the mode of thought which condition the individual for his entire professional career.

Applying this model to the context of using cases in legal education in the Netherlands, this study argues that using cases in legal education makes contributions at three levels at least to the functioning of the case law mechanism. First of all, at the level of the impact of *individual* cases, using cases in legal education can have the effect of enhancing the status of *some particular* cases. As described earlier in this chapter, the syllabi of various law courses require students to study, and in some events even to memorize, many cases that are presented as containing legal innovation. The norms extracted from this type of cases are presented as the law. Accordingly, law students may perceive these particular cases as highly influential, and it is possible that they may continue to entertain this perception throughout their later career.

Obviously, this study does not argue that cases become influential in practice *because* they have been used in legal education. Asserting so would amount to a reversed "one-way street" model that does no justice to the reality. In fact, it follows from the description provided earlier in this chapter that judgments would not be used as legally important cases in legal education, if they had not already gained significant prominence in practice.

This is, however, not to say that, contrary to what the "one-way street" model would imply, selecting a body of cases and presenting them in legal education as the valid law has no further impact on the status of those cases in practice. This study wishes to highlight that presenting a body of cases in legal education as being the law can have the effect of confirming and reinforcing the prominent status of those cases in practice. As the next paragraph will reveal, how a case is received in academic writings and in legal practice is an important factor that judges take into consideration when determining whether a previous case will be followed or not in later decisions.[422] The fact that a case is presented in legal education as being the law can serve as a powerful indication that consensus on the soundness and the desirability of the concerned judicial decision has been reached in scholarly writings and in legal practice, which may in its turn further enhance the likelihood that the case will be followed in future court practice.[423] In this context, it seems that the observation by Nieuwenhuis that the highest status a case can reach is to be incorporated into legislation[424] can be supplemented by a remark that the next highest status that a case can obtain is to be incorporated into a classic law textbook as a judicial decision that has further developed the law. In fact, one may even go one step further and argue that being incorporated into a classic law textbook as a court decision that has further developed the law is a status even higher than being incorporated into legislation, because the latter makes the case redundant but the former further strengthens the authority of the case.[425]

Another contribution that legal education makes to the operation of case law is at the level of skills and techniques. For cases to fulfil the function of a source of law in legal practice, it is crucial that actors such as judges, public prosecutors and lawyers possess the necessary skills and techniques to find, analyse and apply cases to solve legal problems. As the previous paragraph illustrates, two types of cases are used in university legal education in the Netherlands, which can train law students to acquire such skills (see Table 7). At an early stage of a university legal education programme, for example, cases are used that primarily help students to develop the necessary skills to read and analyse judicial decisions. At a relatively advanced stage, students are trained to develop more sophisticated case law techniques and skills, such as

---

[422] See the relevant passages in the following paragraph on the various factors that influence the likelihood that a case is followed in adjudication practice.

[423] See e.g. interviews NL20131008-2, NL20131022 and NL20131107-03.

[424] Nieuwenhuis 2000, p 687.

[425] I would like to thank Van Rooij for inspiring me to derive this insight from the findings of this subparagraph.

searching, evaluating and applying cases to solve legal problems. It can accordingly be said that by using cases, legal education supplies legal practice with law graduates that are armed with the necessary skills to handle cases.

		Types of cases used in legal education		
		Type I: Assigned cases		Type II: Non-assigned cases
		Cases as illustration materials	Cases of legal significance	
Case law techniques and skills	Read and analyse cases	Yes, but thorough analysis not always required	Yes	Yes
	Search for cases through online databases or other media	No	No	Yes
	Apply cases to solve legal problems	No	Yes, but usually only straight-forward application	Yes

Table 7 Types of cases used in legal education and related techniques and skills

The third, and possibly the most fundamental contribution seems to be at the level of awareness. One of the effects of repeated use of cases throughout nearly all courses in a university law programme is that law students gradually develop a "case law awareness", i.e. an internalized conviction that cases are highly relevant materials that ought to be treated seriously and carefully when dealing with legal problems. Given the fact that the key legal professions (judges, public prosecutors and lawyers) in the

Netherlands all require a university law degree as a basic qualification, it would be anything but surprising if one should find a high level of case law awareness among the key players in law in the Netherlands. In this respect, Vranken observed rightly that:[426]

> Without knowledge of case law and legal literature, lawyers are not able to exercise their profession properly. Every lawyer knows this, because it has been hammered into his head from the very first day of his legal education.

By cultivating a strong case law awareness among law students, university legal education becomes an important institution that contributes to forge and maintain a strong perception among the key players in law that cases are a highly important source of law.[427]

4. Use of cases in adjudication

4.1 Method

Two main research methods used in this part of the study include analysis of relevant writings in the existing literature and semi-structured interviews with judges. The relevant literature has been found, in the first place, by searching in online database Picarta[428] and by using Google Scholar.[429] The snowball method was also used. Consulting the bibliographies of publications on this topic has led me to many other relevant scholarly writings.

In addition to text analysis, I conducted semi-structured interviews with 13 judges that are mainly involved in the trial of

---

[426] Vranken 1995, p. 116.

[427] See Vranken 1995, p. 116 and interviews NL20131008, NL20131029, NL20131107-2 and NL20131114.

[428] www.picarta.nl

[429] The search terms include, among other things, "gezag van jurisprudentie" (authority of cases), "arresten lezen" (reading cases), "arresten interpreteren" (interpreting cases) and "jurisprudentie rechtsbron" (cases source of law).

civil cases. These respondents were found through my personal network, as gaining access to judges through the courts turned out to be difficult. Nine of the interviewed judges are appeal judges. Four of the interviewed judges serve in district courts. Out of the nine interviewed appeal judges, seven have previously served in district courts. The sample covers, considering the district courts where seven of the nine interviewed appeal judges have previously served, all the four courts of appeal in the Netherlands[430] as well as seven[431] out of the eleven district courts in the Netherlands.[432] Although the sample covers all the courts of appeal and most of the district courts, doubt can be cast on the representativeness of the sample, because the number of respondents is limited and no Supreme Court judge has participated in the interview. Readers are urged be aware of this methodological limitation of the interviews. This study, as has been pointed out in the introduction, is of an explorative nature. Scholars are welcome to test the representativeness of the interview results by, among other possible methods, conducting systematic studies that include a more representative sample of respondents.

4.2 Findings

The existing literature suggests that cases have been playing an important role in adjudication practice in the Netherlands since at least the early decades of the 20th century.[433] For quite a long time, judges were careful to conceal the influence of previous cases on

---

[430] The four courts of appeal are the Court of Appeal of Amsterdam, Court of Appeal of Arnhem-Leeuwarden, Court of Appeal of Den Bosch and Court of Appeal of The Hague, see http://www.rechtspraak.nl/Organisatie/Gerechtshoven/Pages/default.aspx.

[431] The seven district courts are the District Court of Amsterdam, District Court of The Hague, District Court of Gelderland, District Court of Limburg, District Court of North Holland, District Court of East Brabant and District Court of Rotterdam.

[432] The four district courts that are not covered by the sample are the District Court of Middle Netherlands, District Court of North Netherlands, District Court of Overijssel and District Court of Zeeland-West Brabant. For a complete overview of the district courts in the Netherlands see http://www.rechtspraak.nl/Organisatie/Rechtbanken/Pages/default.aspx.

[433] See e.g. Teixeira de Mattos 1885, p. 31 and Telders 1938.

their decision-making by avoiding citing previous court decisions in judgments.[434] Since the *Bull Calf* case in 1980[435], explicit case citations and discussions in judgments grew steadily and has now become a common practice in the Netherlands.[436]

How judges use previous court decisions to solve legal disputes is a topic that has fascinated Dutch legal scholars for a long time.[437] In particular, academic writings on this topic tend to focus on the question what kind of force previous cases carry in adjudication practice.[438] A commonly used method is to analyse references to previous cases in court judgments.[439] This study, as mentioned in the previous paragraph, experimented with a different method to study the use of cases in adjudication by conducting semi-structured interviews with judges.[440] One of the reasons to choose this method is that the legal reasoning in court judgments may not always completely reveal all the considerations that have influenced the deliberation of judges.[441] Moreover, this study not only investigated the question what kind of force previous cases carry in court practice, but also paid attention to the ways through which judges find and analyse previous cases in their adjudication work. Such data cannot, or at least cannot easily be inferred from the text of judgments. The key findings will be summarized in the following two subparagraphs.

---

[434] Drion 1968b, p. 168.

[435] HR 7 March 1980, *NJ* 1980, 353 (*Stierkalf*).

[436] See e.g. Glastra van Loon e.a. 1968 and Brunner 1994.

[437] See e.g. Scholten 1931, p. 114-124, Glastra van Loon e.a. 1968, Jessurun D'Oliveira 1973 and Haazen 2007.

[438] See e.g. Kottenhagen 1986 and Struycken & Haazen 1993.

[439] See e.g. Jessurun D'Oliveira 1973, Kottenhagen 1986 and Struycken & Haazen 1993.

[440] For details see the previous subparagraph on the mothods used for this part of the research.

[441] Some appeal judges, for example, do not cite cases decided by district courts or other appeal courts even if they have consulted and followed such cases, see interviews NL20131008-1 and NL20131022.

4.2.1 How judges find relevant cases

The findings of this study indicate that when dealing with disputes where consulting previous cases can be necessary or desirable[442], judges rarely have to begin from scratch, as the counsels of the litigating parties usually cite and discuss previous cases that they find relevant to the dispute at hand in their oral and written submissions to the court.[443] The quality of the submissions with regard to previous cases, i.e. whether the scope of the cases cited in the submissions is complete and how relevant the cited cases are for the legal dispute at hand, varies depending on the competence and skills of the lawyers.[444] Where the quality of the submissions by the counsels is high, the efforts that judges need to make in order to find relevant cases are usually fairly limited, so that they can concentrate on verifying the interpretations given by the counsels to the cited cases and evaluating the submitted arguments based on the cited cases. Even where the counsels' submissions do not contain a thorough examination of relevant previous cases, judges still benefit from the submissions as the cases cited by counsels usually provide a fairly good starting point for extra case research that the judges themselves conduct. [445]

When carrying out case research, judges tend to combine two search approaches.[446] The first is to use handbooks or other scholarly writings as a starting point to locate the disputed legal issues and to find the relevant cases. Another way to find possibly applicable cases is to use the search engines in online legal databases. Which one of the approaches a judge would start with

---

[442] The fact that cases play an important role in adjudication practice in the Netherlands does not mean that in every case the judge needs to consult previous court decisions. Many disputes concern solely factual issues, so that the need to consult case law in this type of lawsuits is usually rather limited, see interviews NL20131008-2 and NL20131021.
[443] All respondents indicated that it is quite common that lawyers cite and discuss previous cases in their submissions if consulting previous case law is necessary or desirable to solve the dispute at hand.
[444] See e.g. NL20131008-1, NL20131017, NL20131022, NL20131028, NL20131029 and NL20131107-1.
[445] See e.g. NL20131008-1, NL20131021 and NL20131114.
[446] See e.g. NL20131008-2, NL20131017, NL20131022, NL20131029, NL20131031 and NL20131107-1.

tends to depend on the degree to which he or she is familiar with the legal area(s) that the litigation involves.

Where the litigation involves a legal area that is relatively new to the judge, consulting the relevant handbooks or other system-oriented scholarly works is often the first step to take, as the relevant cases are usually conveniently organized and explained in this type of publications. When they are familiar with the legal area(s) involved in a dispute, judges tend to rely primarily on online databases to find cases that may be relevant to the litigation at hand. A frequently used online search tool is Porta Iuris, a portal website with an integrated search engine that does not only offer access to full-text judgments, but also shows whether and if so in which scholarly publications a case has been commentated.[447] Many of the interviewed judges replied that where a search generates a great number of hits, cases that have attracted many scholarly comments are more likely to catch their attention than those that have not been commented on or those that have attracted but limited or no scholarly attention.[448]

4.2.2 How judges analyse cases

When it comes to analysing the essence of previous cases, the interview results suggest that scholarly writings that discuss cases are generally perceived to be a helpful tool.[449] In particular, where the holding of a case is susceptible to different interpretations, many judges are inclined to consult scholarly writings such as annotations and journal articles that explore the essence and the application scope of the case.[450] For the analysis of Supreme Court cases, the advisory opinions of the Advocates General[451] are also perceived to be valuable, as such opinions usually contain fairly thorough

---

[447] For more information on Porta Iuris see Van Opijnen 2006a.

[448] NL20130923, 20131008-1, NL20131008-2, NL20131017, NL20131021, NL20131022, NL20131028, NL20131029, NL20131107-1 and NL20131107-2.

[449] NL20130923, NL201308-1, NL20131008-2, NL20131022, NL20131029, NL20131031, NL20131107-3 and NL20131114.

[450] Ibid.

[451] For more information on the role of Advocates General, see Bruinsma 1988a and Smits 2012.

references to and analysis of relevant cases and scholarly writings, which can help judges to put the analysed case in a proper context.[452]

The interview results further indicate that when analysing a previous case, judges do not simply focus on possible rules that can be extracted from the case, they also pay attention to the facts and circumstances of the case.[453] One of the reasons why they pay attention to the particular facts and circumstances of previous cases is that when, on the surface, a rule extracted from a previous case is broad enough to cover the dispute at hand but applying the rule may lead to a highly undesirable outcome, judges may try to avoid applying the previous case by seeking differences between the facts and circumstances of the litigated case at hand and those of the previous one.[454] Another reason is that, as some respondents indicated, a previous court decision may be prompted by the particular facts of that specific case (e.g. in order to protect a weaker party in that individual case), so that a possible rule extracted from such a case, if there is one to be extracted, is likely to be interpreted narrowly by judges.[455]

Moreover, the interview results indicate that subtle differences in the wording of judgments may affect how judges interpret cases. A district court judge, for example, replied during the interview that she would not necessarily interpret a judgment that applied the holding of a previous Supreme Court decision with the wording that "as the Supreme Court has decided in the … case, the valid law is that…"[456] in the same way as a judgment that applied the same holding with the wording "the Supreme Court rightly held that…".[457] Even though both judgments applied the

---

452 NL20131008-1, NL20131022, NL20131107-1, NL20131107-3 and NL20131114.

453 NL20130923, NL20131008-1, NL20131108-2, NL20131017, NL20131021, NL20131022, NL20131028, NL20131031, NL20131107-1, NL20131107-2, NL20131107-3 and NL20131114.

454 Ibid.

455 NL20131008-1, NL20131017 and NL20131114.

456 The Dutch wording that the judge used was "zoals de Hoge Raad heeft bepaald in… geldt dat …" See NL20131021.

457 The Dutch wording that the judge used as "de Hoge Raad heeft terecht geoordeeld dat …" See interview NL20131021.

holding of the same case, the second wording unambiguously supports the holding of the Supreme Court, whereas the first one does not explicitly indicate whether the court that has followed the previous case substantively agrees with the holding of the cited case.[458] Such a distinction is subtle but can be relevant, because, as will be further explained in the next subparagraph, how well a previous court decision is received in later court practice can affect the weight that the previous case carries in judicial deliberation. It is possible that a case cited with wordings that explicitly demonstrate endorsement by later courts may, all else being equal, carry, however slightly, more weight than a case that courts have followed in later decisions with neutral wordings that do not express explicit consent to the substantive correctness or desirability of the previous holding.

4.2.3 The force of previous cases in adjudication

4.2.3.1 Various factors jointly determine the influence of a case

What kind of force previous cases carry in adjudication is a question that has led to many scholarly writings in the Netherlands.[459] A commonly used framework to analyse this question is one based on the concept of "binding force".[460] Drion, for example, submits that Supreme Court decisions carry legally binding force upon lower courts.[461] Many other scholars seem to be inclined to the view that Supreme Court cases carry *de facto* binding force, whereas lower court decisions do not carry binding force, except where they constitute a constant court practice.[462]

---

[458] NL20131021.

[459] See e.g. Scholten 1931, p. 114-124, Glastra van Loon e.a. 1968, Drion 1968b, Jessurun D'Oliveira 1973, Kottenhagen 1986, Struycken & Haazen 1993, Brunner 1994 and Drion 2014.

[460] It should be noted that many scholars that use this framework do not make the framework explicit in their writings. For relatively rare examples where the framework is made explicit see Kottenhagen 1986 and Struycken & Haazen 1993.

[461] Drion 1968b.

[462] See e.g. Glastra van Loon e.a. 1968, Jessurun D'Oliveira 1973 and Brunner 1994.

It should be pointed out that a framework based on a distinction between "binding" and "non-binding " cases has significant limitations.[463] To say that a case is binding means, in essence, that judges have to follow the case irrespective of evaluation of the substantive soundness of the previous court decision, i.e. whether judges agree with the holding of the previous case or not, they have to follow it.[464] If one, for example, observes that Supreme Court decisions are binding upon lower courts, it would mean that in order to ascertain whether they should follow a previous case, judges are supposed to observe a formal criterion, i.e. which court has made the judgment, whereas substantive considerations such as the soundness and desirability of the holding of the previous case are not supposed to affect their decision. Moreover, a framework based on a distinction between "binding" and "non-binding" creates a dichotomy. Within such a framework, a case is either binding or not binding, so that it seems nothing could be in between.

A preferable view is that the influence of previous cases in adjudication can be understood as a matter of degree that is jointly determined by an assessment of a number of elements,[465] as the responses by the interviewed judges indicate that the weight that they attribute to a previous case depends on their assessment of a number of factors such as:[466]

---

[463] This view has been inspired by, among other publications, Lund 1997 and Haazen 2007.

[464] See e.g. Cross & Harris 1991, p. 3 and Haazen 2007, p. 238-239.

[465] This view has already been brought forward in, among other scholarly writings, Glastra van Loon e.a. 1968, p. 145 and Nederpel 1985, p.112. However, Glastra van Loon and Nederpel did not specify the evidence for their observation.

[466] It should be noted that this list is not exhaustive. One of the judges mentioned, for example, that he would also pay attention to comparative law elements, i.e. where a solution adopted in an earlier case deviates significantly from the responses to the same issue in neighbouring countries, he would be less inclined to follow the case than if the solution is similar to approaches in neighbouring jurisdictions, see NL20131008-1. Two other judges mentioned that who has/have written the judgment is also a relevant factor, i.e. if the judge(s) that has/have written the judgment is/are known to be expert(s) on the legal area(s) involved in the case, the likelihood that the case will be followed in later adjudication is

(1) the hierarchy of the court that has made the judgment;[467]
(2) the strength of the arguments that the court employs to reach the decision;[468]
(3) legal scholars' reaction to the case (severe criticism by legal scholars on a case may reduce the likelihood that it will be followed in later adjudication practice, whereas endorsement by legal scholars may add to the weight that the case carries in adjudication);[469]
(4) how well the case has been received in court practice (a case that has been constantly followed in later court practice is likely to carry more weight than one that has been constantly deviated from);[470]
(5) whether applying the holding of the previous case would lead to a highly unjust or undesirable outcome in the dispute at hand (many judges indicated that if applying a previous case to solve the dispute at hand would lead to a highly unjust or undesirable outcome, they would refuse to follow the previous case or they would try to find differences between the facts and circumstances underlying the previous court decision and the facts of the dispute at hand in order to demonstrate that the holding of the previous case does not cover the dispute at hand)[471];
(6) whether the holding of the previous case is in conflict with supranational norms such as EU legislation, case law of the Court of Justice of the European Union or provisions of

---

greater than if the judge(s) is/are not known to have particular expertise in the involved legal area(s), see NL20110519 and NL20131021. These responses, however, do not constitute a majority view among the interviewed judges, so that I have not incorporated them in the main text of this paragraph.

[467] All respondents indicated this as a relevant factor.

[468] Ibid.

[469] Ibid.

[470] Ibid.

[471] NL20130923, NL20131008-1, NL20131108-2, NL20131017, NL20131021, NL20131022, NL20131028, NL20131031, NL20131107-1, NL20131107-2, NL20131107-3 and NL20131114.

international treaties that are directly applicable in the Dutch legal order;[472]

(7) whether the case has been decided a long time ago.[473]

4.2.3.2 Analysis of two formal factors

If we make an analysis of these factors, we would discover that five of the above-listed seven factors involve substantive considerations (factor 2 to 6). Factor 1 (hierarchy of the court that has decided the case) and 7 (the age of the case) appear, at first glance, to be purely formal criteria. Whether a case has been decided a long time ago, for example, is a factual question. However, explanations given by the respondents indicate that this factor is also related to substance, as the older a case is, the more likely it is that relevant legislation, court practice and scholarly opinions have changed so that applying the old case may no longer be appropriate.[474] In other words, judges seem to perceive the old age of a case as an alert for them to closely examine the substance of the case. A proper understanding of the relevance of this formal criterion would therefore be that where judges decide to deviate from an older case, they do not do so due to the mere fact that the case is old, but rather because the substance of the holding no longer fits the current legislation, court practice or scholarly views.

Similarly, the first factor, i.e. the hierarchy of the court that has decided the case, also seems be a formal criterion. However, explanations provided by the respondents suggest that this factor also involves considerations that are related to the substance. The following passages will examine a crucial difference between the way the interviewed judges indicate how they treat Supreme Court decisions and the way they treat lower courts' (courts of appeal and district courts) decisions before exploring the reasons why such a difference exists.

Responses by the interviewed judges all indicate that whether a case is decided by the Supreme Court is of crucial

---

[472] NL20131008-1, NL20131031 and NL20131107-3.

[473] NL20130923, NL20131017, NL20131022, NL20131029 and NL20131107-1.

[474] NL20130923, NL20131017, NL20131022, NL20131029 and NL20131107-1.

importance for their decision whether they will follow the case or not. The very fact that a case has been decided by the Supreme Court is likely to, as the interview results suggest, induce the interviewed judges to attribute so much weight to the case that they would normally follow the case, unless one or more of the other factors strongly point to a different direction.[475] Moreover, the interviewed judges indicate that, where they decide to deviate from a Supreme Court decision that can be said to cover the dispute at hand, they perceive a strong duty to justify and explain why the previous Supreme Court decision should not be followed in the particular case that they decide.[476] In other words, the responses by the interviewed judges suggest that when it comes to possibly applicable Supreme Court cases, judges tend to ask themselves why they should *not* follow the Supreme Court decision, and when they decide not to follow, they perceive a heavy duty of argument on their part as to why the Supreme Court decision should not be applied to resolve the dispute at hand.

The fact that a case has been decided by a court of appeal or a district court, on the other hand, does not urge judges to follow the case, as the respondents indicate that they feel much freer to evaluate the substance of a lower court's decision and to deviate from it as soon as they do not substantively agree with the holding, than to assess the soundness of a Supreme Court's case and to avoid applying it merely on the ground that they do not endorse the substance of the ruling.[477] Moreover, where they decide not to follow a previous case decided by a lower court, the respondents indicate that they normally do not perceive a duty to justify or

---

[475] See the responses of the interviewed judges to question 7 of Appendix 4.

[476] See the responses of the interviewed judges to question 10 of Appendix 4.

[477] See e.g. NL20110519, NL20130923, NL20131008-1, NL20131021 and NL20131028 and NL20131022. It should be pointed out that the responses by the interviewed district judges and some appeal judges that have previously worked in district courts did not indicate that they would attribute more weight to cases decided by the court of appeal, which has the power to reverse their judgments than cases decided by other courts of appeal merely due to the risk of reversal, see the interviews cited at the beginning of this footnote. For an exception see NL20131008-2.

explain why they deviate from the previous case, except where the litigating parties explicitly invoke one or more previous decisions of lower courts that bear close relevance to the dispute at hand.[478] Such responses suggest that when dealing with previous cases decided by lower courts, judges tend to ask themselves why they *should* follow such cases instead of why they should *not* follow them, and that it is, where they invoke lower courts' cases in their argumentation, up to the litigating parties to use substantive justifications to convince the judges that the cases they invoke should be applied.

When asked why they make such an important distinction between the fact that a case is decided by the Supreme Court and the one that a case comes from a lower court, and why they attribute so much more weight to the former than the latter, the respondents unanimously identified the threat of reversal of their judgments as one of the key reasons. This is anything but difficult to understand, as the institution of cassation makes sure that the Supreme Court has the final say on matters of law in civil, criminal and tax cases in the Netherlands.[479] The interview results, however, suggest that, contrary to what some commentators assert in the existing literature,[480] it is not due to concerns of their career development that judges are reluctant to deviate from Supreme Court decisions. In fact, respondents indicate that the reversal rate is not used in the Netherlands as a criterion to evaluate judges' performances.[481] The real consideration behind the interviewed judges' reluctance to deviate from Supreme Court decisions purely on the ground that they themselves do not endorse the substantive choices made by the Supreme Court is that they are aware that, other than under exceptional circumstances, the Supreme Court normally adheres to its previous decisions, so that deviating from Supreme Court cases without sufficient justification would impose a heavy burden upon the litigating parties, not only in terms of litigation costs and time, but also in terms of stress and anxiety, to carry on the lawsuit all the

---

[478] See e.g. NL20110519, NL20130923, NL20131008-2, NL20131021 and NL20131028 and NL20131022.

[479] See e.g. Brunner 1994 and Smits 2012.

[480] See e.g. Dedek & Schermaier 2012, p. 362. See also Lawson 1977, p. 85, where the author expressed a more nuanced view than Dedek and Schermaier.

[481] See NL20110519, NL20130923 and NL20131022.

way to the Supreme Court in order to get the lower court's judgment reversed.[482] This is, of course, not to say that concerns for the burden of appeal and cassation would under all circumstances induce judges to abide by previous Supreme Court decisions. Some of the respondents stressed that they are aware that it is undesirable for the law to be fixed forever and that it can be beneficial to get rid of, among other things, out-dated Supreme Court decisions that no longer fit the current social realities.[483] Consequently, they consider it to be one of the responsibilities of lower judges for the development of the law to deviate from out-dated or highly undesirable Supreme Court cases in order to induce an appeal that would offer the Supreme Court an opportunity to reconsider its previous decisions.[484] Once they deem the benefit for the development of the law outweighs the burden of extra litigation all the way to the Supreme Court, these lower judges would be inclined to deviate from Supreme Court decisions.[485] Obviously, whether a previous Supreme Court decision should be deemed as out-dated or undesirable and whether deviating from the case would be beneficial for the development of the law are questions that cannot be answered by applying formal criteria alone, but require substantive considerations of the merits of the previous case.

Another reason why judges make a significant distinction between Supreme Court cases and those decided by lower courts is related to some of the institutional differences between cassation on the one hand and trial procedures in the first and second instances on the other. One of the unique institutional aspects of the cassation procedure is that in every civil case and most criminal cases brought to the Supreme Court, the Court receives an advisory opinion submitted by the Procurator General or one of the Advocates General.[486] It is usually esteemed legal scholars,[487] former judges[488]

---

[482] All the interviewed judges gave this explanation when answering question 11, see Appendix 4.

[483] See e.g. NL20131022 and NL20131031.

[484] Ibid.

[485] Ibid.

[486] In tax cases advisory opinions are not required, but in practice the Supreme Court does hear advisory opinions submitted by Advocates General, see http://www.rechtspraak.nl/ORGANISATIE/

and practising lawyers[489] who are appointed to the position of (deputy) Procurator General or Advocates General.[490] An advisory opinion usually summarizes the facts upon which the Supreme Court must base its judgment, reviews the judgment(s) in the previous instances, points out the legal question(s) that the Supreme Court must answer and provides a thorough summary and analysis of the relevant scholarly writings and cases.[491] Although the Supreme Court is free to concur with or differ from such advisory opinions and is not obliged to account for itself in this respect, the institution of advisory opinions is generally deemed to be of great value for the Supreme Court's work.[492] District and appeal courts, on the other hand, do not have such an institution of advisory opinions by Procurator General, Advocates General or comparable officials.

HOGE-RAAD/SUPREME-COURT/THE-PROCURATOR-GENERAL-OF-THE-SUPREME-COURT/Pages/default.aspx.

[487] The current Procurator General, deputy Procurator General and 23 out of the 26 Advocates General have an academic background, i.e. they have worked as researchers and/or lecturers at law schools. Fifteen out of the current 26 Advocates General have been or are still law professors, see http://www.rechtspraak.nl/ORGANISATIE/HOGE-RAAD/OVERDEHOGERAAD/ORGANISATIE/Pages/Parket.aspx.

[488] The current Procurator General, deputy Procurator General and 16 out of the 26 Advocates General have been judges prior to their appointment to the current position, see http://www.rechtspraak.nl/ORGANISATIE/HOGE-RAAD/OVERDEHOGERAAD/ORGANISATIE/Pages/Parket.aspx.

[489] Thirteen out of the 26 current Advocates General have worked as practising lawyers (either in law firms or as in-house legal counsels in companies), see http://www.rechtspraak.nl/ORGANISATIE/HOGE-RAAD/OVERDEHOGERAAD/ORGANISATIE/Pages/Parket.aspx.

[490] The (deputy)Procurator General and Advocates General enjoy life tenure and are independent from the Government and the Parliament, see http://www.rechtspraak.nl/ORGANISATIE/HOGE-RAAD/OVERDEHOGERAAD/ORGANISATIE/Pages/Parket.aspx.

[491] See e.g. Spier 2010a and Spier 2010b.

[492] See http://www.rechtspraak.nl/ORGANISATIE/HOGE-RAAD/SUPREME-COURT/THE-PROCURATOR-GENERAL-OF-THE-SUPREME-COURT/Pages/default.aspx. See also Bruinsma 1988a, chapter four.

Another unique institution of the Supreme Court is the *Wetenschappelijk bureau*, an in-house research institute staffed primarily by legal researchers who usually have a mixed academic and practising background.[493] Staff of this in-house research institute provide assistance to Procurator General, Advocates General and judges of the Supreme Court by, among other things, making initial analyses of the cases brought to the Supreme Court, carrying out research into relevant legislation, cases and scholarly publications, writing memos and making drafts of advisory opinions.[494] Such an in-house research institute is absent in district and appeal courts.

Still another relevant difference as indicated by the interviewed judges is that cases brought to the Supreme Court are usually decided by a panel of five judges, whereas appeal cases are usually heard by a panel of three judges and district court cases are normally decided by a single judge.[495] Moreover, the overall quality of Supreme Court judges is commonly perceived to be very high, as it is usually top-class legal scholars, former judges or practising lawyers who are appointed to serve as judges in the Supreme Court.[496]

At first sight, such institutional differences appear to be of formal instead of substantive nature. Explanations provided by some of the interviewed judges, however, indicate that they tend to infer from such institutional factors that Supreme Court decisions are the final products of a long and careful process in which the status of the existing law has been, or at least has had a good chance to be, thoroughly investigated and that the wider implications of the choices and decisions made in the final judgments most probably have been carefully considered, whereas judicial deliberation in

---

[493] See http://www.rechtspraak.nl/Organisatie/Hoge-Raad/wetenschappelijk-bureau-hoge-raad/Pages/default.aspx.

[494] See ibid.

[495] See NL20110509, NL20131021, NL20131022, NL20131028 and NL20131107-3.

[496] See the interviews cited in the previous note. For the selection process of Supreme Court judges see http://www.rechtspraak.nl/Organisatie/Hoge-Raad/OverDeHogeRaad/Organisatie/Pages/Wervingenselectieraadsheren.aspx. See also Bruinsma 2003, p. 31-32.

district and appeal courts may tend to be less thorough.[497] Such an inference suggests that the relevance of the formal criterion whether a previous case is decided by the Supreme Court eventually rests on a presumption that judgments reached through the cassation procedure, due to some of the unique institutional features of cassation, are likely to be well-balanced decisions and accordingly deserve to carry significant weight in judicial deliberation as to whether such a case should be followed or not. In other words, the first factor (hierarchy of the court that has made the judgment) listed at the beginning of this subparagraph is related to substantive considerations, even though on the surface this factor seems to involve only a simple formal criterion.

4.2.3.3 Summary

It is doubtful whether the concept of "binding force" combined with distinctions in the court hierarchy is an optimal framework to analyse the influence of cases on judicial decision-making in the Netherlands. Using such a framework may easily lead to a dichotomy, i.e. cases decided by the Supreme Court are *de jure* or *de facto* binding on lower courts, whereas cases decided by other courts are not binding.[498] This kind of observation may raise the impression that the influence of a case depends on its pedigree, i.e. it depends on which court has made the decision, rather than on the substantive soundness of the decision itself. Furthermore, such a framework may raise the impression that the influence of a case is something static and abstract, as within such a framework a case is either binding or not binding. Accordingly, this framework does not quite cater for the possibility that the influence of a case may vary over time or according to the context of the specific disputes to which it may bear relevance.

The findings of this study suggest that in adjudication practice, judges tend to perceive the influence of previous cases as a matter of attributing weight to arguments in a process of deliberation. How much weight a previous case carries in judicial deliberation depends on a series of factors, many of which involve

---

[497] See e.g. NL20110509, NL20131021, NL20131022, NL20131028 and NL20131107-3.

[498] See e.g. Glastra van Loon e.a. 1968 and Brunner 1994.

substantive consideration, such as the strength of the arguments employed by the court to reach the decision in the previous case and how well the case has been received in scholarly writings. Court hierarchy is a significant factor in this context. The relevance of this factor, however, does not purely depend on the threat of reversal caused by the hierarchical structure of the court system, but it also rests upon judges' presumption that cases decided by the Supreme Court, due to some of the unique institutional features of the cassation procedure, are likely to contain well-balanced decisions. Furthermore, the findings of this study indicate that the influence of a previous case on judicial decision-making needs to be ascertained in the context of a concrete dispute to which the previous case may bear relevance, as whether or not a previous case will be followed in the resolution of a legal dispute brought to court depends not only on the weight that judges attribute to the case, but also on arguments that argue against the application of the previous case to the dispute at hand. Where, for example, applying a previous case to resolve a legal dispute may lead to a highly undesirable outcome in light of the concrete circumstances of a specific dispute, judges may attribute so much weight to the consideration of avoiding a highly undesirable outcome that the previous case will not be followed.[499] Accordingly, it seems more appropriate to see the influence of previous cases as something that has a relative and dynamic nature, rather than something that has an absolute and fixed value that is not susceptible to change or adjustment.

4.2.4 Contribution to the case law mechanism

Findings in the previous subparagraph suggest that the development of case law in the Netherlands takes place in, what Kühn calls, "a process of rational discourse".[500] Judges, legal scholars and practising lawyers all participate and exercise a certain degree of influence in this process. By making choices such as which previous cases to follow and which to avoid in adjudication, judges exercise considerable influence on which previous court decisions eventually become the leading cases. This form of contribution by

---

[499] See e.g. NL20131017, NL20131028, NL20132019, NL20131107-2 and NL20131114.

[500] Kühn 2007, p. 379.

judges to the operation of case law, i.e. influence at the level of the influential status of individual cases, is relatively easy to understand, so that it is not necessary to elaborate on this point. What I do wish to further explore is the contribution made by judges to the operation of case law at a methodological level, which will be elaborated in the following passages.

One of the prerequisites for cases to fulfil the role of a source of law in any legal system is that the way judges treat previous cases in adjudication must be reasonably predictable.[501] It is difficult to imagine how cases could provide a desirable degree of certainty in a legal system where judges make random and arbitrary use of previous cases. For the way judges treat previous cases in adjudication to be reasonably predictable, it is crucial that, among other things,[502]

(a) judges follow certain common methodological guidelines when dealing with previous cases in adjudication and

(b) such guidelines must be accessible to the public.

Findings in the previous paragraph reveal that when dealing with disputes in adjudication, judges in the Netherlands do follow a certain common methodological framework in assessing the influence of previous cases. This framework is common, in the first place, in the sense that judges are likely to take the same set of factors into account when assessing the relative weight that should be attributed to previous cases. Obviously, the mere fact that judges are likely to take the same set of factors into account cannot guarantee a completely accurate prediction as to how judges will treat relevant previous cases in each dispute. After all, the different factors that judges take into account may point in different directions in a specific dispute, so that it is not unthinkable that litigants and their counsels may reach different conclusions from the judges, depending on the weight they attribute to each factor. This is, however, not to say that the way judges assess the weight of previous cases in adjudication in the Netherlands is utterly arbitrary and subjective. The existence of such a set of factors that jointly determine the weight of previous cases in judicial deliberation offers litigants and their counsels a useful framework to estimate how judges are likely to react to arguments based on possibly

---

[501] Vogenauer 2006, p. 895.

[502] Ibid.

relevant previous cases. Moreover, the predictability is enhanced by the fact that some patterns have emerged in adjudication practice, one of which is that Supreme Court decisions carry so much weight in judicial deliberation that judges would normally follow Supreme Court decisions in disputes that concern the same legal issues as those decided in earlier Supreme Court cases unless considerations based on other factors would produce a strong justification for deviation.[503] Another pattern, as revealed earlier in this chapter, is that cases decided by district courts and courts of appeal normally carry much less weight than Supreme Court decisions, so that the mere fact that a district court or a court of appeal has decided a previous similar case in a certain fashion is normally not sufficient to justify an expectation that the previous case will be followed in later court practice.[504] This means that where litigants or their counsels, for example, base their argumentation on a previous decision of the Supreme Court that has decided the same legal issue as the one involved in the dispute at hand, to which legal scholars have not expressed severe criticism and lower courts have not demonstrated considerable resistance in adjudication practice, they can be fairly confident that the chances are rather slim that judges would deviate from the previous case, whereas if they cite a previous decision by a district court that has not won much support in scholarly writings or court practice, they would have to be aware that they need to provide strong justification as to why this previous case should be followed in the dispute at hand. From such patterns one can reasonably infer some thumb rules as to how much weight certain types of cases are likely to carry in judicial deliberation under normal circumstances. Such thumb rules are obviously not of such a precise nature to guarantee completely accurate prediction in each case. However, they are nonetheless capable of considerably facilitating the litigants and their counsels to estimate the likelihood that a previous case will be followed in adjudication.

One may of course argue that even if judges in the Netherlands do follow a certain common methodological framework in assessing the influence of previous cases, the way judges treat previous cases would still be unpredictable if this

---

[503] See the responses of the interviewed judges to question 7 (Appendix 4).
[504] See e.g. NL20110519, NL20130923, NL20131008-1, NL20131021 and NL20131028 and NL20131022.

methodological framework is only known within the judiciary, whereas litigants, practising lawyers and legal scholars have no way to gain insight into the contour of the framework. Fortunately, the way judges treat previous cases in adjudication is not a black box in the Netherlands. As mentioned earlier in this paragraph, citing and discussing previous cases in judgments has now become a common practice in the Netherlands.[505] Citation and discussion of previous cases in judgments offer valuable insights into the factors that judges take into consideration when evaluating arguments based on previous cases.[506] In addition to judgments, one can also derive useful insights from scholarly writings that analyse the way judges interpret and apply previous cases in adjudication.[507] Moreover, the law has been highly professionalized in the Netherlands. Key players in law such as judges, practising lawyers and legal scholars have all accomplished academic legal education and have received similar case law trainings at law schools,[508] which helps to forge a shared fundamental mode of thinking with regard to, among other things, how previous cases should be used to solve legal disputes.[509] This is of course not to say that every practising lawyer and every legal scholar in the Netherlands does in fact know the exact details of the method that judges adopt when using previous cases in adjudication. Nor does this mean that the method of using previous cases in adjudication has been thoroughly and clearly articulated in scholarly writings in the Netherlands. What this study does wish to point out is that the methodological guidelines that judges adopt in adjudication with regard to the use of previous cases are *knowable*

---

[505] See e.g. Kottenhagen 1986, Struycken & Haazen 1993 and Brunner 1994.

[506] This is of course not to say that the way judges cite and discuss cases in the Netherlands has become so accurate and elaborate that there is no room for improvement any more. In fact, it is more than desirable that judges be more transparent about the real considerations that have shaped their decisions when providing justification for their decisions in judgments. However, the situation now is undoubtedly much better than that before 1980 when judges almost never cited previous cases in judgments.

[507] See e.g. Haazen 2007, Snijders 2007 and Lubbers 2008.

[508] See the paragraph in this chapter on the way cases are used in legal education.

[509] Ibid.

to other players in law such as practising lawyers and legal scholars, and that the fact that such methodological guidelines are accessible to a broader public than the judges alone contributes to a reasonable degree of predictability as to how likely it is for previous cases to be followed in adjudication practice.

To summarize, the analysis above indicates that judges in the Netherlands adopt certain common methodological guidelines with regard to the use of previous cases in adjudication. Such guidelines are knowable to a broader public than the judges themselves due to, among other things, the practice of citing and discussing previous cases in judgments and the fact that judges, practising lawyers and legal scholars have received similar case law trainings at law schools. The fact that judges follow common methodological guidelines when using previous cases to solve legal disputes in court and the fact that such guidelines are knowable to other players in law are conducive to achieve a reasonable degree of predictability as to how previous cases are likely to be treated when invoked as arguments in legal proceedings. A reasonable degree of predictability, in its turn, contributes to the fact that cases are able to fulfil the role of source of law that offers a fair degree of certainty.

Moreover, the data presented in this paragraph also indicate that judges function as a selective force in the utilization phase that, jointly with other actors such as legal scholars and practising lawyers, influences which court judgments eventually become the law. They do so by following or rejecting cases brought forward by the counsels of the litigating parties in legal proceedings, and by searching for and using other relevant cases. Through these two modes of selection, judges influence how a case is likely to be treated in later court practice as well as in scholarly writings and in legal education.

5. Concluding remarks

The previous chapter illustrated that once cases are selected for publication, they undergo two basic processes before being made available to the public: a rudimentary process of categorization and a relatively simple process of interpretation. An example of categorization is that cases concerning a particular area of the law such as consumer law, real estate law and intellectual property law, get published in commercial periodicals that cover that specific legal area.[510] In this way, published cases are sorted into different categories. As to the process of interpretation, a clear example is that some cases published in commercial periodicals are accompanied by a commentary (case annotation). Even cases that are not annotated in the publication phase rarely get published without any added information. At least some key words are added to each published case in order to help the reader get a quick impression of the essence of the case. In a broad sense, adding such information as key words and summaries to published cases can also be seen as a basic form of interpretation, as such information can help the reader to better understand the essence of a published case.

This chapter revealed that both the process of categorization and the process of interpretation further continue in the utilization phase. The categorization is for the most part done by legal scholars in the utilization phase. This chapter demonstrated that one way to classify scholarly writings involving cases in the Netherlands is to divide them into case-focused and system-oriented publications. In system-oriented publications, for example, legal scholars have developed two basic models to categorize and systemize cases, i.e. adopt the structure of a piece of legislation or follow a doctrinal structure. Furthermore, this chapter illustrated that legal scholars in the Netherlands developed three grouping patterns to sort cases that are relevant for a particular legislative provision or a particular doctrinal component into a certain order. As for interpretation, this chapter demonstrated that legal scholars also perform a very important role in interpreting cases in the utilization phase. System-oriented scholarly writings, for example, often summarize the essence of a case in one or two sentences by distilling a norm from

---

[510] There are nowadays many commercial periodicals in the Netherlands that publish cases in very specific legal areas. See e.g. *Woonrecht (Housing Law), Tijdschrift voor ambtenarenrecht (Journal for Civil Servant Law), Intellectuele eigendom en reclamerecht (Intellectual Property and Advertisement Law), Tijdschrift voor consumentenrecht (Consumer Law Journal), Jurisprudentie sociale voorzieningen (Social Services Cases) etc*. For details see Appendix 1.

the judicial decision.[511] Most case-focused writings, on the other hand, demonstrate even more elaborate efforts of legal scholars to interpret published cases, as they not only distil a norm or norms from a judicial decision, but also summarize the key facts, analyse the legal reasoning that the court employs to reach the decision and explore possible implications of the discussed case for similar or related cases in the future.[512]

Another, and arguably more intriguing process that takes place in the utilization phase is that normative elements are drawn from published cases, and such normative elements are subsequently used and evaluated in various settings by various users. Such normative elements can be rules, principles or assessment frameworks.[513] This chapter illustrated that not only judges, but also legal scholars and even law students distil normative elements from published cases, evaluate them and use them to solve legal problems. This process of retrieving, using and evaluating normative elements from published cases inevitably produces different views and standpoints. Differences of opinion with regard to the content, scope and soundness of the normative elements retrieved from published cases are settled in a relatively transparent fashion, i.e. through a rational discourse that takes place in open forums such as court trials and academic as well as legal professional publications. The Supreme Court has a significant voice in this discourse, but this chapter demonstrated that also other actors such as lower judges, legal scholars and practising lawyers can exercise meaningful influence on the outcome of the discourse. Where the way various users use and evaluate a case converges in the positive direction, the case is more likely to ultimately become the law than where the way one particular actor uses and evaluates the case is questioned or challenged by other users. It can therefore be concluded that, no more than the publication phase is the utilization of cases monopolized by judges, and that the operation of case law in the Netherlands has a dynamic nature that involves the participation by and allows for influence of various actors.

---

511 See e.g. the cases and the comments to them in Nieuwenhuis & Stolker & Valk 2011, Article 6:162, Commentary 5, paragraph a.

512 See e.g. Haas 2010 and Fernhout 2010.

513 The Dutch term for this word is “toetsingskader” or “gezichtspunten”.

Chapter 3

Recognition of cases as a source of law in the Netherlands

Chapter 3 Recognition of cases as a source of law in the Netherlands

1. Introduction

The previous two chapters examined two phases in the operation of the case law mechanism in the Netherlands. The findings demonstrated that far from all court judgments eventually become leadings cases that shape the law and that various actors exercise a certain degree of influence upon the final outcome as to which court judgments ultimately become leading cases that shape the law. The previous chapters essentially inform us how a case becomes the law, but they did not yet tell us whether, and if so, how cases – including not only the leading cases, but also the vast majority of cases that never get published and the many published cases that never get detected and used – *as a whole* acquire the status of a source of law. In order to answer this question, one cannot limit the investigation to study only how cases are published and used in practice, but should also examine the normative views on the status of cases as a source of law and pay attention to the possible dynamics between what happens in practice and what gets normatively accepted as desirable and justified.

In order to gain a comprehensive understanding of the way cases fulfil the role of a source of law in the Netherlands, this chapter will examine the normative views in the Netherlands on the status of cases as a source of law and reflect on the possible dynamics between the practice of publishing and using cases and the normative views on the desirability and acceptability of what happens in practice. A key question that this chapter will investigate is whether cases are explicitly or implicitly recognized as a source of law in the Netherlands. A closely related question that this chapter will also examine is whether judges are explicitly or implicitly accepted to perform a lawmaking role in the Netherlands.[514]

[514] Recognition of cases as a source of law and acceptance of the lawmaking role of the judge are in fact two sides of the same coin, see Adams 1999, p. 466.

The wish to investigate the normative views in the Netherlands on the status of cases as a source of law was furthermore triggered by the fact that in the existing literature it is commonly held that although throughout time cases have in practice acquired a highly influential status in many civil law jurisdictions, they are still not recognized as a source of law.[515] This commonly held observation raises the impression that the actual influence of cases in practice has undergone a remarkable change in many civil law jurisdictions, moving from being relatively insignificant to highly influential, but the normative views on the status of cases as a source of law have remained the same, i.e. cases used to be denied as a source of law in the past and nowadays they are still not recognized as a source of law. Moreover, this commonly held observation raises the impression that the growing significance of cases in practice throughout time does not have an impact on the normative views, i.e. it tends to suggest that despite the rising significance of cases in practice, the normative views on the status of cases as a source of law have not changed. By investigating the normative views in the Netherlands on the status of cases as a source of law, this chapter seeks to ascertain whether the impression raised by this commonly held observation is correct and if not, what nuances can be added to this observation.

1.1 Analytic framework

Although the question whether cases are recognized as a source of law seems to require a yes or no answer, it can be helpful to envisage a sliding scale as an analytic tool in which the answer to this question can be placed. Such a sliding scale can be visualized with an absolute denial of cases as a source of law at one end and an unequivocal acceptance at the other (see Figure 6). It can be useful to use such a sliding scale as an analytic tool, because ascertaining the normative views on the status of cases as a source of law often requires careful analysis and interpretation of various sources, which is a process that may involve a delicate balancing of various competing opinions and arguments. The result of such an analysis may not comfortably fit in a resolute yes or no. Using a sliding scale

[515] See e.g. Loussouarn 1958, p. 255, Baudouin 1974, p. 12, David 1984, p. 116, Kiel & Göttingen 1997, p. 46 and Adams 2007, p. 149.

may enable us to analyse the data and to present the findings with a desirable degree of nuance.

Figure 6 A sliding scale to capture views on the status of cases as a source of law

Moreover, a time dimension is added to the sliding scale (see Figure 7). A time dimension combined with the sliding scale can help to reveal possible changes that the normative views have undergone over time, and it can help to visually present the possible changes in the form of a curve.

Figure 7 A sliding scale combined with a time dimension

As to the question *whose* views will be investigated, this chapter chooses to examine the views of the legislature, the judges and legal scholars, as they are commonly deemed as the three major actors in law in civil law jurisdictions.[516] In accordance with this multi-actor approach, this chapter will present the findings in a graph with three axes x, y and z as shown in Figure 8, which represent the attitude of the legislature, the judges and respectively legal scholars. Although the time dimension is not incorporated in this graph, two different graphs will be presented at the end of this

---

[516] See Van Caenegem 1987.

chapter to illustrate whether, and if so how, the views of the three actors in the Netherlands at present differ from their views around 1838 when the Dutch Civil Code was introduced.

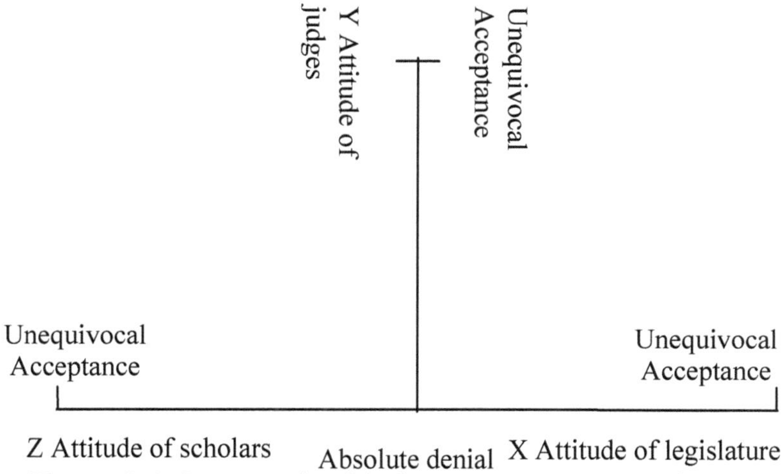

Figure 8 A framework with three axes to capture views on the status of cases as a source of law in a legal system

Of course, the analytic framework developed by this study is not free of limitations. The views of the legislature, judges and legal scholars on the status of cases are a source of law, after all, is something that can hardly be measured in quantity. This means that the value that a researcher assigns to the sliding scale involves subjective evaluation and thus cannot be mathematically accurate. However, this does not mean that the value that a researcher assigns to the sliding scale is necessarily arbitrary and hence entirely unverifiable. Scholars may differ on the question which exact point in the sliding scale should be chosen to represent the degree of normative acceptance of cases as a source of law, but it is possible that, after examining the various sources and arguments, scholars may agree upon a certain margin on the sliding scale that can be reasonably said to represent the degree of acceptance. Despite the difficulty of accurate quantification, the sliding scale framework can still serve to facilitate the analysis of data as well as the presentation of the findings.

Another limitation can be that the sliding scale framework tends to avoid giving a clear-cut answer to a question that requires a yes or no. It should be noted that the sliding scale is not incompatible with a yes or no answer. As Figure 9 illustrates, anything short of an unequivocal acceptance can be categorized as a no, albeit the no answer does not have to be an unqualified negation. In other words, the sliding scale does not have to be seen as a replacement of a yes or no answer, but rather a supplement to it.

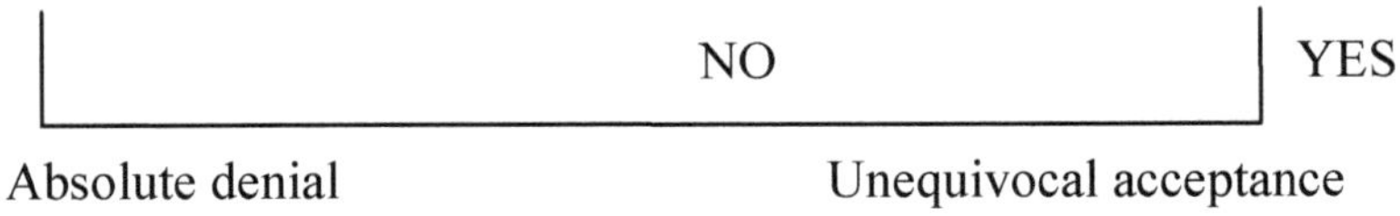

Figure 9 A sliding scale combined with an all-or-nothing framework

1.2 Method

The primary method used in this chapter is analysis of written texts. In addition, one semi-structured interview was conducted with a legal scholar to obtain data that are missing in his writings.[517]

Four types of data have been gathered and analysed:

(1) Legislation and records of legislative history. These sources are primarily used to ascertain the attitude of the legislature towards the recognition of cases as a source of law.

(2) Cases. This source is used primarily to ascertain the views of judges. Due to the huge volume of cases published since 1838 and the limited time for this study, it has not been possible to conduct a systematic research on all published cases. Only cases to which relevant scholarly writings refer have been consulted. This methodological choice is made for two major reasons. The first reason is that existing studies[518] have already demonstrated that for a long time legal reasoning in judgments was very formalistic, so that it is not very

[517] See interview NL 20110519.

[518] See e.g. Fockema Andreae 1904, Polak 1953, p. 54 and Hesselink 2001, p. 9 and 11-13.

likely that older judgments might contain in their legal reasoning explicit recognition that cases are a source of law. Secondly, a number of scholars have already conducted systematic studies on published cases to verify whether the *stare decisis* rule applies in court practice.[519] Data collected by these studies are very useful for the current study. Given these two facts, I have chosen to rely on case law data collected in earlier scholarly writings.

(3) Speeches, interviews and publications by (former) judges. This type of data is primarily used to ascertain the views of judges.

(4) Scholarly writings. This study has primarily focused on three types of scholarly writings:

   (a) Introductory and handbooks of (private) law. This type of books are a valuable source to ascertain the views of scholars on the status of cases as a source of law, because many of these books contain a section that explicitly discusses the question of the sources of law.

   (b) Books and papers that explicitly discuss the sources of law.

   (c) Scholarly writings on the theory and practice of judicial decision-making (*rechtsvinding*). This type of literature also contains valuable data because the lawmaking role of the judge and the authority of case law are two of the frequently discussed topics in this type of publications.

   (d) Scholarly writings that comment on some of the legislative provisions that shed light on views of the legislature. This type of literature is relevant for this study because it provides scholarly interpretations to some of the relevant legislative provisions.

Two search methods have been used to find the above-mentioned data. The first method uses online library catalogues and online databases. In particular, I have made frequent use of Picarta,

---

[519] See e.g. Kottenhagen 1986 and Struycken & Haazen 1993. Two less systematic yet relevant empirical studies also contain useful data, see Jessurun D'Oliveira 1973 and Vranken 1995, p. 170.

a Netherlands-based database that contains references to Dutch and English literature including books and journal articles, and Opmaat, a Dutch legal database that contains Dutch legislation and cases.[520] The second method is the snowball method. Scholarly writings often contain useful references to legislation, cases and other legal literature. Part of the data has been found by verifying these references.

1.3 Structure of the chapter

The main body of this chapter consists of three parts that successively examine the views of the legislature, judges and legal scholars. The key findings will be summarized in the conclusion.

2. The legislature

It is difficult to find a clear-cut answer in Dutch legislation to the question whether the legislature recognizes cases as a source of law. Both arguments pro and contra can be found in various legislative provisions. Some older statutory provisions enacted in the 19th century tend to suggest that originally the legislature was of the view that judges ought only to apply enacted laws and that cases were not supposed to fulfil the role of a source of law. Some later statutes, however, suggest that the attitude of the legislature has changed and that it has deliberately endorsed judges to perform a lawmaking role in some areas. The following subparagraphs will examine the arguments pro and contra that can be drawn from legislative provisions and legislation techniques. The analysis will reveal that the attitude of the legislature is shifting from denial to an increasingly open recognition of the lawmaking role of the judge as well as the status of cases as a source of law.

---

[520] Some of the key words used in the search include: "sources of law", "legalism", "precedent", "*stare decisis*", "precedent system", "case law", "judge-made law" and "lawmaking role of the judge".

2.1 Arguments contra the status of cases as a source of law

2.1.1 The Constitution (De Grondwet)

The Constitution of the Netherlands was introduced in 1815,[521] and has been amended several times since then.[522] A number of significant amendments took place in 1848, which put an end to the nearly absolute power of the King and made the Netherlands a constitutional monarchy.[523]

One of the cornerstones of the 1848 amendments was Montesquieu's theory of the separation of powers.[524] This is reflected in a number of constitutional provisions. Article 81, for example, confers the legislative power to the Government[525] and the Parliament,[526] whereas the adjudication power is conferred to an independent judiciary.[527] Moreover, Article 120 expressly forbids the courts from performing constitutional reviews.[528]

The fact that the Government and the Parliament jointly exercise the legislative power illustrates that the separation of powers in the Netherlands is not as strict as Montesquieu envisaged. However, it is obvious that the Constitution intends to separate the

---

[521] *Staatsblad* 1815, 45.

[522] See e.g. *Staatsblad* 1848, 60, *Staatsblad* 1953, 264, *Staatsblad* 2002, 200, *Staatsblad* 2008, 240 etc.

[523] See e.g. *Staatsblad* 1848, 59 and *Staatsblad* 1848, 60.

[524] Franken 1985, p. 103-105.

[525] The Government consists of the King and the ministers, according to Article 42 Paragraph 1 of the Constitution. The ministers, and not the King, are responsible for acts of parliament, according to Article 42 Paragraph 2 of the Constitution.

[526] "Acts of Parliament shall be jointly enacted by the Government and the State General", according to Article 81. "State General" is the official name of the Dutch Parliament, which consists of a Lower House (*Tweede Kamer*) and an Upper House (*Eerste Kamer*), according to Article 51 Paragraph 1 of the Constitution.

[527] "The adjudication of disputes involving rights under civil law and debts will be the responsibility of the judiciary", according to Article 112 Paragraph 1. "The trial of offences will also be the responsibility of the judiciary", according to Article 113 Paragraph 1.

[528] "The constitutionality of Acts of Parliament and treaties will not be reviewed by the courts", according to Article 120.

legislative and the adjudication powers. This can be interpreted as to mean that the legislature does not recognize cases as a source of law, since such a separation is based on a model that restricts the role of the courts to the application of laws enacted by a legislative body.[529]

2.1.2 The Kingdom Legislation Act (Wet houdende algemeene bepalingen der wetgeving van het koninkrijk)

Together with the old Civil Code, the Kingdom Legislation Act went into force on 1 October 1838.[530] Many articles of this statute bear a clear mark of the 19th century legalism, which held legislation to be the only source of law. Article 3, for example, provided that "customs create no law unless legislation refers to them". This used to be seen as clear evidence that the legislature originally intended legislation to be the only source of law, thus denying that cases ought to be recognized as a source of law.[531] However, in the 1980's, the old legalistic theory became so outdated that the legislature decided to delete this article.[532]

Although Article 3 has been deleted, this statute still contains a number of provisions that tend to deny that cases are a source of law. Article 11, for example, provides that "the judge must adjudicate according to legislation", and that "he may under no circumstance evaluate the intrinsic value and fairness of legislation". Article 12 goes on to provide that "no judge may adjudicate cases submitted to him by way of general ordinances, dispositions or regulations". Furthermore, Article 13 provides that "the judge that refuses to adjudicate, under the pretext of silence, obscurity or incompleteness of legislation, can be prosecuted for the offence of refusing to administer justice".

---

[529] In Montesquieu's view, "judges are no more than the mouth that pronounces the words of the law, mere passive beings, incapable of moderating either its force or rigour", see Montesquieu 2001.

[530] Diephuis 1869, p. 2.

[531] "The doctrine that holds legislation to be the only source of law has led our legislature to enact this rule", according to Van Apeldoorn, see Van Apeldoorn 1939, p. 71.

[532] See *Staatsblad* 1989, 616. The article is no longer in force as of 1 January 1992.

These legislative provisions used to be widely accepted as to mean that the legislature does not recognize cases as a source of law. Article 12, for example, used to be interpreted as restricting the binding force of a judgment to the litigating parties and forbidding judges from playing a lawmaking role.[533] Article 13 used to be understood as a denial by the legislature that legislation could ever be incomplete or ambiguous, as these were in the eyes of the legislature mere “pretexts”.[534]

Such negative interpretations changed over time. Since the 1950s, some scholars argued that Article 12 is not quite relevant for the debate, because this article is copied from Article 5 of the French Civil Code, which was intended to address a problem that had never existed in the Netherlands, namely the practice that during the Ancien Régime French courts were authorized to decide cases by issuing general regulations (*Arrêt de règlements*).[535] Moreover, the assumption that laws enacted by the legislature are never incomplete or obscure has become so unattractive over time that nowadays Article 13 is seen as an “invitation” for cases to fulfil the function of a source of law.[536]

2.1.3 Article 236 Civil Procedure Code (Wetboek van burgerlijke rechtsvordering)

Yet another legislative argument against recognizing cases as a source of law can be drawn from Article 236 of the Civil Procedure Code, which provides that “decisions on the disputed legal relation contained in a legally irreversible judgment has binding force between the parties in another law suit”.[537] This article can be

[533] See e.g. Opzoomer 1865, p. 68, Diephuis 1869, p. 86-87, Teixeira de Mattos 1885, p. 31, Land 1899, p. 198, Suijling 1918, p. 7 and Zonderland 1974, p. 190.
[534] See e.g. Pitlo 1968, p. 16 and Zevenbergen 1925, p. 166-167.
[535] See Drion 1968b, 156. For more elaborate discussion of the meaning of this article see Kottenhagen 1986, p. 113-116.
[536] See Albers e.a. 2009, p. 127. For an earlier similar view see Bellefroid 1937, p. 107.
[537] This article was originally codified in Article 1954 of the old Dutch Civil Code. Later it was moved to Article 67 of the Civil Procedure Code. See Van Hattum 2012, p. 16.

understood to mean that a judgment only has binding force between the litigating parties. However, since the 1950s a number of scholars argued that this article has no bearing with the *stare decisis* rule and thus does not hinder the recognition of cases as a source of law.[538]

2.2 Arguments pro the status of cases as a source of law

2.2.1 Article 424 Civil Procedure Code

In the Netherlands, the Supreme Court can quash a judgment by a lower court without directly making a final decision.[539] When this happens, the Supreme Court refers the case to another lower court with instructions on questions of law. Article 424 of the Civil Procedure Code requires the lower court to which the case is referred, to decide the case in compliance with the judgment of the Supreme Court. This can be seen as evidence that, at least in some cases, lower courts are bound by decisions of the Supreme Court, so that in these cases it can be said that judgments by the Supreme Court function as a source of law.[540]

2.2.2 Article 78 Court Organization Act (Wet op de rechterlijke organisatie)

Article 78 of the Court Organization Act may also lend some support to the proposition that the legislature recognizes cases as a source of law. This article creates an institution called "cassation in the interest of the law".[541] This legal institution authorizes the Procurator General to request the Supreme Court to annul a judgment of a lower court for legal errors or for non-compliance with some crucial formality requirements.[542] This is an

---

[538] See e.g. Drion 1968b, p. 155, Kottenhagen 1986, p. 111-113 and Struycken & Haazen 1993, p. 104-105.

[539] This can happen for example when some facts still need to be ascertained, see Article 421 Civil Procedure Code.

[540] See Drion 1968b, p. 147. C.f. Struycken & Haazen 1993, p. 108-110.

[541] The Dutch term is "cassatie in het belang der wet". For details of this legal institution see Den Hartog Jader 1994.

[542] For details of this legal institution see Den Hartog Jader 1994.

extraordinary remedy at law for a number of reasons. First, it cannot be used by the litigating parties, but only by the Procurator General.[543] Second, it cannot be used until it is no longer possible for the litigating parties to challenge the judgment by way of an ordinary remedy such as an appeal or a cassation procedure.[544] Third, the decision of the Supreme Court in such a case cannot negatively affect the rights of the litigating parties.[545]

The purpose of this legal institution is obviously not to remedy possible wrongs suffered by the litigating parties, but rather to obtain a decision by the highest court in order to maintain uniformity in the application of legislation.[546] Some scholars argue that this purpose cannot be achieved unless it is accepted that Supreme Court judgments are binding on lower courts, so that this legal institution can be seen as recognition by the legislature of the binding force of Supreme Court judgments.[547]

2.2.3 Article 79 Court Organization Act

Another article of the Court Organization Act, namely Article 79, suggests a remarkable change in the attitude of the legislature. This article was previously numbered Article 99 in the Court Organization Act.[548] In 1963, this article underwent an important change. Before 1963, this article provided that one of the grounds for the Supreme Court to annul a judgment by a lower court was "violation of legislation". In 1963, the legislature changed this phrase into "violation of the law".[549] Some scholars argue that "the

---

[543] Article 78 Paragraph 1 Court Organization Act.

[544] Article 78 Paragraph 2 Court Organization Act.

[545] Ibid.

[546] Glastra van Loon e.a. 1968, p. 145.

[547] See e.g. Drion 1968b, p. 159, Glastra van Loon e.a. 1968, p. 145 and Jessurun D'Oliveira 1973, p. 37-38.

[548] *Staatsblad* 2002, 1.

[549] *Staatsblad* 1963, 272. It should be noted that this change of legislation did not cause tremendous changes in practice, because in its adjudication practice the Supreme Court has already expanded the ground of cassation to include, among other things, violation of general legal principles and customary law even before 1963, see Veegens 1971, p. 132-333. This, of course, does not undermine the symbolic value of the change that Article 99 of the Court Organization Act underwent, see Wiarda 1972, p. 43.

law" also includes case law, so that this change confirms the status of cases as a source of law.[550]

2.2.4 Article 80a Court Organization Act

Article 80a of the Court Organization Act can be seen as yet another piece of evidence that the attitude of the legislature has changed in favor of openly recognizing the lawmaking role of the judge, and hence the status of cases as a source of law.

This provision (previously numbered Article 101a[551]), was added to the Court Organization Act in 1988.[552] It authorizes the Supreme Court to dismiss a cassation appeal without providing substantive reasons, if the Supreme Court is of the opinion that the appeal grounds cannot lead to annulment of the challenged judicial decision and "the dismissal of the appeal does not require answering legal questions in the interest of the legal unity or the development of the law".[553] This provision suggests that the legislature regards maintaining legal unity and developing the law as two major tasks of the Supreme Court, whereas maintaining legal unity used to be seen as the only task of the Supreme Court.[554] Developing the law, in turn, suggests playing a lawmaking role, so that this provision can be seen as the legislature's open recognition of the lawmaking role of the Supreme Court. [555]

2.2.5 Article 392 – 394 Civil Procedure Code

In 2012, the legislature added three new articles (Article 392-394) to the Civil Procedure Code, authorizing the Supreme Court in the Netherlands to, by way of preliminary rulings,[556] answer questions

---

[550] Glastra van Loon e.a. 1968, p. 144. Cf. Franken 1985, p. 108-109.
[551] *Staatsblad* 2001, 621
[552] *Staatsblad* 1988, 286.
[553] The text cited within the quotation marks is part of Article 80a in my translation.
[554] See e.g. Hondius 1988b.
[555] See e.g. Snijders 1988, p. 1611, Martens 2000, 747-748 and Asser 2008, p. 10.
[556] The Dutch term for this new legal institution is "prejudiciële vragen aan de civiele kamer van de Hoge Raad", see

of law submitted by lower courts in civil proceedings.[557] According to Article 392, Paragraph 1, a lower court may submit a question of law to the Supreme Court and request a preliminary ruling while the proceeding stays in the lower court itself, if the answer to the question is directly relevant for settling mass claims or for resolving many other proceedings in court that arise from similar facts where the same question of law is involved.

The Explanatory Notes (*Memorie van Toelichting*) to Article 392-394 indicate that the legislature expects that the Supreme Court's answers to questions of law by way of preliminary rulings can prevent lower courts from reaching conflicting judgments in similar cases and that this new legal institution of preliminary rulings will enable the Supreme Court to "optimally fulfil the task of developing the law"[558] in cases where there is a great need in society for a leading decision by the Supreme Court.[559] This can be seen as yet another recognition by the legislature of the lawmaking role of the Supreme Court and the status of Supreme Court decisions as a source of law.

2.2.6 New legislation techniques

Not only can specific legislative provisions shed light on the increasingly favorable attitude of the legislature towards openly recognizing cases as a source of law, some of the new legislation techniques also suggest this trend. One such technique is incorporating case law into legislation. This technique was widely used during the recodification of the civil law in the second half of the 20th century. The new[560] Civil Code of the Netherlands contains

---

http://www.rechtspraak.nl/Organisatie/Hoge-Raad/OverDeHogeRaad/Bijzondere-taken-HR-en-PG/Pages/Prejudici%C3%ABlevragenaandecivielekamervandeHogeRaad.aspx.

[557] *Staatsblad* 2012, 65.

[558] The original Dutch text is "optimale vervulling van de rechtsvormende taak", see Opstelten 2012, p. 5

[559] See Opstelten 2012, p. 5.

[560] Although the current Civil Code has already been in force for more than 20 years, the word "new" is still used here to distinguish the current

many provisions that are based on case law developed since 1838.[561] The wide use of this technique can be seen as an open recognition by the legislature of the authority of case law. Obviously, the authority of some cases proved to be so high in practice that even the legislature followed them.

Another legislative technique that has gained popularity since the second half of the last century is the use of open norms in legislation. Again, the new Civil Code is a good example,[562] as it contains many open norms such as "reasonableness and fairness",[563] "unreasonably onerous",[564] "generally accepted views"[565] and "proper social conduct".[566] A key characteristic of these open norms is that they only provide an abstract framework, thus allowing the judge to develop more detailed substantive legal norms. The increasing use of open norms in legislation illustrates that nowadays the legislature intends to allow judges to play an active lawmaking role in certain areas.[567]

The increasingly favorable attitude of the legislature towards case law is not only reflected in what the legislature does, but also in what it chooses not to do. Sometimes, the legislature explicitly chooses not to regulate an issue in legislation, because it deems it

---

Civil Code from the first Civil Code of the Netherlands introduced in 1838, which is often referred to as the old Civil Code.

[561] Article 6:162 Paragraph 2, for example, comes chiefly from a case *Lindenbaum/Cohen* decided by the Supreme Court in 1919 (HR 31 January 1919, *NJ* 1919, 161). Article 6:228 can be traced to the *Baris/Riezenkamp* case in 1957 (HR 15 November 1957, *NJ* 1958, 67). Article 6:2 Paragraph 2 can be traced back to the *Saladin/HBU* case in 1967 (HR 19 May 1967, *NJ* 1967, 261).

[562] The increasing use of open norms is not limited to private law legislation. The same tendency can be found in administrative legislation as well, see Wiarda 1972, p. 40-42.

[563] Article 6:2 Civil Code.

[564] Article 6:233 Paragraph a Civil Code.

[565] Article 3:4 Paragraph 1 Civil Code.

[566] Article 6:162 Paragraph 1 Civil Code.

[567] By using such open norms, "the legislature implicitly charges the judge with the task of developing the law in many areas", according to Kottenhagen, see Kottenhagen 1986, p. 6. Many scholars share this view, see e.g. Pitlo 1968, p. 34, Nederpel 1985, p. 106 and Giesen & Schelhaas 2008, p. 136.

more desirable for judges to develop the law on that matter. A good example is the pre-contractual liability. Originally, the draft new Civil Code contained a provision regulating pre-contractual liability.[568] However, this provision was later deleted from the draft, because legislators deemed it preferable to allow judges to fully develop the law on this matter.[569]

An even clearer indication that the legislature recognizes cases as a source of law is that sometimes the legislature chooses not to enact laws on a certain matter, because case law has already adequately addressed the issue. In 1928, for example, the minister of justice withdrew a bill submitted earlier to the parliament, which intended to broaden the tort liability grounds contained in Article 1401 of the old Civil Code.[570] One of the reasons to withdraw the bill was that it was no longer necessary, as the Supreme Court had already laid down essentially the same rule in the *Lindenbaum/Cohen* case in 1919.[571]

2.3 Sub-conclusion on the attitude of the legislature

In sum, it can be said that evidence can be found in legislative provisions and techniques that indicates an increasingly favorable attitude of the legislature towards recognizing cases as a source of law. It can also be concluded that the legislature is becoming more aware of the limitations of its lawmaking capacity and that it has been intentionally making use of case law to supplement its legislative work. On the other hand, it should be pointed out that there is evidence of implicit recognition by the legislature of the status of cases as a source of law, but there is no evidence of explicit recognition. Accordingly, it should be concluded that unequivocal recognition of cases as a source of law is still lacking in legislation. The changing attitude of the legislature can be visualized as in Figure 10.

---

[568] Article 6.5.2.8a.

[569] See Hartkamp & Sieburgh 2010, p. 159.

[570] Drion 1968b, p. 159 footnote 79.

[571] Ibid.

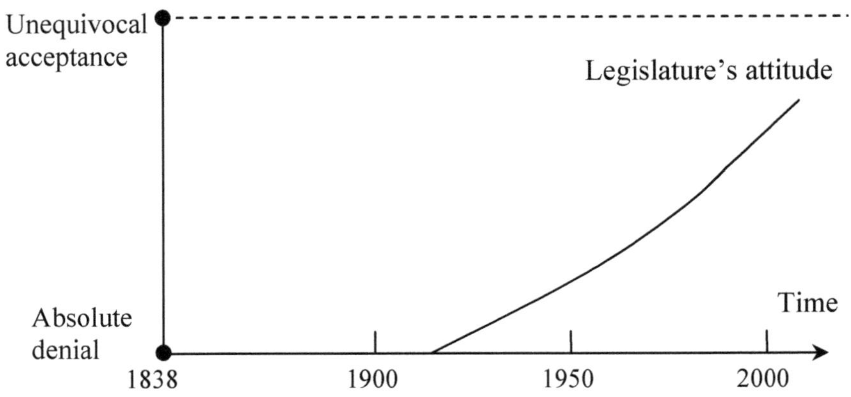

Figure 10 Attitude of the legislature

In this context it is particularly worth noting that the recodification of civil law in the Netherlands did not "kill" case law. Both the technique of incorporating previous case law into the new Civil Code and the wider use of open norms in the new Code conveyed a positive attitude of the legislature towards the status of cases as a source of law.

3. Judges

For quite a long time, judges in the Netherlands were reluctant to openly admit the influence of cases on their decision-making, even though in practice previous decisions of higher courts did have significant impact on judicial deliberation in court practice.[572] This attitude began to change in the 1970s and the 1980s. Although I have not been able to find judgments that explicitly discuss the question whether cases are a formal source of law, I have been able to find evidence that reflects changes in the attitude of judges in two sources: legal reasoning in judgments on the one hand and speeches, publications and interviews by judges on the other.

---

[572] See e.g. Drion 1968b, p. 168.

3.1 Legal reasoning in judgments

The legal reasoning in judgments used to be very formalistic in the Netherlands.[573] References to cases in judgments used to be very rare.[574] Often it seemed as though the decision came entirely from legislative provisions, without the slightest doubt that the case could have been decided otherwise.[575]

In the early decades after the introduction of the old Civil Code in 1838, it was to a certain extent understandable that the legal reasoning in judgments did not cite cases. After all, not so many cases were available at that time and the dominant theory in the 19th century denied that cases could have any authority beyond the specific disputes in which the judicial decisions were made.[576] However, the practice of avoiding citing and discussing cases in judgments continued well into the time when cases in practice played a highly important role and the legal theory no longer denied that cases could have authority beyond the litigating parties. In 1931, for example, Scholten concluded that, although lower courts rarely explicitly cited cases decided by the Supreme Court, influence of earlier cases on their decision-making could be found in the fact that lower courts did repeat the arguments and the phrases that had been used previously by the Supreme Court.[577]

The practice of avoiding citing and discussing cases in the legal reasoning in judgments was misleading in the sense that it obscured one crucial factor, namely cases, that influenced judicial decision-making. Many scholars criticized this practice and argued

---

[573] See e.g. Fockema Andreae 1904, Polak 1953, p. 54 and Hesselink 2001, p. 9 and 11-13.

[574] Glastra van Loon wrote in 1968 that the Supreme Court of the Netherlands *never* explicitly cited its own decisions, see Glastra van Loon e.a. 1968, p. 141. However, later studies proved that Glastra van Loon was wrong. A limited number of examples of explicit references to cases can be found in earlier judgments made by the Supreme Court. The earliest example was a case decided by the Supreme Court in 1873, according to Kottenhagen, see Kottenhagen 1986, p. 14-20. See also Jessurun D'Oliveira 1973, p. 43.

[575] Vranken 1995, p. 110.

[576] For details see the subparagraphs in this chapter that discuss the legal theory in the 19th century.

[577] Scholten 1931, p. 116.

that it is desirable that judges explicitly cite and discuss cases in their judgments.[578]

Old habits, however, die hard. It was not until the *Bull Calf* case[579] decided by the Supreme Court in 1980 that the old habit of keeping silent on the role of cases in judicial legal reasoning began to change significantly.[580] Since 1980, explicit case citations and discussions in judgments increased steadily and has now become a common practice in the Netherlands.[581] From the fact that judges nowadays explicitly cite and discuss relevant cases in their judgments it can be inferred that judges openly admit that cases are capable of furnishing grounds for further judicial decisions, i.e. that cases are a source of law. This can be interpreted as an implicit way of recognizing cases to be a source of law.

3.2 Speeches, publications and interviews by judges

Not only can evidence be found in the legal reasoning in judgments that in recent decades judges have become increasingly willing to openly admit the influence of cases on their decision-making, such evidence can also be found in speeches, interviews and writings published by judges. In his farewell address in 1971, the then president of the Supreme Court, De Jong, explicitly discussed the influence of previous cases on the decision-making of the Supreme Court.[582] Towards the end of the address he said:[583]

> There are of course a number of cases from which we could not deviate without causing serious

---

[578] See e.g. Scholten 1934, p. 116, Polak 1953, p. 60, Kottenhagen 1986, p. 6 and Hondius 1988b, p. 252.

[579] HR 7 March 1980, *NJ* 1980, 353 (*Stierkalf*). This is a case about the liability for damages caused by animals. In this case, the Supreme Court explicitly cited one of its own previous decisions and discussed the relevance of other judicial decisions, including those by lower courts.

[580] Kottenhagen 1986, p. 11-12.

[581] This is shown by a number of empirical studies, see e.g. Kottenhagen 1986, p. 11-12, Struycken & Haazen 1993, p. 112-133 and Vranken 1995, p. 170.

[582] De Jong 1971.

[583] De Jong 1971, p. 577.

> confusion. If the Supreme Court should overrule the case of 1929 where property transfer as a means of providing guarantee was held legal, or the *Harms/De Visser* case of 1945, the consequences would be unforeseeable. People can be assured: the Supreme Court shall always regard itself bound by such cases.

Another former president of the Supreme Court, Martens, discussed the lawmaking role of the judge in his farewell address in 2000. In this address, Martens said that in the 1950s and 1960s, scholars, the legislature and judges no longer regarded the lawmaking role of the judge as a taboo, and they began to openly recognize this role of the judge.[584] Moreover, he argued that although judges are not elected, judicial law-making is justified by the rule of law.[585]

Similar views can be found in interviews given and papers published by judges of the Supreme Court.[586] Roelvink,[587] for example, said in an interview in 1988, that "a lot of judge-made law has been developed in recent years, because the codification does not solve every problem".[588] When asked about the desirability of judicial law-making on controversial issues, he replied:[589]

> I do not think it is so bad that, at a certain moment, the judge is called upon in such cases to solve a problem without the help of a specifically for that problem enacted law. We then try to create a solution that fits in our legal system and that is consistent with the views of the majority of the Dutch people.

---

[584] Martens 2000, p. 747-748.
[585] Martens 2000, p. 751.
[586] See e.g. Bruinsma 1988a, p. 95 and Ras 1988, p. 74.
[587] Former Vice President of the Supreme Court. When he was interviewed in 1988, he was serving as a judge in the Supreme Court.
[588] Mensonides 1988, p. 12.
[589] Mensonides 1988, p. 13.

Twenty years later another judge of the Supreme Court wrote the following passage in a paper:[590]

> The judge, especially the Supreme Court, has become increasingly active in law-making. It has gone far beyond filling in "loopholes in legislation". More than ever, legislation is giving the judge a lot of freedom, and the legislature indicates more than ever that a certain issue should be left to the judges to be further developed. It has thus become an outdated idea that the legislature has the primacy in law-making.

3.3 Sub-conclusion on the attitude of judges

Evidence presented in this subpart demonstrates a remarkable change in the attitude of judges. Instead of carefully concealing the influence of previous cases on judicial decision-making, judges are nowadays more and more open about their lawmaking role and the status of cases as a source of law. It should, however, be noted that the evidence presented in this paragraph indicates largely an *implicit* instead of an explicit recognition by judges of the status of cases as a source of law. The change can be visualized as in Figure 11.

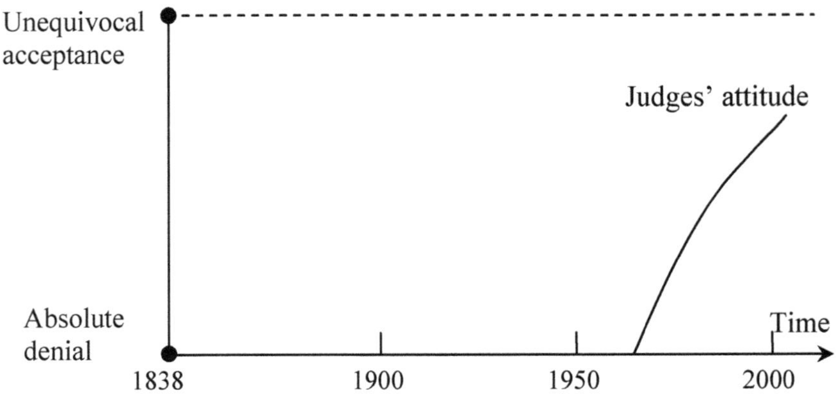

Figure 11 Attitude of judges

[590] Asser 2008, p. 11.

4. Legal Scholars

Prior to the legislature and judges, many legal scholars have long openly recognized the lawmaking role of the judge and the status of cases as a source of law. The following sections will examine how legal scholars' views on the status of cases as a source of law evolved throughout three periods since 1838.

4.1 1838-1900 Legislation is the only source of law

After the introduction of the old Civil Code and the Kingdom Legislation Act in 1838, the dominant view among jurists held that only the legislature was authorized to create law, whereas judges ought only to apply laws enacted by the legislature. Opzoomer,[591] one of the most prominent Dutch legal scholars of the 19th century, wrote in 1865 that "(c)ustoms have ceased to be a source of law; also for the private law all the power is in the hands of the legislature".[592]

The view that only the legislature is authorized to make law lasted well until the end of the 19th century. In 1899, Land,[593] another well-known scholar in the 19th century, wrote that "(i)t should remain the task of the legislature as representative of the community, rather than of the judge, to express the legal consciousness of the community".[594]

The view that all the lawmaking power should be in the hands of the legislature led to another dominant view that legislation is the only source of law. Diephuis,[595] a highly esteemed legal scholar of the 19th century, wrote the following passage in 1869, arguing that legislation is the only source of law:[596]

---

[591] Former professor of law at Utrecht University. In the 19th century, the legal scholarship in the filed of private law was dominated by two law professors: Opzoomer and Diephuis, according to Scholten, see Scholten 1931, p. 239.

[592] Opzoomer 1865, p. VII.

[593] Former professor of law at Groningen University.

[594] Land 1899, p. 12.

[595] Former professor of law at Groningen University.

[596] Diephuis 1869, p. 25.

> The legislature, authorized to enact laws and thus to prescribe what will be the law among us, is also authorized to prescribe whether anything else will be recognized in equal sense as a source of law in addition to legislation…Now our legislation does not recognize any other source of law, which, in addition to legislation, defines the private law. So in our country legislation is the only source of law, as expressed by the Kingdom Legislation Act.

Land endorsed Diephuis' view that legislation is the only source of law. In 1899 he wrote that "(customs) used to be a source of law", implying that they had ceased to be a source of law since the introduction of the national codification.[597]

Of course not everybody in the 19th century accepted that legislation was the only source of law. Van Hall,[598] for example, argued that customs were, in addition to legislation, an independent source of law, especially when legislation was silent on a given question of law.[599] However, even though he denied that legislation was the only source, Van Hall did not say a word about cases being a source of law.

Another dominant view during this period was that cases, even those decided by the Supreme Court, should not have a particular authority higher than opinions of legal scholars, so that judges were not bound by previous cases, not even by those decided by the highest court.[600] Teixeira de Mattos, for example, wrote the following passage in1885:[601]

> The crucial difference between legislation and a judicial decision is that the former is general and binds everyone, whereas the latter only decides a single case and only has force for the

[597] Land 1899, p. 6.
[598] Former professor of law at Utrecht University.
[599] Van Hall 1851, p. 61-62.
[600] See e.g. Diephuis 1869, p. 87.
[601] Teixeira de Mattos 1885, p. 31.

> parties concerned (Article 1954 Civil Code), without being able to be invoked vis-à-vis third parties, not even in a similar case...It should thus be clear how wrong it is to attribute too much weight to the so-called jurisprudence,[602] and to use it to replace legislation, which is an error that, in particular in France, has gained much ground in recent years."

The warning that it is wrong to attribute too much weight to cases and to use them to replace legislation, seems to suggest that towards the end of the 19th century cases were beginning to play an increasingly important role in legal practice,[603] so important that cases were even beginning to threaten the status of legislation as the only source of law. The phrase "in particular in France" seems to imply that such a practice was also growing in the Netherlands, albeit not as fast as in France. At the same time, Teixeira de Mattos' criticism on such a practice, in his words "an error", shows that at the end of the 19th century the mainstream legal theory was still trying to defend the traditional view that cases are not and should not be a source of law. However, it did not take long before this old view began to encounter increasingly strong resistance, which will be illustrated in the following subparagraphs.

4.2 1900-1930 Initial challenges to the 19th-century views

Academic writings in the first three decades of the 20th century demonstrated some initial signs towards an open recognition of the lawmaking role of the judge. In his inaugural lecture *The Sources of Private Law* in 1913, Anema[604] admitted that according to the prevailing theory in his time judges were only supposed to apply

---

[602] The word jurisprudence is used here to denote judicial decisions, not legal theory.

[603] In the same book where the author criticized the practice of attributing too much authority to cases, he admitted that it was crucial for practitioners to know and to use cases, because whether a law suit could be won sometimes depended more on cases rather than on legislation, see Teixeira de Mattos 1885, p. 31.

[604] Former professor of law at the VU University Amsterdam.

enacted laws.[605] However, he argued that history and reality proved that judges had always played and were still playing a lawmaking role, albeit people no longer dared to openly admit it due to Montesquieu's "silly fantasy"[606] of the separation of powers.[607] In 1918, Suijling[608] introduced the notion of "*de facto* law"[609] and argued that judges were able to create factually binding norms, implying that cases were a *de facto* source of law.[610] Bellefroid was of the view that a constant court practice was capable of creating generally binding law.[611]

Despite these initial steps towards an open recognition of cases as a source of law, traces of the 19th-century legalism were still visible. Zevenbergen,[612] for example, refused to accept cases as a source of law and insisted that judges could only "discover",[613] but never create law.[614] Also Suijling insisted that judges were not authorized to create law due to the limitations imposed by Article 12 of the Kingdom Legislation Act.[615] Even Bellefroid, who argued that a constant court practice did create generally binding law, excluded cases from the formal sources of law in his book published in 1927.[616] It was not until 1937 that he changed this view and openly recognized cases as a source of law.[617]

---

605 Anema 1913, p. 8.
606 Anema 1913, p. 12.
607 Anema 1913, p. 13.
608 Former professor of law at Utrecht University.
609 The Dutch term that Suijling used is "feitelijk recht", see Suijling 1918, p. 6.
610 "Ultimately, what is actually being applied as law is what the judge claims to find in enacted laws", see Suijling 1918, p. 12.
611 Bellefroid 1927, p. 192.
612 Former professor of law at the University of Amsterdam.
613 Zevenbergen 1925, p. 326.
614 Even a constant practice of the courts cannot create law, according to Zevenbergen, see Zevenbergen 1925, p. 327.
615 Suijling 1918, p. 7. In 1927 he repeated this view in Suijling 1927, p. 19.
616 In 1927 Bellefroid only recognized three formal sources of law: enacted laws, customs and treaties, see Bellefroid 1927, p. 2.
617 "Customs, enacted laws in the broad sense, treaties and cases are the formal sources of the contemporary Dutch law", see Bellefroid 1937, p. 58.

In sum, the old view that enacted laws were the only source of law was quickly losing ground in the first three decades of the 20th century. However, there was no consensus yet on the lawmaking role of the judge. Open recognition of cases as a source of law was still rare.

4.3 1930 - present: growing recognition for cases as a source of law

In 1931 Paul Scholten[618], one of the most revered legal scholars of the 20th century in the Netherlands, published his masterpiece *The General Part.*[619] In this book Scholten refuted the legalistic doctrine that equated legislation with the law.[620] He also disproved the view that the role of the judge is limited to applying laws enacted by the legislature.[621] Scholten argued that the law is an "open system" to which every judicial decision adds something new.[622] On page 102 of his book Scholten wrote:

> The law is never "finished". It keeps changing, not only as a result of legislation, i.e. deliberate creation of new law, but also by way of its application. We can put it as such: the system should be seen as "dynamic", not as "static". The theory of logical completeness treats the law as a static system that does not change until the legislature takes action. That is where it is mistaken.

After the publication of Scholten's *General Part*, more and more legal scholars began to openly recognize the lawmaking role of the judge. In 1938, for example, Telders[623] made an analysis of

---

[618] Former professor of law at the University of Amsterdam.
[619] Scholten 1931. This book is the general part of the *Asser's Series*, a very influential private law handbook series in the Netherlands, which is widely used by academics, judges and practising lawyers.
[620] Scholten 1931, p. 9-15.
[621] Scholten 1931, p. 1-8 and 100.
[622] Scholten 1931, p. 100-103.
[623] Former professor of law at Leiden University.

the various ways in which judges contributed to the development of the law in the 100 years after the introduction of the old Dutch Civil Code in 1838.[624] The influence of judges on the law was so huge that he used the term "legislative judgments" to refer to the (in his view nearly countless) lawmaking judicial decisions[625] and argued that "every judicial decision, in particular those of the Supreme Court, has for us the meaning of a contribution to the existing law".[626] Two other law professors of the 1930s, Bellefroid[627] and Bregstein[628], also endorsed the view that judges do and ought to be recognized as playing a lawmaking role.

In the following two decades the lawmaking role of the judge continued to gain academic recognition. In 1953, Polak[629] argued that both legislation and adjudication involve law making and that judges should decide as "legislature *ad hoc*".[630] Pitlo[631] wrote in 1968 that deciding a case is by no means purely a matter of finding out the solution that the law dictates in the case at hand, but in the first place an act of creation.[632] "What people call interpretation is not seldom lawmaking rather than application of the law", according to him.[633]

The same trend continued in the 1970s[634] and reached a climax in the 1980s when the Supreme Court openly acknowledged its lawmaking role by organizing a symposium in 1988 on the lawmaking role of the Supreme Court in celebration of the 150th anniversary of its establishment.[635] By this time the lawmaking role

---

624 Telders 1938.
625 Telders 1938, p. 205.
626 Telders 1938, p. 198.
627 Bellefroid 1937, p. 106-107.
628 Former professor of law at the University of Amsterdam. See Bregstein 1939, p. 18.
629 Former professor of law at the University of Wageningen.
630 Polak 1953, p. 17.
631 Former professor of law at the University of Amsterdam.
632 Pitlo 1968, p. 34.
633 Ibid.
634 See e.g. Jessurun D'Oliveira 1973, p. 62, Wiarda 1972, p. 20-43 and Zonderland 1974, p. 134.
635 Papers presented on the occasion of this symposium have been published in the following volume Baardman 1988.

of the judge had been so widely accepted[636] that the Supreme Court was referred to as the "deputy lawgiver" (wetgever-plaatsvervanger) in some academic writings. [637] A large volume of academic publications on the lawmaking role of the judge emerged in the 1980s and afterwards.[638] The academic debates moved far beyond the question whether judges do or ought to create law.[639] Scholars have been debating since on more in-depth questions such as why judicial lawmaking is justifiable in a civil law country,[640] where the boundaries of judicial lawmaking are,[641] how to avoid retroactive

[636] Vranken wrote in 1988 that "(i)t can be said that nowadays the lawmaking role of the civil judges has been generally accepted", see Vranken 1988, p. 1161.

[637] This term is believed to be introduced by Verburg in 1977 and was frequently cited in the 1980s and afterwards. See Verburg 1975, Mensonides 1988, p. 13, Vranken 1988, p. 1161 and Brunner 1994, p. 36.

[638] For a review of the relevant literature in 1988 see Snijders 1988. For examples of later literature on this topic see De Lange 1991, Vranken 2000, Broers & Van Klink 2001, Van Vugt 2005, Bovend'Eert 2009 and Keukens & Van den Nieuwenhuijzen 2008.

[639] By the 1980s only a very limited number of scholars expressed doubts in their writings as to whether judges are authorized to create law, see e.g. Kortmann 2008 and Bovend'Eert 2009.

[640] Martens, for example, argues that, despite the lack of democratic legitimacy, judicial lawmaking is justified by the rule of law, see Martens 2000, p. 751. Rijpkema (professor of law at the University of Amsterdam), on the other hand, disagrees that judicial lawmaking is not democratically legitimated because judges in the Netherlands are not elected. Instead, he gives a fresh interpretation of the term "democratic legitimacy". According to Rijpkema, "the law is democratically legitimate if it is created in accordance with the formal and substantive requirements stemming from the fundamental norms that form the cornerstones of the democratic constitutional state of the Netherlands… As long as judges observe these fundamental principles, judicial lawmaking is not less democratically legitimate than lawmaking by the legislature". See Rijpkema 2001, p. 19.

[641] See e.g. the literature cited in the previous note.

application of judge-made law[642] and how to harmonize judicial lawmaking with legislative work.[643]

The jurists' growing acceptance of the lawmaking role of the judge is accompanied by an increasingly open recognition of cases as a source of law in academic writings. Since the 1930s the majority of scholars[644] argues that, although the Netherlands has no precedent system and judges are under no legal obligation to follow cases decided by themselves or by any other court, [645] the importance of cases in practice has grown to such an extent that they have, contrary to the original intention of the legislature, nonetheless developed into a source of law.[646]

In 1931, Scholten gave a vivid account of the crucial role of cases in practice:[647]

> Someone that attends a pleading in civil cases will notice that a lawyer never feels more confident than when he can base his argument on a case decided by the Supreme Court, and that analysing and comparing judicial

---

[642] See e.g. Smits 2000 and Haazen 2001.

[643] Some scholars propose to create an institution of periodic consultations between the legislature and the Supreme Court in order to coordinate their lawmaking activities, see Giesen & Schelhaas 2008.

[644] A small minority of scholars argues that there is a precedent system in the Netherlands and that judges are under a legal obligation to adhere to the rule of *stare decisis*, see e.g. Drion 1968b and Glastra van Loon e.a. 1968, p. 140-142.

[645] Bellefroid, for example, wrote the following passage in 1937: "The interpretations of legislation given by the judge and the judge-made rules have no general binding force. They are only binding for the specific cases to which they are applied. Therefore the judge is in principle not bound by cases decided by other courts, not even the highest one... Therefore the judge may also deviate from his own previous decisions", see Bellefroid 1937, p. 108. Note that Bellefroid used the term "in principle" and that he emphasized in the following passages of his book that a constant court practice is capable of creating generally binding law. For similar views see Bregstein 1939, p. 7, Van Apeldoorn 1939, p. 86 and Pitlo 1968, p. 36.

[646] See literature cited in the following passages.

[647] Scholten 1931, p. 115.

> interpretation is a second nature to the counsels. It is the list of cases that the judge hearing the pleading will primarily pay attention to as preparation to draft his judgment. It is the case reports that every lawyer keeps up with and treats as the most essential, no matter how little time his daily work allows him to study. The legal scholarship regards it as one of its primary tasks to study the development of case law and to systemize it…When one compares the role that cases play in a current text book with that they had in one of fifty years ago, one will come to understand how much authority cases have won.

The extraordinary importance of cases in practice led Scholten to conclude that "(t)he recognition of cases as authoritative is imposed upon us by the facts."[648] He was so convinced of the authoritative role of cases that he wrote, "If we *have to*[649] follow cases, what sense does it make to say that they are not a source of law?"[650]

Similar accounts and views can be found in many scholarly writings in the following years and decades. In 1939 Van Apeldoorn[651] wrote: [652]

> Whoever thinks that the law can be learned solely from codes and enacted laws shall be disappointed. One finds the law more in case reports than in enacted laws. That is because the law is not simply what "is in the legislation…, but is legislation as interpreted, transformed and supplemented by cases to suit the needs of our time".

[648] Scholten 1931, p. 118.
[649] Italics by Scholten.
[650] Scholten 1931, p. 119.
[651] Former professor at the University of Amsterdam.
[652] Van Apeldoorn 1939, p. 86.

In 1953 Polak argued that "despite Article 12 of the Kingdom Legislation Act, cases have authority".[653] "All in all, it seems justified to say that judge-made norms in case law are equal to statutory ones", according to him.[654]

In 1968 Pitlo wrote, "The value of cases is extraordinarily high. So high that we can say that he who knows enacted laws but does not know the cases in the latest decades, only has a highly insufficient impression of our law".[655]

In 1973, Jessurun d'Oliveira[656] conducted a literature review on the authority of cases and concluded that "(i)t has become a dominant view that, contrary to the original design of our legal system where cases were granted no independent value as a source of law, cases have nevertheless developed into a source of law, at least where there is a constant court practice."[657]

This trend continued in the following decades and in 1993 Struycken[658] and Haazen[659] concluded that "in recent decades a certain consensus has been reached on the recognition of cases as a source of law".[660] Not only did these two authors conclude that a certain consensus had been reached, they went on to argue that it is desirable to revise some of the existing statutes in order to bring legislation in line with the new theoretic insights, so that an explicit recognition of cases as a source of law will no longer be hindered.[661]

---

653 Polak 1953, p. 38.
654 Ibid.
655 Pitlo 1968, p. 37.
656 Former professor of law at the University of Amsterdam.
657 Jessurun D'Oliveira 1973, p. 39.
658 Professor of law at Utrecht University and partner at NautaDutilh, a prominent Dutch law firm.
659 Professor by special appointment of comparative and transnational civil procedure at the University of Leiden, and counsel at Boies, Schiller & Flexner LLP.
660 Struycken & Haazen 1993, p. 103.
661 Ibid.

4.4 Sub-conclusion on the attitude of legal scholars

This subparagraph shows that, although the dominant view among jurists in the 19th century denied cases to be a source of law, the rising importance of cases in practice has eventually led more and more scholars to openly accept the lawmaking role of the judge and to explicitly recognize cases as a source of law. Here, again, it should be stressed that not all evidence points to an *explicit* recognition. It should also be noted that some of the academic writings cited in this subparagraph are of a descriptive nature, i.e. they observe a fact that judges have in fact been playing a lawmaking role and that cases have in practice been functioning as a source of law, whereas other writings express a normative view that judges ought to be allowed to play a lawmaking role and that cases ought to fulfil the role of a source of law. It should therefore be concluded that the evidence examined in this subparagraph does indicate a trend towards an open recognition of cases as a source of law, but the trend has not yet reached such a point that there is an undisputed normative conviction among legal scholars that cases ought to fulfil the role of a source of law and ought to be explicitly recognized as a source of law. This trend can be visualized as in Figure 12.

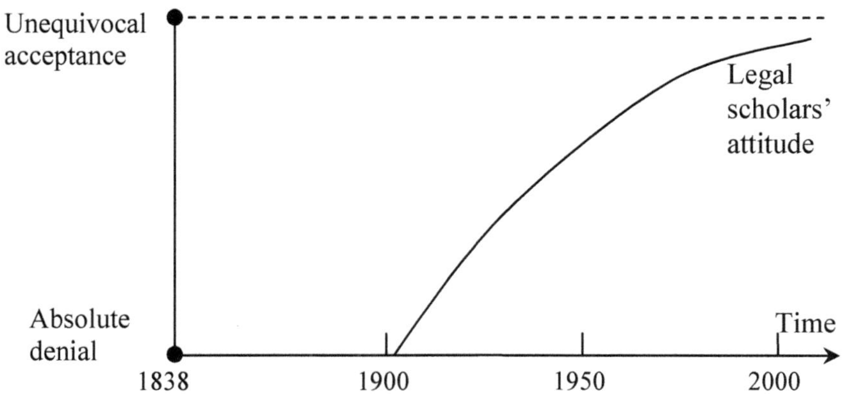

Figure 12 Attitude of legal scholars

5. Concluding remarks

This chapter illustrates that originally, i.e. when the old Civil Code was introduced in the Netherlands in 1838, cases were not designed to fulfil the role of a source of law. The Kingdom Legislation Act enacted in 1838, for example, shows that the legislature intended legislation to be the only source of law.[662] Prominent legal scholars of the 19th century endorsed the original intention of the legislature and commonly denied that cases ought to have normative force beyond the litigating parties.[663] For a long time, judges hardly ever cited cases as a relevant factor for judicial decision-making, even though in practice they did pay attention to previous cases.[664] Accordingly, the formal role of cases around 1838 and the following decades can be seen as very close, if not identical, to the position of an absolute denial. This position can be visualized as in Figure 13.

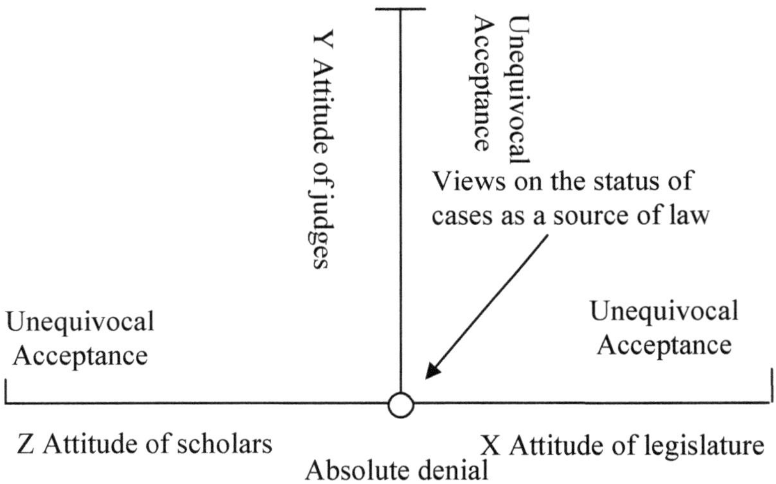

Figure 13 Views on the status of cases as a source of law in the Netherlands in 1838 and the following decades

Nowadays the situation is different. Since 1988, the legislature openly admits that it is one of the chief tasks of the Supreme Court to develop the law, implying that (the highest) judges are authorized to play a lawmaking role.[665] This can be seen as (at least) an implicit recognition by the legislature that judges

---

[662] See in particular Article 3, Article 11 and Article 12 of this Act.

[663] See e.g. Diephuis 1869, p. 87 and Teixeira de Mattos 1885, p. 31.

[664] See e.g. Drion 1968b, p. 168 and Kottenhagen 1986, p. 14-20.

[665] Article 81 Court Organization Act (previously Article 101a of the same Act).

ought to be allowed to play a lawmaking role. Since the 1930s, there is a growing consensus among scholars that it is inevitable and desirable for judges to play a lawmaking role,[666] and cases are nowadays more than ever openly recognized as a source of law in academic writings.[667] Also the views of judges have changed. It has become a common practice that judges explicitly cite and discuss cases in judicial decisions.[668] Moreover, judges are nowadays even willing to openly admit their lawmaking role and the influence of cases on judicial decision-making in speeches, interviews and publications.[669]

Notwithstanding these remarkable changes, an unequivocal acceptance of cases as a source of law has not been reached so far. Some of the old legislative provisions that reflect the 19th century legalism are still in force.[670] There is still no legislative provision that explicitly declares cases to be a source of law. Although more and more scholars recognize cases as a source of law, some of them still put some qualifications on this view.[671] In judgments or other sources that reflect the attitude of the judges, it is also difficult to find unreserved acceptance of cases as a source of law. The current situation can accordingly be visualized as in Figure 14.

---

666 See e.g. Scholten 1931, p. 102, Telders 1938, p. 205, Polak 1953, p. 17, Glastra van Loon e.a. 1968, p. 17 and Vranken 1988, p. 1161.

667 See e.g. Scholten 1931, p. 119, Bellefroid 1937, p. 58, Glastra van Loon e.a. 1968, p. 140, Struycken & Haazen 1993, p. 103 Albers e.a. 2009, p. 107.

668 Kottenhagen 1986, p. 20-50 and Struycken & Haazen 1993, p. 112-133.

669 De Jong 1971, Mensonides 1988 and Asser 2008.

670 E.g. Article 12 Kingdom Legislation Act and Article 120 of the Constitution.

671 Some scholars still see cases as a *de facto* source of law, instead of a formal one, see e.g. Hijma e.a. 2007, p. 19-20. Others recognize cases as a source of law, only where absolutely no legislative provisions, not even open norms, can be found, see e.g. Nederpel 1985, p. 112-113.

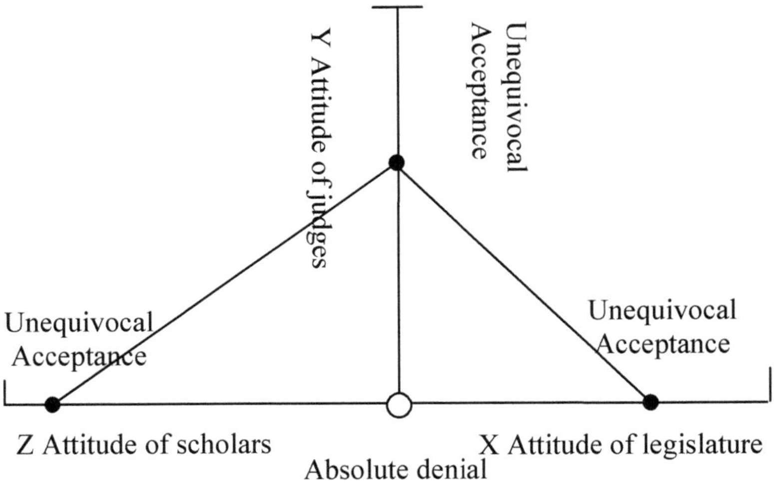

Figure 14 Current views on the status of cases as a source of law in the Netherlands

Moreover, this chapter suggests that normative views that recognize cases as a source of law are not a necessary condition for the development of case law in practice in the Netherlands and, by careful analogy, probably not in other codified legal systems either.[672] In other words, denying that cases ought to fulfil the role of a source of law may not be able to prevent cases from ultimately achieving a highly influential status in practice in a codified legal system. A possible explanation for this phenomenon could be that, due to the limitations of codifications and statutes such as the use of abstract language and the difficulty to amend codes and statutes swiftly to cope with the technical and social development in reality, there is an innate need in practice for cases to fulfil the role of a source of law and to supplement codes and statutes in a codified legal system.[673]

This is, of course, not to say that normative views on the status of cases as a source of law are incapable of exercising any

[672] As the works of some legal scholars indicate, cases already achieved a highly influential status in practice before the 1930s when Scholten and many other legal scholars began to explicitly recognize cases as a source of law, see Teixeira de Mattos 1885, p. 31, Scholten 1931 and Polak 1953.
[673] For similar views see Bellefroid 1927, p. 5, Bellefroid 1937, p. 123 and Polak 1953, p. 58.

influence on the actual functioning of case law in practice. After all, there has been a period of time after the introduction of the Dutch Civil Code in 1838 where cases did not seem to have played a particularly influential role in practice.[674] Moreover, the dominant view in the 19th century that denied cases as a source of law induced judges to carefully conceal the influence of cases on their decision-making for as long as one and a half century by avoiding citing cases in judgments, which has had the effect of complicating the use of cases in practice.[675] These findings suggest that denial of cases as a source of law is capable of delaying the rise of case law in a codified legal system, even though in the long term it may not be able to prevent cases from ultimately acquiring the status of a source of law in practice.[676]

On the other hand, it is worth noting that the actual influence of cases in practice is capable of affecting the normative views. If we synthesize the three graphs showing the attitude of the legislature, judges and respectively legal scholars, we will get a new graph (Figure 15), which clearly indicates that it was legal scholars who took the lead in openly recognizing cases as a source of law in the Netherlands. Careful analysis of the relevant scholarly writings in the early decades of the 20th century shows that such a change was neither the result of initiatives of the legislature or the courts to officially attribute broader normative force to cases,[677] nor the influence of the common law doctrine of precedent.[678] In fact, it was primarily the reality that cases have acquired a highly important

[674] It is in academic writings around the end of the 19th century and the beginning of the 20th century that I have been able to find the earliest signs of cases beginning to play an increasingly influential role in practice, see e.g. Teixeira de Mattos 1885, p. 31 and Anema 1913. It seems that between 1838 and the end of the 19th century, cases did not occupy a particularly authoritative status in practice.

[675] See e.g. Drion 1968b, p. 168.

[676] The findings of this study lend support to the observation by Dawson in Dawson 1970, p. 503.

[677] See the relevant paragraphs that examine the views of the legislature and judges in this chapter.

[678] In fact, I have not been able to find many scholarly writings in the Netherlands that studied the common law doctrine of precedent as a positive model to draw inspiration from. One exception is Kottenhagen 1986.

status in practice that prompted legal scholars in the early 20th century and later to openly recognize cases as a source of law.[679] Later changes in the attitude of the legislature and judges may have been stimulated by increasing scholarly recognition of cases as a source of law combined with further growth of the actual influence of cases in practice.[680]

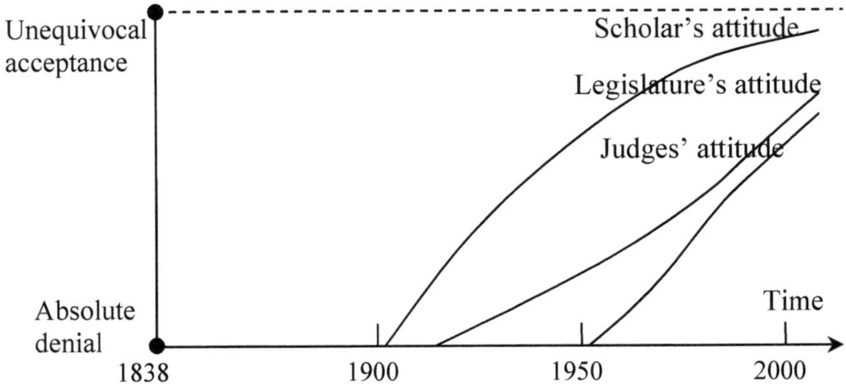

Figure 15 Relative positions of the legislature, judges and scholars

In conclusion, this chapter demonstrates that the normative views on the status of cases as a source of law have not remained static in the Netherlands since 1838, and that there is an interesting dynamic between the normative views and the actual significance of cases in practice. The rising influence of cases in practice has not been the result of an explicit recognition by the legislature or the judiciary of cases as a source of law. Rather, it was the rising importance of cases in practice that has pushed the boundaries of the normative views on the status of cases as a source of law. On the other hand, an increasingly favorable attitude towards openly accepting cases as a source of law, as well as the lawmaking role of the judge, further stimulates and institutionalizes the practice of publishing and using cases, so that not only the leading cases, but also cases as a whole eventually acquire the status of a source of law. In this sense, recognition can be seen as an ultimate step in the case law mechanism in the Netherlands, as it arises from,

[679] Scholten observed, for example, that "if we *have to* follow cases, what sense does it make to say that they are not a source of law", see Scholten 1931, p. 119.

[680] See e.g. Kottenhagen 1986, p. 6 and Asser 2008, p. 11.

strengthens and provides legitimacy to the practice of publishing and using cases to solve legal problems and to further develop the law.

Chapter 4

Implications for literature on cases in civil law jurisdictions

Chapter 4 Implications for literature on cases in civil law jurisdictions

1. Introduction

The previous three chapters concentrated on one jurisdiction, i.e. the Netherlands. From this chapter on, this study will look beyond the Netherlands and explore broader implications of the findings of the first three chapters. This chapter will place the findings of the first part of this study, i.e. chapter one, two and three, in the context of a broader body of English-language comparative law literature related to the role of cases in civil law jurisdictions, whereas the next two chapters will link the first three chapters to a trend in China since the 1980s, i.e. a growing interest in case law among Chinese judges and legal scholars, and reflect on the relevance of the experiences with case law in the Netherlands for China to further enhance the use of cases.

The first three paragraphs of this chapter will put the findings of chapter one, two and three separately in the context of the existing literature related to the role of cases in civil law jurisdictions and reflect on the relevance of the findings of each chapter for this body of literature. The last three paragraphs of this chapter will link the findings of chapter one, two and three as a whole to the existing literature and explore the relevance of these findings for three debates in this body of literature, i.e. whether the common law and the civil law legal families are converging, whether civil law jurisdictions have a case law method and whether civil law jurisdictions should adopt the doctrine of precedent.

This chapter relied on the method of literature analysis. Online search engines and the snowball method have been used to find the relevant literature. In particular, Google Scholar and Picarta were used.[681]

The findings of the first three chapters reflect only the situation in the Netherlands, while it could not be established that the Netherlands is a representative example of all continental European civil law jurisdictions where cases have developed into a

---

681 Some of the search terms included "case law in civil law jurisdictions", "cases in civil law jurisdictions", "stare decisis in civil law jurisdictions" and "case law in codified legal systems".

source of law in practice.[682] Consequently, this chapter will not seek to contribute to the existing literature by generalizing from the Netherlands to all civil law jurisdictions.

The fact that the representativeness of the findings of the first three chapters cannot be firmly established, however, does not mean that no meaningful insights can be drawn from them that may make a contribution to the existing literature. The paper of Seawright and Gerring on case selection techniques[683] in case study research demonstrates that studying representative cases is not the only way to generate new insights, as studying other types of cases, i.e. cases that are not selected due to their representativeness, can be a good method to, among other things, test theories, verify observations in the existing literature and to explore new hypotheses or new research questions.[684]

Accordingly, instead of generalizing from the Netherlands to all civil law jurisdictions, this chapter contributes to the existing literature by, among other approaches and in light of the findings of the first three chapters of this study, questioning the soundness and correctness of some of the assumptions underlying or some of the observations in some of the writings in the existing literature. Paragraph two of this chapter, for example, questions the soundness of the assumption that case publication is a (mere) technical matter, given that chapter one of this study demonstrated that, in the Netherlands at least, case publication has a selective effect and that the design of case publication requires answering a series of important questions that involve value judgments and principle

---

[682] This is of course not to say, as has already been pointed out in the introduction of this study, that the Netherlands is a deviant example that demonstrates essential differences from other continental European civil law jurisdictions. Scholarly writings on the role of cases in France and Germany in the existing literature, for example, do suggest that the case law mechanism in the Netherlands bears many similarities to the way cases fulfil the role of a source of law in these two prominent civil law jurisdictions. See e.g. Loussouarn 1958, Yiannopoulos 1974, Kiel & Göttingen 1997, Troper & Grzegorczyk 1997, Dedek & Schermaier 2012 and Fauvarque-Cosson & Fournier 2012.

[683] The word "case" is used here in a methodological sense to denote an "example" in the method of case study instead of a court judgment.

[684] Seawright & Gerring 2008.

considerations. Another way in which this chapter seeks to contribute to the existing literature is to use the findings of the first three chapters as an entry point to search for questions concerning the role of cases in civil law jurisdictions that may be worth further investigation. Paragraph four, for example, reflects on one of the key findings of chapter three that the legislature, judges and legal scholars in the Netherlands have been demonstrating an increasingly favorable attitude towards openly recognizing cases as a source of law, and raises a series of questions, such as whether other European civil law jurisdictions have been experiencing a similar trend and if so, what the implications of this trend would be for cases to continue to be a criterion in the classification between the common law and the civil law legal families.

2. Is case publication merely a technical matter?

Chapter one of this study carried out an in-depth investigation into various aspects of case publication in the Netherlands. This is an unusual approach compared to the existing literature on the role of cases in civil law jurisdictions. As already has been pointed out at the beginning of chapter one, publication is a basic yet important requirement for cases to fulfil the role of a source of law in any jurisdiction.[685] This obvious requirement, however, appears to have escaped the attention of many scholars who study the role of cases in civil law jurisdictions.[686] While legal scholars never seem to get tired of debating whether cases are or ought to be a source of law in civil law jurisdictions, not so many of them have dealt with case publication.[687] The underlying assumption seems to be that case publication is a dull technical matter that does not deserve much scholarly reflection, i.e. case publication is a mere technical question of making the final result of a legal battle in court available to a public beyond the litigating parties.[688] The fast development of computer and Internet technologies in recent decades may have

[685] See e.g. Kavass 1977, p. 107, Kottenhagen & Kaptein 1989, p.1 and Adams 1999, p. 466.
[686] Kavass 1977, p. 107.
[687] See e.g. Taruffo 1997, p. 451, Deák 1934, p. 341 note 8, Lawson 1977, p. 84-85, Adams 2007, 166 and Bogdan 2013, p. 100.
[688] Kavass 1977, p. 107.

even further strengthened this assumption. After all, nowadays it is very common that judges no longer “write” but “type” their decisions on computers so that publication of judgments seems to have become a really simple matter of uploading already digitally stored judicial decisions to an online database.

The findings of chapter one suggest, however, that case publication is by no means a mere technical matter. A close analysis of the evolution of case publication in the Netherlands and the debates around this topic demonstrate that designing and implementing a good case publication institution requires answering a series of important questions. What should be the purpose(s) of case publication, to facilitate the work of professional actors such as judges and lawyers or to enhance the transparency and the accountability of judicial work? Should case publication be deemed a responsibility of the state or can it be entrusted entirely to commercial entities? Should all cases be published? If so, what would be the positive and negative consequences? If not, which cases should be published? What should be the selection criteria? Who should select cases, judges or actors independent from the judiciary? Is it sufficient to provide the raw text of the judgments or is it desirable to add extra information to the published cases? If adding extra information to published cases is desirable, what extra information should be added and would the added information justify the increased costs and the possible delay in publication? Should the entities that publish cases only be concerned with accumulating judgments in digital databases or paper periodicals that are accessible to the public, or should they make further efforts to devise and improve search mechanisms to help users quickly find the cases that they are interested in and if so, what can be done to enhance the findability of cases?

Obviously, answers to these questions may involve technical considerations. The evolution of search mechanisms in commercial and official case publications in the Netherlands, for example, demonstrates how solutions to enhance the findability of cases benefits from technical improvement.[689] However, it would be wrong to assume that these questions only require considerations of a technical nature. This study shows that answering these questions

[689] See the subparagraphs in chapter one on the search tools in commercial and official case publication in the Netherlands.

also involves value judgments and principle considerations, some of which can even be of a fundamental nature. In the debate on the question whether case publication should be considered a responsibility of the state, for example, chapter one revealed that some commentators invoked a fundamental principle of a constitutional state, i.e. it is a responsibility of the state to make the law accessible to the public.[690] Similarly, when debating whether all cases should be published, some commentators invoked the principle of public oversight on the judiciary as well as a right of every citizen to know how legislation has been interpreted and applied in actual cases. [691] This is of course not to say that whenever such (fundamental) principles are invoked, they will always dictate the outcome of a debate. In fact, this study illustrated that answering the questions that arise in the context of case publication often involves balancing various principle and practical considerations, and that the outcome depends on the relative weight that one assigns to the competing considerations.[692]

The answers to the above-raised questions, as chapter one of this study illustrated, have not remained static in the Netherlands since 1838. There has been, for example, an increasing awareness that case publication is a responsibility of the state and that case publication should not only serve the purpose of facilitating the work of judges and lawyers, but should also serve the purpose of increasing the transparency of judicial decision-making and enhancing public oversight on the work of the judiciary. [693] Moreover, this study shows that case publication in the Netherlands has been moving from simply making cases available towards making them findable, understandable and affordable to the

---

[690] See e.g. Hondius 1973, p. 745-746 and Kottenhagen & Kaptein 1989, p. 99.

[691] See e.g. Matthijssen 2000, p. 10 and De Meij e.a. 2006, p. 8.

[692] See e.g. the debate on the question whether all cases should be published. Compare e.g. De Meij e.a. 2006 and Mommers & Zwenne & Schermer 2010 with Phillippart 2010, Van der Hoek 2010 and Jongeneel 2010.

[693] See e.g. Editors' Board 1982 and Commissie Jurisprudentiedocumentatie (Case Law Documentation Committee) 1994.

users.[694] This study does not present the solutions adopted in the Netherlands as the best practice, but by closely examining how cases are published in the Netherlands this study does wish to identify and highlight the key questions that arise in case publication. Those who are interested in the functioning of cases as a source of law are invited to pay close attention not only to the way cases are or should be used in court practice, but also to the way cases are or should be published.

3. Are legal scholars losing ground to judges in civil law jurisdictions as the significance of case law continues to rise?

As has been mentioned earlier in this study, there is a consensus in the existing literature that the actual influence of cases in practice has risen to such a high level in many continental European civil law jurisdictions that they have in fact become a source of law.[695] On the other hand, some writings in the existing literature observe that the influence of legal scholars in these jurisdictions has been declining.[696] Deák's paper, for example, suggests that in the 20th century scholarly writings in civil law jurisdictions more or less deteriorated into a series of comments on cases.[697] Lawson even contrasted the rising authority of cases directly with the, in his view, shrinking role of legal scholars and observed that:[698]

> French law has become almost as much a system of judge-made law as English law... Gény and other jurists came to the conclusion that there was no longer any point in running an orthodox body of juristic doctrine derived from exegesis of the Civil

---

694 See e.g. the subparagraphs in chapter one on the search tools in commercial and official case publication and on the practice of publishing annotations together with cases.
695 See e.g. Siving 1966, p. 200, Yiannopoulos 1974, p. 76, Merryman 1974, p. 194-196, Kiel & Göttingen 1997, p. 24-25 and Zweigert & Kötz 1998, p. 263.
696 See e.g. Deák 1934, p. 346 and Lawson 1977, p. 82-83.
697 Deák 1934, p. 346.
698 Lawson 1977, p. 82-83.

> Code side by side with a body of unorthodox doctrine actually enforced in the courts. Whatever the jurists might think, the latter was the working law of France, and the new school of jurists ended by accepting it and finding a theoretical basis for it in the custom of the courts. The jurists still reserve to themselves the right to criticize, but more in the spirit of American jurists.

Such scholarly writings may raise the impression that legal scholars are losing ground to judges in civil law jurisdictions and that the influence of legal scholars is declining as a result of the rising significance of cases in practice. The findings of chapter two of this study, however, suggest that, at least in the Netherlands, such an understanding is not entirely accurate.

In the first place, the findings of chapter two indicate that legal scholars in many ways fulfill an important role in the case law mechanism in the Netherlands, although their influence is not always explicit. Evaluative scholarly comments on a case, for example, can influence the likelihood that the case will be followed in later court practice, as scholarly reaction to previous cases is one of the many factors that jointly determine the weight that judges attribute to previous cases in judicial deliberation.[699] Even descriptive scholarly writings that systemize and interpret cases without an explicit value judgment on the desirability and soundness of previous cases exercise a certain influence on, among other things, judicial deliberation, as many of the choices made by legal scholars in such descriptive works may, however subtly, affect which cases are likely to be consulted by judges and other users as well as how judges and other users are likely to interpret and apply such cases.[700] It is through the enormous scholarly efforts of systemizing, analyzing, interpreting and evaluating cases that scattered individual judgments become more structured, better comprehensible and easier to use.[701] One may, of course, rightly

[699] See the paragraph in chapter two that analyses the way cases are used in adjudication.
[700] See the paragraph in chapter two that analyses the contribution of legal scholars to the case law mechanism in the Netherlands.
[701] Ibid.

observe that the ways through which legal scholars influence the law are nowadays no longer the same as the way they influenced the law in the 19th century, but this does not necessarily mean that the influence of legal scholars has declined in the Netherlands or, by careful analogy, in other continental European civil law jurisdictions.[702]

More importantly, the findings of chapter two indicate that it is not accurate to, as the writings of Lawson tend to imply,[703] see legal scholars and judges as two opposing groups that fight for dominance. It is perhaps more in line with the reality to see the relationship between legal scholars and judges in a civil law jurisdiction as a co-operative one, even though legal scholars do express critical comments on court judgments.[704] The findings of chapter two indicate that on the one hand, legal scholars pay close attention to development in court practice and on the other hand, judges derive considerable benefit from scholarly works that select, systemize, interpret and evaluate published cases and that they generally deem such scholarly works valuable.[705] In this respect, I concur with Vranken, who observed rightly that:[706]

> Court practice and legal scholarship are dependent on each other. There is cooperation and interaction between the two. The level of the one also influences the level of the other.

4. Is there a trend in civil law jurisdictions towards explicit recognition of cases as a source of law?

As pointed out earlier in chapter three, in the existing literature it is commonly held that although throughout time cases have in practice acquired a highly influential status in many civil law jurisdictions, they are still not recognized as a source of law in these

---

[702] See e.g. Loussouarn 1958 and Kiel & Göttingen 1997.
[703] Lawson 1977, p. 82-83.
[704] The paper of Loussouarn expressed a similar view, see Loussouarn 1958, p. 268.
[705] See chapter two of this study.
[706] Vranken 1995, p. 115.

jurisdictions.[707] This commonly held observation gives the impression that the normative views on the status of cases as a source of law have remained the same, i.e. cases used to be denied as a source of law in the past and nowadays they are still not recognized as a source of law.

The findings of chapter three illustrated that in the Netherlands it is not true that the normative views on the status of cases as a source of law have remained static. By using an analytic framework consisting of a sliding scale combined with a time dimension to examine the views of the legislature, judges and legal scholars in the Netherlands on the status of cases as a source of law, chapter three of this study demonstrated that the views of these actors have moved away from an absolute denial and are approaching an unequivocal acceptance of cases as a source of law. Moreover, the findings of chapter three suggest that it was the rising significance of cases in practice that has pushed the boundaries of the normative views.

These findings, if we reflect carefully upon them in the context of civil law jurisdictions, can raise important and intriguing questions. Given the persistent influence of cases in practice and the increasingly favorable attitude among the legislature, judges and legal scholars towards openly recognizing cases as a source of law, could it be possible that the legislation in the Netherlands would one day be revised to explicitly recognize cases as a source of law? Are similar changes taking place in other civil law jurisdictions and if so, can we speak of a trend towards an explicit recognition of the status of cases as a source of law in the civil law legal family? And if there is indeed such a trend and the trend eventually leads to an unequivocal recognition of cases as a source of law not only by legal scholars but also by the legislature and judges in (a considerable number of the members) the civil law legal family, can the role of cases still have a distinguishing capacity in the classification between the common law and the civil law?[708] Obviously, it goes beyond the scope of this study to answer all these questions. What this study does aim to do is to stimulate the readers to reflect on these questions and to invite (comparative) legal

---

[707] See e.g. Loussouarn 1958, p. 255, Baudouin 1974, p. 12, David 1984, p. 116, Kiel & Göttingen 1997, p. 46 and Adams 2007, p. 149.

[708] Cf. Baade 2002b.

scholars to carry out further investigation into these questions either by using the analytic framework developed by this study, or by developing and applying more advanced analytic frameworks.

5. Are the common law and civil law legal families converging?

Some scholars argue that there is a trend of convergence between the common law and the civil law legal families.[709] This claim is chiefly based on an observation that the actual authority that cases have in court practice in many continental European jurisdictions no longer differs fundamentally from that of precedents in common law legal systems, i.e. judges in many continental European civil law jurisdictions are in fact bound by certain types of cases, especially those decided by the highest courts.[710] This argument is highly result-driven, and tends to focus solely on the courts. In essence, this argument draws the conclusion of convergence between civil law and common law primarily from the premise that where lawyers in civil law jurisdictions invoke arguments based on previous cases, especially those decided by the highest courts, the *result* that such arguments are likely to achieve in civil law courts would be very similar to what common lawyers would be able to achieve in court by citing precedents.

This study offers a *process*-oriented approach to explore the role of cases as a source of law in civil law jurisdictions, which may yield some fresh insights for the convergence theory debate. It is, after all, not unthinkable that the same result can be achieved through different processes. In other words, even if proponents of the convergence theory have convincingly established that the result of citing cases in court proceedings is the same in civil law courts as in common law courts, doubt can still be cast on their conclusion of

[709] See e.g. Deák 1934, p. 341, David 1984, p. 10-11 and P. 137, Markesinis 1994, p. 30-32, MacCormick & Summers 1997c, p. 2, MacCormick & Summers 1997a, p. 531-535, Zweigert & Kötz 1998, p. 71 and p. 259-265, Baade 2002b, Hondius 2003, De Cruz 2007, p. 98 and p. 499 and Bogdan 2013, p. 75. For different views see e.g. Dainow 1966, p. 427, Cappelletti 1981, Adams 1999, p. 465-466, Haazen 2007, p. 228 and Komárek 2012, p. 67.

[710] See the sources cited in the previous footnote that argue there is a trend of convergence.

convergence if it turns out that the same result is achieved through different processes in these two legal families.

This study reveals that in the Netherlands the result that cases fulfil the role of a source of law is achieved through a process of publication and utilization of cases that involves multiple institutions, practices and actors in each phase of the process. When we adopt such a process-oriented approach to explore the role of cases as a source of law against the background of the convergence theory debate, we would soon see a series of new and intriguing questions arising. Is the fact that cases fulfil the role of source of law in common law jurisdictions the result of a single doctrine of *stare decisis*, or is this result also achieved through a process of publication and utilization of cases that involves multiple institutions, practices and actors? If the latter is true, what kind of institutions, practices and actors jointly contribute to the result of cases fulfilling the role of a source of law in common law jurisdictions? Do legal scholars in common law jurisdictions play a similar role to their counterparts in civil law jurisdictions in the selection process for case publication? Do legal scholars in common law jurisdictions also fulfil a bridge function between the published cases and other users of cases by systemizing, interpreting and evaluating previous court decisions? Is there a similar dynamic in the utilization phase between judges and legal scholars in common law systems as that in civil law jurisdictions, and in particular, do scholarly evaluative comments on a previous case have a similar effect on the influential status of the case in adjudication practice in common law jurisdictions as that in civil law systems? Answers to these questions can enrich our understanding of the differences and similarities between the civil law and the common law legal families, and may shed new light on the convergence theory debate. Obviously, it goes beyond the scope of this study to answer all those questions. However, the approach adopted by this study does make it clear that there is much more to be explored than what has been done in the convergence theory debate so far. Hopefully, this study will encourage comparative legal scholars to further investigate this topic.

Furthermore, the distinction that this study draws between the *result* that cases fulfil the role of a source of law on the one hand and the *process* through which cases fulfil such a role reveals a shortcoming in the convergence theory debate, i.e. comparative legal scholars participating in this debate do not always clearly define the concept and the scope of convergence so that different understandings of and diverse appraisal criteria for convergence occur in the existing literature, which, to say the least, does not facilitate a meaningful debate. Some scholars, for example, endorse the convergence theory by observing that nowadays case law forms a major source of law both in common and civil law countries,[711] whereas other scholars are more cautious to accept the conclusion of convergence because, although as a result cases are indeed a source of law in both legal families, there are still considerable differences between the method of using cases in the common law and that in the civil law legal family.[712] Obviously, the disagreement is related to the fact that the first view defines convergence at the level of the result, whereas the second view examines convergence not only at the level of the result, but also at the level of methodology. If we examine the existing literature, we will also find differences in the scope of convergence that scholars attempt to establish. Some scholarly writings tend to suggest that the two legal families are converging on the whole,[713] whereas others tend to restrict their observation of convergence to specific areas.[714] Moreover, different appraisal criteria are used to assess whether there is a trend of convergence. De Cruz, for example, uses a fairly low criterion. As long as some degree of convergence is taking place and continues to take place, De Cruz would deem the case for convergence already proven.[715] Haazen, on the other hand, denies that there is a trend of convergence, because, although courts in civil law jurisdictions more or less follow the same rules or even cite precedents in their opinions, there is, in his view, no evidence suggesting that any of the civil law jurisdictions recognizes the doctrine of precedent as part of the law.[716] Such an argument

711 See e.g. Markesinis 1994, p. 30-32 and Zweigert & Kötz 1998, p. 71 and p. 259-265.
712 See e.g. Dainow 1966, p. 15 and Baudouin 1974, p. 12-16.
713 See e.g. Markesinis 1994, p. 30-32 and Bogdan 2013, p. 75.
714 See e.g. David 1984, p. 10-11 and MacCormick & Summers 1997a, p. 531-535.
715 De Cruz 2007, p. 503.
716 Haazen 2007, p 230.

implies a very high criterion, as it suggests that Haazen would not accept the theory of convergence until the doctrine of precedent has been accepted in civil law jurisdictions as part of the law. One may rightly doubt whether such a criterion is appropriate, because should the doctrine of precedent indeed be accepted as part of the law in civil law jurisdictions one day, one might as well observe that the civil law legal family has been, at least at the point of the legal authority of precedents, assimilated by the common law family rather than that the two legal families are converging.

This study submits that, for a clear debate on the convergence theory, it is crucial to conduct systematic comparative research where at least the following three questions need to be explicitly addressed. The first is whether a comparative research intends to examine possible convergence between the common law and the civil law families *as a whole*, or does it intend to investigate possible trends within certain legal areas or possible changes with regard to certain legal institutions.[717] An explicit answer to this question can help avoid inappropriate generalization from the findings, and it may also avoid possible misunderstandings on the scope or level of convergence that a scholarly research seeks to verify or establish.

The second question that needs to be clarified is which jurisdictions are to be included in a comparative study on convergence. Some of the existing scholarly writings study only one or two civil law jurisdictions such as Germany and France, but claim or imply that the findings also apply to other civil law jurisdictions.[718] Such an approach is obviously far from ideal. This study submits that, which jurisdictions are to be included in a systematic comparative study that seeks to verify a possible trend of convergence between the common law and the civil law is barely to be answered in abstract, but should rather be assessed in relation to a number of factors, such as the scope of convergence that the research intends to investigate, i.e. convergence between legal systems as a whole or convergence in certain legal areas, the expertise of the researchers, the available time and financial resources etc.[719]

---

[717] Inspiration has been drawn from Mattei & Pes 2008, p. 268-269.

[718] See e.g. Deák 1934, Lipstein 1946, Dainow 1966 and Silving 1966.

[719] This view is inspired in particular by Oderkerk 2001.

The third but certainly not the least important question that needs to be clarified in a comparative study on convergence is how to define convergence. This study submits that a good definition of convergence should explicitly address at least three aspects: time, direction and distance.[720] Convergence, after all, implies a trend of change and the concept of change involves a time dimension, i.e. it involves a comparison between at least two situations: a situation somewhere in the past and the situation now.[721] It is therefore desirable for any study that seeks to participate in the convergence theory debate to make explicit which time span it covers. Moreover, convergence also implies movement. Movement can be analysed in at least two aspects: direction and distance. Such aspects are relevant for the convergence theory debate. It could be helpful to envisage a situation somewhere in the past where the common law and the civil law legal families were situated at the extreme ends of a line. For any scholarly research that seeks to investigate a possible trend of convergence between these two legal families or certain legal areas or legal institutions within these two legal families, it is crucial to identify whether the objects of study have moved, and if so in which direction. Obviously, if the legal families are moving further apart from each other, it would make no sense to conclude that there is a trend of convergence. This study agrees with what has been tacitly assumed or explicitly expressed in many of the existing literature that convergence can be understood as a movement towards a certain central point by the objects of study that were originally separated by a certain distance.[722] In addition to the direction, it is also important for any study that seeks to participate in the convergence debate to define the distance that the studied objects must have covered in order for the conclusion to be drawn that there is a trend of convergence. Does any movement towards a certain central point, no matter how small, justify a conclusion of convergence, or must both legal families have moved fairly close to the central point in order for the conclusion of convergence to be drawn? This question has rarely been explicitly addressed in the

[720] One may also call distance a matter of degree.
[721] Mattei & Pes 2008, p. 268.
[722] See e.g. Haazen 2007, p. 228 and Mattei & Pes 2008, p. 268.

existing literature.[723] It is desirable that future studies be more open about the criterion of distance that they apply to ascertain whether there is a trend of convergence. Obviously, the nature of the studied objects does not quite allow for an accurate quantified measurement. It is nonetheless desirable that future studies at least indicate a margin of distance that they deem acceptable for the conclusion of convergence to be drawn.

To summarize, the role of cases as a source of law in a legal system has often been involved in comparative law studies that debate on the question whether there is a trend of convergence between the common law and the civil law legal families. This study agrees that the role of cases in a legal system is indeed a relevant issue for the convergence theory debate, either as an object of study on its own, or as a component for scholarly research that seeks to explore a possible system-wide scale of convergence. The approach adopted by this study to investigate the functioning of case law in the Netherlands indicates that the role of cases as a source of law can be explored from different perspectives, e.g. as a result or as a process. Adopting a different perspective may lead to different insights into the similarities and differences between the common law and the civil law legal families. In order to avoid misunderstanding and overgeneralization, it is desirable for future scholarly studies that seek to participate in the convergence theory debate to clarify, among other things, from which perspective(s) they study the role of cases as a source of law in a legal system, the scope or level of convergence that they seek to verify and the definition of convergence that they adopt.

6. Do civil law jurisdictions have a case law method?

In the existing literature, some scholars have expressed doubts as to whether civil law jurisdictions have a workable case law method. "[A] relative absence of skills in case analysis", for example, is said to be "the Achilles heel of civil-law methods".[724] Dawson observed that there is no workable case law technique in French law.[725] These

---

[723] De Cruz did explicitly deal with this question, see De Cruz 2007, p. 503.
[724] Glendon 1997, p. 102.
[725] Dawson 1970, p. 413-415.

views were recently challenged by Komárek, who argues that the continental European tradition has its own way of dealing with cases, whose techniques, although different from the common law case law method, are no less rational and intellectually sophisticated.[726] The findings of this study can yield some fresh insights for the debate on case law method in civil law jurisdictions, which will be elaborated in the following passages.

At the outset, this study wishes to emphasize that, for a meaningful debate on case law method in civil law jurisdictions, it is crucial to make a distinction between the question whether civil law jurisdictions have developed a coherent and well-articulated methodological *theory* regarding the use of cases on the one hand, and the question whether a set of methodological standards or guidelines have emerged and been more or less consistently used in *practice* in civil law jurisdictions on the other hand. At the theoretic level, it seems that civil law jurisdictions are indeed lagging behind. In this respect, it is not difficult to accept the observation by Vogenauer that "[t]he highly developed case law theory of Anglo-American jurisdictions has no counterpart on the Continent"[727] to the extent that coherent and in-depth theoretic writings on methods of using cases are at least still scarce in the Netherlands.[728]

However, it is unjustified to jump from the fact that theoretic case law methodological writings are scarce in civil law jurisdictions to the conclusion that there is no workable case law method in these jurisdictions. As Vogenauer rightly pointed out, even a *de facto* source of law that is habitually followed needs to be interpreted and applied according to certain methodological standards.[729] The findings of this study suggest that at least in the Netherlands certain methodological guidelines and thumb rules have indeed emerged in adjudication practice.[730] Of course, it would

---

[726] Komárek 2013.

[727] Vogenauer 2006, p. 895.

[728] This is of course not to say that there are no academic writings that reflect on the method or method(s) of interpreting and using cases in the Netherlands, see e.g. Scholten 1931, p. 114-124, Snijders 2007 and Lubbers 2008.

[729] Vogenauer 2006, p. 895.

[730] See the paragraph that examines the way cases are used in adjudication practice in chapter two of this study.

be more than desirable to further develop and refine these methodological guidelines both in practice and in theory. However, neither the fact that such methodological guidelines have not yet been sufficiently articulated in theoretic methodological writings, nor the fact that in practice they have not yet been thoroughly developed seems to justify the conclusion that these methodological guidelines are not workable.

Perhaps more importantly and more interestingly, this study can stimulate us to reflect on the definition of case law method in the existing literature. Currently, scholarly writings on case law method tend to concentrate largely on ascertaining the ways cases are interpreted and applied in court practice.[731] This study suggests a broader understanding of the case law method. In its basic meaning, method connotes the "path" or "way to achieve and end". [732] From this perspective, case law mechanism in the Netherlands, as revealed by this study, can be seen as a case law method in a broader sense. After all, it is through the case law mechanism that cases have been able to fulfil the function of a *de facto* source of law in the Netherlands, contributing to attain ideals of the law such as legal certainty, legal unity, equality before the law and a desirable degree of flexibility. If we understand case law method in this broader sense, we will see a whole new and promising research area emerging for comparative law. Vogenauer rightly pointed out that there is a huge gap in comparative research on case law, i.e. whilst there is a significant body of literature as to whether cases are or are not a source of law in different legal systems, almost no comparative analysis of the case law method has been done. If we realize that "the case law method" that Vogenauer referred to is defined in a narrow sense[733] instead of the broader sense advanced by this study, it becomes plain how huge the gap actually is. This study has made a modest attempt to fill a tiny portion of the gap by drawing the contours of the case law method in the Netherlands both in a narrow and in a broad sense. Hopefully, this study will encourage comparative legal scholars to explore the case law method/mechanism in other legal systems and to compare their findings.

---

[731] See e.g. MacCormick & Summers 1997b and Vogenauer 2006.
[732] Vogenauer 2006, p. 885.
[733] Vogenauer 2006, p. 885-886.

7. Should civil law jurisdictions adopt the doctrine of precedent?

Still another debate in the existing literature on the role of cases in civil law jurisdictions is whether civil law jurisdictions should adopt the doctrine of precedent or at least a certain variant of the doctrine of precedent, for example, in the sense that previous court decisions are presumed to be rational and correct and should be followed unless a court can find sufficient justification for deviating from previous cases.[734] I doubt whether it would be desirable for civil law jurisdictions to abandon their current practice and to adopt a strict doctrine of precedent or a form of conditional doctrine of precedent where courts are bound by previous cases unless they can find sufficient justification to deviate from them.

Crucial to the doctrine of precedent is the notion of binding force, i.e. judges must follow previous cases that are binding upon them even if they substantively do not agree with those cases.[735] One of the effects of the doctrine of precedent in English law, for example, is that lower courts are bound by previous cases decided by higher courts, which means that lower courts must follow previous cases decided by higher courts that are applicable to later disputes, even if lower courts believe that the previous cases are substantively wrong or undesirable.[736] At first sight, it might be

[734] Compare e.g. Kottenhagen 1986, p. 4 with Hondius 2007a, p. 19-20 and Drion 2014.

[735] There is an elaborate body of literature that discusses the common law doctrine of precedent, see e.g. Schaefer 1967, Hardisty 1979, Cross & Harris 1991, Kalt 2003, Markman 2003, Cartwright 2007, p. 21-24, Nelson 2011 and McLeod 2011. Upon careful analysis of this body of literature, one would realize that the questions addressed in these writings are often related to the notion of binding force, such as what binding force means, which cases have binding force, which part of a case has binding force (i.e. the distinction between *ratio decidendi* and *obiter dictum*), which courts are bound by previous cases, are there exceptions to the rule of binding force and if so, under what circumstances are precedents not binding.

[736] Cross & Harris 1991, p. 5-7. It should be noted that this is not an absolute rule. For a summary of the limited exceptions to this and other

quite appealing to introduce such a rule to a civil law jurisdiction such as the Netherlands. As this study reveals, Dutch judges take various substantive considerations into account when deciding whether a previous case will be followed, such as how well the case has been received in scholarly writings and whether following the previous case would lead to an undesirable or unjust result in a later lawsuit.[737] Such substantive considerations, one may argue, involve a subjective evaluation of the judge and may even point to different directions, so that it would be very difficult for litigants to predict whether judges would follow a previous case or not. Seen in this light, introducing the doctrine of precedent may have a huge benefit of simplifying the prediction of the reaction of judges to previous cases, i.e. whether a previous case will be followed depends on a clear objective criterion: whether the previous case has been decided by a higher court.

It is, however, doubtful whether introducing a strict or conditional doctrine of precedent would indeed eliminate substantive considerations with regard to the merits of previous cases in adjudication practice and subsequently contribute to a higher degree of legal certainty in civil law jurisdictions. In the first place, it should be pointed out that a conditional doctrine of precedent in the sense of a legal obligation for courts to follow previous cases unless they can justify why a previous case that they are supposed to follow is wrong, undesirable or no longer good law, by definition, opens the door for substantive considerations with regard to the merits of previous cases. In other words, under such a conditional doctrine of precedent, judges are still able to avoid following previous cases that they deem undesirable or wrong on substantive grounds, so that litigants still need to estimate whether the judge substantively endorses previous cases. That would mean, in the context of the Dutch legal system, even if a conditional doctrine of precedent were to be introduced, litigants would most probably still have to check the various substantive factors that judges take into account under the current methodological

---

rules based on the doctrine of *stare decisis* see Cross & Harris 1991, p. 163-164.

[737] See the paragraph on the way cases are used in adjudication practice in the Netherlands in chapter two of this study.

framework,[738] in order to assess how likely the judge would substantively endorse previous cases. It is therefore not obvious how such a conditional doctrine of precedent would be able to create an effect of simplifying the prediction of judges' reaction to previous cases in adjudication.

Would, one may rightly wonder, a strict form of unconditional doctrine of precedent eliminate judges' substantive considerations with regard to the merits of previous cases and subsequently make it easier for litigants to predict the reaction of judges to previous cases? The practice in common law jurisdictions tends to suggest that the answer would most likely be negative. It is no longer a secret that judges in common law jurisdictions have developed various ways to avoid following precedents that they do not substantively endorse even though they are formally bound by such previous court decisions.[739] One of the ways to avoid applying binding precedents is to manipulate the distinction between *ratio decidendi* and *obiter dictum.*[740] Another well-known, if not notorious, way to avoid binding precedents that judges do not like is to use the technique of distinguishing, i.e. by demonstrating that there are crucial differences between the facts underlying the binding precedent and those of the dispute at hand so that the precedent is not applicable.[741] It is anything but unthinkable that, if a strict form of doctrine of precedent were to be introduced to a civil law jurisdiction, judges would resort to various technical constructions to avoid applying binding precedents that they do not endorse due to substantive considerations. At least, the interviews with Dutch judges that I conducted indicate that the technique of distinguishing is by no means unique to the common law legal family, as many interviewed judges replied that they would try to avoid applying Supreme Court cases to solve a legal dispute at hand by seeking crucial factual differences between the previous case and the lawsuit at hand, where, among other situations, applying the previous case would lead to a result that they deem highly unjust or

[738] For details of the substantive factors that judges take into account see the paragraph on the way cases are used in adjudication practice in the Netherlands in chapter two of this study.
[739] See e.g. Deák 1934, p. 341 and David 1984, p. 10-11.
[740] See e.g. Stone 1959, Goodhart 1959 and Cross & Harris 1991, p. 39-96.
[741] See e.g. Deák 1934, p. 341 and David 1984, p. 10-11.

undesirable.[742] Accordingly, this study suspects that introducing a strict form of doctrine of precedent to a civil law jurisdiction may have the effect of forcing judges to use technical reasons to conceal the real substantive considerations that underlie their choice not to follow previous cases. One may rightly doubt whether such an effect would be desirable, as a growing trend to resort to technical constructions to avoid applying previous cases would obscure the real substantive considerations that judges take into account, which would neither facilitate an open and rational discourse on the merits of different approaches to solve a legal problem, nor be helpful to enhance the litigants' ability to predict how judges would react to relevant previous cases in adjudication.

One may argue that introducing a conditional or a strict form of the doctrine of precedent will at least impose a burden of argument on judges in the sense that they have to provide substantive or technical justifications for their decision to deviate from possibly applicable previous cases, which is conducive to enhance legal certainty, as judges would no longer be able to ignore relevant previous cases or to deviate from them without any explanation.[743] To this argument I wish to respond, in the first place, that as far as Supreme Court cases are concerned, judges interviewed by this study all indicate that they are fully aware that they in fact bear a burden of argument where they decide to deviate from possibly applicable previous cases decided by the Supreme Court.[744] As far as previous cases decided by the courts of appeal and trial courts are concerned, most judges interviewed for this study indicate that in practice they do perceive a burden of argument where litigants or their counsels explicitly invoke previous cases decided by other courts than the Supreme Court and

[742] E.g. interviews NL20130923, NL20131008-2, NL20131017, NL20131028-1, NL20131028-2 and NL20131114.
[743] Kottenhagen 1986, p. 5-6.
[744] The interview results indicate a strong normative conviction among the respondents that judges ought to provide sufficient justification if they decide to deviate from an applicable case decided by the Supreme Court. Not doing so would be, according to one senior judge, "utterly unprofessional and unacceptable", see interview NL20131008-1. For similar views see NL20131021, NL20131022, NL20131028-1 and NL20131114.

such cases do bear close relevance to the dispute at hand.[745] In other words, the findings of this study suggest that at least in the Netherlands judges already carry a certain degree of burden of argument in practice, so that it is doubtful whether imposing an explicit burden of argument on judges would lead to significant changes in reality.

This is, of course, not to say that nothing needs to or can be done to improve the way cases function as a source of law in civil law jurisdictions. As far as the use of cases in adjudication is concerned, it is crucial, as explained earlier in this study, that judges follow certain common methodological guidelines and that such guidelines be accessible to the public, otherwise it would be highly difficult for litigants to predict how judges are likely to treat possibly relevant previous cases and thus undermining legal certainty.[746] Accordingly, in order to improve the predictability of the way judges treat previous cases in adjudication, it is desirable to refine the method of using cases in adjudication and to make the (application of the) method transparent to the public. This study agrees with Komárek that the case law method developed under the common law doctrine of precedent is neither the only possible nor the most rational or advanced method of using previous cases to solve legal disputes and to develop the law.[747] The findings of this study suggest that, at least in the Netherlands, judges do apply, perhaps not always explicitly, certain common methodological guidelines when using cases in adjudication. Such methodological guidelines are obviously not yet so sophisticated and accurate that no improvement is possible. It is therefore desirable for judges, academic and practising lawyers in the Netherlands and other civil law jurisdictions to pay closer attention to the question of method and to experiment with possible ways to improve their existing method of using cases.

In addition, it is highly desirable that judges shed more light on their judgments on the real considerations that shape the way they treat previous cases by, among other things, providing more

---

[745] See e.g. interviews NL20131008-1, NL20131022, NL20131031 and NL20131107-2.

[746] See the passage that examines the way cases are used in adjudication practice in the Netherlands in chapter two.

[747] Komárek 2013.

elaborate and honest reasoning and argumentation in their judgments. In this context, introducing a strict form of doctrine of precedent may not be a wise move, as doing so is likely to induce judges to avoid substantive discussion of previous cases in judgments by resorting to formalistic and technical argumentation. Perhaps more elaborate and honest reasoning and argumentation in judgments with regard to the use of previous cases is not something to be (easily) achieved by imposing legal sanctions under a strict or conditional doctrine of precedent.[748] After all, the findings of this study suggest that the fact that judges in the Netherlands no longer conceal the influence of previous cases on judicial deliberation has not been induced by a change in legislation, but is related to a gradual change of mentality among the key players in law with regard to the justification of the lawmaking role of the judge and the desirability to have cases as a source of law.[749] Accordingly, more elaborate and honest reasoning and argumentation in judgments with regard to the use of previous cases may very well depend on further changes in the mentality of the key players in law rather than the introduction of a doctrine of precedent.

8. Concluding remarks

The insights presented in this chapter are diverse. They touch upon various topics such as case publication, the role of legal scholars, explicit recognition of cases as a source of law, a possible trend of convergence between the civil law and the common law legal families, case law method and the desirability of adopting the doctrine of precedent in civil law jurisdictions. In substance, there does not seem to be a common theme that runs through all these topics. However, the insights presented in this chapter do have one thing in common, i.e. this study would not have arrived at such insights if it had not questioned and broken away from the dominant approach in the existing literature, which studies the role of cases in civil law jurisdictions from the perspective of the common law

[748] See e.g. Adams 2007, p. 175 and Drion 2014.
[749] See chapter three of this study.

doctrine of precedent by focusing chiefly, if not solely on the question how judges treat previous cases in court practice.[750]

At the outset, it was pointed out that concepts such as "*stare decisis*" or "precedent" would not be used to analyse or describe the way cases fulfil the role of a source of law in the Netherlands and in other civil law jurisdictions, for doing so might cause the readers to, consciously or unconsciously, project a common law understanding of precedent onto the functioning of cases as a source of law in civil law jurisdictions.[751] Subsequently, this study developed the concept of case law mechanism and a new analytic framework, which broadened the scope of investigation from the way judges use cases in court practice to include other aspects such as case publication and the use of cases in legal research and in legal education. If this had not been developed, this study would most probably not have been an in-depth investigation into the way cases are published in the Netherlands and would hence most probably not have reflected on the soundness of the assumption that case publication is a mere technical matter. Similarly, if this study had not broken away from the focus on judges and if it had not broadened the scope of investigation to also include the way legal scholars use cases, it would probably not have been able to discover the subtle ways through which legal scholars influence the development of case law and would hence probably not have been able to question the tendency in the existing literature to de-emphasize the influence of legal scholars on case law in civil law jurisdictions. The last paragraph of the final conclusion of this study will further reflect on this methodological point and will make an appeal to legal scholars to seriously consider the soundness of the dominant common law paradigm in the existing literature related to the role of cases in civil law jurisdictions and to create more neutral and suitable analytic tools to explore this topic.

---

[750] Komárek observes rightly that there is a "dominance of the common law paradigm" in the existing literature on case law method, see Komárek 2013, p. 150. The common law paradigm also seems to dominate in the existing literature that studies the role of cases in civil law jurisdictions, see the paragraph that presented the concept of case law mechanism in the introduction and the last paragraph of the final conclusion of this study.

[751] Komárek 2012, p 54.

Chapter 5

China's quest for case law

Chapter 5 China's quest for case law

1. Introduction

The previous chapter placed the findings of the first part of this study (chapter one, two and three) in the context of the existing English-language comparative law literature related to the role of cases in civil law jurisdictions and explored the relevance of the first part of this study for this body of literature. The remaining part of this study will continue to explore the broader implications of the first three chapters by linking these findings with what has become a trend in China since the 1980s, i.e. a growing interest in developing and using case law in China, and by trying to draw insights from the experiences with case law in the Netherlands that may be useful for China to further enhance the use of cases.

Since the Communist Party founded the People's Republic of China in 1949, cases no longer constitute a source of law in China.[752] Neither in theory nor in practice do judicial decisions have normative force beyond the specific disputes in which the decisions are made.[753] One of the reasons for rejecting cases as a source of law is that under the Chinese constitutional framework, courts are only authorized to apply the law, but not to make law.[754]

Since the 1980s, however, courts and legal scholars in China have been demonstrating a growing interest in developing and using case law.[755] A large volume of journal articles and books emerged that debate on, among other things, the need for and the feasibility of case law in China's codified legal system that formally rejects cases as a source of law.[756] The growing interest in case law eventually led to the introduction of a new legal institution called the "Case Guidance System"[757] by the Supreme People's Court of

---

[752] In Imperial China (prior to 1912) and the Republic of China (1912-1949), cases did constitute a source of law, see Wang 2005 and Wu 2010.

[753] See e.g. Liu 2009, p. 111-112, Rao & Liao 2009, p. 119 and Li 2009a.

[754] Art. 126 Constitution of the People's Republic of China. See also Li 2009a.

[755] See e.g. Wu 2004 and Shen 2009b.

[756] Ibid.

[757] The Chinese term is 案例指导制度(Anli Zhidao Zhidu). The term Case Guidance System is my translation.

China in November 2010.[758] This new legal institution enables the Supreme People's Court to select and publish "guiding cases"[759] from a vast pool of candidate cases sent in by courts at various levels across China through a fairly complicated selection procedure.[760] Once published, the guiding cases are supposed to be followed in later court practice.[761]

This chapter seeks to understand what triggered the growing interest in case law in China and the introduction of a nationwide Case Guidance System by the Supreme People's Court in 2010. Furthermore, this chapter will examine some of the key aspects of the Supreme People's Court's design of the Case Guidance System, as well as the evolution process that has led to this new legal institution in China. The final part of this chapter will briefly summarize the findings and reflect on the question whether the Case Guidance System will be able to successfully solve the problems that it is intended to address. By doing so, this chapter will set the stage for the next chapter, which will explore the question what the relevance of the case law mechanism in the Netherlands could be in the context of China.

The main method used was analysis of the relevant literature. Relevant Chinese-language literature has been found primarily by using online databases and search engines[762] such as China Knowledge Resource Integrated Database (CNKI)[763], China Law Info (Beida Fabao)[764] and Baidu.[765] The snowball method was also used to find relevant literature. Moreover, I conducted

---

[758] See Supreme People's Court of the People's Republic of China 2010b.

[759] The Chinese term is 指导案例(Zhidao Anli). Guiding cases is my translation.

[760] For details, see the relevant paragraph in this chapter that discusses the Supreme People's Court's design of the Case Guidance System.

[761] Art. 7 Provisions Concerning Work on Guiding Cases, see Appendix 5.

[762] Some of the search terms included "Anli Zhidao Zhidu" (Case Guidance System), "tongan bu tongpan" (like cases not being treated alike), "zhidao anli"(guiding cases), "anli yanjiu" (case research) and "anli jiaoxue" (using cases in legal education).

[763] www.cnki.net.

[764] www.vip.chinalawinfo.com.

[765] www.baidu.com.

interviews with seven Chinese legal scholars,[766] five Chinese judges[767] and four Chinese practising lawyers[768] mainly to verify information found in the existing Chinese-language literature.[769] The respondents were found through my personal contacts. Obviously, doubt can be cast on the representativeness of the small sample of respondents. However, it should be noted that literature review was the main source of information for this part of the research, whereas the interviews only played a supplementary role.

In addition to Chinese-language literature, I also consulted relevant English-language publications. These publications were found mainly by using Google Scholar[770] and the snowball method. Also the website of the Stanford Law School China Guiding Cases Project[771] was used as an important source of English-language information related to the Case Guidance System and the case law debate in China.

2. Problems in China that aroused a growing interest in case law

Whether China needs case law is a question that has triggered many publications in China since the 1980s.[772] Proponents of a case law system in China identified various problems to which case law, as they argue, can provide an effective cure, such as the problem that like cases are not treated alike in different courts throughout China, lack of transparency in adjudication as well as corruption within the Chinese judiciary.[773] Before examining these arguments separately,

---

766 Interview codes: CN20110614, CN20110615, CN20110622, CN20110709, CN20110711-1, CN20110711-2 and CN20111205-1.

767 Interview codes: CN20110705, CN20110708, CN20110701-1, CN20110701-2, CN20130408 and CN20130920.

768 Interview codes: CN20110221, CN20110302, CN20110307 and CN20111205-2.

769 I verified, among other things, the workload of judges, the role of research judges and selection procedure for case publication.

770 The main search terms included "Case Guidance System", "case law in China", "guiding cases" and "judicial reforms in China".

771 http://cgc.law.stanford.edu/

772 See e.g. Zhang 2002a and the publications collected in Wu 2004.

773 See the second, third and fourth subparagraph. The proponents' arguments in favor of establishing a case law system in China discussed in

this paragraph will highlight a fundamental problem in the Chinese legal system, i.e. rejecting cases as a source of law causes the legislature in China to face an extremely difficult task of striking a proper balance in lawmaking among four competing requirements: adequacy, feasibility, certainty and adaptability.[774]

2.1 The top-down lawmaking process and difficulty for the legislature to strike a proper balance in legislation

As Van Rooij rightly pointed out, good legislation must strike a proper balance between four requirements: adequacy, feasibility, certainty and adaptability.[775] In China, a large and fast-developing country with a unitary legal system where lawmaking is largely a top-down process dominated by a relatively small group of powerful people, striking a proper balance among these four requirements is an extremely difficult task for the legislature.[776]

As cases are neither recognized nor effectively used as a source of law, legislation in China needs to provide specific rules to attain certainty, because any room for interpretation leaves nearly full discretion to those applying the law.[777] However, China does not have a pluralistic political system that allows for meaningful and broad public participation in the lawmaking.[778] Consequently the end products of a primarily top-down legislation process may end up containing precise and specific rules that look strong and good on paper, but due to the lack of sufficient participation, the law does not enjoy support from the relevant interest groups and the precisely drafted rules do not fit the actual circumstances on the ground.[779] Due to the lack of an institutionalized system through

---

this paragraph are not exhaustive. Enhancing efficiency of adjudication and raising public confidence in the judiciary, for example, have also been used as arguments to justify the necessity of case law in China, see e.g. Zhang 2004, p. 103, Shen 2009a, p. 5-6 and Hu & Yu 2009, p. 7-8.

[774] Van Rooij 2006, p. 25-104.

[775] Van Rooij 2006, p. 32-43.

[776] Van Rooij 2006, p. 44-49.

[777] Van Rooij 2006, p. 47.

[778] See e.g. Alford & Liebman 2001 and Van Rooij 2006, p. 44-49.

[779] The *Land Management Act* 1998 (土地管理法 Tudi Guanlifa) is a good example, see Van Rooij 2006, p. 54-67.

which societal norms can move bottom-up to become part of the national legal system, the legislature in China has to anticipate what happens at the bottom level and in future circumstances.[780] This is an extremely difficult, if not impossible task, given the obstructed vertical information flow that characterizes a non-pluralistic political system and the rapid changes in China's reform society.[781]

Many Chinese legal scholars and judges have realized and pointed out this problem in their writings, although it should be noted that their writings tend to use relatively mild and neutral language to describe this problem, instead of directly criticizing the non-pluralistic political system and the top-down lawmaking process.[782] A frequently used term in the Chinese-language literature to describe this problem is the "limitations of legislation".[783] It has been frequently pointed out that legislation inevitably contains vague norms, flexible rules or even lacunas, and that it is impossible for the legislature to foresee all possible future problems, so that case law is needed as an instrument to counterbalance such limitations of legislation.[784]

2.2 Like cases not treated alike

Treating like cases alike is often deemed as a fundamental principle of justice.[785] In Chinese courts, however, similar cases have often been reported to reach (vastly) different outcomes.[786] The following two examples found in the Chinese-language legal literature may provide a rough impression of the situation in China.

---

[780] Van Rooij 2006, p. 47.

[781] Ibid.

[782] See e.g. Zhao & Liu 2004, p. 533-535, Xu 2004, p. 3-4, Shen 2004, p. 20, Zuo 2004, p. 88, Cui 2004, p. 106, Li & Pan 2006, Liu & Xu 2006, p. 17-19, Su & Li 2009, p. 15 and Xie 2014.

[783] The Chinese term is 成文法的不足(chengwenfa de buzu), see the literature cited in the previous footnote.

[784] See e.g. Xu 2004, p. 4, Shen 2004, p. 20, Gao 2004, p. 103-104 and Chen & Xie 2004, p. 126, Liu & Xu 2006, p. 17-19 and Hu & Yu 2009, p. 6.

[785] Hart 1961, p. 159.

[786] See e.g. Liu 2007b, Xu 2009, Wang 2009 and Rao & Liao 2009, p. 119.

Example 1: *Conditional contract cases in Shenyang city.*[787] Around the year 2002, the Intermediate People's Court in the city of Shenyang in Northeast China decided two cases involving the same defendant (a real estate developer), who signed standardized relocation contracts with owners of houses that were demolished in a real estate development project. One of the key terms of the standardized contract was that the real estate developer would provide comparable housing to the owners of demolished houses. However, the contracts contained one conditional clause: the contracts would be invalid, if the house owners have other properties in Shenyang. Later, it turned out that two house owners did own other properties in Shenyang. The developer refused to perform, insisting that the contracts were void. The two house owners brought separate law suits to the Intermediate Court.

In the first case, the court found judgment for the plaintiff. The reason was that a condition upon which the validity of a contract depends, may only concern possible future facts. The fact that the plaintiff owned another property in Shenyang is one that already existed at the moment when the contract was concluded, which means it cannot constitute a condition for the validity of the contract. Consequently, the court held the contract to be valid and the defendant should perform. In the second case, however, the court gave a totally opposite judgment, holding the contract to be void due to the fulfilment of the condition specified in the conditional clause of the contract.

Example 2: *Counterfeit medicine cases in Zhengzhou city.*[788] In 1998, a citizen of the city Zhengzhou in central China bought counterfeit medicine of the same kind and brand in three drugstores located in three different districts of Zhengzhou. He sued the drugstores in the three corresponding district courts, claiming punitive damages on the basis of Article 55 of the Consumer Protection Law. However, these three cases involved one complicating factor. The plaintiff, Mr Ge Rui, was a well-known

[787] The original court judgments in this example cannot be obtained, since they are not published. A description of the key facts and the outcomes can be found in an empirical report of the Intermediate People's Court of Shenyang city. See Zhang 2009.

[788] For a description of the key facts and court decisions in this example, see Liu 2006.

consumer-rights activist in China, who deployed a strategy of fighting businesses that sold counterfeit goods by intentionally buying counterfeit goods from them and suing them subsequently for punitive damages. In other words, the plaintiff was not under deception when he bought the counterfeit medicine. Rather, he bought the medicine, knowing that it was counterfeited, with the intention to sue the sellers.

The first district court rejected the claim on the ground that the plaintiff did not buy the medicine for personal consumption. The second district court also rejected the claim, but on a different ground, i.e. the plaintiff failed to prove that the medicine was counterfeited. The last district court declared the contract void, because the plaintiff failed to prove that he bought the medicine for medical purposes. At first sight, the three cases seemed to have reached the same outcome, i.e. the plaintiff's claim was rejected. However, the reasons underlying the judgments do demonstrate quite divergent understandings of the law.

I have not been able to find systematic quantitative research in the Chinese-language literature that would be able to firmly establish the representativeness of the above-described examples. However, the vast volume of publications on the desirability and feasibility of case law in China does suggest that these examples are but the tip of an iceberg and that like cases not being treated alike is widely perceived to be a serious problem in China. A district court president, for example, said the following about this problem in an interview with the media:[789]

> It is not uncommon that similar cases reach different outcomes. Like cases may be treated differently by different judges in the same court. Even the same judge may give different judgments in similar cases at different times. This problem is all the more serious in novel and controversial cases.

This problem is perceived to be particularly damaging to the public's confidence in the courts and in the legal system.[790] According to a senior judge of the High Court of Guangdong

---

[789] Liu 2007b.

[790] Zhang 2009, p. 124 and Zhou 2011.

Province, widespread instances of like cases being treated differently, such as awarding different levels of compensation to the loss of lives under similar circumstances (同命不同价) and applying different punishments to similar crimes (同罪不同罚), have become the "primary factor that undermines the authority of the law". [791]

Many legal scholars and judges believe that introducing a case law institution is an effective cure to this problem, and they have conducted a vast amount of research on the desirability, feasibility and specific designs of a case law institution for China.[792] Many publications by Chinese legal scholars and judges indicate that they expect that once a case selected through an official procedure and backed by sufficient coercive force is published, lower courts will follow the case and apply the same standards to decide later similar cases, which will solve the problem that like cases are not treated alike.[793] This expectation has not only been expressed in journal articles and books, but also in official documents issued by the Supreme People's Court. The *Second Five-year Reform Outline* issued by the Supreme People's Court in 2005, for example, says that the Supreme People's Court will attach great importance to the role of cases in "unifying the legal standards applied in adjudication".[794] The very first sentence of the official document issued by the Supreme People's Court in 2010 that marks the birth of the nationwide Case Guidance System says that the rules on the Case Guidance System are enacted with the purpose of "summing up adjudication experiences, *unifying the application of the law*,[795] improving adjudication quality and upholding judicial

[791] Ding 2008b, p. 142.
[792] See e.g. the publications collected in Wu 2004.
[793] See e.g. Zhang 2004, Xu 2009 and Dou & Wang 2009.
[794] The Chinese term is 统一法律适用标准(tongyi falu shiyong biaozhun). See Supreme People's Court of the People's Republic of China 2005.
[795] Italicized by the author of this study. "Unifying the application of the law" indicates that the Case Guidance System is introduced as an instrument to address the problem of like cases not being treated alike.

justice".[796] It seems fair to infer from the academic and official sources cited in this subparagraph that like cases not being treated alike is one of the problems that aroused a growing interest in case law in China.

2.3 Lack of transparency in adjudication

Lack of transparency is a criticism that the Chinese judiciary frequently incurs. It has, for example, long been a point of criticism that court decisions are inaccessible to the public, as many courts (used to) refuse to publish judgments or choose to publish only a small proportion of judgments that they deem "safe" for the public to know.[797] Moreover, judgments in China have been frequently criticized for lacking (sufficient) legal reasoning.[798] Consequently, even when judgments do get published, it is still difficult for the public to ascertain how the courts reached their decisions.

Proponents of a case law system in China argue that stimulating the use of cases in court practice as a source of law can help increase transparency in adjudication. Some authors, for example, submit that doing so would stimulate or even require courts to publish more and more judgments.[799] Some proponents also expect that setting the goal of establishing a case law system in China can have the effect of raising the quality of legal reasoning in court judgments, as they believe that one of the conditions for case law to develop is that judgments must provide reasons.[800]

---

[796] The Chinese text is 总结审判经验，统一法律适用，提高审判质量，维护司法公正(zongjie shenpan jingyan, tongyi falu shiyong, tigao shenpan zhiliang, weihu sifa gongzheng). See Appendix 5.

[797] See e.g. He 2005 and He 2006.

[798] See e.g. Zong 2009 and Cheng 2012.

[799] See e.g. Chen & Li 2003, p. 24.

[800] See e.g. Chen & Li 2003, p. 24 and Chen & Wei 2004, p. 77-78. One may rightly question the validity of this argument, as it seems to rely on circular reasoning or a reserved causal relationship. It is, however, not the intention to engage in a debate with the authors that have explored the question why China needs case law. The purpose of this paragraph is simply to present the views of these authors to the readers and by doing so, to help the readers understand what Chinese legal scholars and judges perceive to be problems that need to be and can be addressed by case law.

2.4 Judicial corruption

Judicial corruption is a frequently reported problem in China. A striking example is the case of Huang Songyou (黄松有), former Vice President of the Supreme People's Court, who was sentenced to life imprisonment due to corruption in 2010.[801] An empirical study in 2010 shows that corruption occurs at almost all levels of the Chinese judicial system, involving all types of judges, regardless of their rank, level of education and income.[802]

Proponents of a case law system in China argue that using cases as a source of law can help curtail judicial corruption.[803] Two of the key assumptions underlying this argument is that abuse of judicial discretion is one of the (most crucial) causes of judicial corruption and that case law is an effective tool to standardize the exercise of judicial discretion, which will lead to less corruption.[804]

3. Basic design and evolution of China's Case Guidance System

The Case Guidance System[805] refers, in a loose sense, to a practice of the Chinese judiciary, which allows higher courts to select cases that are supposed to serve as models for lower courts to decide later similar cases.[806] The selected model cases are called "guiding cases".[807] Guiding cases are not necessarily decided by higher courts themselves, as higher courts are free to appoint cases decided by lower courts as guiding cases.

The operation of the Case Guidance System consists of three phases:

(1) selection,

(2) publication, and

---

801 See http://fanfu.people.com.cn/GB/10796016.html.

802 Li 2010.

803 See e.g. Zhang 2002a, paragraph 4, Liu & Xu 2006, p. 16, Su & Li 2009, p. 12, Hu & Yu 2009, p. 8 and Ma & Cha 2011, p. 59

804 See e.g. Zhang 2002a, paragraph 4, Liu & Xu 2006, p. 16, 20 , 22 and Hu & Yu 2009, p. 8.

805 The Chinese term is 案例指导制度(Anli Zhidao Zhidu).

806 This is my definition based on the analysis of relevant literature. In particular, I consulted Hu & Yu 2009, p. 5 and Chen 2012b.

807 The Chinese term is 指导案例(Zhidao Anli).

(3) application.

How the three phases should exactly be designed has been an issue of debate in China for decades. This paragraph reviews how the debate evolved. The next paragraph will examine the answers of the Supreme People's Court to the debated questions.

During the evolution process of China's Case Guidance System, the Supreme People's Court issued two official documents that are of particular importance. In 2005, the Supreme People's Court issued the *Second Five-year Reform Outline of the People's Courts (2004-2008)* [808], announcing its plan to create a nationwide Case Guidance System. In 2010, the Supreme People's Court issued the *Provisions of the Supreme People's Court Concerning Work on Guiding Cases*, which marks the birth of a nationwide Case Guidance System.[809] Accordingly, this paragraph will be divided into two subparagraphs. The first subparagraph reviews the period prior to 2005, and the second discusses the period between 2005 and 2010.

3.1 Court practices and academic debates prior to 2005

In 1985, the Supreme People's Court started to issue its official publication the *Gazette of the Supreme People's Court of the People's Republic of China.* [810], hereinafter *the Gazette*). *The Gazette* contains not only relevant laws and decrees, but also model cases[811] selected by the Supreme People's Court.[812] Prior to 1985, the Supreme People's Court occasionally instructed lower courts to follow model cases selected by the highest court.[813] However, cases

---

[808] See Supreme People's Court of the People's Republic of China 2005.

[809] See Supreme People's Court of the People's Republic of China 2010b and Jiang 2011a.

[810] The Chinese title of this publication is 中华人民共和国最高人民法院公报(Zhonghua Renmin Gongheguo Zuigao Renmin Fayuan Gongbao). In the rest of this study, this publication will be referred to as the *Gazette*.

[811] The published cases are not necessarily decided by the Supreme People's Court itself. Many of them are decided by lower courts.

[812] *The Gazette* also contains the Supreme People's Court's interpretations of laws, its policy documents and its replies to lower courts' requests for clarification of specific points of law.

[813] Zhou 2009, p. 141.

that lower courts were instructed to follow used to be largely shrouded in secrecy before 1985, since they were mainly distributed to lower courts through internal channels within the judiciary, so that the public could not gain access to them.[814]

It should be noted that the Supreme People's Court has at no point declared the cases published in the *Gazette* to be binding precedents. The official position of the Supreme People's Court on the status of the cases published in the *Gazette* is that these selected cases have reference value and can be used as an important tool to guide the adjudication practice in lower courts.[815] The impact of the cases published in the *Gazette* on the adjudication practice in China is generally perceived to be rather limited.[816] This is of course not to say that publishing cases through the Gazette is a meaningless act. In fact, some Western observers regarded the *Gazette* as "probably the most important new publication on law" in China in the 1980s, as it was the first institutionalized channel through which cases selected by the Supreme People's Court were made public.[817]

Another interesting development within the Chinese judiciary prior to 2005 is that a number of lower courts took the initiative to experiment with what they called "Precedent Decision System" [818] or "Precedent Guidance System". [819] These local experiments all involved selection and publication of certain earlier decided cases that are supposed to serve as a source of inspiration for courts to decide later similar cases.[820]

The publication of cases in the *Gazette* as well as the local experiments were, generally speaking, positively received in the Chinese academic world, although a number of commentators did

---

[814] Ibid.

[815] Zhou 2009, p. 143.

[816] See e.g. Zhu 2008, p. 44 and Mou 2014. In fact, some lower courts have such a limited budget that they cannot even afford a subscription to the *Gazette*, let alone consulting and using the cases published in it, see Rao & Liao 2009, p. 119.

[817] Tsia & Johnson, p276.

[818] The Chinese term is 先例判决制度(Xianli Panjue Zhidu), see Chen & Li 2003.

[819] The Chinese term is 判例指导制度(Panli Zhidao Zhidu), see Li & Meng 2002.

[820] Chen & Li 2003 and Li & Meng 2002.

question the authority of lower courts to select model cases.[821] Between the mid-1980s and 2005, creating a precedent system in China was a hot topic among legal scholars. One of the key questions that attracted much attention was whether it is desirable and feasible for China to create a precedent system within its codified legal system.[822] Another question of debate was how a Chinese precedent system should be designed.[823]

It is noteworthy that prior to 2005 the term "precedent system"[824] was frequently used in the case law discourse in China to refer to an envisaged new legal institution that would enable cases to fulfil the role of a *de facto* source of law in China.[825] In the Chinese legal language, terms such as "precedent"[826] and "precedent system" carry a strong common law connotation and are closely associated with the doctrine of *stare decisis*.[827] Frequent use of the terms "precedent" and "precedent system" in the case law discourse may give the impression that judges and legal scholars in China were trying to transplant the common law doctrine of precedent. However, a closer look at the court experiments and the academic publications prior to 2005 reveals that the common law doctrine of *stare decisis* was not seen as an ideal model for China to copy. What most people had in mind was an institution that would allow higher courts to select model cases that do not have formal binding force, but are supposed to be followed by lower courts when deciding later similar cases.[828]

3.2 Court practices and academic debates from 2005 till 2010

In 2005 the Supreme People's Court issued the *Second Five-year Reform Outline of the People's Courts*.[829] It was in this Reform

[821] See e.g. Zhang 2008b and Jing e.a. 2005.
[822] See e.g. Gao 1991, Zhang 2002b and Zhang 2004.
[823] See the academic publications prior to 2005 collected in Wu 2004.
[824] The Chinese term is 判例制度 (Panli Zhidu)。
[825] See the academic publications prior to 2005 collected in Wu 2004.
[826] The Chinese term is 判例 (Panli).
[827] See e.g. Liang 1991, Rao & Yan 2004 and Zhu 2008, p. 35.
[828] See e.g. Wang 2004a and Zhao & Liu 2004, p. 536-537.
[829] See Supreme People's Court of the People's Republic of China 2005.

Outline that the term "Case Guidance System"[830] first appeared in an official policy document of the Supreme People's Court. The *Outline* announced that the Supreme People's Court will issue an official document on a nationwide Case Guidance System, specifying guiding cases selection criteria, selection procedure, publication channels as well as application principles.[831]

The 2005 *Reform Outline* opened a new chapter in the evolution of China's Case Guidance System. As of 2005, the key issue is no longer *whether* case law is necessary or possible in China, but rather *how* a nationwide Case Guidance System should be designed. The Supreme People's Court, local courts at various levels and legal scholars all joined this quest. A series of research projects and court experiments were launched soon after the publication of the 2005 Reform Outline.

Continuing its existing practice of selecting and publishing model cases, the Supreme People's Court launched three research projects in 2005 on the use of cases in court practice,[832] which generated some of the first nationwide empirical reports.[833] Drawing upon these research results, the Research Department of the Supreme People's Court made a first draft document in 2006, containing rules on operation of a nationwide Case Guidance System.[834] The draft was circulated to judges, academics and the Standing Committee of the National People's Congress for comments and suggestions.[835] Legal Scholars were invited to submit academic draft versions.[836] In five years' time, the Research Department of the Supreme People's Court produced about 40

[830] The Chinese term is 案例指导制度(Anli Zhidao Zhidu).

[831] See Supreme People's Court of the People's Republic of China 2005, paragraph 2.

[832] The Supreme People's Court did not carry out the research projects itself, but instructed three institutes that are affiliated to the Supreme People's Court to conduct the research, see Jiang 2011a.

[833] The research results were published in Research Department of the Supreme People's Court 2007.

[834] Jiang 2011a.

[835] Huang & Cao 2010, Jiang 2011a and interviews CN20110615, CN20110622, CN20110709.

[836] Huang & Cao 2010 and interviews CN20110615, CN20110622, CN20110709.

drafts,[837] before the final document was released in November 2010.

While the Supreme People's Court was busy drafting rules on selecting and publishing model cases, lower courts at various levels started to experiment with their own Case Guidance Systems. It was reported that more than ten Higher People's Courts as well as some Intermediate People's Courts and District Courts devised their own case selection and publication mechanisms.[838]

The courts' efforts to explore various designs of a Case Guidance System concurred with animated debates in the Chinese legal academic world. The remaining part of this subparagraph will examine some of the most debated issues.

I. Which courts should be authorized to select guiding cases?

The Chinese judiciary has a hierarchy of four levels:

(1) The Supreme People's Court

(2) Higher People's Courts (the highest court in each province)

(3) Intermediate People's Courts (courts in cities) and

(4) District People's Courts (courts in districts and counties)

Everyone agrees that the Supreme People's Court should have the power to select guiding cases. The key issue of debate is whether courts of any other level(s) should also be authorized to select guiding cases. Roughly three opinions can be discerned:

Opinion 1: Only the Supreme People's Court should be authorized to select guiding cases, because otherwise conflicts between guiding cases selected by different courts may erode the unity of the law, thus defeating the very purpose of the Case Guidance System.[839]

Opinion 2: Higher People's Courts should also be authorized to select guiding cases.[840] The key argument is that there are vast regional differences in China. Insufficient account will be taken of

[837] Jiang 2011a.
[838] Shen 2009a, p. 5.
[839] Chen 2006, p. 101, Yan 2009, p. 142 and Ding 2008b, p. 145.
[840] Shen & Liu & Fan 2009, p. 97 and Liu 2009, p. 112.

these regional differences, if the Supreme People's Court is the only court authorized to select model cases.[841]

Opinion 3: Not only the Supreme People's Court and Higher People's Courts, but also Intermediate Courts in some large cities should be authorized to select guiding cases.[842] One of the key arguments is again the vast regional differences in China.[843]

II. What should be the selection criteria?

Various criteria have been put forward for the selection of guiding cases. The common ones are:

(1) Guiding cases should be representative/typical.[844] This is believed to be one of the selection criteria used by the *Gazette*.[845]

(2) Guiding cases should concern new issues.[846] This is also believed to be one of the selection criteria used by the *Gazette*.[847]

(3) Guiding cases should be those that deal with difficult issues.[848]

(4) Guiding cases should be of significant influence.[849]

(5) Guiding cases should be of general guiding value for the application of the law.[850]

In general, it seems that there is a majority view that guiding cases can be most valuable where[851]

(1) they fill loopholes in the law, i.e. they provide a good solution to a question of law to which the existing sources of law provide no answer, or

---

841 Li 2009b, p. 90 and Huang & Jiang 2009.

842 Shen & Liu & Fan 2009, p. 97 and Huang 2009, p. 50

843 Huang 2009, p. 50.

844 The Chinese term is 典型性(Dianxingxing).

845 Ding 2008b, p. 141.

846 The Chinese term is 新颖性(Xinyingxing).

847 Research Group of the Higher People's Court of Beijing 2007, p. 345.

848 The Chinese term is 疑难性(Yinanxing). See Qin 2007.

849 The Chinese term is 重大影响性(Zhongda Yingxiangxing). See Li 2009b, p. 88.

850 The Chinese term is 在法律适用上具有普遍指导意义(Zai falu shiyong shang you pubian zhidao yiyi). See Huang 2009, p. 54.

851 Research Group of the Higher People's Court of Beijing 2007.

(2) they provide sensible interpretations to vague terms or rules in legislation.

III. What kind of force should be attributed to the selected guiding cases?

What kind of force should be attributed to the selected guiding cases is probably the most sensitive and difficult question in the debate on China's Case Guidance System, because it touches upon the constitutional limits of the power of the judiciary in China. According to the Chinese constitution, the judiciary only possesses the power to *apply* the law, but not to *make* law.[852] A conservative view in China holds that, attributing binding force to selected guiding cases would promote the selected cases to the status of a (quasi) source of law.[853] Such a practice would be equal to granting lawmaking power to the judiciary, which is incompatible with the Chinese constitution.[854]

The constitutional restraints contrast with a much felt practical need to attribute more than pure reference status to selected model cases. The fact that selected model cases do not have clearly defined binding force upon judges is perceived to be a key problem in local courts' experiments.[855] As the model cases do not have clearly defined force, lower judges do not take them seriously, according to some empirical reports.[856] An empirical research on the experiments in Sichuan Higher People's Court suggests that, given the weak force of the selected cases, it is unrealistic to expect lower judges to voluntarily consult and follow them.[857] Another empirical report suggests that, as long as selected model cases do not have clearly defined force, they will eventually end up having no more value than cases in textbooks.[858]

---

852 See Art. 126 of the Chinese Constitution.

853 Li Shichun sees this as a "constitutional risk" of the Case Guidance System, see Li 2009a.

854 Li 2009a.

855 See the literature cited in the following three footnotes.

856 Research Group of the Higher People's Court of Beijing 2007, Zhu 2008, p. 36-37, Li 2009b; Zhu 2008, p 93 and Liu 2009, p. 112.

857 Li 2009b, p. 93.

858 Liu 2009, p. 112.

As a compromise between the constitutional limits and the practical need, attributing *de facto* binding force to selected guiding cases gained much support in the debate. Proponents of *de facto* binding force generally based their standpoint on three arguments:[859]

(1) Although there is no sufficient legal basis to grant legal binding force to model cases, the current legal framework does not exclude the possibility of granting *de facto* binding force to guiding cases.

(2) The purpose of the Case Guidance System will be defeated if selected model cases are of no more than reference value.

(3) It is a common practice in civil law jurisdictions that cases (decided by the highest judges) have *de facto* binding force.

IV. Should judges be allowed to cite guiding cases in their judgments?

A question that is related to the force of selected guiding cases is whether judges should be allowed to cite guiding cases in judgments. It has been a long-standing practice among Chinese judges that they do not cite previous cases in judgments, even if they have followed or drawn inspiration from previous judgments.[860] In fact, some local courts that have experimented with selecting and publishing model cases (e.g. in Shanghai,[861] Shenyang[862] and Tianjin[863]) explicitly forbid judges from citing published model cases in judgments. The courts seem to be concerned that the selected model cases, once cited, would rise to the status of precedents, thus giving the impression that the courts are making law.

However, proponents of a nationwide Case Guidance System realize that the purpose of the Case Guidance System may not be achieved if judges would not be allowed to cite the selected

[859] Deng 2007, Ding 2008b, p. 145, Yuan 2009, p. 108 and Li 2009b, p. 93.
[860] Wang 2006, p. 15.
[861] Research Department of the Higher People's Court of Shanghai 2009, p. 65.
[862] Zhang 2009, p. 133.
[863] Rao & Liao 2009, p. 114.

guiding cases in judgments.[864] As a compromise, it was suggested that guiding cases could be cited as arguments or reasons in a judgment, but not as the (sole) legal basis upon which a judicial decision is made.[865]

V. What should be the sanctions if judges refuse to follow applicable guiding cases?

Proponents of *de facto* binding force suggest that when lower judges refuse to follow applicable guiding cases, they must state in their judgments the reason(s) why they do not apply the guiding cases.[866] Some of them even suggest that lower courts, if they do not follow a guiding case, should report to the higher courts that had selected the guiding case.[867]

Possible sanctions could, according to these proponents, include: [868]

(1) Litigants should be allowed to appeal a judgment on the ground that the judgment did not follow one or more applicable guiding case(s).
(2) Higher courts should be authorized to reverse a judgment made by a lower court in an appeal procedure, if the judgment did not follow applicable guiding case(s) and reached an unjust result.
(3) Refusing to follow applicable guiding case(s) should be made a relevant factor that could negatively influence the evaluation of judges.

In sum, creating a nationwide Case Guidance System involves a number of complicated issues. It took the Supreme People's Court six years to draft an official policy document that clarifies the highest court's position on some of the debated issues. The next subparagraph will examine the *Provisions of the Supreme People's Court Concerning Work on Guiding Cases* released in November 2010 to ascertain the choices made by the Supreme

[864] Liu 2009, p. 112 and Hou 2008.
[865] Hu & Yu 2009, p. 18 and Research Department of the Supreme People's Court 2007.
[866] Hu & Yu 2009, p. 43.
[867] Research Group of the Higher People's Court of Beijing 2007.
[868] Li 2009b, p. 93 and Research Group of the Editor's Office of People's Court Daily 2007.

People's Court and the possible considerations that have shaped the Supreme People's Court's choices.

3.3 The Supreme People's Court's design of a nationwide Case Guidance System

The Provisions of the Supreme People's Court Concerning Work on Guiding Cases contains only 10 articles and 892 words. Obviously, it is impossible for such a short document to specify all the details of a nationwide Case Guidance System. It has been reported that the Supreme People's Court is now drafting another document called the *Implementation Details to the Provisions Concerning Work on Guiding Cases*,[869] which contains more detailed rules on the operation of the Case Guidance System. When the *Implementation Details Document* will be released was yet unknown at the time when this study was concluded in July 2014. The next subparts will take a closer look at the Provisions released by the Supreme People's Court in 2010 by examining its legal basis and the specific rules contained in it.

3.3.1 The legal basis of the Case Guidance System

The *Provisions Concerning Work on Guiding Cases* refers to the *Organic Law of the People's Courts* (hereinafter the *Organic Law*)[870] and other laws as its legal basis, without further specifying which article(s) of the *Organic Law* or which other laws serve(s) as its legal basis. It can be reasonably inferred that the Supreme People's Court at least intends to use Article 32 of the *Organic Law* as a legal basis.[871] This article provides that "the Supreme People's Court interprets questions concerning the specific application of laws and decrees in judicial proceedings."[872] The underlying reasoning seems to be that the Supreme People's Court sees the

[869] The Chinese term is 案例指导工作规定实施细则(Anli Zhidao Gongzuo Guiding Shishi Xize), see Yuan 2013. This document will be referred to as the *Implementation Details Document* in the remaining part of this study.
[870] The Chinese term is 人民法院组织法(Renmin Fayuan Zuzhi Fa).
[871] Gao & Cao 2010, paragraph 1.
[872] My translation.

practice of selecting and publishing guiding cases as a way of interpretating laws and decrees.[873] This reasoning seems particularly attractive, as it tends to suggest that the Case Guidance System merely enables the Supreme People's Court to *interpret* laws and decrees, but not to make law. The border between interpretation and judicial lawmaking is of course not clear-cut. However, by addressing the Case Guidance System as a mechanism of legal interpretation, the Supreme People's Court at least avoids openly challenging the formal restraints on its power.

3.3.2 Details of the Supreme People's Court's design

The Supreme People's Court's design follows the existing three-phase pattern,[874] dividing the operation of the Case Guidance System into selection, publication and application phases. The *Regulations Concerning Work on Guiding Cases* provides relatively clear rules on the selection and publication phases, but remains vague on the application phase. As will be discussed in greater detail below, in the 2010 document the Supreme People's Court does not provide a clear answer to the crucial question as to what kind of force should be attributed to guiding cases.

3.3.2.1 The selection phase

The *Regulations Concerning Work on Guiding Cases* addresses three key aspects of the selection phase: case selection power, case selection criteria and case selection procedure. The remaining part of this subparagraph will examine these three aspects in greater details.

I. Case selection power

Article 1 of the *Provisions* makes it clear that only the SPC has the power to select guiding cases. One of the earlier drafts intended to extend case selection power to higher people's courts

[873] Gao & Cao 2010.

[874] See the paragraph on the basic design and evolution of China's Case Guidance System in this chapter.

and the military court,[875] but obviously the Supreme People's Court eventually decided not to go that far.

Restricting the case selection power to the Supreme People's Court may be largely induced by the fact that the *Organic Law of the People's Courts* only authorizes the Supreme People's Court to interpret laws and decrees. Since the Supreme People's Court seems to portray the Case Guidance System as a mechanism to fulfil its task of interpreting laws and decrees, it is not surprising that the case selection power is restricted to the Supreme People's Court.

II. Case selection criteria

A minimum formal criterion is that a judgment must have taken legal effect[876] before it can be considered as a candidate guiding case.[877] In addition, a guiding case must meet at least one of the following substantive criteria:[878]

(1) it is of widespread concern in society;[879]
(2) it concerns issues on which legal provisions are of relatively general nature;[880]
(3) it is of a typical nature;[881]
(4) it involves difficult, complicated or new types of legal issues;[882]
(5) it can have a guiding effect in other ways.[883]

The last criterion is obviously intended as a catch-all, so that the Supreme People's Court will have the flexibility to develop new criteria in the future. The second, the third and the fourth criterion

---

875 Zhao 2009.

876 "Taking legal effect" means, in the Chinese legal language, that a judgment can no longer be reversed by a regular appeal procedure.

877 Article 2 Provisions Concerning Work on Guiding Cases.

878 Ibid.

879 The Chinese term is 社会广泛关注的 (Shehui Guangfan Guanzhude).

880 The Chinese term is 法律规定比较原则的 (Falu Guiding Bijiao Yuanzede).

881 The Chinese term is 具有典型性的 (Juyou Dianxingxingde).

882 The Chinese term is 疑难复杂或者新类型的(Yinan Fuza huozhe Xin Leixingde).

883 The Chinese term is 其它具有指导作用的案例 (Qita Juyou Zhidao Zuoyong de Anli).

are not surprising, as both the Supreme People's Court and local experimenting courts appear to have been using these criteria for years in their practice of selecting model cases.[884] It is fairly plain that these criteria are relevant, as they concern cases that usually require interpreting legislative rules.

The relevance of the first criterion, however, is not self-evident. If a nationwide Case Guidance System is an instrument for interpreting laws and decrees, it is not evident why extensive public attention or widespread public concern should be a decisive factor in the selection of guiding cases. After all, a case that attracts extensive public attention or raises widespread concern in society does not necessarily involve complicated issues of legal interpretation. Furthermore, it is striking that the social concern-criterion is placed at the top of the list. Such a prominent place may be related to the recent populist trend in the Chinese judiciary. As Liebman rightly observes, after three decades of legal reforms, there is a public perception in China that the law is inaccessible to the public and that the legal system served only those with power or influence.[885] Courts in China are trying to ease the widespread public discontent with the judiciary by being more responsive to the needs and opinions of the public.[886] Placing the public attention criterion as a top criterion may be induced by the Supreme People's Court's wish to portray itself as being responsive to the needs of the people.

III. Case selection procedure

A case normally needs to go through three stages before obtaining the status of a guiding case: the recommendation, the preliminary review, and the final decision stages.[887] The *Provisions Concerning Work on Guiding Cases* provides that the Supreme People's Court will set up a coordinating office called the Case

---

[884] See the relevant passages in the previous subparagraph that review different proposals of selection criteria in the case law debate in China.
[885] Liebman 2011b, p. 171.
[886] See e.g. Liebman 2011a and Liebman 2011b.
[887] Art. 4 and Art. 5 Provisions Concerning Work on Guiding Cases.

Guidance Work Office[888] to take care of, among other things, the administrative work of selection.[889]

(1) The recommendation stage

It appears that the Supreme People's Court intends to encourage broad participation in the recommendation stage. Article 4 of the *Provisions* allows courts at all levels to recommend cases for selection.[890] Moreover, article 5 allows wide public participation: virtually everyone outside the judiciary is allowed to recommend cases for selection.[891] This public participation approach seems to be an interesting innovation by the Supreme People's Court. Up till the release of the *Provisions*, the public had not been able to participate in the selection of cases, as both the Supreme People's Court and local experimenting courts have relied solely on cases recommended by their own judges or by lower courts.[892]

(2) The preliminary review stage

All recommended cases arrive at the Case Guidance Work Office, which conducts a preliminary review.[893] This Office makes an initial selection using the criteria in article 2 of the *Provisions*. Cases that, in the opinion of the Office, meet the criteria are then presented to the President or one of the Vice Presidents of the Supreme People's Court, who will decide whether or not to present these cases to the Adjudication Committee[894] of the Supreme People's Court for final selection.[895]

(3) The final decision stage

---

[888] The Chinese term is 案例指导工作办公室 (Anli Zhidao Gongzuo Bangongshi).

[889] Art. 3 Provisions Concerning Work on Guiding Cases.

[890] Technically speaking, only Higher People's Courts and the Military Court are allowed to recommend cases *directly* to the Supreme People's Court, whereas Intermediate People's Courts and district courts must recommend cases to their immediate upper-level courts, see Art. 4 of the Provisions Concerning Work on Guiding Cases.

[891] For a critical discussion of this provision see Duan 2012.

[892] See e.g. Chen & Li 2003, Li & Meng 2002 and Fan 2009.

[893] Art. 6 Provisions Concerning Work on Guiding Cases.

[894] The Chinese term is 审判委员会 (Shenpan Weiyuanhui).

[895] Art. 6 Provisions Concerning Work on Guiding Cases.

It is the Adjudication Committee of the Supreme People's Court that has the final say in the selection procedure. The Adjudication Committee discusses the cases that have passed the preliminary review and makes a final selection decision, according to Art. 6 of the *Provisions*.[896]

Every court in China has an Adjudication Committee, which is the highest decision-making body in a court.[897] The Adjudication Committee of the Supreme People's Court consists of the president, the vice presidents, the chief judges of all the trial divisions and a number of senior judges of the Supreme People's Court.[898] The Supreme People's Court's Adjudication Committee is particularly powerful within the judiciary, since it is the only body that possesses the power to issue judicial interpretations.[899] Judicial interpretations issued by the Adjudication Committee of the Supreme People's Court can be cited as the legal basis in judgments[900], so they have acquired the status of a source of law in China.[901]

For a long time, the Adjudication Committee of the SPC used to be the only body that had the power to decide which cases could get published in the *Gazette*.[902] In 1998 however, the SPC relaxed the case selection procedure.[903] As of that year, cases could get published in the *Gazette* with the approval of merely one vice president so that no discussion or approval by the Adjudication Committee was required any more.[904]

---

[896] Art. 6 Provisions Concerning Work on Guiding Cases.
[897] Art. 10 Organic Law of the People's Courts.
[898] Art. 6 of the *Opinions of the Supreme People's Court on the Reform and Improvement of the Institution of Adjudication Committee*, see Supreme People's Court of the People's Republic of China 2010c.
[899] Wang 2006, p. 24 footnote 68. The Chinese term for judicial interpretations is 司法解释(Sifa Jieshi). For more details on judicial interpretations see Keith & Lin 2009.
[900] Art. 7 Provisions of the Supreme People's Court on the Work of Judicial Interpretation, see Supreme People's Court of the People's Republic of China 2007.
[901] Wang 2006.
[902] Zhou 2009, p. 142-143.
[903] Zhou 2004, p. 5.
[904] Ibid.

The *Provisions Concerning Work on Guiding Cases* reinstalls the Adjudication Committee's discussion and approval procedure in a nationwide Case Guidance System. Reinstalling this "heavier" procedure is probably meant to strengthen the authority of the selected guiding cases.[905] The underlying reasoning seems to be that cases selected by the highest decision-making body of the highest court should be taken very seriously. This procedure may also serve to enhance the formal legitimacy of the Case Guidance System. Since the Adjudication Committee already possesses the power to issue judicial interpretations, it can be argued that selecting guiding cases is but another way to exercise the power of judicial interpretation, so that the Supreme People's Court does not exceed limits on its power by introducing a nationwide Case Guidance System.

3.3.2.2 The publication phase

Cases selected by the Adjudication Committee of the Supreme People's Court will be published through three channels: the *Gazette*, the website of the Supreme People's Court and the *People's Court Daily*, according to Art. 6 Para. 2 of the *Provisions Concerning Work on Guiding Cases*.[906] In addition, the Case Guidance Work Office will make a compilation of guiding cases every year, as Art. 9 of the *Provisions* prescribes.[907]

3.3.2.3 The application phase

There is only one vague rule in the *Provisions* that concerns the application of guiding cases: when deciding similar cases, courts at all levels should "*Canzhao* (参照)" guiding cases issued by the Supreme People's Court.[908] This rule is confusing, as the term "*Canzhao*" is susceptible to different interpretations.[909]

---

905 Interviews CN20110615, CN20110622 and CN20110709.

906 The Chinese term is 人民法院报(Renmin Fayuanbao).

907 Art. 9 Provisions Concerning Work on Guiding Cases.

908 Art. 7 Provisions Concerning Work on Guiding Cases.

909 See the various views expressed in Li 2011.

Literally, the term *Canzhao* can be translated as "consult" or "refer to".[910] Accordingly, a literal interpretation suggests that although judges must consult guiding cases, they have discretion as to whether or not they eventually follow the guiding cases. However, the director of the Research Department of the Supreme People's Court, Hu Yunteng, expressed a different view in an interview with the media.[911] Hu breaks the term *Canzhao* into two parts. The first part *Can* (参) means *Cankao* (参考, literal meaning: consult, refer), whereas the second part *Zhao* (照) means *Zunzhao* (遵照, literal meaning: obey, follow), according to him. *Cankao* means that, as Hu explains, while deciding cases that are not similar to guiding cases, judges may consult guiding cases for inspiration. While deciding cases that are similar to guiding cases, lowers courts must follow (*Zunzhao*) guiding cases, explains Hu. He continues to stress that judges must state convincing reasons where they refuse to follow applicable guiding cases, otherwise litigants may appeal on that ground.[912] In the interview Hu stresses that he was merely expressing his personal opinions.[913] It is uncertain whether his personal views correspond with the official position of the Supreme People's Court.

Furthermore, it is noteworthy that in the *Provisions* the Supreme People's Court does not touch upon two of the most debated questions concerning the application of guiding cases: whether judges are allowed to cite guiding cases in judgments and what the sanctions are if judges refuse to follow applicable guiding cases. The future will tell whether the *Implementation Details Document*, which was still being drafted at the time this study was concluded, will provide more clarity on these crucial points.

---

[910] See The English translation of Provisions Concerning Work on Guiding Cases in Appendix 5.
[911] See Jiang 2011b.
[912] Jiang 2011b.
[913] Jiang 2011b

4. Functioning of the Case Guidance System since 2010

By the time this study was concluded in July 2014, the Supreme People's Court published 31 guiding cases.[914] These cases cover civil, criminal and administrative law.[915] As Figure 16 illustrates, the vast majority of the guiding cases was decided by lower courts, while the Supreme People's Court itself only decided two of the guiding cases.[916]

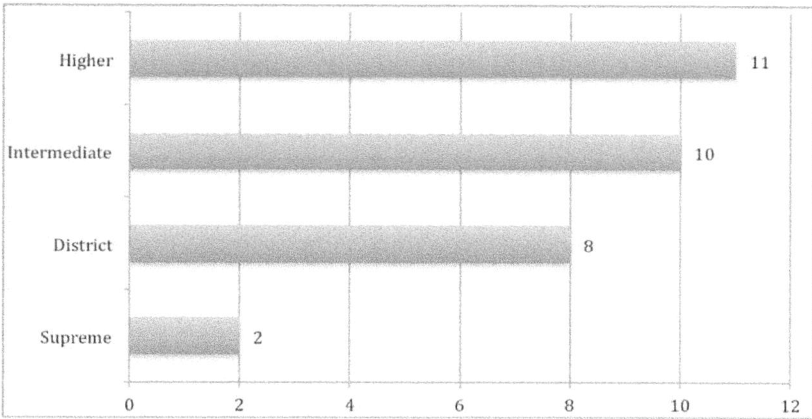

Figure 16 Number of guiding cases per level of court

The guiding cases are published in a format that consists of six parts:[917]

(1) Key words
(2) Main points of the judgment
(3) Relevant legal rule(s)
(4) Basic facts
(5) Results of the judgment
(6) Reasons for the judgment

---

914 English translation of all the published guiding cases can be found on the website of the Stanford China Guiding Cases Project, http://cgc.law.stanford.edu/guiding-cases/.

915 For details see Gechlik 2014, chart 2.

916 For details see Gechlik 2014, chart 3.

917 For details see the example guiding cases in the Appendix 6 and 7 of this study.

It should be noted that the published guiding cases are not the original judgments, but are summaries of the original judgments edited by the Supreme People's Court. Not only the main points of the judgment where a rule or principle is drawn from the judgment, but also the facts of the case and the reasons for the judgment have been edited by the Supreme People's Court. The final part of every guiding case (reasons for the judgment) does not tell the readers why the Supreme People's Court chose the judgment as a guiding case, but gives a summary of the reasons employed by the court that has made the judgment to justify its decision. In a sense, the Supreme People's Court fulfils the role of a narrator that tells the reader what a guiding case is about and what rules or principles can be distilled from it, but it should be noted that the published guiding cases do not contain the Supreme People's Court's comments on the guiding cases, nor any explanation as to whether other courts have adopted alternative approaches in similar cases and if so, why the solution chosen by the court that has made the selected judgment is preferable.

The impact of published guiding cases on court practice in China is yet largely unknown.[918] After all, the first batch of guiding cases were not published until late December 2011, which means that Chinese judges have had barely three years' experience with guiding cases. Due to limited time and resources, I have not been able to carry out systematic fieldwork in China to investigate how Chinese judges deal with published guiding cases. An empirical study by the China Guiding Cases Project of Stanford Law School indicates that the impact of published guiding cases on court practice in China has thus far been rather limited.[919] The results of this study indicate that nearly half of the Chinese judges that have participated in the research have never read the *Provisions Concerning Work on Guiding Cases*.[920] The results also show that

---

[918] Academic publications on the Case Guidance System have continued to emerge in China since 2010, but these publications contain largely normative discussions on, among other things, the interpretation of the *Provisions Concerning Work on Guiding Cases* and methods of using guiding cases, rather than empirical data on the actual application of guiding cases in court practice.

[919] Stanford Law School China Guiding Cases Project 2013.

[920] Stanford Law School China Guiding Cases Project 2013, p. 3.

43.8% of the participating judges have never discussed a guiding case with other judges, attorneys or legal experts, and that 61.8% of the judges reported that they had never considered guiding cases in their adjudication practice.[921]

5. Reflections on the Case Guidance System

Media reports in China are largely very enthusiastic about the Case Guidance System. The *Legal Daily*, a newspaper controlled by the Central Political-Legal Committee of the Communist Party, praises the Supreme People's Court's *Provisions Concerning Work on Guiding Cases* as a "symbol of epoch-marking significance".[922] The title of another report in the same newspaper also radiates optimism, which says "Case Guidance, Adjudication Says Farewell to Like Case Being Treated Differently".[923]

The reaction of Chinese legal scholars to the nationwide Case Guidance System introduced by the Supreme People's Court is less one-sided than the media. Some legal scholars did express critical thoughts on this newly introduced legal institution.[924] The focus of the case law discourse is, however, on the improvement and refinement of the selection and application of guiding cases under the framework of the Case Guidance System instead of seeking alternative or supplementary instruments.[925]

This study, however, doubts whether the Case Guidance System *alone* would be sufficient to solve the problems that it is intended to address. It is, in the first place, doubtful whether the Case Guidance System is able to produce a sufficient amount of guiding cases that can meet the vast demand in legal practice throughout China. As has been revealed in the previous paragraph, the Supreme People's Court has only published 31 guiding cases in nearly four years. Given the fact that courts across China normally

---

921 Stanford Law School China Guiding Cases Project 2013, p. 3-4.
922 Jiang 2011a.
923 Cao 2010.
924 See e.g. Huang 2011 and Lu 2011.
925 See e.g. Huang 2011, Lu 2011 and Mou 2014.

handle more than 12 million cases each year,[926] it does not seem very likely that the very small number of guiding cases selected through the Case Guidance System would be able to eliminate all the possible uncertainties in court practice throughout China.

One may of course argue that the reason why only a very small number of guiding cases has been published so far is that the Supreme People's Court has yet but limited experience with selecting guiding cases so that it adopts a cautious attitude towards case selection at the beginning. Once the Supreme People's Court has gained sufficient experience with case selection, one may continue to argue, the number of published guiding cases is likely to increase.

This argument, however, is not convincing. In the first place, it is not true that the Supreme People's Court has but limited experience with selecting guiding cases. As has been revealed previously in this chapter, the Supreme People's Court has been selecting model cases for the *Gazette* for almost three decades.[927] One may of course argue that the case selection procedure for publication in the *Gazette* is different from that for the nationwide Case Guidance System. However, it should be noted that the purpose of and criteria for case selection for the *Gazette* do not differ fundamentally from those for the Case Guidance System. It is not unlikely that the Supreme People's Court indeed adopts a particularly cautious approach towards case selection in the early years of the Case Guidance System. However, this cautious attitude is neither the only nor the most fundamental obstacle that prevents the Case Guidance System from producing a sufficient amount of guiding cases. The complicated and time-consuming selection procedure, as will be further analysed in the following passages, is a much more fundamental obstacle, which makes it unlikely that the Case Guidance System will be able to produce a sufficient amount of guiding cases that can satisfy the demand in court practice.

Art. 6 of the *Provisions Concerning Work on Guiding Cases* prescribes that a candidate case must ultimately be approved

---

[926] According to the statistics provided by the Supreme People's Court, courts in China handled 12,396,632 cases in 2012, see http://www.court.gov.cn/qwfb/sfsj/201312/t20131213_190137.htm.

[927] See the paragraph of this chapter on the evolution of the Case Guidance System.

by the Adjudication Committee of the Supreme People's Court before it can become a guiding case and gets published. As revealed earlier in this chapter, the Adjudication Committee of the Supreme People's Court consists of the president, the vice presidents, the chief judges of all the trial divisions and a number of senior judges of the Supreme People's Court.[928] This is a group of around 30 persons.[929] The *Working Rules of the Adjudication Committee of the Supreme People's Court* provides that decisions of the Adjudication Committee are to be made at Committee meetings, and that no Committee meeting is to take place unless more than half of the members are present.[930] A decision of the Adjudication Committee must be approved by more than half of the members of the Committee.[931] Moreover, the Adjudication Committee is entrusted with a series of highly important tasks and responsibilities such as discussing and deciding death penalty cases submitted by higher people's courts and the military court, discussing and deciding retrial cases, discussing and deciding counter appeal cases brought by the Supreme People's Procuratorate under the adjudication supervisory procedure as well as discussing and approving judicial interpretations.[932] Given these procedural prescriptions and the heavy tasks and responsibilities of the Adjudication Committee, it is doubtful whether the Adjudication Committee of the Supreme

---

[928] Art. 6 of the *Opinions of the Supreme People's Court on the Reform and Improvement of the Institution of Adjudication Committee*, see Supreme People's Court of the People's Republic of China 2010c.

[929] For a partial list of the members of the Adjudication Committee of the Supreme People's Court and their responsibilities see http://www.court.gov.cn/jgsz/zgrmfyld/.

[930] Art. 4 of the *Working Rules of the Adjudication Committee of the Supreme People's Court*. The Chinese title of this official document is 最高人民法院审判委员会工作规则(Zuigao Renmin Fayuan Shenpan Weiyuanhui Gongzuo Guize), see Supreme People's Court of the People's Republic of China 1993.

[931] Art. 9 of the *Working Rules of the Adjudication Committee of the Supreme People's Court*. It should be noted that this article provides that a decision needs the approval of more than half of the Committee members instead of half of the members that are present at a Committee meeting.

[932] This list is not exhaustive. For a complete list of the tasks and responsibilities of the Adjudication Committee see Art. 2 of the *Working Rules of the Adjudication Committee of the Supreme People's Court*.

People's Court is able to convene frequently enough and to have enough time to discuss and approve a sufficient amount of guiding cases each year to meet the demand in court practice throughout China.

In addition, it should be stressed that only a tiny proportion of guiding cases comes from judgments made by the Supreme People's Court itself.[933] The vast majority of guiding cases are selected from judgments made by lower level courts. According to the *Provisions Concerning Work on Guiding Cases*, candidate cases decided by a lower level court need to go through a selection procedure in the decision-making court itself and a selection procedure at each upper level court, which means that a case decided by a district level court needs to go through as many as four rounds of selection before it can ultimately become a guiding case and gets published. Given the fact that in each round of selection a positive decision by the Adjudication Committee of a lower level court is required and the Adjudication Committees of lower level courts not only need to follow practically the same working procedure as the Adjudication Committee of the Supreme People's Court, but also are entrusted with many important tasks and responsibilities,[934] it is plain that the vast majority of guiding cases need to go through a complicated and time consuming selection procedure, which further casts doubt on the ability of the Case Guidance System to generate a sufficient amount of guiding cases that are capable of meeting the vast demand for leading cases to clarify uncertainties and to enhance uniform application of the law in legal practice across China.

Not only is the selection procedure complicated and time-consuming, it is also a procedure shrouded in secrecy that lacks a transparent discourse. Although the public is allowed, at least in theory, to participate in the selection procedure by recommending candidate cases to the courts that have made the recommended

---

[933] So far, only two of the 31 published guiding cases are decided by the Supreme People's Court itself, see Gechlik 2014.

[934] For an impression of the tasks and the working procedures of the Adjudication Committees of lower level courts in China, see e.g. Intermediate People's Court of Zhengzhou City 2003 and Higher People's Court of Guangdong Province 2008.

judgments,[935] the selection procedure is nearly an entire black box to the outside world. It is, for example, nearly impossible for the public to know how many candidate cases have been considered during the selection procedure and what kind of cases have been involved in the selection.[936] It is also highly difficult, if not impossible, for the public to know whether courts have adopted alternative solutions to the legal problem(s) addressed in a guiding case and if so, why the approach of the guiding cases is preferable.[937] In fact, even the full facts of a guiding case and the legal reasoning of the court that has originally made the judgment are not plainly available to the public, as the published guiding cases are not the original judgments, but rather summaries of the original judgments edited by the Supreme People's Court.[938]

Such a non-transparent selection procedure may prevent the Case Guidance System from adequately achieving its desired effects. Due to the secrecy of the selection procedure and a lack of rational discourse, it is difficult for judges to know the full facts and the legal reasoning of the original judgment of a guiding case and it is also difficult for them to ascertain why a guiding case is selected and what purpose(s) the Supreme People's Court exactly intends to achieve with a selected guiding case. Consequently, judges may have difficulty in interpreting and applying the guiding cases, which means that different judges may interpret and apply the same guiding case differently, thus reducing the role of guiding cases in promoting consistent judgments.[939]

Another uncertainty that the non-transparent selection procedure causes is that guiding cases selected through such a

---

[935] Art. 5 Provisions Concerning Work on Guiding Cases.

[936] Occasionally, there are news reports that report how many cases have been considered, but they do not shed light on the exact type and content of the candidate cases that have been considered, see e.g. Zhang 2011.

[937] The discussion within the Adjudication Committee is to be kept secret and the minutes of the Committee meetings are classified documents that are not accessible to the public, see Art. 13 of the *Working Rules of the Adjudication Committee of the Supreme People's Court*.

[938] See paragraph 4 of this chapter.

[939] The analysis of guiding cases no. 26 by Gechlik and Dai illustrates, for example, how important the full facts of the original judgment are for the interpretation of a guiding case, see Gechlik & Dai 2014.

procedure may not have the support of the relevant legal communities, thus having limited effect in practice. In the Netherlands, as has been revealed in chapter two of this study, the fact that the Supreme Court decisions are particularly influential is related to two factors.[940] In the first place, the existence of a cassation system in the Netherlands makes sure that the Supreme Court has the final say in matters concerning legal points, so that judgments that ignore relevant Supreme Court decisions run the risk of being reversed in cassation appeal.[941] Moreover, the selection of leading cases in the Netherlands takes place in a process of rational discourse, which means that pros and cons of previous cases are often discussed in later cases and in scholarly writings.[942] Cases that win the most support in such a rational discourse are likely to be repeatedly followed and ultimately grow into leading cases. In other words, leading cases selected through such a process derive their influential status not only from the power of the author of the leading cases to reverse deviating judgments, but also from the substantive merits of the cases as evidenced in a certain consensus in the legal community expressed in a process of rational discourse. The Case Guidance System, however, does not involve an open discourse on the pros and cons of the candidate cases. The selection scheme is essentially top-down, putting considerable emphasis on the hierarchical status of the selectors, rather than on substantive arguments. It seems therefore fair to observe that the status of guiding cases selected under the Case Guidance System relies largely on the power of the selectors, but it is uncertain whether the selected cases do in fact enjoy support among the legal community. One of the reasons why many laws in China are poorly implemented is that they do not enjoy the support of the relevant (local) communities.[943] Given the non-transparent and the rather top-down style of case selection, it is not unlikely that guiding cases selected through the Case Guidance System will not enjoy the support of the relevant communities and will face similar difficulties in the application phase as many statutes do.

---

[940] See the paragraph on the way cases are used in adjudication in the Netherlands in chapter two of this study.
[941] Ibid.
[942] Ibid.
[943] See e.g. Van Rooij 2004 and Van Rooij 2006.

One last remark that needs to be made in this context is that, contrary to the Netherlands, China does not have a cassation system. Art. 11 of the *Organic Law of the People's Courts* provides that "(i)n the administration of justice, the people's courts adopt the system whereby the second instance is the last instance".[944] This means that a litigant may launch an appeal against a judgment of the court of first instance, but there is in principle no legal remedy any more against a judgment of the court of second instance. Which level of court has jurisdiction in first instance depends on various factors. In ordinary civil cases, for example, district courts are usually the court of first instance, but if a civil case has a significant international aspect, it must be tried by an intermediate people's court in first instance.[945] Under circumstances, higher people's courts and the Supreme People's Court can try civil cases in first instance.[946] In criminal cases, district courts normally have jurisdiction in first instance, but if a case concerns national security matters or terrorism, or if a case is likely to result in a sentence of life imprisonment or death penalty, it must be tried in first instance by an intermediate people's court.[947] Higher people's court and the Supreme People's Court may also try criminal cases in first instance, where the case can be deemed as "of major importance" in a province, respectively, in the entire country.[948]

China's trial system whereby the second instance is the final instance means that many cases may never have the possibility of reaching the Supreme People's Court. Accordingly, it is not apparent how the Supreme People's Court will be able to directly enforce the supposedly coercive force of guiding cases selected through the Case Guidance System. At least it does not seem

---

[944] Translation by the National People's Congress of China, see http://www.npc.gov.cn/englishnpc/Law/2007-12/13/content_1384078.htm.

[945] See Art. 18 and Art. 19 of China's Civil Procedure Code. When the Supreme People's Court tries a case in first instance, its judgment is the final judgment that is not susceptible to appeal, see Art. 11 Para. 4 Organic Law of the people's courts.

[946] See Art. 20 and Art. 21 of China's Civil Procedure Code.

[947] See Art. 19 and Art. 20 of China's Criminal Procedure Code.

[948] The Chinese term used in the Criminal Procedure Code is 重大刑事案件(Zhongda Xingshi Anjian), see Art. 21 and Art. 22 of China's Criminal Procedure Code.

possible for the Supreme People's Court to enforce the supposedly coercive force of guiding cases by reversing judgments made by district courts and intermediate people's courts that refuse to follow applicable guiding cases, as the existing trial system does not allow litigants to bring an appeal against judgments of these two levels of courts to the Supreme People's Court. In other words, even if the *Implementation Details Document* that the Supreme People's Court is drafting would eventually allow a court in second instance to reverse a judgment that refuses to follow an applicable guiding case as a sanction to courts that do not take guiding cases seriously, the power to enforce the supposedly coercive force of guiding cases through reversal of judgments would rest in the hands of hundreds of different courts across China.[949] This raises the questions how consequently, willingly and effectively these various courts would exercise this power to enforce the supposedly coercive force of guiding cases that they themselves did not select or substantively endorse. Of course, it is not unthinkable that the Supreme People's Court would design other instruments to enforce the coercive force of guiding cases, but even if the Supreme People's Court does come up with such instruments to sanction courts and judges that refuse to follow guiding cases, the concerns raised earlier in this subparagraph on the limited amount of guiding cases, the risk of conflicting interpretations of guiding cases and the uncertainty of sufficient support in the legal community still cast considerable doubt on the ability of the Case Guidance System to achieve the desired effects.

What has been said in this paragraph does not mean that the Case Guidance System will have any positive effect at all. What should be stressed is that it may not be wise for Chinese legal scholars, courts and media to focus *solely* on the Case Guidance System. Such a focus may lead to an attitude that treats the vast body of cases that have not been selected through the Case Guidance System as wastes, i.e. unusable remains of an official case selection procedure. A better view is to see the vast body of unselected cases as a hidden goldmine that may provide valuable materials for counterbalancing the limitations of legislation and for promoting consistency in judgments in China. A crucial question is

[949] For and extensive yet still incomplete list of intermediate courts in China see http://www.court.gov.cn/jgsz/qgfyml/.

how to develop proper ways to find and to make use of the treasures hidden in this vast body of unselected cases. The next chapter will elaborate on this point and will examine whether, and if so, what insights can be drawn from the experiences with case law in the Netherlands for China to further enhance its case law practice.

6. Concluding remarks

This chapter revealed that due to the lack of case law, the legislature in China has to take on an extremely difficult, if not impossible task of striking a proper balance in lawmaking among four competing requirements: adequacy, feasibility, certainty and adaptability.[950] This fundamental problem in the Chinese legal system as well as some specific problems such as like cases not being treated alike, lack of transparency in adjudication and judicial corruption, caused Chinese legal scholars and judges to actively search for a new legal institution to enhance the use of cases in adjudication.[951] In this quest, legal scholars and courts in China demonstrated considerable interest in the common law doctrine of precedent, but have not transplanted it to China.[952] Instead, courts and legal scholars designed and experimented with a practice of allowing higher courts to select and publish model cases, which are supposed to be followed in later court practice.[953] Such a practice is commonly referred to as the "Case Guidance System".[954] These efforts eventually resulted in a new legal institution, i.e. a nationwide Case Guidance System that allows the Supreme People's Court to select and publish guiding cases from candidate cases recommended by courts at all levels throughout China.[955]

It is doubtful whether the Case Guidance System alone would be sufficient to solve the problems that it is intended to address. The top-down case selection scheme and the exclusion of other actors such as legal scholars and practising lawyers cast doubt on the ability of the Case Guidance System to function as an

[950] Van Rooij 2006, p. 25-104.
[951] See paragraph 3 of this chapter.
[952] Ibid.
[953] Ibid.
[954] The Chinese term is 案例指导制度(Anli Zhidao Zhidu).
[955] Ibid.

institution through which societal norms can move bottom-up to become part of the national legal system.[956] Due to the rigid and time-consuming case selection procedure, it is doubtful whether the Case Guidance System would be able to produce a sufficient amount of guiding cases that is able to satisfy the demand for case law in court practice throughout China. Moreover, it is doubtful whether the non-transparent case selection procedure that restricts the power to select guiding cases to a small group of people within the judiciary that occupy high positions would be able to generate guiding cases that can count on a desirable degree of consensus and support in the legal community. It was submitted that it would not be wise for Chinese judges and legal scholars to focus solely on the Case Guidance System and the selected guiding cases. The vast body of unselected cases may actually be a hidden treasure, containing valuable materials that, if used properly, can supplement the Case Guidance System to achieve the purpose of counterbalancing the limitations of legislation and to enhance consistency in court judgments in China. The next chapter will elaborate on this last point.

---

[956] For an analysis of the need for an institution in China through which societal norms can move bottom-up to become part of the national legal system see Van Rooij 2006, p. 25-49.

Chapter 6

Case law mechanism, insights for China

Chapter 6 Case law mechanism, insights for China

1. Introduction

As has been analysed in the previous chapter, the Case Guidance System *alone* would probably not be sufficient to adequately solve the problems that it is intended to address.[957] A fundamental problem is that, as the previous chapter revealed, due to the lack of an institutionalized system through which societal norms can move bottom-up to become part of the national legal system, the legislature in China bears virtually all the burden and responsibility to make the law not only adequate and certain, but at the same time also feasible and adaptable.[958] This is an extremely difficult, if not impossible task for the legislature in such a large and fast-developing country as China with a unitary legal system where lawmaking is largely a top-down process dominated by a relatively small group of powerful people.[959] The Case Guidance System does not significantly change all this, as this new legal institution also works top down and runs through a single actor, i.e. the judiciary, without engaging a broader system of research and education that spreads cases beyond the confines of the court system.[960]

Another reason for this study to doubt whether the Case Guidance System alone would be adequate is that, due to its rigid and time-consuming case selection procedure, it is unlikely that the Case Guidance System would be able to produce a significant amount of guiding cases that can satisfy the need for leading cases in court practice across China. This means that the vast majority of cases will not be chosen as guiding cases and may thus be excluded from the Case Guidance System. This study submits that it can be very helpful to make effective use of the vast body of unselected cases in order to supplement the Case Guidance System and to mitigate the limitations of its top-down case selection scheme.

---

[957] See the last paragraph in the previous chapter that reflects on the limitations of the Case Guidance System.

[958] Van Rooij 2006, p. 47.

[959] Van Rooij 2006, p. 44-49.

[960] I wish to thank Van Rooij for inspiring me to derive these insights from the data presented in the previous chapter.

For an optimal use of the vast body of unselected cases, this study argues that it is very important to look beyond the courts and to mobilize other actors to further strengthen and develop not only the Case Guidance System, but also other relevant institutions and practices. It is, for example, important to keep investing in and improving case publication in China.[961] More importantly, this study argues that it is crucial for Chinese scholars to conduct systematic research into cases, and that legal education also has a meaningful role to play in the development of a well-functioning case law practice in China. The following two paragraphs will reflect on the case law mechanism in the Netherlands and explore the possible contribution by legal scholars and legal education in China in greater detail. The last paragraph of this chapter will further reflect on the experiences with case law in the Netherlands and add some final observations and remarks that may be helpful for enhancing the case law practice in China.

[961] This chapter will not elaborate on case publication. This is not only due to limited time and resources, but also because the Chinese judiciary has been making increasing efforts to enhance case publication in recent years. A noteworthy and positive initiative in this regard is that at the beginning of 2014 the Supreme People's Court launched a website "Judicial Opinions of China" (中国裁判文书网, Zhongguo Caipan Wenshu Wang, http://www.court.gov.cn/zgcpwsw/bj/), where all courts in China are supposed to publish all their judgments except those that satisfy one of the conditions not to be published as specified in Art. 4 of the *Supreme People's Court's Rules on Internet Publication of Judgments of People's Courts* (最高人民法院关于人民法院在互联网公布裁判文书的规定, Zuigao Renmin Fayuan Guanyu Renmin Fayuan zai Hulianwang Gongbu Caipan Wenshu de Guiding), see Supreme People's Court of the People's Republic of China 2013. Many courts have already been using this website to publish judgments. It is, however, nearly impossible to ascertain whether the courts that have been publishing judgments on this website do indeed adopt an active case publication policy and faithfully implement the Supreme People's Court's Rules on Internet Publication of Judgments, as outside researchers do not have access to the full judgment archives of these courts and therefore cannot verify the implementation of the Supreme People's Court's Rules by these courts.

2. Possible contributions by legal scholars to the development of case law in China

In the case law debate in China there is a clear emphasis on the role of courts and judges, as the debate chiefly focuses on questions such as which courts should be authorized to select cases, what kind of criteria judges should use to select cases and what kind of force should be attributed to selected guiding cases in court practice.[962] This study does not deny that courts and judges do have an important role to play in the functioning of case law, but it would be unwise to overlook the contribution that legal scholars can make to the development of a well-functioning case law mechanism. In the Netherlands, for example, legal scholars play an important role both in the publication and in the utilization phase of the case law mechanism.[963] This study argues that for the development of case law in China, it can be very helpful if Chinese legal scholars get involved and conduct similar research into cases as their colleagues in the Netherlands do. This argument is not based on copy-paste reasoning, i.e. Dutch scholars' research into cases makes a contribution to the functioning of the case law mechanism in the Netherlands, therefore Chinese scholars should adopt this practice. Instead, this argument is based on an analysis that consists of three steps. First, this study explores why extensive and systematic scholarly case research constitutes an important component of the case law mechanism in the Netherlands. Then it seeks to ascertain whether similar needs for scholarly case law research also exist in China. The final step is to assess whether it is feasible for Chinese legal scholars to contribute to the development of case law in China by doing systematic and extensive research into cases. Based on the answers to these three questions, this study argues that it is highly desirable for Chinese legal scholars to conduct systematic and extensive research into cases and to integrate such research results in their publications such as journal articles, handbooks and textbooks.

While exploring the question why scholarly case law research is an important component of the case law mechanism in

---

[962] See the paragraph that reviews the evolution of China's Case Guidance System in the previous chapter.
[963] See chapter one and chapter two.

the Netherlands, this study wishes to make a comparison between enacted laws and case law. When it comes to the functioning and development of enacted laws in codified legal systems, scholarly efforts to systemize, interpret and evaluate legislative provisions are commonly accepted as valuable in many of these legal systems.[964] Comparing the characteristics of enacted laws with those of case law reveals that, for the functioning and development of case law in codified legal systems, scholarly efforts to interpret, systemize and evaluate cases are equally needed as, if not more necessary than, their efforts to interpret, systemize and evaluate enacted laws.

A similarity between enacted laws and case law is that they both need systemization. Enacted laws need to be systemized, because it is hardly avoidable that the vast body of legislation in a codified legal system may contain conflicting provisions, and the relationship among various legislative provisions is not always self-evident.[965] The degree of systemization among previously decided cases is lower than that among legislative provisions. Whereas enacted laws in codified legal systems are usually drafted in a more or less systematic fashion, published cases in their raw form are mere *ad hoc* decisions in individual disputes. Moreover, unlike the legislature which enjoys a fairly high degree of discretion as to what to lay down in a piece of legislation, judges are often restricted in their decision-making by, among other things, the specific facts of the case as well as the claims and defences submitted by the litigating parties.[966] Accordingly, it is not surprising that judicial lawmaking takes place in a haphazard or even accidental way. It can take a series of cases that have a timespan of years or even decades to develop a set of more or less comprehensive rules that address a specific legal issue.[967] Therefore, in order to correctly appreciate the value of a particular previous court decision for the solution of a new legal problem, it is crucial to put the earlier decision in a proper context that involves not only relevant legislative provisions, but also related cases. Given the vast amount of previously decided

---

[964] See e.g. Yiannopoulos 1974, p. 82-83, David 1984, p. 142-144, Vranken 2005, p. 120 and De Cruz 2007, p. 72.
[965] See e.g. Ferdinandusse 2001, Heemskerk 2005, p. 129 and Raad van State 2013, p. 43.
[966] Vranken 1995, p. 9.
[967] See e.g. Owsia 1991, p. 43 and Giesen 2008, p. 565.

cases and the heavy workload of judges,[968] it is unrealistic to expect judges to do all the work of systemization by themselves. Nor is it, due to similar reasons, realistic to expect the legislature or practising lawyers to fulfil a major role in systemizing previous cases. Against this background, it is not surprising that legal scholars in the Netherlands have been playing a crucial role in case systemization.

Another similarity between enacted laws and case law is that they both need interpretation, although the specific techniques to interpret them are not the same.[969] Scholarly efforts to interpret legislative provisions have long been appreciated as valuable in the Netherlands and many other codified legal systems.[970] Again, given the heavy workload of judges, it is unlikely that they would have sufficient time to thoroughly analyse the meaning of each legislative provision that is susceptible to multiple interpretations in each dispute brought to court. Similarly, it is unlikely that judges would have sufficient time to thoroughly analyse and ascertain the essence of each previous case that is relevant for the resolution of a legal dispute in court. Scholarly efforts to explore the various interpretations of previous cases and their debates on the merits of each possible interpretation offer valuable assistance to judicial decision-making.[971] Thanks to scholarly interpretation of cases, judges no longer have to start from scratch while trying to ascertain the essence of a previous case. They can, for example, adopt a scholarly interpretation that has won the most support in scholarly debates. Of course, they can also make other choices, such as developing a new interpretation on the basis of the existing scholarly interpretations or adopting a scholarly interpretation that, although not having won the most support in scholarly debates, offers the most desirable solution in a specific dispute. In any event,

---

[968] See Fruytier e.a. 2013.

[969] For a comparison between the techniques of interpreting legislation and those of interpreting cases see Snijders 2007.

[970] Scholarly works in the early decades after the codification in the 19th century in France and the Netherlands, for example, were largely comments on legislative provisions that sought to reveal the meaning of the commented legislation, see Scholten 1931, p. 237-240.

[971] See interview with judges NL20131008-1, NL20131008-2, NL20131017, NL20131021, NL20130122 and NL20131031.

it seems fair to say that scholarly interpretations of cases offer valuable insights for judicial decision-making.

Still another aspect in which enacted laws and case law are similar is that neither of them can be flawless and both of them need to be constantly improved. One of the core activities of legal scholars in the Netherlands and other codified legal systems is to critically evaluate the work of the legislature by, among other things, checking for inconsistencies, ambiguities and loopholes in legislation.[972] There is no reason to assume that the work of judges never contains defects. No more than the legislature can judges foresee all the consequences of their decisions.[973] Nor is it uncommon that judgments contain imprecisely drafted expressions that cause ambiguities.[974] Legal institutions such as appeal and cassation can undoubtedly correct some mistakes in judicial decisions. However, it is unrealistic to expect the judiciary to remove all flaws in judicial decision-making through appeals and cassation.[975] After all, even the highest judges are capable of making mistakes or overlooking certain consequences of their decisions.[976] Given such limitations of judicial work, it is not surprising that scholarly efforts to critically evaluate cases make an important contribution to the functioning of case law in the Netherlands. Just as their critical examination of legislation helps the legislature to improve the quality of enacted laws, scholarly evaluation of cases offers valuable feedback to judges and stimulates them to improve the quality of adjudication, which leads

---

[972] Scholten 1931, p. 237-246 and Vranken 1995, p. 114.

[973] See e.g. Oldenhuis 2010 and Hartlief 2011.

[974] See e.g. Hartlief 2008, p. 896 and Kottenhage 2010b.

[975] In fact, whether or not appeal judges get a chance to correct mistakes made in first instance depends on whether at least one of the litigating parties initiates an appeal procedure. Whether the Supreme Court gets a chance to correct mistakes made by lower judges primarily depends on whether at least one of the litigating parties files a cassation appeal, although the law does allow the Procurator General to initiate a special cassation procedure called "cassatie in het belang der wet" (cassation in the interest of the law) according to Art. 78 Para. 1 Wet op de rechterlijke organisatie (Judicial Organisation Act).

[976] See e.g. Schutgens 2009, p. 854 and Oldenhuis 2010, p. 2460.

to better production and better application of cases in court practice.[977]

Having explored why scholarly efforts to systemize, interpret and evaluate cases play an important role in the case law mechanism in the Netherlands, this study continues to examine whether such needs also exist in China. Do court decisions in China constitute a coherent and easy to understand system so that no efforts of systemization would ever be required? Are court decisions in China drafted in such clear language that they would never be susceptible to different interpretations? It is difficult to imagine that these questions could be answered affirmatively. After all, cases produced by Chinese judges in their raw form are also mere *ad hoc* decisions in individual disputes. Moreover, it is not difficult to find examples where Chinese judgments contain ambiguities that may give rise to different interpretations.[978] Obviously, systemization and interpretation of cases are equally needed in China.

Is it possible, one might ask, that Chinese judges are able to fulfil this need by themselves so that no scholarly efforts to systemize and interpret cases would be needed? After all, contrary to the situation in the Netherlands, many Chinese courts have a research department staffed by judges who are allowed to do research without the burden to try cases.[979] In fact, research and trial judges in China have been making important contributions to the experiments with and the development of case law in China since the 1980s by, among other things, selecting cases for publication and by organizing them in a certain form.[980] Some of them even

---

[977] See the paragraph on the role of legal scholars in the case law mechanism of the Netherlands in chapter two.

[978] See e.g. Gechlik & Dai 2014.

[979] Interview CN20130408.

[980] Two examples of case reports selected and edited by judges in China are *China Law Reports* (中国审判案例要览 *Zhongguo Shenpan Anli Yaolan*) and *Selection of Cases Decided by People's Courts* (人民法院案例选 *Renmin Fayuan Anlixuan*), see http://njc.chinacourt.org/old/jxky/spyl.php.

take the initiative to write explanatory notes to published cases.[981] Why would scholarly efforts to systemize and interpret cases be needed, if Chinese judges are doing such work?

The efforts by Chinese judges to systemize and interpret cases are certainly more than welcome. However, given the vast amount of cases produced in China each year,[982] it is doubtful whether efforts by judges alone would be sufficient. The core task of the majority of Chinese judges is to resolve disputes brought to court, instead of conducting systematic and extensive legal research. Accordingly, the time that they are able to invest in case research is likely to be rather limited. Even the supposedly full-time research judges have to spend a lot of time handling bureaucratic tasks, such as drafting speeches for the leadership of the courts and processing court statistical information.[983] Consequently, their ability to fulfil the need for case systemization and interpretation should not be overestimated.

In addition to scholarly efforts to systemize and interpret cases, developing a well-functioning case law mechanism in China also requires scholarly efforts to evaluate cases. No more than their colleagues in the Netherlands are Chinese judges able to foresee all possible consequences of their decisions or to avoid making mistakes entirely.[984] The Chinese judiciary seems to be fairly aware

---

981 Some cases published in *Selection of Cases Decided by People's Courts* (人民法院案例选 *Renmin Fayuan Anlixuan*) are accompanied by comments written by judges, see Song 2009.

982 According to the statistics provided by the Supreme People's Court, all courts in China handled 12,396,632 cases in 2012, see http://www.court.gov.cn/qwfb/sfsj/201312/t20131213_190137.htm.

983 Interview CN20130408 and Chen 2012a.

984 In fact, even guiding cases selected by the Supreme People's Court are not completely flawless. Guiding case no. 1, for example, is about the question whether a clause in a brokerage contract is enforceable, which specifies liquidated damages in the event that the client, after obtaining some information and service from the broker, concludes a transaction with another broker or party. The judgment cites Art. 424 of the *Contract Law* (合同法 Hetong Fa) of China as its legal basis. This article only gives a definition of brokerage contract, but says nothing about the issue in question. A more relevant legislative provision and more accurate legal basis for the judgment is in fact Art. 426 of the Contract Law, which, although rather generally, specifies the conditions for the client's

of the fact that not all flaws in judicial work can be eliminated through appeal or other formal institutions within the courts. The leadership of the Supreme People's Court, for example, highly emphasises the need to submit the work of the courts to public oversight.[985] If monitoring and evaluation by the general public is accepted as valuable for the improvement of judicial work, it seems all the more reasonable to accept that evaluation by legal scholars, i.e. a group of people with legal expertise who operate in a academic forum, can offer valuable feedback to the courts in China and can stimulate them to improve the way they produce and use cases.[986]

Of course, the mere fact that scholarly efforts to systemize, interpret and evaluate cases are desirable in China does not in itself mean that it is possible for Chinese legal scholars to contribute to the development of case law in China. One possible obstacle for Chinese legal scholars to fulfil a substantial role in developing case law in China, one might argue, is that too few cases are published in China so that legal scholars do not have sufficient materials to work with.[987] However, it should be pointed out that the mere fact that not a large volume of cases have been published in China does not have to be an insurmountable obstacle for Chinese legal scholars to contribute to the development of case law. The case publication rate in the Netherlands, after all, has long remained less than half a per cent.[988] Even with the latest Internet technologies, the case publication rate in the Netherlands still has not exceeded 2%.[989] Such a low case publication rate has not prevented legal scholars in

---

obligation to pay for the broker's service. I wish to thank Dr Jin Zhenbao for contributing the analysis on this shortcoming in guiding case no. 1.

[985] Supreme People's Court of the People's Republic of China 2009 and Supreme People's Court of the People's Republic of China 2014, paragraph 7.

[986] In fact, the Chinese judiciary is increasingly appreciating the value of legal scholars. This is reflected in, among other things, a recent initiative of the judiciary to appoint law professors as part-time judges, see Wang & Gong 2013.

[987] For critical views on case publication in China see He 2005 and He 2006.

[988] See the paragraph on commercial case publication in the Netherlands in chapter one.

[989] Ibid.

the Netherlands from conducting meaningful case research. It is difficult to see why a low case publication rate in China would make scholarly case research impossible. In any event, the possibilities that Chinese legal scholars nowadays have do not seem to be much worse than what their Dutch colleagues had in the early decades of the 20th century. Since the 1980s, many courts in China have adopted the practice of selecting and publishing cases, either on paper or on their websites.[990] At the beginning of 2014, the Supreme People's Court launched a website where all courts in China are required to publish in principle all decided cases except those that meet the conditions not to be published.[991] In addition, Chinese legal scholars can nowadays make use of online commercial legal databases in China that contain a reasonable collection of cases.[992] Therefore, it seems fair to say that, although the case publication practice in China is still far from optimal, the situation is not so bad that no meaningful scholarly case research would be possible in China.

Another obstacle, one might argue, is that, contrary to the elaborate judgments in common law jurisdictions, Chinese judgments are drafted in a rigid and formalistic style, which rarely contains substantial legal reasoning or analysis, so that there is not much for legal scholars to find in such judgments.[993] This, again, does not have to render scholarly case research impossible. Dutch judgments also used to be drafted in a rigid and formalistic style. The *Lindenbaum/Cohen* case[994] decided by the Supreme Court in 1919, for example, was drafted in such a way that the decision seems to flow naturally from the Civil Code, although in fact the Supreme Court has drastically modified the law of tort by broadening the definition of unlawful act from violation of someone

[990] See e.g. Zhang & Zhu 2007, p. 66-67 and Han 2009.

[991] The website is called "Judicial Opinions of China"中国裁判文书网 (Zhongguo Caipan Wenshu Wang), see http://www.court.gov.cn/zgcpwsw/. For the rules on case publication on this website see Supreme People's Court of the People's Republic of China 2013.

[992] See e.g. http://china.findlaw.cn/case, http://law.cnki.net and http://china.findlaw.cn/case and http://www.chinalawedu.com/web/1900.

[993] For critical views on insufficient legal reasoning in Chinese judgments see Zong 2009 and Cheng 2012.

[994] HR 31 January 1919, *NJ* 1919, 161 (*Lindenbaum/Cohen*).

else's rights and breach of duties imposed by legislations to acts that are to be regarded as improper social conduct according to unwritten law.[995] Even though nowadays citing previous cases in judgments has become a common practice in the Netherlands, Dutch judges still do not seem to have come close to the elaborate and discursive drafting style of their counterparts in common law jurisdictions.[996] Despite the relatively brief and formalistic judgment drafting style, Dutch legal scholars have been able to retrieve valuable information from cases by, among other things, carefully analysing the legal issues involved in the disputes and by comparing the analysed cases with relevant previous court decisions. Similarly, the fact that Chinese judges seem reluctant to shed much light on how they reach their decisions does require legal scholars to develop methods and strategies to analyse cases drafted in a formalistic fashion, but it does not necessarily mean that there is nothing for Chinese legal scholars to discover in Chinese judgments.

Still another obstacle could be that Chinese legal scholars do not have sufficient incentives to carry out extensive and systematic case research, because such research is unlikely to be treated seriously by the courts and hence do not help them advance their career.[997] One may, for example, argue that scholarly case research in China would be useless, because in court practice Chinese judges do not treat cases as authorities and will therefore not pay attention to scholarly case research. This argument, however, has a chicken-and-egg flavour. In China there is currently indeed a correlation between the fact that Chinese judges do not treat cases as authorities on the one hand, and that scholars do not carry out extensive and systematic case research on the other. However, it is not convincing to infer that the former *caused* the latter. It is not unthinkable that cases have not been able to fulfil the role of legal authorities in court practice in China, because, among other reasons, Chinese legal scholars have not yet produced a sufficient body of literature that systemizes, interprets and evaluates previous cases. In fact, the findings of this study on the way case law functions in the

---

[995] Van Maanen 2009.

[996] For criticisms on legal reasoning in judgments of Dutch courts see Bruinsma 1988a, p. 120 and Drion 2009.

[997] See interview CN20111205.

Netherlands demonstrate exactly how important scholarly case research is for cases to fulfil the role of a source of law.[998] Given the possibility that the causal relationship could be the other way round, it is not obvious why one should assume that judges in China would never pay serious attention to scholarly case research, even if Chinese legal scholars could produce a serious body of literature that systemizes, analyses and evaluates previous cases.

A more fundamental obstacle could be that in an authoritarian country such as China, legal scholars do not have sufficient space to develop case law.[999] In a country where the freedom of expression is not guaranteed, one may argue, academic freedom may be threatened, so that legal scholars are not able to pursue unhindered case research.[1000] This argument touches upon a crucial difference between the Netherlands and China, i.e. Dutch legal scholars operate in a constitutional democratic state where they are free to pursue their academic interest and to express critical opinions on court decisions, whereas such freedom is not guaranteed in China. However, the restrictions imposed upon Chinese legal scholars are not of such a nature that any type of scholarly research into any type of cases would be impossible. Although Chinese scholars may have to exercise a certain degree of self-censorship by, for example, avoiding certain legal issues that the regime deems sensitive[1001] or by softening their criticism on certain court decisions, it is still possible for them to conduct at least meaningful descriptive case research in many areas of the law that are not deemed sensitive. In any event, if Chinese legal scholars are able to conduct research on enacted laws in non-sensitive areas of the law, it is not obvious why they would not be able to do research into cases in these areas.

In conclusion, there are undoubtedly considerable challenges for legal scholars to carry out systematic and extensive

---

[998] See the paragraph in chapter two on the contribution of legal scholars to the case law mechanism in the Netherlands.

[999] For discussions on the authoritarian nature of the regime in China see Weatherley 2006 and Stockmann & Gallagher 2011.

[1000] For discussions on academic freedom in China see Shen 2000 and Wang 2012a.

[1001] For a discussion on the types of cases that the regimes deems sensitive see Fu & Peerenboom 2010.

case research in China, such as a low case publication rate, formalistic judgment drafting style, old habits among judges that neglect to pay proper attention to previous cases and an authoritarian environment that does not guarantee academic freedom. However, none of these obstacles is of such a nature that it would render scholarly case research impossible or meaningless in China. The real question is probably whether legal scholars in China are *willing* to invest their time and energy in systematic and extensive case research. After all, combing through hundreds or even thousands of published cases to find judgments that are possibly relevant for the solution of legal problems and for the development of the law, ascertaining the essence of those cases and systemizing them could be tough work, whereas such work, given the old habits among judges or even legal scholars that do not pay particular attention to the possible relevance of previous cases, may not be immediately helpful for legal scholars to gain prestige or to advance their career. An optimist may, of course, respond to the assumption of such an unwilling or hesitant attitude by interpreting the introduction of the Case Guidance System in 2010 as a grand opportunity for Chinese legal scholars to intensify case research. It is possible that, one may argue, this new case law institution will have the effect of stimulating the case law awareness among Chinese judges, so that they will begin to pay more attention to relevant previous cases in court practice, which may subsequently create fresh incentives for Chinese legal scholars to generate case research products in order to meet the rising demand in legal practice for usable case law materials. However, it is not unthinkable that the Case Guidance System triggers an opposite effect. A narrow understanding of the Case Guidance System may lead Chinese judges to believe that *only* cases selected by the Supreme People's Court through the Case Guidance System have special normative force, so that all other cases can be ignored, including those highlighted in scholarly writings. Such an attitude may consequently discourage legal scholars from exploring and systemizing the vast body of unselected cases.

It seems fair to say that Chinese legal scholars are now facing a crucial moment for their role in shaping the future case law practice in China. If Chinese legal scholars do not start to research the vast body of unselected cases and extract materials that can provide valuable assistance to legal practice from the unselected cases, their future role in the development of case law in China may become limited.[1002] Once a narrow understanding of the Case Guidance System takes root in court practice in China, it may generate a path dependency pattern that has the effect of marginalizing the role of legal scholars. Fortunately, some Chinese legal scholars have already started to conduct case research.[1003] It is highly desirable that more and more Chinese legal scholars join this initiative to explore possible treasures hidden in the vast body of unselected cases, as the future of a well-functioning case law mechanism in China may very well depend on how efficiently and effectively the vast body of unselected cases is used.

3. Possible contributions by legal education to the development of case law in China

In addition to the role of legal scholars, this chapter highlights the possible contribution of legal education to the development of case law in China. It is highly desirable for law schools in China to enhance the use of cases in legal education, not merely as examples to illustrate abstract legislative provisions, but also as materials that can be used to solve legal problems and to further develop the law.

As explained earlier, in order for cases to fulfil the role of a source of law in a legal system, the way that judges treat previous cases in adjudication must be reasonably predictable.[1004] The

[1002] It should be noted that although the *Provisions Concerning Work on Guiding Cases* does not explicitly allocate a role for legal scholars in the case selection procedure, some courts do consult prominent legal scholars during the process of case selection for advice, but the opinions provided by legal scholars to the courts are not published, see Zhang 2011 and Tan & Chen 2014.

[1003] See e.g. articles published in *Case Law Review* (判例评论 Panli Pinglun), an academic journal edited by the China Case Law Research Centre of Nanking University (南京大学中国法律案例研究中心 Nanjing Daxue Zhongguo Falu Anli Yanjiu Zhongxin), available at http://www.njucasereview.com/web/research/review/31_1.shtml.

[1004] This passage summarizes what has been said about legal education in the chapter on the utilization of cases in the Netherlands. For a detailed description and sources, see the relevant paragraphs in chapter two.

findings of this study suggest that in the Netherlands a reasonable degree of predictability as to how judges are likely to treat previous cases is achieved by, among other things, two facts, i.e. judges follow certain common methodological guidelines when using previous cases to solve legal disputes in court and such guidelines are accessible to other players in law such as practising lawyers and legal scholars.[1005] Furthermore, the findings of this study suggest that the way cases are used in legal education in the Netherlands contributes both to the fact that judges follow certain common methodological guidelines with regard to the use of previous cases and to the fact that such methodological guidelines are accessible to other players in law, as the key players in law in the Netherlands such as judges, practising lawyers and legal scholars have all accomplished academic legal education and have received similar case law trainings at law schools.[1006] Throughout their education at law schools, law students are required to learn a large body of cases by heart and to treat these cases as heavy-weight legal authorities.[1007] This body of cases constitutes a common core of case law authorities among law students, which helps to forge a strong awareness among future judges, lawyers and legal scholars that cases are not mere illustration materials, but are capable of carrying a normative force that helps to shape the law. Through repeated use of cases in the entire curriculum at law schools, law students acquire fundamental case law methodological skills such as analysing, interpreting, finding and evaluating cases.[1008] They also learn how to develop legal arguments based on previous cases and how to evaluate the strengths and weaknesses of such argumentation through activities such as moot court and thesis writing.[1009] All these case law training activities ultimately cultivate a case law methodological framework among law graduates, which continues to exercise a long-standing influence on their mode of thinking throughout their careers as judges, lawyers and legal scholars.[1010] It should be emphasized that this study does not submit

---

[1005] Ibid.
[1006] Ibid.
[1007] Ibid.
[1008] Ibid.
[1009] Ibid.
[1010] Ibid.

that it is the use of cases in legal education that has *created* a shared case law methodological framework among the key players in law in the Netherlands. It is surely not unthinkable that certain case law methodological approaches had already emerged in legal practice before cases began to be incorporated into university legal education in the Netherlands in the early decades of the 20th century.[1011] However, the findings of this study do suggest that legal education is an important link in a chain of possible causes that ultimately contribute to the forming and the strengthening of a shared case law methodological framework among the key players in law in the Netherlands.[1012]

If cases were to be used as an effective tool to enhance legal certainty and legal unity in China without losing a desirable degree of flexibility,[1013] it is crucial that the way Chinese judges treat previous cases in adjudication must be reasonably predictable. In the current situation, however, it is highly unpredictable how judges will treat cases in their deliberation, even though judges in China occasionally do consult previous cases in court practice and lawyers sometimes do submit cases as part of their argumentation[1014] It is nearly impossible to ascertain from judgments produced by Chinese courts whether previous cases have influenced the judicial decision-making and if so, what factors judges have taken into account to evaluate the relevance of previous cases, as Chinese judges hardly ever cite or discuss previous cases in judgments.[1015] Nor is there evidence suggesting that certain thumb rules have emerged in practice as to what types of cases are likely to be followed in

---

[1011] Fockema Andreae 1938, p. 73.

[1012] This observation is in particular inspired by Dainow 1966, p. 428.

[1013] Flexibility must be highlighted in this context. Enacting very detailed legislation would be able to strengthen legal unity and certainty, but doing so without a proper case law mechanism would render the law inflexible. For a deep analysis on this issue see Van Rooij 2004 and Van Rooij 2006.

[1014] See e.g. Research Department of the Supreme People's Court 2007 and interviews CN20111205, CN20110221, CN20110302, CN20110307, CN20110705 and CN20110708.

[1015] See Wang 2006, p. 24, footnote 68.

court.[1016] The introduction of a nationwide Case Guidance System may help to create some clarity to the extent that guiding cases selected through the Case Guidance System may be more likely to be followed in court practice than other cases. However, as stated earlier in this study, the amount of guiding cases is likely to be so limited that they alone will most probably not be able to meet the vast demand of legal practice.[1017] Accordingly, it is crucial to exploit the vast body of unselected cases. In order to make effective use of the vast body of unselected cases, it is crucial to develop a shared case law methodological framework among judges, lawyers and legal scholars in China, otherwise the use of unselected cases will remain unpredictable and will consequently not be able to provide a desirable degree of legal certainty. Of course, studying and further developing legal methodology including methodological guidelines for using cases is an important task of scholarly legal research, but legal education also has a role to play, because proper use of cases in legal education, as the experiences with case law in the Netherlands illustrate, can contribute to the forming of a shared case law methodological framework among the key players in law.

One possible objection could be that the findings of this study do not prove that it is the use of cases in legal education that has *created* a shared case law methodological framework among judges, lawyers and legal scholars in the Netherlands, as it is possible that a set of methodological guidelines had already evolved in legal practice before cases began to be incorporated in legal education in the Netherlands. One could therefore say that the role of legal education is merely to teach students what has already been long established in legal practice instead of creating something new. Accordingly, one may continue to argue, as no shared case law methodological guidelines have yet been developed in legal practice in China, legal education has nothing to teach.

This argument is unconvincing for a number reasons. First, it overlooks or at least downplays the possibility that, although legal education alone may not be sufficient to create a case law methodological framework among the key players in law, it is still

[1016] See Research Group of the Higher People's Court of Beijing 2007 and interviews CN20111205, CN20110221, CN20110302, CN20110307, CN20110705 and CN20110708.

[1017] See reflections on the Case Guidance System in the previous chapter.

capable of fulfilling the role of a link in a causal chain that ultimately leads to the forming and the strengthening of such a framework.[1018] Secondly, the fact that no shared case law methodological framework has yet been established in legal practice in China can be interpreted positively as to mean that law professors, teachers and students have a grand opportunity to fully use their creativity and to experiment with various methodological approaches to use cases that have not been selected through the Case Guidance System. Thirdly, it is highly doubtful whether there is indeed nothing to teach. After all, the Supreme People's Court has already selected and published a small body of guiding cases. This small body of guiding cases, of course, does not offer sufficient teaching materials that satisfy the need of all the courses taught in a law curriculum. However, the guiding cases can be used at a methodological level, i.e. they can be used as models to teach students how to analyse cases. A careful study of the published guiding cases suggests that the Supreme People's Court seems to be using a four-step method to analyse cases. The first step is to ascertain the facts of the case. The second step is to identify the core disputed question of law in the analysed case. The third step is to find out and summarize the court's answer to the disputed question of law and the last step is to ascertain and summarize the reasons why the court has provided this answer. It can be a good exercise to ask students to analyse cases that have not been selected through the Case Guidance System by using this four-step method derived from the guiding cases, and to write case summaries in a similar format as the one adopted by the Supreme People's Court in the published guiding cases. Moreover, nowadays there are both official court websites in China that publish cases which can be consulted free of charge[1019] and online commercial case databases to which many law schools have a subscription.[1020] It can be a good exercise to encourage students to search for cases in these databases and to use them in, among other things, moot court and thesis writing. In other

---

[1018] See the paragraph in chapter two on the contribution of legal education to the case law mechanism in the Netherlands.
[1019] See e.g. http://www.court.gov.cn/zgcpwsw/ and http://www.chinacourt.org/paper.shtml.
[1020] See e.g. http://china.findlaw.cn/case, http://law.cnki.net, http://china.findlaw.cn/case and http://www.chinalawedu.com/web/1900.

words, case law teaching could focus on cases that students need to actively search for and analyse, as this is good legal training. These are but two examples of how the available resources in China can be used in legal education to stimulate students to explore the use of unselected cases and to develop case law methodological skills. If law professors, teachers and students are willing to fully use their creativity, they may find many other possible ways to make meaningful use of cases in legal education in China, so that the fact that no shared case law methodological framework has yet emerged in legal practice does not have to be an insurmountable obstacle.

Another possible objection could be that, if all the law schools in China were to experiment with case law methodological approaches, many different case law methodological approaches could emerge, which would render the use of unselected cases unpredictable. This concern is certainly not groundless, given that there are more than 600 law schools in China.[1021] However, it seems to overlook the fact that it can take a long period of time before a shared case law methodological framework evolves and takes root in any legal system. During the long evolution process, it is neither surprising nor undesirable that different methodological approaches exist. Indeed, it can even be healthy for the development of a shared methodological framework to have various approaches compete with each other. Such a competition can lead to the survival of the fittest. Or, if the courts in China would like to play a decisive role in case law method engineering, competing case law methodological approaches developed by various law schools can at least offer candidate options for the courts to choose. In fact, the evolution of the nationwide Case Guidance System has experienced a period where various courts in China experimented with their own methods of selecting, publishing and using cases.[1022] These experiments have offered valuable materials to the Supreme People's Court for its design of a nationwide Case Guidance System.[1023] Similarly, competing methodological approaches to use unselected cases developed by different law schools can be a

[1021] See Sun 2011.
[1022] See the paragraph on the evolution of China's Case Guidance System in the previous chapter.
[1023] Shen 2009a, p. 5.

constructive step towards a more or less standardized nationwide case law methodological framework.

Still another challenge for making effective use of cases in legal education in China is that systematic and extensive scholarly research into published previous cases is still relatively rare in China.[1024] The findings of this study indicate that two types of cases are used in legal education in the Netherlands, i.e. cases that students are assigned to study either due to their normative impact as leading cases or as illustration materials on the one hand, and cases that students must actively search for and apply to complete assignments. Systematic and extensive scholarly research into previous cases is helpful for the choice of the first type of cases, i.e. such research can help law professors and law teachers in deciding which cases they would assign students to study. Without systematic and extensive scholarly case research, it could be difficult for law professors and teachers to, among other things, ascertain which cases actually represent a dominant approach in court practice across China towards a certain legal issue and should therefore be assigned as studying materials. To this challenge this study does not have a proposal for a quick solution, as whether this challenge can be met may very well ultimately depend on the willingness of legal scholars in China to engage in systematic and extensive case research. This is in fact yet another reason why this study stresses the importance of scholarly case research for the development of case law in China and why this study makes an appeal to Chinese legal scholars to intensify their efforts to systemize and analyse the vast body of cases that have not been selected as guiding cases through the Case Guidance System.

To summarize, this study submits that, despite the many challenges, it is desirable for law schools in China to enhance the use of cases in legal education, as proper use of cases in legal education may help raise the case law awareness among law students and it may help them develop the necessary methods and

[1024] This situation is gradually changing in recent years. See e.g. the articles published in *Case Law Review* (判例评论 Panli Pinglun), an academic journal edited by the China Case Law Research Centre of Nanking University (南京大学中国法律案例研究中心 Nanjing Daxue Zhongguo Falu Anli Yanjiu Zhongxin), available at http://www.njucasereview.com/web/research/review/31_1.shtml.

skills to use cases to solve legal problems and to develop the law. This study does not argue that Chinese law schools should copy the way cases are used at Dutch law schools or the case law education mode in any other legal system. Instead, it encourages law schools in China to experiment with their own methods of using cases and to engage in an open debate on the merits of competing case law methodological approaches, as this can be an important step towards forming a common methodological framework in China with regard to the use of previous cases to solve legal problems, which in its turn may help to enhance legal certainty without losing a desirable degree of flexibility by improving the predictability as to how judges are likely to treat previous cases in adjudication.

4. Some further observations

4.1 Methodological observations

The case law debate in China since the 1980's has led to a considerable body of literature.[1025] Comparative law is a frequently used method in this body of literature.[1026] One of the methodological choices that each comparative law research project needs to treat carefully is the selection of legal systems/jurisdictions to be studied and compared.[1027] When reviewing the Chinese-language literature that adopts the method of comparative law to participate in the case law debate in China, one could hardly avoid the impression that there is a selection bias, i.e. the experiences with case law in common law jurisdictions tend to receive more attention than the role of cases in civil law jurisdictions.[1028]

[1025] The author of this study searched for 案例指导(Case Guidance) and 判例(Precedent) in the largest academic online database in China 中国知网(China Knowledge Resource Integrated Database www.cnki.net. The search rendered nearly 2200 journal articles and dissertations that have been published since 1980.

[1026] See, just to cite a few examples, Zhang 2002a, Zeng 2004, Jiang 2004, Rao & Yan 2004, Pan 1998, Ge & Hu 2007, Liu 2007a, Zhang 2008a, Ding 2008a, p. 28-41 and Yuan 2012.

[1027] See Oderkerk 1999 and Oderkerk 2001.

[1028] This is of course not to say that the role of case law in civil law jurisdictions with case law has been totally ignored in the Chinese legal

It is doubtful whether it is wise for Chinese legal scholars and other actors that participate in the case law debate to focus heavily on common law jurisdictions in order to gain comparative insights for China to enhance the use of cases. At first sight, it seems more than natural for Chinese researchers to pay close attention to the functioning of case law in common law jurisdictions, not only because these jurisdictions have a long tradition of using cases to solve legal disputes and to develop the law,[1029] but also due to the fact that in common law jurisdictions there is a body of literature on the method and techniques of using cases.[1030] This, however, does not mean that the experiences with case law in civil law jurisdictions are less relevant or valuable for China and therefore deserve less attention. In fact, as far as the tradition is concerned, it should not be neglected that before the codification wave in the 19th century, continental European civil law jurisdictions also had a long history of using previous cases to solve legal disputes and to further develop the law.[1031] Another reason to doubt the wisdom of focusing primarily on common law jurisdictions as a source to draw inspiration for China to enhance the use of cases is that the current Chinese legal system seems to be much more influenced by and to bear more similarities with the continental European civil law legal family than the common law.[1032] Moreover, continental European civil law legal systems have had a stage in their history of development where, similar to

---

literature. For publications that refer to the role and functioning of case law in civil law jurisdictions see e.g. Zhang 2002a, Zeng 2004, Pan 1998 and Zhang 2008a. It should, however, be noted that accounts of case law in civil law jurisdictions are generally (much) less detailed and in-depth than studies on case law in common law jurisdictions in the Chinese legal literature that uses comparative legal research as a method to participate in the case law debate. Compare e.g. literature cited in this note with Zhong 1989, Liang 1991, Meng 2004, Jiang 2004, Chen 2004, Lin 2009 and Lü 2010.

[1029] See e.g. Frederick 1959, Cross & Harris 1991 and Cartwright 2007, p. 3-13.

[1030] See e.g. Goodhart 1959, Stone 1959, Dworkin 1962, Schaefer 1967, Hellman 1989, Cross & Harris 1991, Markman 2003, Kalt 2003, Duxbury 2008 and Nelson 2011.

[1031] Drion 1968b, p. 149-154 and Dawson 1970.

[1032] See e.g. He 2010 and Xu 2012.

today's China, cases were explicitly rejected as a source of law, and where courts did not use cases in their argumentation, legal scholars did not care to analyse cases in their writings and law students were not required to study cases,[1033] whereas nowadays the importance of cases has reached such an extent in these jurisdictions that they have become a source of law in practice.[1034] Given these facts, it seems fair to say that, if comparative law is accepted as a useful method in the case law debate in China, the experiences with case law in continental European civil law jurisdictions are at least equally relevant as the functioning of case law in common law jurisdictions, so that a selection bias in favor of common law jurisdictions may not be conducive to a balanced debate.

By conducting an in-depth investigation into the way cases fulfil the role of a source of law in a continental European civil law jurisdiction, i.e. the Netherlands, this study wishes to offer a fair amount of descriptive materials for Chinese researchers that are capable of reading English to examine and to reflect upon. It is hoped that the data provided by this study may be useful for Chinese researchers to gain fresh insights that could be useful for the case law debate in China. It is also hoped that this study will arouse the interest among Chinese researchers to carry out more research into the way case law functions in civil law jurisdictions.

4.2 Misconceptions on the role of cases in civil law jurisdictions

As has been pointed out in the previous subparagraph, comparative law has been used as an important method in the Chinese-language literature that participates in the case law debate in China. When closely examining this body of literature, one would notice some curious assumptions underlying some of the comparative law arguments advanced in the debate. One of the arguments to justify the use of cases as an instrument to enhance legal certainty and legal unity in China, for example, is that doing so would fit a global trend of convergence between the civil law and the common law where each legal family learns from the other's strong points to

---

[1033] See e.g. Dawson 1970, p. 375-386 and Hondius 2007a, p. 12.

[1034] See e.g. Loussouarn 1958, p. 255, David 1984, p. 116, Van Caenegem 1987, p. 40, MacCormick & Summers 1997a and Zweigert & Kötz 1998, p. 263.

supplement its limitations.[1035] Such an argument seems to involve at least two assumptions. First, China is assumed to be a civil law jurisdiction, or at least a jurisdiction with a codified legal system that bears considerable similarities with civil law jurisdictions. Another assumption appears to be that case law is originally something alien to the civil law legal family and that it is through a process of convergence where the two legal families learn from each other that cases come to fulfil an increasingly prominent role in civil law jurisdictions.

This study does not wish to extensively discuss the first assumption, because although one can doubt whether China can be said to belong to the civil law legal family, it seems at least acceptable to say that China does have a codified legal system that bears similarities with civil law jurisdictions.[1036] What this study does wish to point out is that serious doubt can be cast on the second assumption, because it is neither true that cases are alien to civil law jurisdictions, nor justified to infer from a possible trend of convergence between the civil law and the common law that it is *due to the influence*[1037] of the common law doctrine of precedent that cases become influential in civil law jurisdictions.

As has been explained in the previous subparagraph, before the codification wave in the 19th century, civil law jurisdictions already had a long history of using cases as legally relevant materials to solve disputes in court and to further develop the

[1035] See e.g. Zeng 2004, Shen 2004, p. 19, Wang 2004b, p. 61, Guo 2004, Liu 2007a and Xie 2014.

[1036] See e.g. He 2010 and Xu 2012.

[1037] The Chinese term "相互借鉴" (learning from each other) is frequently used in the body of Chinese-language literature on the case law debate, see e.g. Guo 2004, p. 147, He & Hong & Sun 2008, p. 140, Xu 2009, Jiang 2011a and Yuan 2014. The use of this term in this context is misleading, as this term does not merely describe a factual converging trend, but also implies a pattern of influence and a process of intentional learning. Some Chinese authors even explicitly indicate that legal scholars and judges in civil law jurisdictions turned to the doctrine of precedent in common law jurisdictions for inspiration in order to find remedies that could compensate the limitations of codification, see Pan 1998, p. 52 and Kong 2004, p. 96.

law.[1038] The codification movement in the 19th century did interrupt this long tradition, but this interruption does not justify the conclusion that case law is originally something alien to civil law jurisdictions. Moreover, it is highly doubtful whether the fact that cases nowadays fulfil the role of a *de facto* source of law in civil law jurisdictions is indeed induced by efforts to learn from the common law doctrine of precedent. The findings of this study suggest that, at least in the Netherlands, it is neither through formal instruments such as legislation or court orders that explicitly attribute binding force to certain types of cases upon future judges, nor through comparative legal research that draws inspiration from the common law doctrine of precedent that cases became influential in practice and eventually grew into a source of law.[1039] Rather, it was the fact that cases in practice became influential in the first place that prompted legal scholars, the legislature and judges to reflect upon the soundness of some of the assumptions underlying the codification movement in the 19th century and to adjust their views towards the question whether cases should be accepted as a source of law.[1040] In other words, it seems more appropriate to say that using cases in court as legally relevant materials to solve legal problems is a practice that more or less grew naturally in civil law jurisdictions out of a need in practice for proper instruments to supplement the limitations of codes and legislation,[1041] rather than that case law is something that is originally alien to civil law jurisdictions but has been later imported from common law jurisdictions during the 20th century. Accordingly, this study is inclined to concur with the view of Komárek that the increasing importance of cases should perhaps not be seen as an instance of civil law's convergence with common law, but rather as the coming back of cases from illegality to a place it once occupied in the civil law tradition as an important type of law.[1042]

This study wishes to clarify this point of misunderstanding, because doing so may be relevant for the practice of using cases in China. One of the arguments against using cases as legally relevant

---

1038 See e.g. Drion 1968b, p. 149-154 and Dawson 1970.
1039 See chapter three.
1040 Ibid.
1041 MacCormick & Summers 1997c, p. 2.
1042 Komárek 2012, p. 67.

materials for solving disputes in court and for further developing the law in China tends to rely on a form of syllogistic reasoning, i.e. the conclusion that judges do not need to treat cases as legally relevant materials in court is drawn from two propositions: case law is alien to civil law jurisdictions and unique to common law as the major premise and China is a civil law jurisdiction or at least a jurisdiction with a codified legal system that bears more similarities with civil law jurisdictions than common law jurisdictions as the minor premise.[1043] The findings of this study combined with insights drawn from some of the existing English-language comparative law literature[1044] indicate, as illustrated in the previous passage, that the major premise is not true, so that doubt can be cast on the soundness of the conclusion that judges in China are justified to ignore outright and do not have any obligation to respond to arguments submitted by litigating parties or their counsels that invoke or rely on similar previous cases.

One may argue that the introduction of the Case Guidance System has already put an end to the debate as to whether cases can be used in adjudication in China, because if the Supreme Court did not believe that cases should be treated as legally relevant materials in judicial deliberation, it would not have introduced such a legal institution that requires judges to follow the guiding cases that the Supreme Court selects. Accordingly, one may continue to argue that since the introduction of the Case Guidance System in 2010, it is no longer necessary to clarify the misunderstanding that case law is alien to civil law jurisdictions and that the rising importance of cases in civil law jurisdictions throughout the 20th century is the result of learning from the common law doctrine of precedent.

It should, however, be pointed out that, although the Case Guidance System may have the effect of coercing judges to take the guiding cases selected by the Supreme Court into consideration in adjudication practice, it does not explicitly provide how judges are supposed to treat unselected cases.[1045] Accordingly, it is not

---

[1043] See e.g. Li 2009a and Zhu 2010.

[1044] See e.g. Loussouarn 1958, p. 255, Silving 1966, p. 141, Merryman 1974, p. 193-198, David 1984, p. 116, Van Caenegem 1987, p. 40, MacCormick & Summers 1997a and Hondius 2007a.

[1045] Article 9 of the *Provisions Concerning Work on Guiding Case* touches upon a small aspect of the status of unselected cases, i.e. the status of

unthinkable that the misunderstanding that case law is alien to civil law jurisdictions or codified legal systems such as the Chinese legal order may induce judges to narrowly interpret the Case Guidance System as a signal by the Supreme Court that *only* guiding cases selected through the Case Guidance System deserve particular attention in adjudication. Such an understanding may subsequently induce judges to believe that they are justified to continue to ignore arguments submitted by the litigating parties or their counsels that involve merely previous cases that have not been selected as guiding cases. Such a narrow interpretation could hardly be conducive to strengthening the use of cases as an effective instrument to counterbalance the limitations of legislation. As has been pointed out in the previous chapter, the Case Guidance System *alone* may not be sufficient to address the problem that like cases are not treated alike, because, among other reasons, the amount of guiding cases selected through the Case Guidance System is unlikely to be sufficient to meet the vast demand in practice for leading cases, so that it is desirable to explore the vast body of unselected cases for usable materials that may supplement the Case Guidance System.[1046] If a narrow understanding of the Case Guidance System were to take root in China, it could lead to an attitude that treats unselected cases as irrelevant materials for judicial decision-making, which would render it difficult to make effective use of unselected cases in adjudication, whereas the difficulty to use unselected cases in adjudication may in its turn discourage legal scholars to explore and systemize the vast body of unselected cases.

Obviously, it is undesirable for such a vicious circle to occur. Therefore, this study wishes to clarify this misunderstanding and to emphasize that using cases to solve legal disputes in court and to further develop the law is not unique to the common law, but is actually something quite natural in codified legal systems.[1047] As

---

cases that the Supreme People's Court has selected and published prior to the introduction of a nationwide Case Guidance System, but remains silent on the status of other cases that have not been selected as guiding cases after November 2010.

[1046] See the last paragraph of the previous chapter.

[1047] See e.g. MacCormick & Summers 1997c, p. 2 and Komárek 2012, p. 67.

MacCormick and Summers rightly observed, case law is a form of law of great antiquity, not only in common law jurisdictions, but also in civil law jurisdictions.[1048] In other words, case law is not something imported from the common law legal family, but is rather something that is inherent in civil law jurisdictions themselves, although its prominence has been suppressed for a brief period of time since the codification wave of the 19th century.[1049] If Chinese judges and legal scholars do regard China as a civil law jurisdiction or at least as a codified legal system that bears similarities to civil law jurisdictions, it seems more appropriate to infer from such an understanding that it is natural for Chinese judges to take relevant previous cases into account in adjudication, rather than categorically denying the relevance or usability of cases unless there is a certain form of official recognition that explicitly confirm their possible influence on judicial-decision making. Accordingly, I wish to call upon Chinese judges and legal scholars to abandon the misconception refuted in this subparagraph and to treat not only guiding cases selected through the Case Guidance System, but also relevant unselected cases as usable materials for solving legal disputes in adjudication and for further developing the law.

4.3 Limitations of cases

In the Chinese-language literature that participates in the case law debate in China, there is considerable optimism about the possibilities of using cases to enhance consistency in judgments. Of course there are critical writings that question the ability of case law to deal with the problem of conflicting judgments,[1050] but the general attitude towards to the possibilities of enhancing legal certainty and legal unity through a case law institution has been positive and hopeful.[1051]

When used properly, cases can indeed be a valuable instrument to supplement the limitations of codes and statutes and

---

[1048] MacCormick & Summers 1997c, p. 1-2.
[1049] See e.g. Drion 1968b, Dawson 1970 and Hondius 2007a.
[1050] See e.g. Gao 1991, Zhu 2010, Wu 2011a and Wu 2011b.
[1051] See e.g. Wu 2004, Shen 2009b, Cao 2010, Jiang 2011a, Lu 2011 and Wang 2012b.

to help curb conflicting judgments, which can be conducive to enhance legal certainty and unity in codified legal systems.[1052] However, it should be pointed out in the context of the case law debate in China that the ability of cases to enhance consistency in judgments should not be overestimated. Inconsistency in judgments, after all, can have many different causes.[1053] One of the causes of conflicting judgments could, for example, be related to ambiguous or broad norms in legislation that are susceptible to different interpretations.[1054] In the Netherland, the cassation system has been introduced to address this cause of conflicting judgments by making it possible for the Supreme Court, which is a court of cassation, to reverse judgments of lower courts that do not conform to interpretations of legislation adopted by the Supreme Court as expressed in its previous cases.[1055]

However, inconsistency in judgments may also be related to the way judges exercise discretionary power of, among other things, awarding damages or imposing criminal sanctions.[1056] The exercise of such discretionary power does not always involve interpretation of legislation, so that the ability of the Supreme Court in the Netherlands to reduce inconsistency caused by the exercise of judicial discretion through deciding cassation appeals is limited.[1057] Accordingly, judges in the Netherlands have developed other mechanisms to enhance consistency in judgments. Labour law judges in the Netherlands, for example, have developed a formula to calculate the amount of severance pay that a laid-off employee is

---

[1052] This study will not elaborate on this point, as it has already been established in many existing writings, see e.g. Zhang 2002a, Van Rooij 2004, Wang 2004a, Liu 2006 and Xu 2009.

[1053] See e.g. Xu 2009 and Su & Li 2009, p. 14.

[1054] Ibid.

[1055] There is a consensus in the legal scholarship in the Netherlands that enhancing legal unity is one of the key purposes of the institution of cassation, see e.g. Korthals Altes & Groen 2005, p. 156-162 and the sources cited in this book.

[1056] See e.g. Noordam 2008, p. 180-186, De Groot 2008, p. 142-143 and Verburg 2009, p. 111-113.

[1057] Korthals Altes & Groen 2005, p. 236-240.

entitled to.[1058] Family law judges have developed recommendations to standardize the award of alimony.[1059] Criminal judges have developed sentencing guidelines with regard to some common offences as well as agreements on, among other things, the amount of damages to be awarded in case of detention on remand according to Article 89 of the Code of Criminal Procedure.[1060] Such instruments, although not officially binding as judges are allowed to deviate from them, are devised to enhance consistency in judgments in areas where the effect of using previous cases to standardize judicial decision-making is likely to be limited.[1061]

A close examination of the guiding cases selected by the Supreme People's Court in China through the Case Guidance System reveals that such cases are mainly intended to clarify ambiguities in or caused by legislation.[1062] It is not obvious how this type of cases can fulfil a prominent role in eliminating inconsistency in judicial decision-making caused by, among other things, the exercise of judiciary discretion in awarding damages or imposing criminal sanctions. This is, of course, not to say that there is no mechanism in China other than the Case Guidance System that is capable of enhancing consistency in judgments.[1063] Nor does this imply that it would be impossible for Chinese judges and legal scholars to fully use their creativity and to develop proper ways to use unselected cases to standardize judicial decision-making caused by the exercise of judicial discretion. What this study does wish to point out is that, instead of generally asserting or expecting that using cases will solve the problem of like cases not being treated

---

[1058] See http://www.rechtspraak.nl/Procedures/Landelijke-regelingen/Sector-kantonrecht/Aanbevelingen-van-de-kring-van-kantonrechters/Pages/Kantonrechtersformule.aspx.

[1059] See Dijksterhuis 2008.

[1060] See http://www.rechtspraak.nl/Procedures/Landelijke-regelingen/Sector-strafrecht/Documents/Orientatiepunten-en-afspraken-LOVS.pdf

[1061] http://www.rechtspraak.nl/Procedures/Landelijke-regelingen/Pages/default.aspx

[1062] See http://cgc.law.stanford.edu/guiding-cases/.

[1063] The Supreme People's Court, for example, issued a policy document to standardize criminal sentencing in September 2010, see Supreme People's Court of the People's Republic of China 2010a.

alike, it would be wise for participants in the case law debate in China to bear the limitations of cases as an instrument to promote consistency in judicial decision-making in mind, to closely analyse the various causes that lead to the problem of conflicting judgments, and to carefully consider, with regard to each cause, whether using previous cases would be the most suitable instrument to standardize judicial decision-making and if not, what other instruments could be used to achieve the goal of promoting consistency in judgments. This study understands the enthusiasm in China about the Case Guidance System, as this legal institution could indeed be a very positive step towards a well-functioning case law mechanism in China. However, it would not be particularly helpful for the development of case law in China to raise too high an expectation among the participants of the case law debate and the public. Instead, it seems wiser for those who wish to further explore the use of case law in China to carefully consider and to make explicit what case law can and cannot achieve, so that the Case Guidance System or possible ways developed by judges and legal scholars to exploit the vast body of unselected cases will not be unjustly blamed for possible problems that persist in the future, which the method of using previous cases is neither intended nor suitable to solve.

5. Concluding remarks

This chapter reflected on the relevance of the experiences with case law in the Netherlands for the development of case law in China. It was submitted that in order to make optimal use of the vast body of cases that have not been selected as guiding cases through the Case Guidance System, it is highly desirable that legal scholars in China conduct systematic research into published cases and integrate such research results into their publications such as handbooks, textbooks and journal articles. It was also submitted that law schools can make a meaningful contribution to the development of a well-functioning case law practice in China by enhancing the use of cases in legal education, as doing so may help to forge overtime a common methodological framework with regard to the use of cases among law students, i.e. future judges, lawyers and legal scholars. Moreover, this chapter clarified a misconception among many Chinese judges and legal scholars and pointed out that, contrary to what some of the Chinese-language publications assert, case law is not something imported from common law to continental European civil law jurisdictions, but has grown naturally in civil law jurisdictions.

As has been pointed out in the introduction of this study, there are considerable differences between China and European civil law jurisdictions including the Netherlands. Accordingly, it is not the intention to present the case law mechanism in the Netherlands as the best practice for China to copy. Nor does this study purport to be able to provide a road map for China to build a well-functioning case law mechanism. Instead, this study hopefully will fulfil the humble role of supplying descriptive materials that have been so far largely missing in the case law debate in China. The thoughts presented in this chapter are neither meant as instructions nor as policy recommendations, but rather as an invitation for those who are interested in further enhancing the use of cases in China to reflect on some of the assumptions, approaches and commonly held perceptions in the case law debate in China and to fully use their creativity to develop practices and methods of using cases that are most suitable for China.

Conclusion

Conclusion

This study explored three main questions. In the first place, it investigated how cases fulfil the role of a source of law in the Netherlands. The findings were then linked to the existing English-language literature related to the role of cases in civil law jurisdictions in order to seek new insights that may enrich this body of scholarly writings. The last two chapters linked the findings of the first part of this study to efforts in China since the 1980s to create a case law system, and explored the possible implications that can be drawn from the experiences with case law in the Netherlands for China to further enhance its case law practice. The final conclusion of this study will summarize the key findings with regard to these three questions, put them in an interrelated context, reflect upon them and seek insights at an overarching level.

1. Case law mechanism in the Netherlands, summary and reflections

The introduction of this study presented the concept of case law mechanism and an analytic framework that identifies the operation of a case law mechanism as a process that consists of two major phases, i.e. the publication and utilization of cases (see Figure 17).

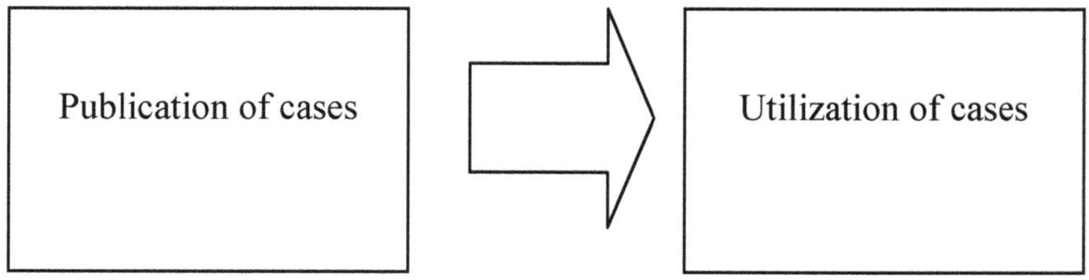

Figure 17 Case law mechanism as a process of publication and utilization of cases

Using this framework, it was discovered that in the publication phase, cases undergo a remarkable and rigorous selection process in the Netherlands. Even in today's Internet age, 98.5% of all decided cases never get published in the

Netherlands.[1064] The lucky tiny proportion of 1.5% that does get selected for publication subsequently undergoes some further treatment in order to make it not only available to the public, but also findable and better comprehensible. The cases that are selected for publication are categorized and supplemented with keywords, headnotes or a summary (the Dutch term for this process is "*ontsluiting*" [1065]). Some of the cases that are published in commercial periodicals even receive a luxurious treatment of being escorted by a commentary (case annotation) written by a (prominent) legal scholar or a practising lawyer.

In the utilization phase, as chapter two of this study revealed, published cases become building materials or ingredients for various users such as judges, legal scholars and law students to produce various products, such as judgments, legal academic publications as well as bachelor's and master's theses. One of the remarkable things that happen during the utilization phase is that normative elements, such as rules, principles and assessment frameworks[1066] are drawn from published cases. These normative elements are subsequently evaluated and applied in various settings such as adjudication, scholarly legal research and legal education. In this process of drawing normative elements from published cases as well as evaluating and using them, not only judges, but also legal scholars play a significant role, as scholarly works that systemize, interpret and evaluate published cases exercise in various ways direct or indirect influence on judicial decision-making.[1067]

The two-phase framework as presented in the introduction of this study has been a useful analytic tool to disentangle the processes and actors involved in the case law mechanism. This, however, does not mean that the two-phase framework is the only possible approach. As this study is of an explorative nature, the concluding part of this study will put the findings of the various parts of this study together and reflect on possible alternative approaches. The following subparagraphs will present two alternative approaches, i.e. case law mechanism as one continuous

---

[1064] See Table 3 in chapter one.

[1065] This term can be translated as "indexing" or "disclosing".

[1066] The Dutch term for this word is "toetsingskader" or "gezichtspunten".

[1067] See chapter two of this study.

selection process and case law mechanism as a process that consists of three phases: publication, utilization and recognition.

1.1 Case law mechanism as a continuous selection process

When the findings of chapter one (case publication) and chapter two (utilization) are put together, it becomes plain that a crucial process that takes place in both phases is "case selection". Chapter one revealed that far from all decided cases are published. Chapter two revealed that far from all published cases actually catch the attention of legal scholars, judges and practising lawyers and are eventually able to become leading cases that shape the law. Accordingly, an alternative approach could be to define the operation of a case law mechanism as one continuous process of selecting leading cases that shape the law.

If case law mechanism is defined as one continuous process of selecting leading cases that shape the law, what does this process look like? The findings of chapter one and chapter two of this study indicate that, at an abstract level, a selection process that moves from case to law has at least three crucial steps (see Figure 18). The first step is selection for publication. As many authors have pointed out, it is difficult to imagine how an unpublished case can have a significant impact on the development of the law.[1068] Accordingly, the first battle that a case needs to win in its journey from case to law is to catch the attention of the actors that select cases for publication and convince them that it has an added value beyond the specific dispute in which the judicial decision was made. This first battle, as has been revealed in chapter one, is a tough one to win, because only a tiny proportion of 1.5% of all decided cases gets the approval from judges and editors of commercial case reporting periodicals to appear in the official online judgment database of the

[1068] See e.g. Loussouarn 1958, p. 259, Kavass 1977, p. 107, Lawson 1977, p. 84, Adams 1999, p. 466 and Kottenhagen & Kaptein 1989, p. 1.

judiciary and in commercial periodicals.[1069]

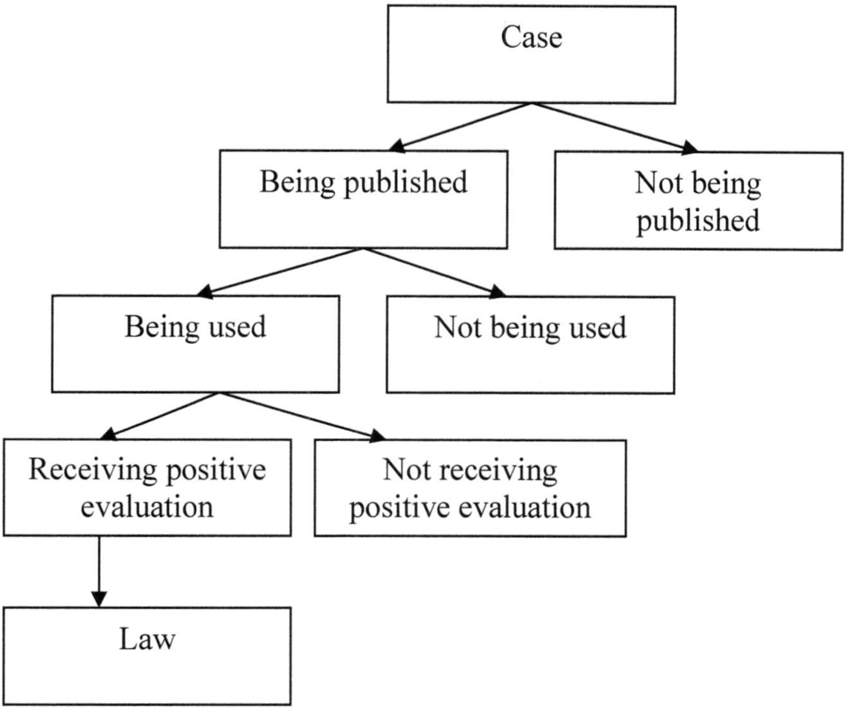

Figure 18 Case law mechanism as a continuous selection process

After publication, the struggle of a case to become the law continues. The second battle that it needs to win is to catch the attention of the various users of cases and to convince them that it can offer these users valuable materials that can help them to attain their goals, be it deciding a new case in court, developing a new legal doctrine in scholarly publications or writing an academic thesis. Obviously, if a published case never gets detected and used by legal scholars, practising lawyers or judges, it cannot significantly influence the law, any more than an unpublished case.

Being used and cited in judgments and scholarly writings prevents a case from being forgotten or neglected, but it does not guarantee a final victory in its journey from case to law. As chapter two revealed, not all cases cited in scholarly writings receive

[1069] See Table 3 in chapter one.

positive comments from legal scholars. In fact, there are plenty of cases, even those decided by the Supreme Court, that are severely criticized in legal academic publications.[1070] Such severe criticisms, as chapter two revealed, can (significantly) reduce the weight that a case carries in judicial deliberation. Also how judges evaluate a case can significantly influence the chance that a case is followed in court practice. As the study of Haazen indicates, a severe critical attitude expressed by lower courts towards Supreme Court decisions can in some instances even induce the Supreme Court to abandon and change a position adopted in its earlier cases.[1071] Accordingly, the final hurdle that a case needs to clear in its journey from case to law is to win positive evaluation from as many users as possible. Only when a case receives sufficient normative endorsement from the users of cases, can it become a legal authority.[1072]

Even if a case has won all the three battles and has become a leading case, its victory is not secured forever. Social changes and evolving moral standards may lead to the birth of new cases that challenge the existing leading cases and may even eventually defeat them in a battle to win the most positive normative endorsement from the users. In this sense, the selection process is a dynamic and continuous one.

An advantage of this continuous selection approach is that it can integrate the findings of chapter one and two into a fairly fluent whole. Moreover, this approach can lead to deeper insights, if one goes one step further to explore some questions that are related to any form of selection. A crucial question that any form of selection involves is who select(s). Another essential question is what the selection criteria are. The remaining passages of this subparagraph will examine these two questions and explore the implications of the answers to them for our understanding of the case law mechanism in the Netherlands.

If we examine the first question, i.e. who select(s), in each step of the selection process, the findings of this study tell us that multiple actors are involved in each of the three steps. In case publication, for example, judges have played an increasingly

[1070] See e.g. Schutgens 2009, Kottenhage 2010b, Van Dam 2010, Hartlief 2011 and De Groot 2011.

[1071] Haazen 2007, p. 236.

[1072] Haazen 2007, p. 246-251.

dominant role since the launch of the official online judgment database by the judiciary in December 1999, but legal scholars and practising lawyers are still capable of exercising a certain degree of influence in determining which cases will be published.[1073] In the step of determining which published cases will be used, not only judges but also legal scholars and practising lawyers play a role. Cases that are not cited by practising lawyers in oral or written submissions to the court or by legal scholars in academic publications are less likely to attract the attention of judges than those that do get cited in such materials.[1074] Also in the third step, namely evaluation, judges are not the only actors who determine the outcome, as scholarly evaluative comments are one of the factors that jointly influence the status of a case in adjudication practice.[1075]

The second question, i.e. what the selection criteria are, has been explicitly addressed in chapter one on case publication. It was discovered that the selection criteria for case publication are becoming more and more transparent, detailed and objective in the Netherlands, in particular since the launch of the official online judgment database of the judiciary.[1076] The selection criteria in the second step, i.e. in determining which cases will be used and which will not, have not been explicitly dealt with in this study. Most probably, the selection criteria in this step may not be uniform, but may vary from user to user and may depend on the goal(s) that a user wishes to attain. As to the selection criteria in the third step, i.e. whether a case receives positive normative evaluation from the users, chapter three revealed a number of criteria that legal scholars explicitly or implicitly use, which can be summarized as a checklist (see Table 8). It seems highly probable that other actors such as

---

[1073] See the subparagraph in chapter one that examines the actors who are involved in the case selection for commercial publication.

[1074] See the paragraph in chapter two that analyses the way cases are used in adjudication practice in the Netherlands.

[1075] See the subparagraph in chapter two on the factors that influence the weight that a case carries in adjudication practice.

[1076] Compare the commercial case publication criteria cited in chapter one with the criteria adopted in official case publication in Appendix 2 and 3. Also a comparison between the old and the new case publication criteria adopted by the judiciary leads to this conclusion. See Appendix 2 And 3.

judges and practising lawyers (implicitly) use a similar set of criteria to evaluate court judgments.

A. How does the court arrive at its decision?		
	1. Has the court made mistakes in its legal reasoning?	
		(1) Has the court correctly identified, interpreted and applied relevant legislative provisions?
		(2) Has the court correctly identified, interpreted and applied norms established in earlier cases?
		(3) Has the court made logic errors such as circular or self-contradictory reasoning?
	2. Has the court violated procedural norms while arriving at its decision?	
B. How has the court justified and explained its decision?		
	1. Has the court provided justification for its decision?	
	2. Has the court ignored certain crucial elements in the justification that it provided?	
C. Quality of the court's answer to the disputed issue		
	1. If the court explicitly or implicitly devises a rule in its answer to a disputed point of law, is the rule vague?	
	2. If the court imposes a sanction on one or more of the litigating parties, is the sanction disproportional?	
	3. Is the decision likely to cause undesirable consequences?	

Table 8 Evaluation criteria used by legal scholars

From the analysis above it can be concluded that, contrary to what some scholars assert, [1077] case law in the Netherlands is not simply what the Supreme Court decides. The forming of case law is not a top-down process. The result of this process is not single-handedly determined by one actor who has the highest rank in the judicial hierarchy and the final power to reverse judgments. Instead, the forming of case law is a process that involves various actors such as judges, legal scholars and practising lawyers, and the outcome is determined by a process of selection that is becoming increasingly transparent both in the step of case publication, i.e. by publishing the selection criteria and making them more detailed and

[1077] See e.g. Draaisma & Duynstee 1988, p. 25.

objective, and in the third step (determining which cases receive positive normative evaluation) by citing previous cases in, among other things, judgments and scholarly writings and by openly discussing the substantive merits of previous cases. All in all, it seems fair to conclude that the selection of leading cases takes places in a rational discourse.[1078] In this discourse, court judgments that, owing to their substantive merits, win a (large degree of) consensus among the legal community stand the best chance of becoming leading cases that shape the law.[1079]

This conclusion has significant relevance for the normative justification of case law in the Netherlands, and by analogy, in other codified legal systems. One of the objections to case law in codified legal systems is that, contrary to legislation, case law lacks democratic legitimacy, because judges are not elected.[1080] The analysis in this subparagraph, however, demonstrates that case law formed through a case law mechanism as that in the Netherlands, does not necessarily lack democratic legitimacy.[1081] After all, which cases become the law is determined through a relatively transparent and rational process in which various actors take part and exercise influence, while the winners of this process derive their status as leading cases ultimately from a certain consensus in the legal community. Accordingly, the mere fact that judges are not elected does not justify that case law formed through such a process mechanism lacks democratic legitimacy. This can perhaps be yet another reason to explicitly recognize cases as a source of law, which will be further discussed in the following subparagraph.

1.2 Case law mechanism in three phases: publication, utilization and recognition

The first part of this study not only investigated how cases are published and used in the Netherlands, it also examined the

[1078] The term rational discourse is borrowed from Kühn 2007, p. 379.
[1079] Loussouarn's paper suggests that the situation in France is quite silimar to that in the Netherlands in this respect, see Loussouarn 1958, p. 261.
[1080] Rijpkema 2001, p. 14.
[1081] The argument in this passage has been particularly inspired by Rijpkema 2001.

normative views of the legislature, judges and legal scholars towards the question whether cases ought to be recognized as a source of law. Chapter three revealed that a distinction can be made between explicit and implicit recognition of cases as a source of law. Moreover, the findings of chapter three indicate that the legislature, judges and legal scholars in the Netherlands are increasingly inclined to openly recognize cases as a source of law.

The findings of chapter three, when combined with those of chapter one and two, reveal that an explicit and unequivocal recognition of cases as a source of law by official actors such as the legislature and judges is not a necessary condition for cases to fulfil the role of a source of law in practice. After all, cases were already playing a very influential role in practice towards the end of the 19th and the beginning of the 20th century in the Netherlands,[1082] but it was not until the end of the first half of the 20th century that increasing evidence became apparent in legislative provisions and in legislation techniques that indicates an implicit recognition of cases as a source of law by the legislature.

Moreover, the findings of the first three chapters indicate that it was the increasing significance of cases in practice that pushed the boundaries of normative views on the status of cases as a source of law. Scholten, for example, observed in 1931 that "(t)he recognition of cases as authoritative is imposed upon us by the facts".[1083] The impact of the rising significance of cases in practice upon normative views on their status as a source of law is also reflected in a rhetorical question raised by Scholten: "(i)f we *have to*[1084] follow cases, what sense does it make to say that they are not a source of law?"[1085]

These findings suggest that case law mechanism in the Netherlands can also be seen as a process that consists of three, instead of two steps as illustrated in Figure 19. In this process, cases are first published and then used by certain types of actors in such a way that it becomes possible for litigants to reasonably rely on certain types of cases to defend legal propositions in court. Once the publication and the utilization of cases have reached such a level in

---

[1082] See e.g. Teixeira de Mattos 1885, p. 31 and Telders 1938.
[1083] Scholten 1931, p. 118.
[1084] Italicizing by Scholten.
[1085] Scholten 1931, p. 119.

practice that cases become capable of significantly influencing judicial decision-making, a third step follows whereby normative views become increasingly favorable towards openly recognizing cases as a source of law.

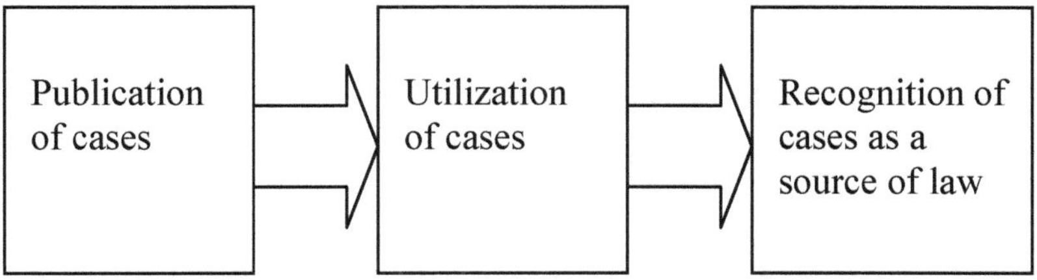

Figure 19 Case law mechanism as a process consisting of three steps

An advantage of using such a three-step framework is that it can integrate descriptive data and normative views and it can help to draw the attention of the researcher and the readers to the possible dynamics between the actual significance of cases in practice and the normative views on the status of cases as a source of law. A drawback of the three-step framework as presented in this subparagraph is, however, that it tends to imply that the influence pattern is like a one-way street, i.e. increasing significance of cases in practice pushes the boundaries of normative views, but in reality it is not unthinkable that the influence can be mutual, i.e. increasingly favorable normative views towards explicitly recognizing cases as a source of law can in turn further stimulate the use of cases in practice and thus further strengthen the influence of cases in practice. Again, this study is of an explorative nature. The findings that this study has generated are not of such a nature that they can accurately reveal the exact influence patterns between the significance of cases in practice on the one hand and the normative views on the status of cases as a source of law on the other. This study encourages other researchers to develop more rigorously designed methods and analytic tools to further investigate the dynamics between the two.

2. Implications for comparative law literature related to the role of cases in civil law jurisdictions

Chapter four of this study linked the findings of the first three chapters to the existing English-language literature related to the role of cases in civil law jurisdictions. For example, it pointed out that in the debate on the question whether the common law and the civil legal families are converging, many scholars adopt a *result*-oriented argumentation, i.e. the conclusion that the two legal families are converging often relies on an observation that where lawyers in civil law jurisdictions invoke arguments based on previous cases, especially those decided by the highest courts, the *result* that such arguments are likely to achieve in civil law courts would be very similar to what common lawyers would be able to achieve in court by citing precedents. Using a *process*-oriented approach as the one developed by this study to explore the role of cases as a source of law may possibly shed new light on the similarities and differences between the common law and the civil law legal families and may contribute new insights to the convergence debate.

As a result of the findings of the first part of this study as well as the analysis made in the first paragraph of this final conclusion, this paragraph will highlight one final key argument, i.e. case law is *not* purely judge-made law in the Netherlands, and by careful analogy, nor in many other continental European civil law jurisdictions.

As the introduction of this study already pointed out, the existing literature on the role of cases in civil law jurisdictions tends to focus primarily on the role of judges and court-related institutions in the functioning of case law in civil law jurisdictions.[1086] When reviewing this body of literature, one can hardly avoid the impression that case law in civil law jurisdictions is judge-made law,[1087] i.e. whether cases are capable of functioning as a source of law in practice and if so, which cases eventually become the law depend on how judges treat them. Some authors, for example, initially submitted that only constant court practice (*jurisprudence constant*) was capable of creating law, i.e. only when courts repeatedly decided a question of law in a certain fashion, would this

---

[1086] See e.g. Deák 1934, Lipstein 1946, Cappelletti 1981, MacCormick & Summers 1997b and Zweigert & Kötz 1998, p. 256-275.

[1087] Some authors explicitly use the term "judge-made law" to refer to case law in civil law jurisdictions, see e.g. Lawson 1977, p. 82 where the author observed that "French law has become almost as much a system of judge-made law as English law", Eorsi 1996, p. 76, Kiel & Göttingen 1997, p. 45 and Dedek & Schermaier 2012, p. 362.

position adopted by the courts become the law.[1088] Later on, it was recognized that even a single case decided by a court of last resort in a civil law jurisdiction can become the law.[1089]

This tendency to equate case law with judge-made law seems to be related to the fact that the role of cases in civil law jurisdictions is usually studied from the perspective of the common law doctrine of precedent.[1090] As case law and judge-made law are commonly used as interchangeable terms in common law jurisdictions,[1091] scholars that adopt the paradigm of the common law doctrine of precedent to study the role of cases in civil law jurisdictions may have simply taken over this usage in their writings.

In a formal sense, there is of course an argument to be made for the proposition that case law is judge-made law. One may, for example, define case law as legal principles and rules enunciated and embodied in judicial decisions.[1092] As judges make judicial decisions, one may subsequently argue that judges can also be considered to be the authors, at least in a formal sense, of the principles and rules enunciated and embodied in such decisions.

However, it is doubtful whether it is appropriate to assert that in civil law jurisdictions case law is entirely made by judges, or to use a terminology borrowed from the common law doctrine of precedent that, without further qualification, may raise an inaccurate impression. Chapter two demonstrated, for example, that some case law norms were originally developed in scholarly writings,[1093] so that it is doubtful whether it would be fair to say that, in substance, such norms are entirely made by judges. Moreover, this study demonstrated that which previous judicial decisions eventually become the leading cases that shape the law depends on the

---

[1088] See e.g. Silving 1966, p. 198 and Kiel & Göttingen 1997, p. 44-45.
[1089] See e.g. Lipstein 1946, p. 36 and 42 and Glastra van Loon e.a. 1968, p. 140.
[1090] See e.g. MacCormick & Summers 1997c, p. 13 and Komárek 2013, p. 150.
[1091] See e.g. Pound 1908, Landis 1930, Deák 1934, p. 340, Currier 1965 and Scott 1999.
[1092] Hargreaves 2013, p. 307 footnote 7.
[1093] See the subparagraph in chapter two that analyses the contribution by legal scholars to the case law mechanism in the Netherlands.

outcome of a process of rational discourse in which not only judges, but also other actors such as legal scholars and practising lawyers participate and exercise influence.[1094] Persistent and severe scholarly criticism on a previous judicial decision may, for example, reduce the likelihood that the decision will be followed in later court practice, as scholarly reactions to judicial decisions are an important factor that together with a number of other factors jointly determine the weight that judges attribute to previous court decisions when using them in adjudication practice.[1095]

One may, of course, argue that, although legal scholars and other actors do participate in a process of rational discourse that determines the development of case law, the voice of judges, and in particular that of Supreme Court judges, carries significantly more weight than the opinions of other actors, because judicial decisions are backed by state coercion and can be enforced to affect the actual legal rights and obligations of the litigating parties, whereas the views of legal scholars and practising lawyers are mere opinions that have no particular coercive force.[1096] Such an observation is not necessarily wrong. However, even if this observation was accurate, it could only serve to emphasize a particularly important influence of judges in the forming and development of case law, but it does not justify the assertion that case law is *purely* made by judges in civil law jurisdictions.

The purpose of this study, it should be stressed, is not to engage in a wordplay. Rather, the aim is to add some nuance to many of the existing writings that concentrate on the role of judges in the operation of case law in civil law jurisdictions, by pointing out that the role of judges, important as it is, should not be isolated from a proper context, as judges are not the only actors who shape the development of case law and they derive considerable benefit from the work of other players in law such as legal scholars, practising lawyers and, in the case of Supreme Court judges in the

[1094] See the subparagraph in chapter two that examines the way cases are used in adjudication in the Netherlands.
[1095] See the subparagraph in chapter two that examines the various factors that influence the weight a case carries in judicial deliberation.
[1096] See e.g. Lawson 1977, p. 82-83.

Netherlands, advisory officers such as the Procurator General and the Advocates General.[1097]

Moreover, this study wishes to draw attention to one of the limitations of adopting a concept or a paradigm from one legal family to describe or analyse a phenomenon in another legal family without careful qualifications, as such a practice may cause confusion or lead to inaccurate understandings.[1098]

This study experimented with the use of a relatively neutral concept to capture the functioning of cases as a source of law in civil law jurisdictions, i.e. the concept of case law mechanism. In addition, this study developed an analytic framework that does not rely on the common law doctrine of precedent to explore the functioning of case law in a civil law jurisdiction.[1099] When describing the way cases fulfil the function of a source of law in the Netherlands, this study tried its best to use neutral terms as much as possible instead of concepts that are typically associated with the doctrine of precedent in the common law legal family. For example, the term "previous cases" is used instead of "precedents" to refer to judicial decisions made in the past.[1100] Also, the neutral term "influence" is used instead of "binding force" or "persuasive force" to describe the impact of previous cases on judicial decision-making.[1101] By making such efforts, this study strives to avoid causing the readers to (unintentionally) project their understandings of the common law doctrine of precedent on the functioning of cases in the Netherlands. Hopefully these methodological attempts will stimulate legal scholars to reflect on the soundness of the common approach in the existing literature to examine the role of cases in civil law jurisdictions from the perspective of the common law doctrine of precedent, and to design more suitable analytic tools to explore the role of cases in civil law jurisdictions.

[1097] See the subparagraph in chapter two that examines the way cases are used in adjudication in the Netherlands.

[1098] See Komárek 2012, p. 54.

[1099] See the paragraph in the introduction of this study that presents the concept of case law mechanism and the analytic framework.

[1100] This approach is inspired by MacCormick & Summers 1997c, p. 13 and Komárek 2012, p. 54.

[1101] Ibid.

3. Implications for China's quest for case law

Chapter five of this study examined a relatively recent phenomenon in China, i.e. a growing interest among judges and legal scholars in developing and using case law, despite the fact that China's codified legal system does not allow judges to fulfil a lawmaking role and hence does not recognize cases as a source of law. The growing interest in case law, as chapter five revealed, was triggered by a number of problems to which many Chinese legal scholars and judges believe that case law can offer an effective cure. A fundamental problem is that due to the lack of an institutionalized system through which societal norms can move bottom-up to become part of the national legal system, the legislature in China has to take on the task of striking a proper balance in lawmaking between four competing requirements: adequacy, feasibility, certainty and adaptability, which is extremely difficult in such a large and fast developing country as China with a unitary legal system where lawmaking is largely a top-down process dominated by a relatively small group of powerful people.[1102] Another widely perceived problem in China is that like cases reach different outcomes in different courts across China, thus undermining the legal unity and the public confidence in the courts.[1103] Many Chinese legal scholars and judges argue that case law can be an effective tool to counterbalance the limitations of legislation, enhance consistency in court judgments, increase transparency in adjudication and curb judicial corruption.[1104]

After decades of debates and court experiments, the Supreme People's Court of China finally introduced a new legal institution called the "Case Guidance System" in November 2010.[1105] The essence of this new legal institution is that it creates an exclusive power for the Supreme People's Court to select so-called "guiding cases"[1106] from candidate cases recommended by courts at all levels throughout China. Once selected and published,

[1102] Van Rooij 2006, p. 25-104.

[1103] See the paragraph in chapter five that discusses the problems that triggered a growing interest in case law in China.

[1104] Ibid.

[1105] The Chinese term is 案例指导制度(Anli Zhidao Zhidu).

[1106] The Chinese term is 指导案例(Zhidao Anli).

the guiding cases are supposed to be followed in all courts across China.

These findings, when compared with those summarized in the first paragraph of this final conclusion, reveal that both China's Case Guidance System and the case law mechanism in the Netherlands can be seen as a process of selecting leading cases. The way leading cases are selected in China, however, differs considerably from the way leading cases are selected in the Netherlands.

In the Netherlands, as revealed in the first paragraph of this final conclusion as well as in chapter two, the selection takes place in a relatively transparent rational discourse, in which various actors such as judges, legal scholars and practising lawyers have a chance to influence the outcome of the selection by conducting a relatively visible and traceable debate on the merits of published cases in open forums such as court adjudication and academic or legal professional publications. The outcome of such a selection process can be reasonably said to rely on a (certain degree of) consensus among the legal community.

The selection procedure in China, as revealed in chapter four, is largely non-transparent and lacks an open and traceable debate on the pros and cons of the candidate cases by relevant actors such as judges, legal scholars and practising lawyers. The candidate cases do not have to be published before they enter the selection procedure. The selection process takes place entirely within the judiciary. All courts lower than the Supreme People's Court are required to select and recommend candidate cases to the Supreme People's Court. It is a small group of people who occupy high positions, such as the president, the vice presidents and the chief judges of various sections within a court, that decides which cases will be selected and recommended as candidate cases to the Supreme People's Court. Within the Supreme People's Court, a final selection takes place. The final decision is again made by a small group of powerful people who occupy high positions in the Supreme People's Court. Discussions on the pros and cons of the candidate cases are kept secret in all courts and are therefore inaccessible to actors who are not authorized to select cases. This means that not only actors outside the judiciary such as legal scholars and practising lawyers, but even many actors within the judiciary, i.e. the vast majority of judges that do not occupy high positions in a court, have no way to ascertain which candidate cases have been considered and what the substantive considerations have been during the selection procedure. It is, consequently, very doubtful whether the outcome of such a non-transparent selection procedure can be said to rely on a certain degree of consensus among the legal community.

Chapter five of this study reflected on some of the limitations of the Case Guidance System and expressed doubts as to whether the Case Guidance System alone would be able to successfully solve the problems that it is intended to address. It was submitted that the rigid selection procedure might make it very unlikely for the Case Guidance System to produce a sufficient amount of guiding cases that can satisfy the demand for case law in court practice throughout China. Consequently, it was submitted that making effective use of the vast body of unselected cases can be a crucial supplement to the Case Guidance System. Chapter six subsequently argued, among other things, that for an optimal use of the vast body of unselected cases, it is highly desirable that legal scholars in China conduct extensive and systematic research into unselected cases and that law schools in China intensify the use of cases in legal education.

This paragraph, as part of the final conclusion of this study, will not repeat what has already been put forward in chapter six. Instead, prompted by the analysis in the first paragraph on the way leadings cases are selected in the Netherlands and the comparison made earlier in this paragraph, this paragraph will draw the reader's attention to one crucial question that the development of case law in China still needs to address, i.e. the normative justification for case law in a codified legal system that officially denies cases to be a source of law.

One of the most fundamental normative objections to case law, both in the Netherlands and in China, is that case law lacks democratic legitimacy because judges are not elected. [1107] Obviously, in reality China is an authoritarian country where no open, fair and meaningful general elections take place, so that even the official legislature in China, i.e. the National People's Congress

[1107] See e.g. Li 2009a and Rijpkema 2001, p. 14.

and the People's Congresses at various local levels, can hardly be said to enjoy sufficient democratic legitimacy.[1108] However, at least in theory, the legislature in China is an elected representative body. The courts in China, on the other hand, are not even in theory elected. This means that the normative objection that case law lacks democratic legitimacy in China because judges are not elected is certainly not groundless and ultimately needs to be addressed.

Up till now the Supreme People's Court seems to be very unwilling to openly engage with this question. The Supreme People's Court is, for example, extremely vague about the legal basis of the Case Guidance System that it introduced in November 2010. The Court only refers very generally to the *Organic Law of the People's Courts* without specifying which provision(s) of this legislation justifies or justify this new legal institution that is supposed to create case law.[1109] The Supreme People's Court's answer seems to rely on a theory of mandate, i.e. the Supreme People's Court obtained a mandate from the legislature to interpret legislation via the *Organic Law of the People's Courts* and the Case Guidance System is a way through which the Supreme People's Court interprets legislation.[1110]

This study wishes to point out that the mandate theory is not the only possible solution. In fact, this study highly doubts whether the mandate theory chosen by the Supreme People's Court is the most satisfactory response. In the first place, it should be pointed out that this theory relies on a mandate to *interpret* legislation. It can be doubted whether such a theory is entirely honest and accurate. In fact, the Case Guidance System not only enables the Supreme People's Court to *interpret* existing legislation, but also to *create* new rules that can hardly be said to rely on existing legislation. Accordingly, even if the mandate theory justifies guiding cases that do nothing more than interpreting existing legislation, it *cannot* sufficiently justify cases that create new rules.

Another, and much more fundamental reason why it is doubtful whether the mandate theory is a desirable answer, is that

---

[1108] For discussions on the authoritarian nature of the regime in China see Weatherley 2006 and Stockmann & Gallagher 2011.
[1109] See the relevant passages in chapter five that discusses the legal basis of the Case Guidance System.
[1110] Ibid.

the National People's Congress has only mandated the Supreme People's Court to interpret legislation, which means that this theory only justifies the legitimacy of guiding cases selected by the Supreme People's Court, but does not recognize any general normative force of cases decided or selected by any other actor. In other words, this theory can easily lead to a conclusion that *only* cases selected by the Supreme People's Court have particular normative force, so that judges are justified to ignore all the unselected cases. Such an understanding would induce an attitude to treat unselected cases as a waste and would accordingly render the use of the vast body of unselected cases in court extremely difficult. This would be highly undesirable, as explained in chapter five, because the vast body of unselected cases may contain valuable materials that, if used properly, can meaningfully supplement the Case Guidance System to satisfy the demand for case law in China.

An alternative approach is not to hide, but to recognize the fact that case law can be or is already a lawmaking mechanism in China. The objection to case law based on a lack of democratic legitimacy can be weakened, if the process through which case law is formed in China can be designed or can evolve in such a way that the selection of leading cases takes place in a transparent discourse in which various actors can exercise meaningful influence through rational debates, so that the outcome can be reasonably said to rely on a certain consensus in the legal community.[1111] If this can be achieved, then the lack of democratic legitimacy due to the fact that judges are not elected can be, at least to a certain degree, compensated by an open and transparent leading case selection process, which is likely to generate case law that is in conformity with the dominant values and norms in the society.

The Case Guidance System introduced by the Supreme People's Court, however, seems to go exactly in the opposite direction. Under this new legal institution, the selection process is designed in such a way that only a small group of powerful people within the judiciary who occupy high positions exercise decisive influence on the selection of guiding cases in a process that largely takes place in secrecy. Such a design does not weaken, but rather further *strengthens* the normative objection to case law in China due

[1111] Inspiration for this argument has been drawn from Rijpkema 2001.

to a lack of democratic legitimacy. It can therefore be rightly questioned whether the mandate theory and the non-transparent selection process would be conducive eventually to the development of case law in China.

It should, once again, be noted that it is not true that the Case Guidance System introduced by the Supreme People's Court is unlikely to induce any positive effect. This new legal institution can, for example, raise the overall case law awareness among Chinese judges, legal scholars and practising lawyers and can produce at least a small body of cases that may prove to be useful for court practice in China. By reflecting on some of the limitations of the Case Guidance System, this study wishes to draw the attention of those who participate in the case law debate in China or are interested in the development of case law in China to some of the overlooked aspects in China's quest for case law, and to invite them to look beyond the courts and to seek creative approaches that may ultimately lead to an effective case law mechanism in China.

Appendices

Appendix 1 Overview of periodicals containing case reports in the Netherlands[1112]

I. Periodicals that started in the 19th century

Nr.		Title of Periodical	Start/End Year
1	*	Periodiek woordenboek van administratieve en gerechtelijke beslissingen (Periodic Dictionary of Administrative and Judicial Decisions)[1113]	1829-present
2	*	Verzameling van gewijsden in zaken van Zee-assurantie (Collection of Judicial Decisions in Sea Insurance Cases)	1838-1859
3	*	Nederlandsche regtspraak (Netherlands Court Judgments)	1839-1913
4	*	Het regt in Nederland, Regtsgeleerd tijdschrift (The Law in the Netherlands, Legal Journal)	1839-1850
5	*	Weekblad van het regt (Law Weekly)	1839-1943
6	*	Verzameling van Arresten van den Hoogen Raad der Nederlanden (Collection of Judgments by the Supreme Court of the Netherlands)	1840-1904
7		De gemeente-stem (The Voice of Municipalities)	1851-present
8	*	Magazijn van handelsregt (Journal of Commercial Law)	1859-1875
9	*	Nederlandsche Pasicrisie (Netherlands Pasicrisie)	1871-1917

[1112] This is not a complete overview of all case reporting periodicals in the Netherlands, see the methodological notes at the end of this overview.
[1113] The title of this periodical underwent a number of changes. The current title is *Rechtspraak notariaat (Public Notary Cases)*.

10	*	Paleis van justitie (Palace of Justice)	1872-1910
11		Weekblad voor de administratie der directe belastingen, in- en uitgaande rechten en accijnzen (Weekly for the Administration of Direct Taxes, Import and Export Tariffs and Duties)[1114]	1872-present
12	*	De juridische spectator (The Legal Spectator)	1874-1876

II. Periodicals that started in the first half of the 20th century

Nr.		Title of Periodical	Start/End Year
1	*	Militair-rechterlijk tijdschrift (Military Law Journal)	1905-present
2	*	Rechterlijke beslissingen inzake de wet op de arbeidsovereenkomst (Judicial Decisions on the Labor Contract Act)	1909-1942
3	*	Beslissingen in belastingzaken[1115] (Decisions in Tax Cases)	1910-present
4	*	Nederlandse jurisprudentie: uitspraken in burgerlijke en strafzaken (Netherlands Cases: Judgments in Civil and Criminal Cases)	1913-present
5	*	Periodieke verzameling van beslissingen op de Nederlandsche staatswetten (Periodic Collection	1916-present

[1114] The title of this periodical underwent a number of changes. The current title is *Weekblad voor fiscaal recht (Tax Law Weekly)*.

[1115] The title of this periodical underwent a number changes. The current title is *BNB: beslissingen in belastingzaken, Nederlandse belastingrechtspraak (BNB: Decisions in Tax Cases, Netherlands Tax Cases)*.

		of Judicial Decisions on Netherlands State Laws)[1116]	
6		Advocatenblad (Lawyers' Magazine)	1918-present
7		De Naamlooze vennootschap: maandblad voor den ondernemingsvorm en het bedrijfswezen in Nederland en Nederlandsch Indië[1117] (The Public Limited Company: Monthly for Business Enterprises and Companies in the Netherlands and the Dutch East Indies)	1923-present
8		Nederlands juristenblad (Netherlands Jurists' Magazine)	1923-present
9	*	Bijblad bij De industrieele eigendom (Supplement to the Industrial Property)[1118]	1933-present
10	*	Rechtspraak van de week (Cases of the Week)	1939-present
11	*	Losbladig fiscaal weekblad FED[1119] (Loose-leaf Fiscal Weekly FED)	1940-present
12	*	Tribunalen in Nederland en andere na-oorlogsche rechtspraak	1945-1951

[1116] The title of this periodical underwent a number of changes. The current title is *AB rechtspraak bestuursrecht (AB Administrative Law Cases)*.

[1117] In 2009, this periodical merged with *TVVS: maandblad voor ondernemingsrecht en rechtspersonen (TVVS: Monthly Magazine for Business Law and Legal Personals)*. After the merge the title changed to *Tijdschrift voor ondernemingsrecht (Magazine for Business Law)*.

[1118] The title of this periodical underwent a number changes. The current title is *Berichten industriële eigendom (Industrial Properties Messages)*.

[1119] The title of this periodical underwent a number of changes. The current title is *Fiscaal tijdschrift (Fiscal Magazine)*.

		(Tribunals in the Netherlands and Other Judgments after the War)[1120]	
13	*	Vakstudie nieuws: documentatie op het gebied van het fiscaal recht (Professional Study News: Documentation in the Field of Tax Law)	1948-present
14		Het personeel statuut: maandblad gewijd aan het personen- en nationaliteitsrecht (The Personal Statute: Personal and Nationlality Law Monthly)[1121]	1950-present

III. Periodicals that started in the second half of the 20th century

Nr.		Name of Periodical	Start/End Year
1	*	Verkeersrecht (Traffic Law)	1953-present
2	*	Sociaal maandblad arbeid (Labour Social Monthly)[1122]	1954-present
3	*	Schip en schade (Ship and Damage)	1957-present
4	*	Rechtspraak sociale verzekering (Social Insurance Cases)	1958-present
5		Tijdschrift voor vennootschappen, verenigingen en stichtingen (Magazine for Companies, Associations and Foundations)[1123]	1958-2009
6	*	Bouwrecht (Construction Law)	1963-present

[1120] In 1948, the title of this periodical changed to *Na-oorlogse rechtspraak (Judgments after the War)*.
[1121] In 1993, this periodical merged with *Burgerzaken (Civil Cases)*. After the merge, the title changed to *Burgerzaken & recht (Civil Cases & Law)*.
[1122] The title of this periodical underwent a number of changes due to merges. The current title is *Tijdschrift recht en arbeid (Law and Labour Magazine)*.
[1123] The title of this periodical underwent a number of changes. In 2009, it merged with *De naamloze vennootschap* (*The Public Limited Company*) to form a new periodical *Tijdschrift voor ondernemingsrecht* (*Business Law Journal*).

7		Delikt en delinkwent (Delict and delinquent)	1970-present
8	*	De praktijkgids (The Practice Guide)	1971-present
9	*	Rechtspraak ondernemingsraad (Employees Council Cases)	1971-present
10	*	Rechtspraak Ziekenfondswet en Algemene Wet Bijzondere Ziektekosten (Cases on National Health Service Act and General Act Special Health Care Costs) [1124]	1972-present
11	*	Verkeersrecht Jurisprudentie ANWB (Traffic Law Cases ANWB)	1972-present
12		Werkgroep Rechtsbijstand in vreemdelingenzaak (Study Group Legal Aid in Immigration Cases)[1125]	1972-present
13		Tijdschrift voor milieu en recht (Magazine for Environment and Law)[1126]	1974-present
14		Auteursrecht (Copy Right)[1127]	1977-present
15		Tijdschrift voor gezondheidsrecht (Health Care Law Journal)	1977-present
16	*	Jurisprudentie algemene bijstandswet en rijksgroepsregelingen (Cases on	1978-present

[1124] The title of this periodical underwent a number of changes. The current title is *Rechtspraak zorgverzekering* (*Health Insurance Cases*).
[1125] The title of this periodical underwent a number of changes. The current title is *Asiel en migrantenrecht* (*Asylum and Migration Law*).
[1126] In 1995, the title changed to *Milieu en recht* (*Environment and Law*).
[1127] The title of this periodical underwent a number of changes. The current title is *AMI: tijdschrift voor auteurs-, media- en informatierecht* (*Journal for Copy Right, Media and Information Law*).

		the General Social Security Act and the National Group Rules)[1128]	
17		Tijdschrift voor familie- en jeugdrecht (Family and Youth Law Journal)	1979-present
18		Tijdschrift voor arbitrage (Arbitration Journal)	1980-present
19	*	Kort geding (Interim Injunction Proceedings)	1981-2003[1129]
20	*	Belastingblad: tijdschrift voor provinciale, gemeentelijke en waterschapsbelastingen (Tax Magazine: Journal for Provincial, Municipal and District Water Board Tax)	1982-present
21	*	Woonrecht (Housing Law)	1982-present
22	*	Nederlands internationaal privaatrecht (Dutch International Private Law)	1983-present
23		Computerrecht: tijdschrift voor informatica en recht (Computer Law: Journal for Computer Science and Law)	1984-present
24		Kwartaalbericht Nieuwe BW[1130] (Quarterly Bulletin New Civil Code)	1984-present
25	*	Tijdschrift voor ambtenarenrecht (Journal for Civil Servant Law)	1984-present
26	*	Intellectuele eigendom en reclamerecht (Intellectual Property	1985-present

[1128] The title of this periodical underwent a number of changes. The current title is *Jurisprudentie wet werk en bijstand* (*Cases on Work and Social Security Act*).

[1129] In 2003, this periodical merged with *NJ Kort* (*NJ Short*) and formed a new periodical called *Nederlandse jurisprudentie feitenrechtspraak: civiele uitspraken* (*Netherlands Cases Adjudication by Lower Courts: Civil Cases*).

[1130] In 1992, the title changed to *Nederlands tijdschrift voor burgerlijk recht (Dutch Civil Law Journal).*

		and Advertisement Law)	
27	*	Tijdschrift voor consumentenrecht (Consumer Law Journal)[1131]	1985-present
28		Verzekeringsnieuws: focus op rechtspraak (Insurance News, Focus on Cases)	1985-present
29		Journaal NV/BV (Journal NV/BV)[1132]	1986-present
30		Nederlands tijdschrift voor sociaal recht (Dutch Journal for Social Law)[1133]	1986-2009
31	*	Jurisprudentie sociale voorzieningen (Social Services Cases)	1987-2005[1134]
32		Stichting en vereniging (Foundation and Association)[1135]	1987-present
33		Tijdschrift voor milieu aansprakelijkheid (Journal for Environmental Liability)[1136]	1987-present
34		Tijdschrift voor pensioenvraagstukken (Journal for	1987-present

[1131] In 2005, the title of this periodical changed to *Tijdschrift voor consumentenrecht en handelspraktijk (Journal for Consumer Law and Trade Practice)*.

[1132] The title of this periodical underwent a number of changes. The current title is *Journaal ondernemingsrecht (Journal Business Law)*.

[1133] In 2009, this periodical merged with *Tijdschrift over arbeid en sociale zekerheid (Journal for Labour and Social Security)*. After the merge, the title changed to *Tijdschrift recht en arbeid (Law and Labour Journal)*.

[1134] In 2005, this periodical was absorbed by another periodical called *Jurisprudentie Wet werk en bijstand (Cases on Work and Social Security Act)*.

[1135] The title of this periodical underwent a number of changes. The current title is *Tijdschrift voor ondernemingsbestuur (Journal for Corporate Governance)*.

[1136] The title of this periodical underwent a number of changes. The current title is *Tijdschrift gezondheidsschade, milieuschade en aansprakelijkheidsrecht (Journal for Health Law, Environment Damage and Liability Law)*.

		Pension Issues)	
35	*	Uitspraken College van Beroep voor het bedrijfsleven (Cases decided by the Administrative Court for Trade and Industry)[1137]	1987-present
36	*	Fiscale berichten voor het notariaat (Tax Bulletin for the Notarial Profession)	1989-present
37		Verzekeringsrechtelijke berichten (Insurance Law Bulletin)[1138]	1989-2000
38	*	Juridische berichten voor het notariaat (Legal Bulletin for the Notarial Profession)	1990-present
39		Sancties: tijdschrift over straffen en maatregelen (Sanctions: Journal for Punishments and Non-punitive Orders)	1990-present
40	*	Jurisprudentie voor gemeenten (Cases for Municipalities)	1990-present
41	*	Jurisprudentie arbeidsrecht (Labour Law Cases)	1992-present
42	*	Jurisprudentie burgerlijk procesrecht (Civil Procedural Law Cases)	1992-present
43	*	NJ Kort	1992-2003[1139]
44	*	EchtscheidingBulletin: tijdschrift over de fiscale en juridische aspecten van echtscheiding (Divorce Bulletin: Journal on the	1993-present

[1137] The title of this periodical underwent a number of changes. The current title is *Het CBb in (The CBb in)*.

[1138] In 2001, this periodical merged with *Aansprakelijkheid en verzekering (Liability and Insurance)*. After the merge, the title changed to *Aansprakelijkheid, verzekering en schade (Liability, Insurance and Damage)*.

[1139] In 2003, this periodical merged with *Kort geding (Interim Injunction Proceedings)* and formed a new periodical called *Nederlandse jurisprudentie feitenrechtspraak: civiele uitspraken (Netherlands Cases Adjudication by Lower Courts: Civil Cases)*.

		Fiscal and Legal Aspects of Divorce)	
45	*	Conclusies rechtspraak van de week (Conclusions Cases of the Week)	1993-2000
46		Aansprakelijkheid en verzekering (Liability and Insurance)[1140]	1993-present
47	*	BOPZ jurisprudentie (BOPZ Cases)[1141]	1994-present
48	*	Jurisprudentie bestuursrecht (Administrative Law Cases)	1994-present
49	*	Rechtseenheidskamer Vreemdelingenzaken (Legal Unity Section in Migration Cases)	1994-1997
50	*	Pensioen jurisprudentie (Pension Cases)	1995-present
51		Tijdschrift voor insolventierecht (Insolvency Law Journal)	1995-present
52	*	Jurisprudentie onderneming en recht (Business and Law Cases)	1996-present
53	*	Jurisprudentie ontnemingswetgeving (Depossession Law Cases)	1996-present
54	*	Jurisprudentie aanbesteding (Tender Cases)	1996-present
55	*	Jurisprudentie nationaliteitsrecht (Nationality Law Cases)	1996-present
56		Tijdschrift vervoer en recht (Transport and Law Journal)	1996-present
57		Vastgoed fiscaal: fiscaal nieuwsbulletin voor de	1996-present

[1140] In 2001, this periodical merged with *Verzekeringsrechtelijke berichten (Insurance Law Bulletin)*. After the merge, the title changed to *Aansprakelijkheid, verzekering en schade (Liability, Insurance and Damage)*.

[1141] The title of this periodical underwent a number of changes. The current title is *Jurisprudentie verplichte geestelijke gezondheidszorg (Compulsory Mental Health Care Cases)*.

		vastgoedsector (Real Estate Tax: Tax News Bulletin for the Real Estate Sector)[1142]	
58	*	Jurisprudentie milieurecht (Environment Law Cases)	1997-present
59	*	Jurisprudentie vreemdelingenrecht (Migration Law Cases)	1997-present
60		Nieuwsbrief strafrecht: actuele informatie over wetgeving, beleid, jurisprudentie (Newsletter Criminal Law: Current Information on Legislation, Policy, Case Law)	1997-present
61	*	Uitspraken sociale zekerheid (Social Security Cases)	1997-present
62		Letsel en schade (Injury and Damages)	1997-present
63		Nieuwsbrief mededingingsrecht (Newsletter Competition Law)[1143]	1998-present
64		Privacy en informatie (Privacy and Information)	1998-present
65		Tijdschrift voor vergoeding personenschade (Journal for Compensation of Personal Damages)	1998-present
66	*	Jurisprudentie Online (Online Cases)	1999-2008
67	*	Nieuwsbrief vreemdelingenrecht (Migration Law News Letter)[1144]	1999-present
68		Praktisch procederen (Practical Litigation)[1145]	1999-present

[1142] In 2003, the title changed to *Vastgoed fiscaal en civiel (Real Estate Tax and Civil)*.
[1143] The title of this periodical underwent a number of changes. The current title is *MP: tijdschrift mededingingsrecht in de praktijk (MP: Journal of Competition Law in Practice)*.
[1144] In 2002, the title of this periodical changed to *Journaal vreemdelingenrecht*.
[1145] In 2008 the title changed to *Tijdschrift voor de procespraktijk*.

69		Tijdschrift voor effectenrecht (Securities Law Journal)[1146]	1999-present
70	*	Uitspraken studiefinanciering (Student Grants Cases)	1999-1999
71		Nederlands tijdschrift voor fiscaal recht (Dutch Journal for Tax Law)	2000-present

IV. Periodicals that started in the 21st century

Nr.		Name of Periodical	Start/End Year
1	*	Jurisprudentie geneesmiddelenrecht (Medicine Law Cases)	2000-present
2	*	ARO: Actuele rechtspraak ondernemingspraktijk (ARO: Current Business Practice Cases)	2002-present
3	*	Jurisprudentie burgerlijk procesrecht (Civil Procedure Law Cases)	2002-present
4	*	Jurisprudentie huur en verhuur (Rent en Let Cases)	2002-present
5		Overheid en aansprakelijkheid (Government and Liability)	2002-present
6	*	Nederlandse jurisprudentie feitenrechtspraak: civiele uitspraken (Netherlands Cases Adjudication by Lower Courts: Civil Cases)	2003-present
7		Journaal bestuursrecht (Administrative Law Journal) [1147]	2004-present
8	*	Jurisprudentie in Nederland (Case Law in the Netherlands)	2004-present
9	*	Jurisprudentie aansprakelijkheid (Tort Law Cases)	2004-present
10	*	Gezondheidszorg jurisprudentie (Health Law Cases)	2004-present

[1146] In 2005 the title changed to *Tijdschrift voor financieel recht.*
[1147] In 2010, the title changed to *Tijdschrift voor praktisch bestuursrecht.*

11	*	Jurisprudentie wegenverkeersrecht (Traffic Law Cases)	2004-present
12		Nederlands tijdschrift voor handelsrecht (Netherlands Journal for Commercial Law)	2004-present
13	*	Rechtspraak familierecht (Family Law Cases)	2004-present
14	*	StAB: jurisprudentietijdschrift op het gebied van ruimtelijke ordening, milieubeheer en water (Case Law Journal in the Field of Spacial Planning, Environment and Water Management)	2004-present
15		Journaal insolventie, financiering en zekerheden (Insolvency, Financing and Securities Journal)[1148]	2004-present
16	*	Jurisprudentie bodem (Soil Cases)	2005-present
17	*	Jurisprudentie personen- en familierecht (Personal and Family Law Cases)	2005-present
18	*	Nederlandse jurisprudentie feitenrechtspraak strafzaken (Netherlands Cases in Lower Instances, Criminal Law Cases)	2005-present
19	*	Rechtspraak arbeidsrecht (Labor Law Cases)	2005-present
20	*	Rechtspraak financieel recht (Financial Law Cases)	2006-present
21	*	Jurisprudentie omgevingsrecht (Environmental Law Cases)	2006-present
22	*	Rechtspraak ondernemingsrecht (Company Law Cases)	2006-present
23	*	Regelingen onderwijs totaal (Education Regulations)	2006-2010
24		Tijdschrift voor de	2006-present

[1148] In 2009, the title of this periodical changed to FIP: *tijdschrift financiering, zekerheden en insolventiepraktijk.*

		ondernemingsrechtpraktijk (Journal for the Practice of Company Law)	
25	*	Rechtspraak insolventierecht (Insolvency Law Cases)	2007-present
26	*	Rechtspraak Aansprakelijkheids- en verzekeringsrecht (Tort and Insurance Law Cases)	2007-present
27	*	Jurisprudentie levensmiddelenrecht (Food Law Cases)	2008-present
28	*	Rechtspraak contractenrecht (Contract Law Cases)	2008-present
29	*	Rechtspraak vastgoedrecht (Real Estate Law Cases)	2008-present
30		Tijdschrift arbeidsrecht praktijk (Journal for Labor Law Practice)	2008-present
31	*	Tijdschrift voor bouwrecht (Construction Law Journal)	2008-present
32	*	Vooropgestelde arresten (Priority Cases)	2008-present
33	*	Tijdschrift voor sport en recht (Journal for Sport and the Law)	2009-present

Methodological notes to this appendix:

1. Two sources have been searched to obtain this overview: the database portal *Rechtsorde*[1149] and the periodicals archive of the law library of the University of Amsterdam.[1150] *Rechtsorde* is a well-known legal information portal that incorporates, among other things, periodicals published by the most prominent commercial publishers of legal materials in the Netherlands such as Kluwer, SDU, Boom Juridische Uitgevers, Uitgeverij Paris and Ars Aequi.[1151] The periodicals archive of the law library of the

[1149] www.rechtsorde.nl
[1150] http://cf.uba.uva.nl/jb/tijdschriftenlijsten/alfabetische-tijdschriften.htm
[1151] http://www.rechtsorde.nl/index.php/product/bronnen/uitgeversbronnen/

University of Amsterdam was searched because it hosts many case report periodicals of the 19th century, which cannot be found in the database portal *Rechtsorde*. However, it should be noted that the collection of the law library of the University of Amsterdam is not necessarily complete. Readers are therefore reminded that this list is not exhaustive.

2. The start/end year of each periodical is based on the data provided by the database Picarta.[1152]

3. Periodicals marked by a star are publications that in principle only contain case reports (including case annotations), whereas others are periodicals that contain, in addition to regular case reports, other information such as journal articles, book reviews and news. Periodicals that do not contain regular case reports (i.e. periodicals that do not report cases or only incidentally report cases) have been excluded from the list.

[1152] www.picarta.nl

Appendix 2 Old case publication criteria used by the judiciary in the Netherlands

Selection Criteria Judgments Database Rechtspraak.nl[1153]
(December 1999 - March 2012)
The Judgments Database Rechtspraak.nl contains judgments that are selected because they:

- have attracted public attention;
- are important for public life;
- can affect the application of enacted laws and regulations;
- can be of value to interest groups;
- can be of value to indirectly interested parties (residents of a neighbourhood, village, city or region where the litigated issue takes place);
- can be of value to the press targeted at the legal profession.

Judgments can be of value to the press targeted at the legal profession in, for example, those cases where:

- for the first time a position is adopted with regard to a certain issue;
- previous cases are brought together to form a case law line, including, among other things, judgments containing legal reasoning and justification that can serve as an example;
- an existing case law line is abandoned;
- an existing case law line is refined;
- an existing case law line is applied by analogy with other cases;
- a case law line is extended to other fields or categories;
- the answer to a question of law is formulated or justified in a different way and opposite special circumstances occur in the context of the nature of the procedure, regardless whether the judgment has a special verdict.

[1153] My translation from Dutch into English. The original text of the old selection criteria is no longer available on the official website of the judiciary, but is on file.

In principle, no judgment will be selected:

- in cases that have been concluded in a simple way (court has apparently no jurisdiction/claim is apparently inadmissible/claim is apparently groundless/claim is apparently valid);
- in civil cases that have been concluded in absentia;
- in cases in the field of personal and family law that have been concluded in first instance without an appeal being lodged;
- in cases that have been concluded in the context of the administrative settlement of enforcement of traffic measures (the *Mulder Act*) without an appeal being lodged.

Appendix 3 New case publication criteria used by the judiciary in the Netherlands

Resolution Selection Criteria Judgments Database Rechtspraak.nl[1154]

The Council for the Judiciary, the Supreme Court of the Netherlands, the Administrative Law Division of the State Council, district courts, courts of appeal, the Central Appeals Court for the Public Service and for Social Security Matters [1155] and the Administrative Court for Trade and Industry[1156] have decided to adopt the following resolution.

Article 1
In this resolution the following terms are defined as:

a. publication: making something accessible to the public by adding it to the database on the website Rechtspraak.nl created for this purpose;
b. anonymizing: removing information that, separately or in connection, can reveal the identity of natural or legal persons that are not professionally involved in a case;
c. judgments: all judicial decisions, under whatever name and in whatever form.

Article 2
Only judgments of the following courts will be published on Rechtspraak.nl:

a. the Supreme Court of the Netherlands;
b. the Administrative Law Division of the State Council;
c. the Central Appeals Court for the Public Service and for Social Security Matters;

[1154] My translation from Dutch into English. The original Dutch version is availabe on the official portal website of the Judiciary, see http://www.rechtspraak.nl/Uitspraken-en-Registers/uitspraken/Selectiecriteria/Pages/default.aspx.
[1155] Translated according to J.H.M. Van Erp, *Nederlandse rechtsbegrippen vertaald, Frans, Engels, Duits (Dutch Legal Jargons Translated, French, English, German),* The Hague: T.M.C. Asser Press 1992.
[1156] Ibid.

d. the Administrative Court for Trade and Industry;
e. Courts of Appeal;
f. District Courts;
g. the Common Court of Justice of Aruba, Curaçao, Sint Maarten and van Bonaire, Sint Eustatius and Saba;
h. the Courts of first instance as defined in article 1 subparagraph f of the Common Court of Justice Act
i. the Court of Appeal for Tax Cases as defined in article 8:97 Tax Act BES;
j. the Court of Appeal for Civil Servants Cases as defined in article 17 of the Civil Servant Adjudication Act 1951 BES;
k. predecessors of the above-mentioned courts.

Article 3
Every judgment of the following courts/panels will be published:
a. the Supreme Court of the Netherlands;
b. the Administrative Law Division of the State Council;
c. the Central Appeals Court for the Public Service and for Social Security Matters;
d. the Administrative Court for Trade and Industry;
e. the Company Law Section of the Court of Appeal in Amsterdam;
f. the Intellectual Property Law Division of the Civil Law Section of the District Court in The Hague;
g. the Lease Section of the Court of Appeal in Arnhem;

as long as the case has not been held obviously groundless or inadmissible and/or has been dismissed by way of a standard formula.

Article 4
Paragraph 1 A judgment in the following legal proceedings will always be published:
a. Article 267 of the Treaty on the Functioning of the European Union concerning a request to the Court of Justice of the European Union for a preliminary ruling. This includes both the judgment that requests the preliminary ruling, and the judgment in the subsequent national legal proceeding after the preliminary ruling of the Court of Justice has been obtained;

b. Article 6:241 of the Civil Code concerning the right of collective litigation of consumer organizations against unreasonable consumer terms of companies, as far as the Court of Appeal in The Hague, applying paragraph 3 subparagraph c of the said article, has decided to publish the judgment;
c. Article 3:305d of the Civil Code concerning the Consumer Protection Enforcement Act, as far as the Court of Appeal in The Hague, applying paragraph 3 of the said article, has decided to publish the ruling.
d. Article 101 or 102 of the Treaty on the Functioning of the European Union concerning competition cases;
e. Legal proceedings concerning the Convention on Jurisdiction and the Recognition and Enforcement of Judgments in Civil and Commercial Matters (Convention of Lugano 2007) and all the instruments mentioned in article 64 paragraph 1 of this convention, unless they are apparently of no importance for the interpretation and the application of these instruments;
f. Request for the return of a child on the basis of the Hague Convention on the Civil Aspects of International Child Abduction 1980.

Paragraph 2 A judgment will always be published if:

a. a claim relying on the European Convention on Human Rights, International Convention on Civil and Political Rights, the UN Convention on the Rights of the Child or a convention that has been reached under the International Labour Organization, has been admitted or dismissed other than by way of a standard formula;
b. a judgment of a previous instance within the same procedure has already been published;
c. it involves a criminal case in which the charge is based on an offence defined in Title XIX of the Criminal Code, regardless of the nature of the judgment;
d. the judgment contains a sentence of imprisonment of four years or more and/or a hospital order;
e. it involves a ruling on a challenge to one or more judges.

Article 5

A judgment will always be published if:

a. before, during or after the court session, the case has attracted attention of the public media in the broadest sense;
b. the judgment has been published or discussed in a medium aimed at the legal profession;
c. the judgment is of particular importance for a certain professions or interest groups;
d. the judgment also affects the interests of natural or legal persons that were no party to the case;
e. the case has a precedent-forming character, for example because it changes, refines, limits or broadens an earlier case law line, or because a certain fact complex or a legislative provision has been submitted to the judgment of the court for the first time.

Article 6

Paragraph 1 Judgments of district courts and courts of appeal, in particular those made by panels consisting of more than one judge, will be published as much as possible, where they have not been published under articles 3, 4 or 5 and in so far as they do not contain mere standard formulas.

Paragraph 2 If a court decides to use additional selection criteria that give priority to certain categories of the judgments defined in paragraph 1, such additional criteria will be published on Rechtspraak.nl; in any event they will be added as attachment to this resolution, and possibly on the webpages of the court itself.

Article 7

Paragraph 1 All published judgments will be anonymized in accordance with an anonymization guideline that will be set for this purpose.

Paragraph 2 Judgments that attract media attention will, in accordance with the Press Guideline, be published on the day when the judgment is announced. Other judgments will be published as much as possible within one month.

Article 8

Paragraph 1 This resolution can be cited as "Resolution selection Criteria Judgment Database Rechtspraak.nl 2012".
Paragraph 2 This resolution, including the explanatory notes, will be published on Rechtsrpaak.nl.

Explanatory notes

General explanatory notes

The website Rechtspraak.nl was launched in December 1999 and has contained from the very beginning of its existence a database of judgments. For the construction of this database, the Supervision Committee Electronic Counter of the Judiciary[1157] laid down a guideline with selection criteria. In practice, the application of this guideline turned out not to be easy, because, among other things, the criteria contained in it were difficult to objectify and failed to provide sufficient guidance for the everyday decision-making on case publication. The abstract selection criteria have also incurred frequent criticisms from outside the judiciary. For the purpose of better facilitating the selection process and increasing the transparency of the selection policy for society, it has been decided to revise the section criteria.

Legal framework

In 1997, the policy note of the cabinet *Towards Accessibility of Government Information* laid down the foundation for the publication of the "basic information for the democratic constitutional state": legislation, parliamentary information and court judgments. With regard to court judgments the cabinet stated that a "representative picture" of court judgments should be published. This Resolution has sought alliance with Recommendation R (95)11 of the Committee of Ministers of the Council of Europe in order to concretize the concept of "a representative picture".

[1157] The original Dutch name of this committee is Begeleidingscommissie Elektronisch Loket Rechterlijke Organisatie (ELRO).

Structure of the Resolution

In the above-mentioned recommendation of the Council of Europe, a distinction is made between a positive and a negative selection. In the case of negative selection, all judgments are published, unless they meet specific criteria on the basis of which publication can be deemed not valuable. In the case of a positive selection, judgments are in principle not published, unless they meet certain criteria that justify publication. Subsequently, it was recommended to apply the negative selection to the highest courts, and the positive selection to other courts. This approach has been adopted and further refined in this Resolution. A distinction is made among a number of categories of cases. The first category (article 3) contains judgments of the highest courts and a few special sections. The negative selection criterion applies fully to these courts and sections. Judgments that should be published based on the positive criterion can be found in articles 4, 5 and 6. In this category, a distinction is, in the first place, made between judgments whose publication is compulsory (articles 4 and 5) and judgments that should be published as much as possible (article 6). This last category includes judgments that are possibly interesting, because they do not contain mere standard formulas, but do not satisfy the explicit criteria of article 4 or article 5. What distinguishes article 4 from 5 is the possibility to objectify the criteria. It is possible to objectively ascertain whether a judgment meets the criteria contained in article 4, but the selection criteria of article 5 are less unambiguous. This is in itself not problematic: in many cases it will be evident that a judgment satisfies one or more of the criteria; for the other cases these criteria are chiefly intended to offer the selector assistance in deciding which judgments are worthy of publishing.

Explanatory notes on specific articles

Article 3

Article 3 includes (sections) of courts whose judgments are presumed to be in principle so relevant for the society that they are worthy of publishing. An exception is made for judgments in cases that are held apparently groundless or inadmissible, and/or otherwise are disposed of by way of a standard formula. This, however, does not mean that a case held inadmissible never needs to be published: such a judgment can after all satisfy the requirements of article 4 or 5.

Article 4 Paragraph 1

The first paragraph of article 4 includes a number of legal proceedings whose publication is indicated on the grounds of legislation or their social importance. In the procedures named under (b) and (c), the judge can on the grounds of legislative provisions order the publication of his judgment. It is logical to use, among other things, Rechtspraak.nl for the publication of such judgments. Publication of judgments in competition cases on the basis of article 101 or 102 of the Treaty on the Function of the European Union – as defined under subparagraph (d) – is based on article 28 paragraph 8 of the Civil Procedure Code, which provides that, in accordance with article 15 paragraph 2 of Regulation (EC) no. 1/2003 of the Council of the European Union of 16 December 2002 on the Implementation of the rules on competition laid down in Articles 81 and 82 of the Treaty, the Supreme Court of the Netherlands and the Council for the Judiciary will provide the European Commission with a copy of all the judgments with regard to these Treaty articles. It is logical that these judgments are not only made accessible in the database administered by the European Commission, but are also published on Rechtspraak.nl. The publication of the judgments defined under subparagraph (d) is based on article 3 of the Second Protocol of the Convention of Lugano 2007. This article provides that member states will send all the judgments of the court of final instance and important judgments of other courts made in the context of this convention and the in article 64 paragraph 1 of the convention defined instruments, to the European Commission for the purpose of being added to a public accessible database. It is also logical that these judgments are likewise published on Rechtspraak.nl. In order to simplify the selection, it is decided that in principle all judgments with regard to these legal procedures are qualified for publication. Only where the judgments are apparently unimportant for the interpretation of these instruments can they remain unpublished.

Article 4 Paragraph 2

This article includes four categories of judgments that are worthy of publishing. The first group (a) includes cases where a claim is made that relies on the European Convention on Human Rights, International Convention on Civil and Political Rights, the UN Convention on the Rights of the Child or a convention that has been reached under the International Labour Organization. These judgments should be published if the claim has been admitted or dismissed other than by way of a standard formula. The second group (b) does not concern the substance of the case, but turns on the publication of a judgment in an earlier instance within the same legal procedure. Publication is required in such a case not only because the judgment in a later instance can be deemed worthy of publishing on the same grounds as the judgment in the earlier instance, but particularly because the user of Rechtspraak.nl can only judge the value of the judgment in earlier instance if he or she knows the judgment in later instance. The third and fourth category (c and d) include severe criminal cases, for which – given the disruptive effect of the facts – there is a particular concern in society. The fifth group (e) involves judgments on challenges to judges. For the purpose of transparency, the Judiciary decides to publish all judgments on challenges to judges.

Article 5

Selection criteria contained in article 5 bear a common characteristic that it is not always possible to easily and objectively determine whether a judgment satisfies these criteria. Subparagraph (a) uses the interest of general press as the criterion. When the media attention is generated is of no relevance; it can be before, during or after the court session. Even where media attention arises some time after the judgment was made, it should still be published. Media attention is only taken to mean attention directed at a specific case. Where a journalist attends the entire session of a police court, it cannot be seen as a sign of media attention for all the cases that have been handled during the session. Even though many media that are targeted at the legal profession can be can be seen as components of public media under subparagraph (a), a separate subparagraph (b) has nevertheless been created for this category of media. Criterion (b) implies that all the judgments that have been published or discussed in professional law magazines, websites, weblogs or other media targeted at lawyers (still) ought to be published if that has not yet happened. Importance for professions or interest groups – the criterion contained in subparagraph (c) – can be presumed to exist if an interest group was one of the litigation parties, if the procedure was an obvious test case, or if the interest of a certain group or profession was the point of the procedure. This importance should also be deemed to exist where the judgment has been discussed in a medium that is targeted at an interest group or profession. Subparagraph (d) is comparable to (c), but is more targeted at (groups of) individuals, even without the direct presence of an interest group. It can, for example, involve residents of a neighbourhood who are affected by a traffic measure, or a criminal procedure which many victims have not been able to join. Subparagraph (e) is particularly important for the development of the law. A broad interpretation of this subparagraph is appropriate, since the selector is not always able to ascertain to what extent a judgment indeed has a precedent-forming character: in fact, doubt about the legal importance of a judgment is by itself already sufficient for deciding to publish it.

Article 6

As already stated in the general part of the explanatory notes, this article involves judgments that neither fall under the previous articles, nor contain mere standard formulas. Publication of these judgments can be interesting for lawyers in practice, scholars and others, for example to see how the judge reaches his decision, how the sub-district court judges apply the *kantonrechtersformula* in practice, how evidence is evaluated and how the penalty is justified. The second paragraph of this article aims to allow users of the database to gain insight into the additional publication policy of particular courts.

Article 7

This article regulates two subjects that are related to the publication of judgments, but do not concern the selection. The anonymization of judgments is regulated by the Anonymization Guideline. With regard to the speed of publication, a distinction is made between judgments that attract much media attention and the other cases.

The Press Guideline (respectively adopted by the Presidents Conference and the Supreme Court) provides with regard to the first category of judgments that they must be published on the day when the judgments are announced. For the second category a time limit of one month has been adopted in this Resolution. This time limit should be understood as a target period.

Adopted during the Presidents Conference on 26 March 2012.

Appendix 4 Questions of the interviews with Dutch judges

1 Background of respondent

(1) When were you appointed to the judiciary?
(2) How did your career develop before you were appointed to the judiciary?
(3) Are you currently serving in a court of appeal or a district court? If you are currently serving in a court of appeal, have you served in one or more district courts before, and if so, in which district court(s)?
(4) In which legal area(s) are you currently working? In which legal area(s) have you worked before after being appointed to the judiciary?

2 Use of cases in adjudication practice

2.1 Method of using cases in adjudication

(5) In his inaugural lecture, Professor Drion argued that Supreme Court decisions are legally binding upon lower judges.[1158] Do you perceive Supreme Court cases to be legally binding? (If the respondent's reply is affirmative, go to question 6; if not, go to question 7.)
(6) You have just indicated that you perceive Supreme Court cases to be legally binding. Does that mean that you follow Supreme Court decisions under all circumstances or is it possible that under certain circumstances you would be prepared to deviate from Supreme Court decisions? If the latter is true, under what circumstances do you deviate from Supreme Court cases? (Continue to question 10.)
(7) You have just indicated that you do not perceive Supreme Court cases to be legally binding. Do you nonetheless routinely follow Supreme Court decisions in adjudication practice even if you substantively disagree with the holding(s) of the Supreme Court, unless you are convinced that there are proper grounds for deviating from such Supreme Court decisions? Would you point out in the following Table what you normally do with regard to previous cases

[1158] Drion 1968b, p. 149, p. 155 and p. 158-160.

decided by the Supreme Court? (If the respondent chooses option 5, go to question 9. Otherwise, go to question 8.)

	Follow the previous case	Not follow the previous case
Substantively agree with a previous case decided by the Supreme Court	Substantively agree and follow (option 1)	Substantively agree but not follow (option 2)
Substantively disagree with a previous case decided by the Supreme Court	Substantively disagree but follow (option 3)	Substantively disagree, only under special circumstances not follow (option 4)
		Not follow as long as substantively disagree (option 5)

Table 9 Options that judges can adopt with regard to Supreme Court cases

(8) Under what circumstances do you deviate from previous cases decided by the Supreme Court? What are the factors that you take into consideration when assessing whether there are proper grounds for deviating from Supreme Court decisions? (Go to question 10.)
(9) Your answer suggests that you would deviate from a Supreme Court decision as long as you substantively disagree with it. What do you take into consideration to determine whether a Supreme Court decision is right or wrong?
(10) If you substantively disagree with a previous case decided by the Supreme Court but still follow it, do you usually make it explicit in the judgment that you in fact do not substantively endorse the Supreme Court decision but have chosen to follow it due to other considerations?[1159] If you decide not to follow a Supreme Court

[1159] The questions listed under number 10 are related to the way judges write judgments and explain their decisions. As appeal court decisions are made by a panel instead of individual judges, appeal judges are requested to answer these questions under the assumption that they are chosen as the

decision, do you explain in your judgment why you do not follow the previous case? Would you please point out your choice in the following table? If another judge deviates from a Supreme Court decision but does not explain the reasons for refusing to apply the previous case in the judgment, what do you think of such a practice?

	Follow	Not follow
Substantively agree with a previous case decided by the Supreme Court	Substantively agree, follow and explain why follow (option 1)	Substantively agree, not follow, but explain why not follow (option 2)
	Substantively agree, follow, but not explain why follow (option 3)	Substantively agree, not follow, and not explain why not follow (option 4)
Substantively disagree with a previous case decided by the Supreme Court	Substantively disagree, follow, and explain why follow (option 5)	Substantively disagree, not follow, but explain why not follow (option 6)
	Substantively disagree, follow, but not explain why follow (option 7)	Substantively disagree, not follow, and not explain why not follow (option 8)

Table 10 Options that judges can adopt as to whether or not to explain the reasons why they follow or do not follow Supreme Court decisions

(11) In the literature it is commonly held that Supreme Court decisions are particularly influential.[1160] Below are some of the factors mentioned in the existing literature that may account for the highly influential status of Supreme Court decisions. Which factor(s) do you think does/do contribute to the highly influential status of Supreme Court decisions? Is any factor missing in the list?

---

judge that is responsible for writing the draft version of a judgment that will later be discussed by the panel.

[1160] See e.g. Glastra van Loon e.a. 1968, p. 140, Draaisma & Duynstee 1988, p. 25, Brunner 1994, p. 37-38.

A. Threat of reversal

(1) Extra costs of appeal for the litigating parties

(2) Reversal would aversely influence the career development of the judge

B. Esteem of the judges sitting in the Supreme Court

C. Legal education

(12) Do your replies to the questions with regard to Supreme Court decisions also apply to cases decided by courts of appeal and district courts? If not, what are the main differences? Could you use the previous two tables in analogy to explain the main differences? Do or did you normally attribute more weight to cases decided by the court of appeal that has the power to reverse your judgment? (The last sub-question is only put to district court judges or appeal judges that have served in district courts)?

(13) Two analytic frameworks have been presented in the existing literature to analyse the influence of previous cases on judicial decision-making (see the following table). Do you (implicitly) use one or both of these analytic frameworks in practice? If you use one of them, which one do you use? If you use the second analytic framework, do you take any other factor(s) into account in addition to or instead of the factors listed in the following table? Do you explicitly or implicitly use any other analytic framework(s) in addition to or instead of these two analytic frameworks?

Analytic framework 1	This framework is based on a distinction between binding and non-binding cases.[1161] One of the results of applying this analytic framework could be: 1. Supreme Court cases are *de jure*[1162] or *de facto*[1163] binding whereas 2. Cases decided by other courts are not binding[1164]
Analytic framework 2	This framework does not make a sharp distinction between binding and non-

[1161] See e.g. Drion 1968b, p. 149 and Brunner 1994, p. 37-38.

[1162] Drion 1968b, p. 149 and p. 158.

[1163] Brunner 1994, p. 37-38.

[1164] Brunner 1994, p. 37.

	binding cases. The influence of a case is seen as a sliding scale. According to this framework, how much influence a case carries depends on various factors, such as:[1165] - hierarchy of the court that made the decision - strength of the arguments that the court used to justify its decision - reaction of the legal scholarship to the case - reaction of judges to the case (e.g. whether the case has been constantly followed in court practice) - other factors

Table 11 Two analytic frameworks presented in the existing literature to analyse the influence of previous cases

(14) What has/have contributed to the forming of the way you treat previous cases in adjudication practice? Do you think that the counsels of the litigating parties know or are able to know the way you treat previous cases in adjudication?

2.2 Role of counsels of the litigating parties and legal scholars

(15) Do counsels of the litigating parties often refer to previous cases in their oral and written submissions to the court in cases where resolving the legal dispute could potentially involve considering previous cases?
(16) If (the counsel) of a litigating party explicitly invokes a previous case in his/her argumentation but the judge is not convinced that this previous case ought to be followed, can the judge ignore the invoked case in the judgment, or must the judge explain in the judgment why the previous case should not be followed? Does it make a difference whether the invoked previous case is a Supreme Court decision or not?

1165 See e.g. Glastra van Loon e.a. 1968, p. 145 and Nederpel 1985, p. 112.

(17) Do you often need to carry out case research on your own in the cases that you decide, or do the submissions by the counsels of the litigating parties usually provide sufficient (analysis of) previous cases so that you rarely need to carry out case research?
(18) If you carry out case research on your own, how do you find relevant cases? Do you usually use online search engines and databases to find relevant cases, or do you usually use handbooks or other scholarly works to find relevant cases? Are there particular reference and handbooks that you frequently use to find cases?
(19) When litigating parties do not agree on the interpretation of a previous case or when you are not sure about the essence of a previous case, how do you ascertain what should be the right interpretation?
(20) Do you agree with the proposition that, when it comes to the use of cases, it can be said that judges are in fact assisted by the counsels of the litigating parties and legal scholars who perform preparatory work such as collecting, organizing and analysing relevant previous cases?

3 Selection of cases for publication through the official website of the judiciary

(21) Are there still judges and staff in your court that select and send cases to the editorial board of commercial case reporting periodicals or databases?
(22) Does the court where you serve have a team of judges and/or court staff that collectively decide which cases will be published through the official website of the judiciary or is it the individual judges that determine which cases that they have decided will be published through the official website of the judiciary?
(23) Does the judiciary have a judgment database to which the public has no access? If so, what kind of cases are stored in this database?

Appendix 5 Provisions of the Supreme People's Court Concerning Work on Guiding Cases

Provisions of the Supreme People's Court Concerning Work on Guiding Cases[1166]

Fa Fa (2010) No. 51

Promulgated on November 26, 2010

In order to summarize adjudication experiences, unify application of law, enhance adjudication quality, and safeguard judicial justice, the Supreme People's Court, pursuant to such legal provisions as the Organic Law of the People's Courts of the People's Republic of China, hereby formulates this set of Provisions to carry out the work on Guiding Cases.

Article 1

The Supreme People's Court shall determine and uniformly release as Guiding Cases those cases that have the effect of guiding adjudication and enforcement work in courts throughout the country.

Article 2

The Guiding Cases referred to in this set of Provisions mean the rulings and judgments that have taken legal effect and which are cases that meet the following conditions:

(i) are of widespread concern in society;

(ii) legal provisions are of relatively general nature;

(iii) are of a typical nature;

(iv) are difficult, complicated, or of new types; [or]1

(v) Other cases having a guiding effect.

Article 3

The Supreme People's Court establishes the Guiding Cases Work Office, which is responsible for the selection, examination and submission for approval of Guiding Cases.

[1166] Translated by Garret Anderson, Brian Timm-Brock and Ralph Wang, reviewed by Mei Gechlik. Available at http://cgc.law.stanford.edu/supreme-peoples-court-concerning-work-on-guiding-cases/.

Article 4

Any adjudication unit of the Supreme People's Court may recommend to the Guiding Cases Work Office any ruling or judgment that is made by the Supreme People's Court or local people's courts at any level and that has taken legal effect, so long as such ruling or judgment is deemed by the said unit to meet the requirements set out in Article 2 of this set of Provisions.

Any Higher People's Court or the Military Court of the People's Liberation Army may, following discussion and decision by the adjudication committee of the said court, recommend to the Guiding Cases Work Office of the Supreme People's Court any ruling or judgment that is made by the said court or by a people's court in its jurisdiction and that has taken legal effect, so long as such ruling or judgment is deemed by the said court to meet the requirements set out in Article 2 of this set of Provisions.

Any Intermediate People's Court or Basic People's Court may, following discussion and decision by the adjudication committee of the said court, report to the Higher People's court level by level and suggest that the Higher People's Court recommend to the Guiding Cases Work Office of the Supreme People's Court any ruling or judgment that is made by the said court and that has taken legal effect, so long as such ruling or judgment is deemed by the said court to meet the requirements set out in Article 2 of this set of Provisions.

Article 5

Representatives of people's congresses, members of committees of the Chinese people's political consultative conference, experts and scholars, lawyers, and other people from all circles of society who care about the adjudication and enforcement work of people's courts may recommend any ruling or judgment that has taken legal effect to the original trial people's court which rendered such ruling or judgment, so long as such ruling or judgment is deemed by the said individual to meet the requirements set out in Article 2 of this set of Provisions.

Article 6
The Guiding Cases Work Office should promptly put forward examination opinions on the recommended cases. If a case meets the requirements set out in Article 2 of this set of Provisions, the Office should report to the President or the Vice President-in-charge, who then submit the case to the Adjudication Committee of the Supreme People's Court for discussion and decision.

The guiding cases discussed and determined by the Adjudication Committee of the Supreme People's Court shall be uniformly released in the form of notices in the Gazette of the Supreme People's Court, on the website of the Supreme People's Court, and in the People's Court Daily.

Article 7
People's courts at all levels should refer to the Guiding Cases released by the Supreme People's Court when adjudicating similar cases.

Article 8
The Guiding Cases Work Office of the Supreme People's Court carries out the compilation of Guiding Cases annually.

Article 9
Those cases that have significance in guiding the adjudication and enforcement work of courts throughout the country and that have been released by the Supreme People's Court prior to the implementation of this set of Provisions shall be sorted out and compiled in accordance with this set of Provisions and then issued as Guiding Cases.

Article 10
This set of Provisions shall be implemented from the date of promulgation.

Appendix 6 Guiding Case No. 1 released by the Supreme People's Court on 20 December 2011

Shanghai Centaline Property Consultants Limited vs TAO Dehua, **An Intermediation Contract Dispute**[1167]

Guiding Case No. 1 (Discussed and Passed by the Adjudication Committee of the Supreme People's Court Released on December 20, 2011)

Keywords

Civil Intermediation Contract, Sale and Purchase of Second-Hand Housing, Breach of Contract

Main Points of the Ruling(s) and/or Judgment(s)

In a housing sale intermediation contract, terms that concern prohibiting a buyer from using housing information provided by an intermediary company to conclude a housing sale contract with the seller while bypassing the intermediary company are legal and valid. But when a seller lists the same house for sale through multiple intermediary companies and the buyer can obtain the same housing information by other legitimate means that are accessible by the public, the buyer has a right to choose an intermediary company with a lower quoted price and better service to facilitate formation of a housing sale contract. Such acts do not [entail the] use of housing information from the intermediary company with whom [the buyer] has previously contracted; therefore, they do not constitute a breach of contract.

[1167] http://cgc.law.stanford.edu/guiding-cases/guiding-case-1/. This document was primarily prepared by Hans Anderson, Dai Di, Richard Jiang, Liu Qingyu, and Randy Wu and was reviewed by Beijing Tsidu Translation Co., Ltd., Dr Mei Gechlik, Director of the China Guiding Cases Project, and a team of proofreaders led by Jennifer Ingram, Managing Editor of the China Guiding Cases Project. Minor editing, such as splitting long paragraphs, adding a few words included in square brackets, and boldfacing the headings to correspond with those boldfaced in the Chinese Guiding Case (CGC1), was done to make the piece more comprehensible to readers.

Related Legal Rule(s)

Article 424 of the *Contract Law of the People's Republic of China*

Basic Facts

The plaintiff, Shanghai Centaline Property Consultants Limited (上海中原物业顾问有限公司) (hereinafter referred to as "Centaline Company"), claimed: The defendant, TAO Dehua (陶德华), used sale information provided by Centaline Company on a certain-numbered house on Zhuzhou Road, Hongkou District, Shanghai Municipality, intentionally bypassed the intermediary, and privately signed a housing purchase contract directly with the seller, violating the terms of the *Confirmation of Request to Buy Real Estate.* [This act] belonged to [a category of] malicious "bypassing" acts, [for which] the plaintiff requested that the court order TAO Dehua, to, in accordance with the contract, pay Centaline Company liquidated damages of RMB 16,500.

Defendant TAO Dehua defended his position, claiming: The original property right holder of the house involved in this case, a certain LI, had entrusted multiple intermediary companies with selling the house. Centaline Company neither exclusively controlled the housing information nor acted as an exclusive agent in the sale. TAO Dehua did not use the information provided by Centaline Company; there existed no "bypass" breaching act.

The court heard the case and ascertained: In the second half of 2008, the original property right holder, LI, went to multiple housing intermediary companies to list for sale the house involved in this case. On October 22, 2008, a certain real-estate brokerage limited company in Shanghai took TAO Dehua to see the house; on November 23, a certain real-estate consulting limited company in Shanghai (hereinafter referred to as "a certain real-estate consulting company") took TAO Dehua's wife, a certain Ms. CAO, to see the house; and, on November 27, Centaline Company took TAO Dehua to see the house and signed a *Confirmation of Request to Buy Real Estate* with TAO Dehua on the same day.

The terms of the *Confirmation's* Article 2.4 stipulated that if, within six months after TAO Dehua examined the real estate, TAO Dehua or persons associated with TAO Dehua including his principal, agent, representative and undertaker used information, opportunities or other such conditions provided by Centaline Company but not through Centaline Company reached a sale transaction with a third party, [then] TAO Dehua should, based on 1% of the actual closing price reached with the seller in this real-estate sale, pay Centaline Company liquidated damages. At the time, Centaline Company quoted RMB 1.65 million for the house, while the [above-mentioned] real-estate consulting company quoted RMB 1.45 million and actively negotiated with the seller on price. On November 30, under intermediation by this real- estate consulting company, TAO Dehua and the seller signed a housing sale contract with a closing price of RMB 1.38 million. Later, the buying and selling parties completed the procedure for transferring registration, and TAO Dehua paid the real-estate consulting company a commission of RMB 13,800.

Results of the Ruling(s) and/or Judgment(s)

On June 23, 2009, the Hongkou District People's Court of Shanghai Municipality rendered the (2009) Hong Min San (Min) Chu Zi No. 912 Civil Judgment:

Defendant TAO Dehua should, within ten days after this judgment comes into effect, pay plaintiff Centaline Company liquidated damages of RMB 13,800.

After the judgment was pronounced, TAO Dehua appealed. On September 4, 2009, the No. 2 Intermediate People's Court of Shanghai Municipality rendered the (2009) Hu Er Zhong Min Er (Min) Zhong Zi No.1508 Civil Judgment:

(1) Repeal the (2009) Hong Min San (Min) Chu Zi No. 912 Civil Judgment of the Hongkou District People's Court of Shanghai Municipality; (2) Centaline Company's litigation claim requesting that TAO Dehua pay liquidated damages of RMB 16,500 is not supported.

Reasons for the Ruling(s) and/or Judgment(s)

In its effective ruling/judgment, the court opined: [1168] The *Confirmation of Request to Buy Real Estate* signed by Centaline Company and TAO Dehua was of the nature of an intermediation contract, in which the terms of Article 2.4 were standard clauses prohibiting "bypassing" commonly found in housing sale intermediation contracts. The intent of these terms was to prevent the buyer from using housing information provided by the intermediary company but "bypassing" the intermediary company in purchasing the house, making the intermediary company unable to obtain the commission that it deserved. These terms did not include circumstances that exempted one party from liability, increased the other party's liability, or ruled out the other party's primary rights, and [, thus, they] should be determined to be valid.

According to the terms of this article, the key to weighing whether the buyer breached the contract due to "bypassing" was to see whether the buyer used housing information, opportunities, or other such conditions provided by the intermediary company. If the buyer did not use the information, opportunities, or other such conditions provided by the intermediary company, but obtained the same housing information by other legitimate means that were accessible by the public, then the buyer has the right to choose an intermediary company with a lower quoted price and better service to facilitate formation of a housing sale contract without constituting a "bypass" breach of contract. In this case, the original property right holder listed the same house for sale through multiple intermediary companies; TAO Dehua and his family members respectively came to know the same housing information through different intermediary companies and facilitated formation of the housing sale contract through another intermediary company. For these reasons, TAO Dehua did not use information or opportunities provided by Centaline Company; therefore, [his acts] did not constitute breach of contract; Centaline Company's litigation claim was not supported.

[1168] Translators' Note: The Chinese version does not specify which court opined. But given the context, this should be the No. 2 Intermediate People's Court of Shanghai Municipality.

Appendix 7 Guiding Case No. 3 released by the Supreme People's Court on 20 December 2011

PAN Yumei and CHEN Ning, A Bribe-Accepting Case[1169]

Guiding Case No. 3 (Discussed and Passed by the Adjudication Committee of the Supreme People's Court Released on December 20, 2011)

Keywords

Crime of Accepting Bribes, Accepting Bribes through "Jointly Organizing" a Company, Accepting Bribes through Purchase of Houses at Low Prices, Promise to Seek Benefits, Calculation of Amount of Bribes, Accepted Return Illicit Money to Conceal Acceptance of Bribes

Main Points of the Ruling(s) and/or Judgment(s)

1. A state functionary who exploits the advantages of office to seek benefits for an entrusting person and, together with the entrusting person, obtains "profits" in the name of "jointly organizing" a company but does not actually contribute capital or participate in the operation and management shall be punished for accepting bribes.
2. A state functionary who knows that a person has an entrusted matter and yet accepts his property shall be regarded as having promised to "seek benefits for others." The determination of "accepting bribes" is not affected by whether benefits were actually sought for the other person or whether benefits were actually obtained.

1169 https://cgc.law.stanford.edu/guiding-cases/guiding-case-3/. This document was primarily prepared by Liu Qingyu and Randy Wu and was reviewed by Beijing Tsidu Translation Co., Ltd., Dr Mei Gechlik, Director of the China Guiding Cases Project, and a team of proofreaders led by Jennifer Ingram, Managing Editor of the China Guiding Cases Project. Minor editing, such as splitting long paragraphs, adding a few words included in square brackets, and boldfacing the headings to correspond with those boldfaced in the Chinese Guiding Case (CGC3), was done to make the piece more comprehensible to readers.

3. A state functionary who exploits the advantages of office to seek benefits for an entrusting person and purchases goods like houses from the entrusting person at obviously below-market prices shall be punished for accepting bribes.[1170] The amount of bribes accepted is calculated in accordance with the difference between the local market price at the time of the transaction and the price actually paid.
4. The determination of the crime of accepting bribes is not affected by the fact that after a state functionary has accepted property, she, due to the investigation of individuals and matters connected to her acceptance of bribes, returns it to conceal the crime.

Related Legal Rule(s)

Article 385, Paragraph 1 of the *Criminal Law of the People's Republic of China*

Basic Facts

Between August and September of 2003, the defendants, PAN Yumei (潘玉梅) and CHEN Ning (陈宁), respectively exploited the advantages of their office as Secretary of the Street Working Committee of Maigao Bridge, Qixia District, Nanjing Municipality, Jiangsu Province and Director of the Office of Maigao Bridge to help a certain CHEN, General Manager of a real estate development limited company in Nanjing, among other things, obtain 100 mu of land in Maigao Bridge's Innovation Park District at low prices.[1171] Furthermore, on September 3, the defendants respectively used the names of their relatives to jointly register and form Nanjing Duohe Industry and Trade Co., Ltd. (hereinafter referred to as "Duohe Company") with CHEN in order to "develop" the above-mentioned

[1170] Translators' Note: The original Chinese expression is " 房屋等物品" (goods like houses), which, unfortunately, suggests that houses are goods. The Supreme People's Court probably meant to use " 财物"(property), instead of "物品" (goods), to group "houses", a type of real property, under "property".
[1171] Translators' Note: 1 mu = 0.165 acre.

land. PAN Yumei and CHEN Ning neither actually contributed capital nor participated in the operation and management of this company.

In June 2004, CHEN, in the name of Duohe Company, transferred the company and its land to a sporting goods limited company in Nanjing. PAN Yumei and CHEN Ning, in the name of participating in profit-sharing, respectively accepted RMB 4.8 million offered by CHEN. In March 2007, because PAN Yumei was being investigated, CHEN Ning, while on a business trip to the United States, arranged for his driver to return RMB 800,000 to CHEN. After this case was exposed, the illicit money and gains generated from such money obtained by PAN Yumei and CHEN Ning were all recovered in accordance with the law.

From February to October of 2004, the defendants, PAN Yumei and CHEN Ning, respectively exploited the advantages of their office as Secretary of the Street Working Committee of Maigao Bridge and Director of the Office of Maigao Bridge to help a property placement and development limited company in Nanjing purchase land in Maigao Bridge's Innovation Park. At four different times, each of them accepted RMB 500,000 offered by a certain WU, General Manager of the company.

In the first half of 2004, defendant PAN Yumei exploited the advantages of office as Secretary of the Street Working Committee of Maigao Bridge to help a development limited company in Nanjing have a fee waiver of RMB 1 million on the project of transferring Jin Qiao Building. When purchasing the real estate developed by the company, PAN Yumei accepted over RMB 610,000, an amount paid on behalf of her by a certain XU, General Manager of that company, to cover the difference between the house price and the amount she paid and related taxes (the price of the house including taxes was RMB 1,210,817; PAN paid RMB 600,000). In April 2006, because procuratorial organs had already grasped from XU's company accounts the situation that she had merely made partial payment for the purchase of the house, PAN Yumei reimbursed XU RMB 550,000.

Furthermore, from the time prior to the 2000 Chinese New Year to December 2006, defendant PAN Yumei exploited the advantages of office to accept first RMB 2.01 million and USD 490,000 from a certain GAO, Secretary of a Party Branch in the

Maigao Bridge Office and General Manager of a certain commerce and trade limited company in Nanjing, and then USD 10,000 from a certain FAN of a Nanjing property placement limited company of a real estate group in Zhejiang. Between 2002 and 2005, defendant CHEN Ning exploited the advantages of office to accept first RMB 210,000 from GAO, Secretary of a Party Branch in the Maigao Bridge Office, and then RMB 80,000 from a certain LIU, Deputy Director of the Maigao Bridge Office.

In summary, defendant PAN Yumei accepted bribes of over RMB 7.92 million and USD 500,000 (equivalent to RMB 3,981,234), totaling RMB 11.902 million; defendant CHEN Ning accepted bribes of RMB 5.59 million.

Results of the Ruling(s) and/or Judgment(s)

On February 25, 2009, the Intermediate People's Court of Nanjing Municipality, Jiangsu Province, by the (2008) Ning Xing Chu Zi No. 49 Criminal Judgment, determined that defendant PAN Yumei was guilty of the crime of accepting bribes and was sentenced to death with a two- year suspension of execution, deprived of political rights for life, and confiscated of all of her property; defendant CHEN Ning was guilty of accepting bribes and was sentenced to life imprisonment, deprived of political rights for life, and confiscated of all of his property. After the judgment was pronounced, PAN Yumei and CHEN Ning appealed. On November 30, 2009, the Higher People's Court of Jiangsu Province, based on the same facts and reasons, rendered the (2009) Su Xing Er Zhong Zi No. 0028 Criminal Ruling. It rejected the appeal, upheld the original judgment, and examined and approved the first-instance criminal judgment, in which, based on the crime of accepting bribes, defendant PAN Yumei was sentenced to death with a two-year suspension of execution, deprived of political rights for life, and confiscated of all of her property.

Reasons for the Ruling(s) and/or Judgment(s)

In the effective ruling(s) and/or judgment(s), the courts opined:

With respect to the defence views put forward by the defendants, PAN Yumei and CHEN Ning, as well as their defenders[1172] that the defendants' acts of jointly organizing Duohe Company with CHEN and reaping a "profit" of RMB 4.8 million through the development of land should not be determined to be accepting bribes: According to investigation, at the time, PAN Yumei was Secretary of the Street Working Committee of Maigao Bridge while CHEN Ning was Director of the Maigao Bridge Street Office, and they were responsible for leading or coordinating business invitations and land transfers in Maigao Bridge Innovation Park District. The two persons respectively exploited the advantages of their office to help CHEN obtain land etc. in Innovation Park District at low prices and this was [a type of] exploitation of the advantages of office to seek benefits for others. During this period, PAN Yumei, CHEN Ning, and CHEN held discussions to jointly organize Duohe Company for developing the above- mentioned land. All of the registered capital of the company came from CHEN; PAN Yumei and CHEN Ning neither actually contributed capital nor participated in the operation and management of the company. Therefore, PAN Yumei and CHEN Ning respectively exploited the advantages of their office to seek benefits for CHEN, and the RMB 4.8 million that each gained in the name of jointly organizing a company with CHEN to develop that piece of land were not so-called corporate profits, but were a portion of benefits generated from the resale of the land obtained for CHEN at a low price by exploiting the advantages of their office. This exemplified the power-in-exchange-for-money nature of the crime of accepting bribes and belonged to a disguised form of accepting bribes occurring in the name of jointly organizing a company, and [the defendants] should be punished for accepting bribes.

With respect to the defence views put forward by defendant PAN Yumei and her defender that PAN Yumei had not actually sought benefits for XU: According to investigation, when the entrusting person XU bribed PAN Yumei and requested a fee waiver of RMB 1 million in the project of transferring Jin Qiao Building, PAN Yumei accepted the bribes, knowing that XU had an

[1172] Translators' Note: In China, a defender (辩护人) is not necessarily an attorney. For more information, see Article 32 of the *Criminal Procedure Law of the People's Republic of China*, adopted on July 1, 1979 and amended on Mar. 17, 1996.

entrusted matter. Although the entrusted matter was not realized, "seeking benefits for others" includes acts of different stages, such as promise, implementation and realization, and the existence of any of these acts [made the situation] properly categorized as seeking benefits for others. The promise to "seek benefits for others" could be determined from an explicit or implicit expression of intent to seek benefits for others. PAN Yumei, who knew that another person had an entrusted matter and yet accepted his property, should be regarded as having promised to seek benefits for that person. The determination of "accepting bribes" was not affected by whether benefits were already actually sought for the other person or whether benefits were actually obtained because these were only issues concerning the circumstances of the bribe acceptance.

With respect to the defence views put forward by defendant PAN Yumei and her defender that PAN Yumei's purchase of XU's real estate should not be determined to be accepting bribes: According to investigation, the market price, together with taxes, of the real estate purchased by PAN Yumei should exceed RMB 1.21 million, but PAN Yumei only paid RMB 600,000, which was obviously below the local market price of that real estate at the time of the transaction. PAN Yumei's acts of exploiting the advantages of office to seek benefits for the entrusting person and purchasing real estate at obviously below-market prices from the entrusting person was a way of concealing the power-in-exchange-for-money nature of her accepting of bribes by formally paying a certain amount of the price, and she should be punished for accepting bribes. The amount of bribes accepted was calculated in accordance with the difference between the local market price at the time of the real estate transaction in question and the price actually paid.

With respect to the defence views put forward by PAN Yumei and her defender that, in her purchase of the real estate developed by XU, PAN Yumei had already paid XU the price difference on the real estate before the case was exposed and hence should not be determined to have accepted bribes: According to investigation, in April 2006, and before the case was exposed, PAN Yumei had reimbursed XU for RMB 550,000 of the price difference in the purchase of the real estate developed by XU. It had been nearly two years since she purchased the house at a low price in the first half of 2004, and thus she had not promptly reimbursed the huge price difference. PAN Yumei's reimbursement acts were acts of returning illicit money undertaken for the purpose of concealing the crime because XU was found by procuratorial organs to have discussions about other cases, and procuratorial organs had already grasped from XU's company accounts the situation that PAN Yumei merely made partial payment for the purchase of the house. Therefore, PAN Yumei's reimbursement of the price difference on the house in order to conceal the crime did not affect the determination of her being guilty of the crime of accepting bribes.

In summary, the aforementioned defence views put forward by defendants, PAN Yumei, CHEN Ning, and their defenders could not stand and were not adopted. PAN Yumei and CHEN Ning, as state functionaries, respectively exploited the advantages of their office to seek benefits for others and accepted others' property; these acts already constituted the crime of accepting bribes. Furthermore, the amounts of the bribes accepted were especially enormous. But, at the same time, in view of the mitigating circumstances that the two defendants possessed – including that they both gave truthful accounts of their crimes and confessed their crimes with good attitudes after being apprehended, that they took the initiative to account remaining crimes of the same type that judicial organs had not grasped, that they returned part of the illicit money before the case was exposed, and that they cooperated in the recovery of all of the illicit money in question after the case was exposed – the courts of first and second instances rendered the above ruling and judgment in accordance with the law.

References

Adams 1999
M. Adams, 'The Rhetoric of Precedent and Comparative Legal Research', *The Modern Law Review* 1999, p. 464-467.
Adams 2007
M. Adams, 'Precedent versus Gravitational Force of Court Decisions in Belgium: Between Theory, Law and Facts', in: E. Hondius (ed.), *Precedent and the Law,* Brussels: Bruylant 2007, p. 149-175.
Albers e.a. 2009
C.I.G.F.H. Albers e.a., *Van Apeldoorn's Inleiding tot de Studie van het Nederlandse recht (Van Apeldoorn's Introduction to the Study of the Dutch Law),* Deventer: Kluwer 2009.
Alford & Liebman 2001
W.P. Alford & B.L. Liebman, 'Clean Air, Clear Process? The Struggle over Air Pollution Law in the People's Republic of China', *Hastings Law Journal* 2001, p. 703-748.
Anema 1913
A. Anema, *De bronnen van het privaatrecht (The Sources of Private Law),* Utrecht: G.J.A. Ruys 1913.
Arons 2012
T.M.C. Arons, 'Annotatie bij Rechtbank Utrecht, 15 februari 2012, LJN BV 3753 (Annotation to District Court Utrecht 15 February 2012, LJN BV 3753)', *Nederlands tijdschrift voor burgerlijk recht* 2012, p. nr. 37.
Asser 2008
W.D.H. Asser, 'Rechtsvorming door de Hoge Raad: enkele inleidende opmerkingen (Lawmaking by the Supreme Court of the Netherlands: Several Introductory Remarks)', in: W.M.T. Keukens & M.C.A. Van den Nieuwenhuijzen (eds.), *Raad & Daad, Over de rechtsvormende taak van de Hoge Raad (Court & Action, On the Lawmaking Task of the Supreme Court of the Netherlands),* Nijmegen: Ars Aequi Libri 2008, p. 9-29.
Baade 2002a
H.W. Baade, 'Stare Decisis in Civil Law Systems', in: J.A.R. Nafziger & S.C. Symeonides (eds.), *Law and Justice in a Multistate World, Essays in Honor of Arthur T. von Mehren,* New York: Transnational Publishers 2002a, p. 533-554.

Baade 2002b
H.W. Baade, 'Stare Decisis in Civil-Law Countries: The Last Bastion', in: P. Birks & A. Pretto (ed.), *Themes in Comparative Law,* Oxford: Oxford University Press 2002b, p. 3-20.
Baardman 1988
B. Baardman (ed.), *De plaats van de Hoge Raad in het huidige staatsbestel (The Place of the Supreme Court in the Current Constitutional System of the Netherlands)*, Zwolle: W.E.J. Tjeenk Willink 1988.
Bartman 2011
S.M. Bartman, 'Bestuurdersaansprakelijkheid wegens selectieve (wan)betaling [Directors' Liability Due to Selective Payment (default)]', *Ars Aequi* 2011, p. 126-130.
Baudouin 1974
J.-L. Baudouin, 'The Impact of the Common Law on the Civilian Systems of Louisiana and Quebec', in: J. Dainow (ed.), *The Role of Judicial Decisioins and Doctrine in Civil Law and in Mixed Jurisdictions,* Baton Rouge: Louisiana State University Press 1974, p. 2-22.
Bellefroid 1927
J.H.P. Bellefroid, *De bronnen van het stellig recht en haar onderlinge verhoudingen (Sources of the Postive Law and Their Mutual Relations),* Nijmegen: F.G.C. Richellle 1927.
Bellefroid 1937
J.H.P. Bellefroid, *Inleiding tot de rechtswetenschap in Nederland (Introduction to Legal Science in the Netherlands),* Nijmegen: Dekker & Van de Vegt 1937.
Bergwerf & Houweling 2008
V.G.G. Bergwerf & A.R. Houweling, 'Arbeidsrechtelijke jurisprudentie op rechtspraak.nl: foliojurisprudentie exit? (Labour Law Cases on Rechtspraak.nl: End of Paper Case Reports?)', *ArbeidsRecht* 2008, p. 3-9.
Bloembergen 2002
A.R. Bloembergen, 'Over het annoteren van arresten (On Annotating Cases)', *Nederlands tijdschrift voor burgerlijk recht* 2002, p. 88-99.
Bogdan 2013
M. Bogdan, *Concise Introduction to Comparative Law,* Groningen: Europa Law Publishing 2013.

Bovend'Eert 2009
P.P.T. Bovend'Eert, 'Wetgever, rechter en rechtsvorming, 'Partners in the business of law?' (The Legislature, the Judge and the Creation of Law, 'Partners in the Business of Law?')', in: P.P.T. Bovend'Eerte.a. (ed.), *De staat van wetgeving, Opstellen aangeboden aan prof. mr. C.A.J.M. Kortmann (The State of Lawmaking, Essays in honour of Prof. C.A.J.M. Kortmann),* Deventer: Kluwer 2009, p. 27-45.
Bregstein 1939
M.H. Bregstein, *Het gezag van de rechtspraak tegenover het geldende recht (The Authority of Cases vis-à-vis the Positive Law)* Haarlem: De Erven F. Bohn 1939.
Brocx & Stuart 1839
A. Brocx & J.C. Stuart, *Nederlandsche Regtspraak (Netherlands Court Judgments),* The Hague: De Gebroeders van Cleef 1839.
Brocx & Stuart 1855
A. Brocx & J.C. Stuart, *Alphabetisch register der Nederlandsche Regtspraak, Jaargang 1846 tot en met 1852 (Alphabetical Index of the Netherlands Court Judgments, Volume 1846 until 1852)* The Hague: De Gebroeders Van Cleef 1855.
Broers & Van Klink 2001
E.-J. Broers & B. Van Klink (ed.), *De rechter als rechtsvormer*, The Hague: Boom Juridische uitgevers 2001.
Bruinsma 1988a
F. Bruinsma, *Cassatierechtspraak in civiele zaken, Een rechtssociologisch verslag (Cassation in Civil Cases, A Report from the Perspective of Sociology of Law),* Zwolle: W.E.J. Tjeenk Willink 1988a.
Bruinsma 1988b
F. Bruinsma, 'Schijn en werkelijkheid van de Hoge Raad (Appearance and Reality of the Supreme Court)', in: M. Beerepoot, M. Draaisma & B. Duynstee (eds.), *Hoge Raad 150 jaar (Supreme Court 150 Years),* Alphen a.d. Rijn: Samson H.D. Tjeen Willink 1988b, p. 4-5.
Bruinsma 2003
F. Bruinsma, *Dutch Law in Action,* Nijmegen: Ars Aequi Libri 2003.
Brunner 1994

C.J.H. Brunner, 'Over precedenten in het Nederlandse recht (On Precedents in Dutch Law)', in: W. Snijders & H. Stein (eds.), *Voorontwerp burgerlijke rechtsvordering (Preliminary Sketch of the Civil Procedure Code),* Zwolle: W.E.J. Tjeenk Willink 1994, p. 31-41.

Brunner 2011

C.J.H. Brunner, *Verbintenissenrecht algemeen (General Law of Obligations),* Deventer: Kluwer 2011.

Butler 2002

W.E. Butler, 'Judicial Precedent as a Source of Russian Law', in: J.A.R. Nafziger & S.C. Symeonides (eds.), *Law and Justice in a Multistate World, Essays in Honor of Arthur T. von Mehren,* New York: Transnational Publishers 2002, p. 583-593.

Cao 2010

S. Cao, 'Anli Zhidao, Sifa Zouchu Tong'an Butongpan (Case Guidance, The Judicature Says Farewell to the Problem of Like Cases Being Decided Differently)', *Fazhi Ribao (Legal Daily),* 2010.

Cappelletti 1981

M. Cappelletti, 'The Doctrine of Stare Decisis and the Civil Law: a Fundamental Difference or No Difference at all?', in: K. Zweigerte.a. (ed.), *Festschrift für Konrad Zweigert zum 70. Geburtstag,* Tubingen: Mohr 1981, p. 381-393.

Cartwright 2007

J. Cartwright, *Contract Law, An Introduction to the English Law of Contract for the Civil Lawyer,* Oxford: Hart Publishing 2007.

Chen 2006

C. Chen, 'Anli Zhidao Zhidu Zhong Caozuoxing Nandian Wenti Tantao (Discussion of Difficult Practical Issues concerning the Case Guidance System)', *Faxue Zazhi (Law Science Magazine)* 2006, p. 101-103.

Chen & Wei 2004

D. Chen & Q. Wei, 'Lun Panlifa Fangfa zai Woguo Fazhi Jianshe Zhong de Jiejian Zuoyong (Implications of the Method of Case Law for Constructing China's Legal System)', in: S. Wu (ed.), *Panli Zhidu Yanjiu (Research on Case Law Systems),* Beijing: Remin Fayuan Chubanshe (Court Press) 2004, p. 68-80.

Chen & Xie 2004

G. Chen & Z. Xie, 'Guanyu Woguo Jianli Panli Zhidu Wenti de Sikao (Reflections on a Precedent System for China)', in: S. Wu (ed.), *Panli Zhidu Yanjiu (Research on Case Law Systems),* Beijing: Remin Fayuan Chubanshe (Court Press) 2004, p. 121-131.
Chen 2004
J. Chen, 'Yingguo Putongfa de Xingcheng (Evolution of Common Law in England)', http://www.ckni.net.
Chen 2012a
J. Chen, 'Renmin Fayuan Yuanjiushi Gongzuo Fansi (Reflections on the Work of Research Office of the people's courts)', http://faxuemeili.fyfz.cn/b/699794.
Chen & Li 2003
W. Chen & X. Li, 'Xianli Panjue, Panli Zhidu, Sifa Gaige (Precedent Judgment, Case-law System and Judicial Reform)', *Falu Shiyong (Application of Law)* 2003, p. 20-24.
Chen 2012b
X. Chen, 'Cong Guize Tixi Shijiao Kaocha Zhongguo Anli Zhidao Zhidu (China's Case Guidance System from the Perspective of Rules System)', http://article.chinalawinfo.com/Article_Detail.asp?ArticleId=69400.
Cheng 2012
Q. Cheng, 'Panjueshu, Qing Geige Shuofu de Liyou (Court Judgments, Please Give a Convincing Reason)', *Dongfang Zaobao (Dengfang Daily),* 2012.
Commissie Jurisprudentiedocumentatie (Case Law Documentation Committee) 1994
Commissie Jurisprudentiedocumentatie (Case Law Documentation Committee), 'Advies van de commissie jurisprudentiedocumentatie (Advice of the Case Law Documentation Committee)', in: J.M. Van Dunné & R.J.P. Kottenhagen (eds.), *Symposium Toegankelijkheid van Rechtspraak (Symposium Accessibility of Court Judgments),* Arnhem: Gouda Quint 1994, p. 13-25.
Committee of Ministers of the Council of Europe 1995
Committee of Ministers of the Council of Europe, 'Recommendation No. R (95) 11 of the Committee of Ministers to Member States Concerning the Selection, Processing, Presentation and Archiving of Court Decisions in Legal Information Retrieval Systems', https://wcd.coe.int/ViewDoc.jsp?id=538429&Site=COE.
Crommelin 1988

R.G.C. Crommelin, 'De Nederlandse Jurisprudentie (The Netherlands Cases)', *Ars Aequi* 1988, p. 752-755.
Cross & Harris 1991
R. Cross & J.W. Harris, *Precedent in English Law,* Oxford: Clarendon Press 1991.
Cui 2004
M. Cui, '"Panlifa" Shi Wanshan Fazhi de Zhongyao Tujing ("Case Law" is an Important Tool to Improve the Legal System)', in: S. Wu (ed.), *Panli Zhidu Yanjiu (Research on Case Law Systems),* Beijing: Remin Fayuan Chubanshe (Court Press) 2004, p. 106-112.
Currier 1965
T.S. Currier, 'Time and Changes in Judge-Made Law: Prospective Overruling', *Virginia Law Review* 1965, p. 201-212.
Dainow 1956
J. Dainow, 'Civil Code Revision in the Netherlands: The Fifty Questions', *The American Journal of Comparative Law* 1956, p. 595-610.
Dainow 1966
J. Dainow, 'The Civil Law and the Common Law: Some Points of Comparison', *The American Journal of Comparative Law* 1966, p. 419-435.
Dainow 1974
J. Dainow (ed.), *The Role of Judicial Decisioins and Doctrine in Civil Law and in Mixed Jurisdictions*, Baton Rouge: Louisiana State University Press 1974.
David 1984
R. David, 'Chapter 3 Sources of Law', in: R. David (ed.), *International Encyclopedia of Comparative Law, Volume II The Legal Systems of the World, Their Comparison and Unification,* Tübingen: Mohr 1984, p. 1-209.
Dawson 1970
J.P. Dawson, *The Oracles of the Law,* Westport: Greenwood Press 1970.
De Lange 1991
R. De Lange, *Publiekrechtelijke rechtsvinding (Judicial Decision-Making in Public Law),* Zwolle: W.E.J. Tjeenk Willink 1991.
De Cruz 2007
P. De Cruz, *Comparative Law in a Changing World,* London: Routledge Cavendish 2007.

De Groot 2008
G. De Groot, *Het deskundigenadvies in de civiele procedure (Expert Advice in Civil Procedure),* Deventer: Kluwer 2008.
De Groot 2011
G. De Groot, 'Aansprakelijkheid van deskundigen: regulier beroepsrisico of chilling factor? (Liability of Experts: Regular Professional Risk or Chilling Factor?)', *Nederlands tijdschrift voor burgerlijk recht* 2011, p. nr. 58.
De Jong 1980
C.J. De Jong, 'Enige aspecten van een inventarisatie van de toegankelijkheid van de rechtspraak in Nederland (Several Aspects of an Investigation on the Accessiblility of Court Judgments in the Netherlands)', *De juridische bibliothecaris* 1980, p. 2-5.
De Jong 1981
C.J. De Jong, 'Enige aspecten van een inventarisatie van de toegankelijkheid van de rechtspraak in Nederland (Vervolg) [Several Aspects of an Investigation on the Accessiblility of Court Judgments in the Netherlands (Continuation)]', *De juridische bibliothecaris* 1981, p. 2-5.
De Jong 1971
F.J. De Jong, 'Enkele aspecten van de civiele cassatie (Several Aspects of Civil Cassation)', *Nederlandsch Juristenblad* 1971, p. 572-579.
De Meij e.a. 2006
J.M. De Meij e.a., 'Toegang tot rechterlijke uitspraken, Rapport van de VMC-studiecommissie Openbaarheid van rechtspraak (Access to Court Judgments, Report of the VMC Research Committee Publication of Judgments)', *Mediaforum* 2006, p. 1-20.
De Mulder 1996
R.V. De Mulder, 'De kracht van het Internet en de zwakte van het Recht (The Strength of the Internet and the Weakness of the Law)', *Nederlandsch Juristenblad* 1996, p. 1717-1723.
De Pinto 1840
A. De Pinto, 'Boekbeoordelingen en verslagen, Verzameling van Arresten van den Hoogen Raad der Nederlanden, door Joan van den Honert (Book Reviews and Reports, Collection of Cases of the Supreme Court of the Netherlands, by Joan van den Honert)', *Themis* 1840, p. 357-361.
De Vries & Molster 1860

A. De Vries & J.A. Molster, 'Verzameling van Gewijsden in zaken Zee-Assurantie, sedert 1838, bearbeid door Mr. F. Kuijper van Happen, Amsterdam, M. Schooneveld & Zs, 1839 (Annoucements, Collection of Judicial Decisions in Sea Insurance Cases, since 1838, Edited by Mr. F. Kuijper van Happen, Amsterdam, M. Schooneveld & Zs, 1839)', *Magazijn van Handelsregt* 1860, p. 1-6.

Deák 1934

F. Deák, 'The Place of the "Case" in the Common and the Civil Law', *Tulane Law Review* 1934, p. 337-357.

Dedek & Schermaier 2012

H. Dedek & J. Schermaier, 'German Law', in: J.M. Smits (ed.), *Elgar Encyclopedia of Comparative Law,* Cheltenham: Edward Elgar 2012, p. 349-370.

Den Hartog Jader 1994

W.H. Den Hartog Jader, *Cassatie in het belang der wet: een buitengewoon rechtsmiddel (Cassation in the Interest of the Law: An Extraorndinary Remedy at Law),* Arnhem: Gouda Quint 1994.

Deng 2007

X. Deng, 'Sifa Panli Jizhi de Lixing Sikao (Rational Thinking of the Judicial Adjudication Mechanism)', *Falu Shiyong (Application of Law)* 2007, p. 36-41.

Diephuis 1869

G. Diephuis, *Het Nederlandsch burgerlijk regt (The Dutch Civil Law),* Groningen: J.B. Wolters 1869.

Dijksterhuis 2008

B.M. Dijksterhuis, *Rechters normeren de alimentatiehoogte (Judges Standardize the Maintainance Allowance),* Leiden: Leiden University Press 2008.

Ding 2008a

H. Ding, 'Anli Zhidao Zhidu Yanjiu (A Study of the Case Directing System)', http://www.cnki.net.

Ding 2008b

H. Ding, 'Woguo "Anli Gongbu Zhidu" de Shizheng Kaocha ji qi Qishi (An Empirical Investigation and Its Implicaitons on China's "System of Published Cases"', *Dangdai Faxue (Contemporary Law Review)* 2008b, p. 141-146.

Dou & Wang 2009

Y. Dou & J. Wang, 'Zhongguo Anli Zhidao de Fazhan yu Xianshi Yiyi (The Evolution and the Practical Significance of China's Case

Guidance System)', http://hnfy.chinacourt.org/public/detail.php?id=85458.
Draaisma & Duynstee 1988
M. Draaisma & B. Duynstee, 'Hoge Raad en wetenschappers, Een poging om de beïnvloedingsmechanismen in kaart te brengen (The Supreme Court and Legal Scholars, An Attempt to Reveal the Influencing Mechanisms)', in: M. Beerepoot, M. Draaisma & B. Duynstee (eds.), *Hoge Raad 150 jaar (Supreme Court 150 Years),* Alphen a.d. Rijn: Samson H.D. Tjeenk Willink 1988, p. 25-29.
Drion 2009
C.E. Drion, 'De civiele kamer van de Hoge Raad: een paar obversaties vanaf de wal (The Civil Section of the Supreme Court: A Couple of Observations from the Quay)', *Nederlands juristenblad* 2009, p. nr. 268.
Drion 2014
C.E. Drion, 'Stare decisis', *Nederlands juristenblad* 2014, p. 759.
Drion 1968a
J. Drion, 'Common Law and Continental Law', in: A.R. Bloembergene.a. (ed.), *Verzamelde geschriften van J. Drion (Collected Writings of J. Drion),* Deventer: Universitaire Pers Leiden 1968a, p. 235-243.
Drion 1968b
J. Drion, 'Stare Decisis, Het gezag van precedenten (Stare Decisis, The Authority of Precedents)', in: A.R. Bloembergen e.a. (ed.), *Verzamelde geschriften van J. Drion (Collected Writings of J. Drion),* Deventer: Universitaire Pers Leiden 1968b, p. 142-170.
Duan 2012
L. Duan, 'Zhidaoxing Anli Shehui Tuijian Moshi Chulun, Yi Zuigao Renmin Fayuan Guanyu Anli Zhidao Gongzuo de Guiding Weili (Initional Thoughts on Public Recommendation for Guiding Cases, Using the Supreme People’s Court's Provisions Concerning Work on Guiding Cases as an Example)', *Shehui Kexue Yanjiu (Social Science Research)* 2012, p. 105-110.
Duxbury 2008
N. Duxbury, *The Nature and Authority of Precedent,* Cambridge: Cambridge University Press 2008.
Dworkin 1962
G. Dworkin, 'Stare Decisis in the House of Lords', *Modern Law Review* 1962, p. 163-178.

Editors' Board 1982
Editors' Board, 'Redactioneel (Editorial)', *Recht en Kritiek* 1982, p. 3-4.
Editors' Board 2012
Editors' Board, 'Criteria voor publicatie rechterlijke uitspraken (Criteria for Publication of Court Judgments)', *Nederlandsch Juristenblad* 2012, p. 1436-1437.
Editors' Board Rechtsgeleerde Magazijn 1913
Editors' Board Rechtsgeleerde Magazijn, 'Boekbespreking Nederlandsche Jurisprudentie (Book Review Netherlands Cases)', *Rechtsgeleerde Magazijn* 1913, p. 13-14.
Eng 2000
S. Eng, 'The Doctrine of Precedent in English and Norwegian Law - Some Common and Specific Features', *Scandinavian Studies in Law* 2000, p. 275-324.
Enneking 2013
L. Enneking, 'Zorgplichten van multinationals in Nederland (Duties of Care of Multinationals in the Netherlands)', *Nederlands juristenblad* 2013, p. 744-750.
Eorsi 1996
G. Eorsi, 'Comparative Civil (Private) Law: Law Types and Law Groups, the Road of Legal Development', in: V. Gessner, A. Hoeland & C. Varga (eds.), *European Legal Cultures,* Aldershot: Dartmouth 1996, p. 74-77.
Fan 2009
C. Fan, 'Shenyang: Yong Dianxing Anli Zhidao, Jianshao "Tongan Bu Tongpan" (Combating "Like Cases Not Being Treated Alike" by Using Guiding Cases)', http://202.84.17.54/content/20090227/Articel22702005BB.htm.
Fauvarque-Cosson & Fournier 2012
B. Fauvarque-Cosson & A. Fournier, 'France', in: J.M. Smits (ed.), *Elgar Encyclopedia of Comparative Law,* Cheltenham: Edward Elgar 2012, p. 344-348.
Ferdinandusse 2001
W.N. Ferdinandusse, 'De strafbaarheid van een grondrecht. De Wet Openbare Manifestaties en het grondrechtelijk karakter van de betoging (The Criminal Liability of a Fundamental Right. The Public Demonstration Act and the Nature of Protest as a Fundamental Right)', *Nederlandsch juristenblad* 2001, p. 615-619.

Fernhout 2010
F. Fernhout, 'Onrechtmatige rechtspraak herzien (Unlawful Adjudication Revised)', *Nederlands juristenblad* 2010, p. nr. 2191.
Fockema Andreae 1904
J.P. Fockema Andreae, *Tien jaren rechtspraak van den Hoogen Raad (Ten Years Cases of the Supreme Court of the Netherlands),* Leiden: S.C. van Doesburgh 1904.
Fockema Andreae 1938
J.P. Fockema Andreae, 'De methode van interpretatie van het B.W. van 1838 tot heden (The Interpretation Method of the Civil Code from 1838 till Present)', in: P. Scholten & E.M. Meijers (eds.), *Gedenkboek burgerlijk wetboek 1838-1938 (Commemorative Volume Civil Code 1838-1938),* Zwolle: W.E.J. Tjeenk Willink 1938, p. 65-96.
Franken 1981
H. Franken, 'Automatisering en juridische informatie (Computerization and Legal Information)', *Advocatenblad* 1981, p. 392-394.
Franken 1985
H. Franken, *Inleiden tot de rechtswetenschap (Introduction to the Legal Science),* Arnhem: Gouda Quint 1985.
Frederick 1959
G.K.J. Frederick, 'Precedent and Stare Decisis: The Critical Years, 1800-1850', *The American Journal of Legal History* 1959, p. 28-54.
Fruytier e.a. 2013
B. Fruytier e.a., *Werkdruk bewezen, Eindrapport werkdrukonderzoek rechterlijke macht (Work Load Proven, Final Report Research on the Workload of the Judiciary),* Nijmegen: Radboud Universiteit Nijmegen 2013.
Fu & Peerenboom 2010
Y. Fu & R. Peerenboom, 'A New Analytic Framework for Understanding and Promoting Judicial Independence in China', in: R. Peerenboom (ed.), *Judicial Independence in China, Lessons for Global Rule of Law Promotion,* Cambridge: Cambridge University Press 2010, p. 95-133.
Gao & Cao 2010
T. Gao & S. Cao, 'Jianchi Nengdong Sifa Linian, Tansuo Anli Zhidao Zhidu (Uphold the Ideal of Judicial Activism, Explore the

Case Guidance System)', *Renmin Fayuanbao (People's Court Daily)*, 2010.
Gao 1991
Y. Gao, 'Woguo Buyi Caoyong Panlifa Zhidu (Precedent System is Not Suitable for China)', *Zhongguo Faxue (China Legal Science)* 1991, p. 43-48.
Gao 2004
Z. Gao, 'Yunyong Panlifa zhi Wojian (On the Use of Case Law)', in: S. Wu (ed.), *Panli Zhidu Yanjiu (Research on Case Law Systems)*, Beijing: Remin Fayuan Chubanshe (Court Press) 2004, p. 101-105.
Ge & Hu 2007
L. Ge & Y. Hu, 'Shixi Zunxun Xianli Yuanze zai Woguo de Goujian (On the Establishment of Stare Decisis in China)', http://article.chinalawinfo.com/Article_Detail.asp?ArticleId=40508.
Gechlik 2014
M. Gechlik, 'Guiding Cases Analytics', 2014,
Gechlik & Dai 2014
M. Gechlik & D. Dai, 'Guiding Cases No. 26 and China's Open Government Information System', http://cgc.law.stanford.edu/wp-content/uploads/2014/03/CGCP-English-Commentary-10-Gechlik-and-Dai.pdf.
Gerards & Fleuren 2013
J. Gerards & J. Fleuren, *Implementatie van het EVRM en de uitspraken van het EHRM in de nationale rechtspraak, Een rechtsvergelijkend onderzoek (Implementation of the ECHR and the case law of the ECHR in the National Adjudication)*, Nijmegen: Radboud Universiteit Nijmegen 2013.
Giesen 2008
I. Giesen, 'Causaliteit en toerekening naar redelijkheid: geduld is, en blijft, een schone zaak... (Causality and Attribution Based on Reasonableness: Patience is, and Remains, a Good Virtue)', *Weekblad voor Privaatrecht, Notaris-ambt en Registratie* 2008, p. 563-565.
Giesen & Schelhaas 2008
I. Giesen & H.N. Schelhaas, 'Samenwerking bij rechtsvorming, De instelling van een periodiek overleg van rechtsvormers (Cooperation in Lawmaking, Creating of an Institution of Periodic Consultations between the Lawmakers)', in: W.M.T. Keukens & M.C.A. Van den Nieuwenhuijzen (eds.), *Raad & Daad, Over de*

rechtsvormende taak van de Hoge Raad (Court & Action, On the Lawmaking Task of the Supreme Court of the Netherlands), Nijmegen: Ars Aequi Libri 2008, p. 131-154.
Glastra van Loon e.a. 1968
J.F. Glastra van Loon e.a., *Guide to Foreign Legal Materials, Belgium, Luxembourg, Netherlands,* New York: Oceana Publications 1968.
Glendon 1997
M.A. Glendon, 'Comment', in: A. Scalia (ed.), *A Matter of Interpretation, Federal Courts and the Law,* Princeton: Princeton University Press 1997, p. 95-114.
Goodhart 1934
A.L. Goodhart, 'Precedent in English and Continental Law', *Law Quarterly Review* 1934, p. 40-65.
Goodhart 1959
A.L. Goodhart, 'The Ratio Decidendi of a Case', *Modern Law Review* 1959, p. 117-124.
Griffiths 2011
L. Griffiths, 'Legal Framework for Foreign Investment & Establishment of Business Entities in Vietnam with Alex Larkin', http://www.zenlegalnetworking.com/2011/03/articles/conferencewebinar-session-reca/legal-framework-for-foreign-investment-establishment-of-business-entities-in-vietnam-with-alex-larkin/.
Groenendijk 1981
C.A. Groenendijk, *Bundeling van belangen bij de burgerlijke rechter (Joining Interests in the Civil Courts),* Zwolle: W.E.J. Tjeenk Willink 1981.
Guo 2004
Y. Guo, 'Dalu Fa yu Yingmei Fa de Ronghe Ji Dui Woguo Fazhi de Yingxiang (Convergence between the Civil Law and the Common Law and its Influence on Chinese Law)', *Lanzhou Xuekan* 2004, p. 147-148.
Haas 2010
D. Haas, 'Een verklaring voor recht als vorm van genoegdoening, Heeft de Hoge Raad de deur opengezet? (A Declaratory Judgment as a Form of Redress, Has the Supreme Court Opened the Gate?)', *Maandblad voor vermogensrecht* 2010, p. 158-162.
Haazen 2001

O.A. Haazen, *Algemeen deel van het rechterlijk overgangsrecht: een verhandeling over de terugwerkende kracht van rechtspraak, de rechtsdwaling en de democratische rechtsvindingsleer (General Part of Judge-Made Transitional Provisions in Law: a Thesis on the Retroactive Force of Case Law, Miscarriage of Justice and the Doctrine of Democratic Judicial Decision-Making),* Deventer: Kluwer 2001.

Haazen 2007

O.A. Haazen, 'Precedent in The Netherlands', in: E. Hondius (ed.), *Precedent and the Law,* Brussels: Bruylant 2007, p. 227-251.

Han 2009

Y. Han, '"Fei Dianxing Yuanzhang" Tuidong Henan Panjueshu Shangwang ("Atypical Court President" Stimulates Online Publication of Court Judgments in Henan Province)', http://magazine.sina.com/gb/chinanewsweek/2009040/2009-11-09/ba78928.html.

Hardisty 1979

J. Hardisty, 'Reflections on Stare Decisis', *Indiana Law Journal* 1979, p. 41-69.

Hargreaves 2013

A. Hargreaves, 'Professional Capital and the Future of Teaching', in: T. Seddon & J.S. Levin (eds.), *Educators, Professionalism and Politics,* New York: Routledge 2013, p. 290-310.

Hart 1961

H.L.A. Hart, *The Concept of Law,* Oxford: Clarendon Press 1961.

Hartkamp 1992

A.S. Hartkamp, 'Judicial Discretion under the New Civil Code of the Netherlands', *The American Journal of Comparative Law* 1992, p. 551-571.

Hartkamp & Sieburgh 2010

A.S. Hartkamp & C.H. Sieburgh, *Mr. C. Assers Handleiding tot de beoefening van het Nederlands Burgerlijk Recht, Verbintenissenrecht, Deel III Algemeen overeenkomstenrecht (Mr. C. Asser's Guidebook to the Practice of Dutch Civil Law, Law of Obligations, Part III General Contract Law),* Deventer: Kluwer 2010.

Hartkamp & Sieburgh 2011a

A.S. Hartkamp & C.H. Sieburgh, *Mr. C. Assers Handleiding tot de beoefening van het Nederlands Burgerlijk Recht,*

Verbintenissenrecht, Deel 6-IV Verbintenis uit de wet (Mr. C. Asser's Guidebook to the Practice of Dutch Civil Law, Law of Obligations, Part 6-IV Obligations resulting from Enacted Laws), Deventer: Kluwer 2011a.

Hartkamp & Sieburgh 2011b

A.S. Hartkamp & C.H. Sieburgh, *Mr. C. Assers Handleiding tot de beoefening van het Nederlands Burgerlijk Recht, Verbintenissenrecht, Deel 6-IV Verbintenis uit de wet (Mr. C. Asser's Guidebook to the Practice of Dutch Civil Law, Law of Obligations, Part 6-IV, Obligations based on Enacted Laws),* Deventer: Kluwer 2011b.

Hartkamp 1981

D. Hartkamp, 'Huurrecht woonruimte, Jurisprudentie-overzicht 1 juli 1979-1 juli 1981 (Housing Rent Law, Case Law Overview 1 July 1979 - 1 July 1981)', *Advocatenblad* 1981, p. 356-366.

Hartlief 2008

T. Hartlief, 'Vergoeding van overlijdensschade: abstract of concreet? (Compensation for Death Damages: Abstract or Concrete?)', *Ars Aequi* 2008, p. 896-901.

Hartlief 2010

T. Hartlief, 'Een eenvoudige casus stelt het recht voor problemen (A Simple Case Puzzles the Law)', *Nederlands juristenblad* 2010, p. 2071.

Hartlief 2011

T. Hartlief, 'In afwachting van de Franse slag (Expecting the French Solution)', *Nederlands juristenblad* 2011, p. 17-18.

Hartlief 2013

T. Hartlief, 'Proportionele aansprakelijkheid voor juristen en echte wetenschappers (Proportional Liability for Lawyers and Real Scientists)', *Nederlands juristenblad* 2013, p. 289.

He 2010

Q. He (ed.), *Dalu Faxi Ji Qi Dui Zhongguo de Yingxiang (The Civil Law Legal Family and Its Influence on China)*, Beijing: Falu Chubanshe 2010.

He 2005

W. He, 'Panjueshu Shangwang Nan Zai Hechu? (Why is Publishing Judgments Online So Difficult?)', *Fazhi Ribao (Legal Daily),* 2005.

He 2006

W. He, 'Fu Huxia Boshi, Zaitan Panjueshu Shangwang Shi (A Reply to Dr Hu Xia, Discussion Online Publication of Court Judgments Again)', http://www.civillaw.com.cn/article/default.asp?id=24385.
He, Hong & Sun 2008
Z. He, D. Hong & P. Sun, 'Woguo Guoji Sifa Caiyong Panli Zhidu Kexingxing Yanjiu (A Study on the Feasibility of Introducing a Precedent System in China's International Private Law)', *Shanghai Daxue Xuebao (Journal of Shanghai University)* 2008, p. 137-144.
Heemskerk 2005
M. Heemskerk, 'Ontslagrecht voor 65-plussers is onduidelijk (Dismissal Law for People Aged over 65 is Unclear)', *SMA Tijdschrift over arbeid en sociale zekerheid (SMA Journal of Labour Law and Social Security)* 2005, p. 127-135.
Hellman 1989
A.D. Hellman, 'Jumboism and Jurisprudence: The Theory and Practice of Precedent in the Large Appellate Court', *The University of Chicago Law Review* 1989, p. 541-601.
Henssen 1998
E.W.A. Henssen, *Twee eeuwen advocatuur in Nederland (Two Centuries of the Bar in the Netherlands),* Deventer: Kluwer 1998.
Hesselink 2001
M.W. Hesselink, *The New European Legal Culture,* Deventer: Kluwer 2001.
Higher People's Court of Guangdong Province 2008
Higher People's Court of Guangdong Province, 'Guangdong Sheng Gaoji Remin Fayuan Shenpan Weiyuanhui Gongzuo Guiding (Working Rules of the Adjudication Committee of the higher People's Court of Guangdong Province)', http://wenku.baidu.com/view/9f252636396801 1ca300911d.
Hijma e.a. 2007
J. Hijma e.a., *Rechtshandeling en Overeenkomst (Juridic Act and Contract),* Deventer: Kluwer 2007.
Hijma e.a. 2010
J. Hijma e.a., *Rechtshandeling en Overeenkomst (Juridic Act and Contract),* Deventer: Kluwer 2010.
Hoefer-van Dongen 1988

P. Hoefer-van Dongen, 'Van kaartenbak tot CD-Rom, 75 jaar Nederlandse Jurisprudentie (From Card Boxes to CD-Rom, 75 Years Netherlands Cases)', *Nederlandsch Juristenblad* 1988, p. 942.
Hondius 1973
E. Hondius, 'Publikatie van rechterlijke uitspraken; een kanttekening bij het rapport van de commissie-Wiersma (Publication of Court Judgments; A Comment on the Report of the Wiersma Committee)', *Nederlandsch Juristenblad* 1973, p. 745-747.
Hondius 1988a
E. Hondius, 'Nieuw burgerlijk wetboek: Novum voor West-Europa? (New Civil Code: New for West Europe?)', *Nederlandsch Juristenblad* 1988a, p. 669-674.
Hondius 2003
E. Hondius, 'Precedent, Something of the Past', in: M. Fontaine (ed.), *Mélanges offerts à Marcel Fontaine,* Brussels: Larcier 2003, p. 415-423.
Hondius 2004
E. Hondius, 'Precedent in East and West', *Penn State International Law Review* 2004, p. 521-533.
Hondius 2005
E. Hondius, 'Toegevoegde waarde van publicatie van rechtspraak (Added Value of Case Publication)', *Tijdschrift voor Consumentenrecht en handelspraktijken* 2005, p. 37-38.
Hondius 2007a
E. Hondius, 'General Report', in: E. Hondius (ed.), *Precedent and the Law,* Brussels: Bruylant 2007a, p. 1-24.
Hondius 2007b
E. Hondius (ed.), *Precedent and the Law*, Brussels: Bruylant 2007b.
Hondius 1988b
E.H. Hondius, 'De Hoge Raad in rechtsvergelijkend perspectief, van rechtseenheid naar rechtsvorming (The Supreme Court of the Netherlands in the Perspective of Comparative Law, From Legal Unity to Lawmaking)', in: B. Baardman (ed.), *De plaats van de Hoge Raad in het huidige staatsbestel (The Place of the Supreme Court in the Current Constitutional System of the Netherlands),* Zwolle: W.E.J. Tjeenk Willink 1988b, p. 241-253.
Hou 2008

M. Hou, 'Zuigao Renmin Fayuan Niandu Fenxi Baogao (Analytical Report on the Supreme People's Court's Work in 2007)', *Falu Shiyong (Application of Law)* 2008, p. 27-33.
Hu & Yu 2009
Y. Hu & T. Yu, 'Anli Zhidao Zhidu Ruogan Zhongda Yinan Zhengyi Wenti Yanjiu (A study of Several Important, Difficult and Controversial Issues on the Case Guidance System)', in: D. Shen (ed.), *Zhongguo Tese Anli Zhidao Zhidu Yanjiu (A Study of the Case Guidance System with Chinese Characteristics),* Beijing: Court Press (Renmin Fayuan Chubanshe) 2009, p. 2-45.
Huang & Jiang 2009
J. Huang & Y. Jiang, 'Gaoji Fayuan Ying Wei Zhidao Anli Fabu de Zhuti (High Courts Should Be Authorized to Issue Guiding Cases)', http://oldfyb2009.chinacourt.org/public/detail.php?id=126960.
Huang 2009
W. Huang, 'Anli Zhidao Zhidu de Tansuo yu Sikao, Yi Nanjing Diqu de Shijian Weili (Experimentation of and Reflections upon the Case Guidance System, Using the region of Nanjing as an example)', in: D. Shen (ed.), *Zhongguo Tese Anli Zhidao Zhidu Yanjiu (Research on Case Guidance System with Chinese Characteristics),* Beijing: Renmin Fayuan Chubanshe (Court Press) 2009, p. 48-59.
Huang 2011
X. Huang, 'Xuezhe, Lushi Reyi Guanyu Anli Zhidao Gongzuo de Guiding (Scholars and Lawyers Discusisng the Provisions of the Supreme People's Court Concerning Work on Guiding Cases)', http://www.iolaw.org.cn/showNews.aspx?id=25696.
Huang & Cao 2010
X. Huang & J. Cao, 'Yong "Xuting" Panjue Tongyi "Xutingmen", Zhongguoshi Panli Zhidu Shiyan Zaiji (Unify "Xutings" by the "Xuting"-judgment, Experiments with Chinese Style Case Law System are About to Begin', *Nanfang Zhoumo (Southern Weekly),* 2010.
Innis & Jaihutan 2014
M. Innis & Z. Jaihutan, 'Indonesia - Corporate Governance 2014', http://www.iclg.co.uk/practice-areas/corporate-governance/corporate-governance-2014/indonesia.
Intermediate People's Court of Zhengzhou City 2003

Intermediate People's Court of Zhengzhou City, 'Zhengzhou Shi Zhongji Renmin Fayuan Shenpan Weiyuanhui Gongzuo Guize (Working Rules of the Adjudication Committee of the Intermediate People's Court of Zhengzhou City)', http://zzfy.hncourt.org/public/detail.php?id=189.

Jansen 1967

C.H.M. Jansen, 'Twee baanbrekende arresten (Two Groundbreaking Cases)', *Nederlands juristenblad* 1967, p. 482-483.

Jansen 2009

C.H.M. Jansen, *Monografieën BW, B 45 Onrechtmatige daad: algemene bepalingen (Monographs Civil Code, Part B45, Tort: General Provisions),* Deventer: Kluwer 2009.

Jansen & Zwalve 2013

C.H.M. Jansen & W.J. Zwalve, *Publiciteit van jurisprudentie (Publicity of Cases),* Deventer: Kluwer 2013.

Jansen 2003

C.J.H. Jansen, 'De Nederlandse bakermat van het annoteren (The Dutch Cradle of Case Annotation)', 2003, p. 1757-1759.

Jansen 2012

K.J.O. Jansen, 'Groene Serie Onrechtmatige daad, Burgerlijk Wetboek Boek 6, Artikel 162 (Green Serie Tort, Civil Code Book 6, Article 162)', http://www.kluwernavigator.nl.

Jessurun D'Oliveira 1973

H.U. Jessurun D'Oliveira, *De meerwaarde van rechterlijke uitspraken (Arrêt de règlement en precedenten) (The Added Value of Judicial Decisions, Arrêt de règlement and Precedents),* Deventer: Kluwer 1973.

Jiang 2011a

A. Jiang, 'Anli Zhidao Zhidu Guiding: Yige Juyou Huashidai Yiyi de Biaozhi (Provisions on Case Guidance System, a Symbol of Epochmaking Significance)', *Fazhi Ribao (Legal Daily),* 2011a.

Jiang 2011b

A. Jiang, 'Zuigao Renmin Fayuan Yanjiushi Zhuren Hu Yunteng – Renmin Fayuan Anli Zhidao Zhidu de Goujian (Director of the Research Department of the Supreme People's Court Hu Yunteng – Construction of the People's Courts' Case Guidance System)', *Legal Daily,* 2011b.

Jiang 2004

X. Jiang, 'Panlifa Yanjiu (A Study on Case Law)', http://www.cnki.net.
Jing e.a. 2005
C. Jing e.a., 'Tongan Yipan Cuisheng Xinzhi, Xianli Panjue Tuiguang Jiazhi Jiujing You Duoda (The Problem of Like Cases Being Treated Differently Led to a New Institution)', http://cms40.legaldaily.com.cn:7001/servlet/PagePreviewServlet?siteid=4&nodeid=4789&articleid=208323&type=1.
Jongeneel 2010
R.H.C. Jongeneel, 'U weet niet wat u niet weet - ik wel (You do not Know What you do not Know - I do)', *Nederlandsch Juristenblad* 2010, p. 2414-2416.
Kalt 2003
B.C. Kalt, 'Three Levels of Stare Decisis: Distinguishing Common-Law, Constitutional, and Statutory Cases', *Texas Review of Law & Politics* 2003, p. 277-281.
Kavass 1977
I.I. Kavass, 'Law Reporting: Comparisons Between Western Europe and Common Law Countries', *International Journal of Law Libraries* 1977, p. 104-120.
Keith & Lin 2009
R. Keith & Z. Lin, 'Judicial Interpretation of China's Supreme People's Court as "Secondary Law" with Special Reference to Criminal Law', *China Information* 2009, p. 223-255.
Kelk & De Jong 2013
C. Kelk & F. De Jong, *Studieboek materieel strafrecht (Text Book Substantive Criminal Law),* Deventer: Kluwer 2013.
Keukens & Van den Nieuwenhuijzen 2008
W.M.T. Keukens & M.C.A. Van den Nieuwenhuijzen (eds.), *Raad & Daad, Over de rechtsvormende taak van de Hoge Raad (Court & Action, On the Lawmaking Task of the Supreme Court of the Netherlands)*, Nijmegen: Ars Aequi Libri 2008.
Kiel & Göttingen 1997
R.A. Kiel & R.D. Göttingen, 'Precedent in the Federal Republic of Germany', in: D.N. MacCormick & R.S. Summers (eds.), *Interpreting Precedents, a Comparative Study,* Dartmouth: Ashgate 1997, p. 17-64.
Klaassen 2012

C.J.M. Klaassen, 'De reikwijdte van de werkgeversaansprakelijkheid voor arbeidsongevallen na TNT/Wijenberg en De Rooyse Wissel/Hagens en hoe nu verder? (The Scope of the Employer's Liability for Work-Related Accidents after TNT vs Wijenberg en De Rooyse Wissel vs Hagens and How to Proceed Ahead?) ', *Nederlands tijdschrift voor burgerlijk recht* 2012, p. Nr 53.

Kolder 2010

A. Kolder, 'Begrenzing van kwalitatieve aansprakelijkheid; functioneel verband binnen artikel 6:181 BW (Defining the Boundaries of Qualitative Liability; Functional Connection in Article 6:181 of the Civil Code)', *Nederlands tijdschrift voor burgerlijk recht* 2010, p. Nr. 36.

Komárek 2012

J. Komárek, 'Reasoning with Previous Decisions', in: M. Adams & J. Bomhoff (eds.), *Practice and Theory in Comparative Law,* Cambridge: Cambridge University Press 2012, p. 49-73.

Komárek 2013

J. Komárek, 'Reasoning with Previous Decisions: Beyong the Doctrine of Precedent', *Americal Journal of Comparative Law* 2013, p. 149-171.

Kong 2004

X. Kong, 'Panli yu Shensi: Xifang Liangda Faxi Guojia he Zhongguo zai Panli Wenti Shang de Bijiao Yanjiu (Reflections on Case Law: A Comparative Study on the Two Major Legal Families in the West and China)', in: S. Wu (ed.), *Panli Zhidu Yanjiu (Research on Case Law Systems),* Beijing: Remin Fayuan Chubanshe (Court Press) 2004, p. 86-96.

Konijnenbelt & Van Male 2014

W. Konijnenbelt & R.M. Van Male, *Hoofdstukken van bestuursrecht (Chapters of Administrative Law),* Deventer: Kluwer 2014.

Korthals Altes & Groen 2005

E. Korthals Altes & H.A. Groen, *Cassatie in burgerlijke zaken (Cassation in Civil Cases),* Deventer: Kluwer 2005.

Kortmann 2008

C.A.J.M. Kortmann, 'De rechtsvormende taak van de Hoge Raad (The Lawmaking Task of the Supreme Court of the Netherlands)', in: W.M.T. Keukens & M.C.A. Van den Nieuwenhuijzen (eds.),

Raad & Daad, Over de rechtsvormende taak van de Hoge Raad (Court & Action, On the Lawmaking Task of the Supreme Court of the Netherlands), Nijmegen: Ars Aequi Libri 2008, p. 31-38.
Kottenhagen 2010a
R.J.P. Kottenhagen, 'Schockschade en het vereiste van de directe confrontatie, Enkele rechtsvergelijkende kanttekeningen (Shock Damage and the Requirement of Direct Confrontation, Several Comments from a Comparative Law Perspective)', *Nederlands tijdschrift voor burgerlijk recht* 2010a, p. nr. 41.
Kottenhagen 2010b
R.J.P. Kottenhagen, 'Schockschade en het vereiste van directe confrontatie, een gemiste kans (Shock Damage and the Requirement of Direct Confrontation, a Missed Chance)', *Nederlands tijdschrift voor burgerlijk recht* 2010b, p. nr. 17.
Kottenhagen 2011
R.J.P. Kottenhagen, 'Het Hangmat-arrest (Verheijen Achmea-Van Oss): een nieuwe route naar schadevergoeding [The Hammock Case (Verheijen Achmea vs Van Oss): a New Route towards Compensation]', 2011, p. nr. 33.
Kottenhagen 1986
R.J.P. Kottenhagen, *Van precedent tot precedent, Over de plaats en functie van het rechtersrecht in een gecodificeerd rechtsstelsel (From Precedent to Precedent, On the Place and Function of Judge-made Law in a Codified Legal System),* Arnhem: Gouda Quint 1986.
Kottenhagen 1994
R.J.P. Kottenhagen, 'Selectiecriteria en de representativiteit van toegankelijk gemaakte rechtspraak, Enkele recente ontwikkelingen (Selection Criteria and the Representativeness of Court Judgments that Have been Made Accessible, Several Recent Developments) ', in: J.M. Van Dunné & R.J.P. Kottenhagen (eds.), *Symposium Toegankelijkheid van Rechtspraak (Symposium Accessibility of Court Judgments),* Arnhem: Gouda Quint 1994, p.
Kottenhagen & Kaptein 1989
R.J.P. Kottenhagen & M.C. Kaptein, *Toegankelijkheid van Rechtspraak (Accessiblity of Court Judgments),* Arnhem: Gouda Quint 1989.
Kühn 2007

Z. Kühn, 'Precedent in the Czech Republic', in: E. Hondius (ed.), *Precedent and the Law,* Brussels: Bruylant 2007, p. 371-396.

Land 1899

N.K.F. Land, *Inleiding tot de verklaring van het burgerlijk wetboek (Guidebook to the Understanding of the Civil Code),* Haarlem: De Erven F. Bohn 1899.

Landis 1930

J.M. Landis, 'A Note on "Statutory Interpretation"', *Harvard Law Review* 1930, p. 886-893.

Lawson 1977

F.H. Lawson, *A Common Lawyer Looks at the Civil Law,* Westport: Greenwood Press 1977.

Leiden Law School 2011

Leiden Law School, *Tentamen Verbintenissenrecht 11 november 2011 (Exam Law of Obligations 11 November 2011),* Leiden: Leiden Law School 2011.

Leiden Law School 2012a

Leiden Law School, *Leidraad Master civiel recht (Guide to Master Programme Civil Law),* Leiden: Leiden Law School 2012a.

Leiden Law School 2012b

Leiden Law School, *Syllabus Bachelor Verbintenissenrecht (Syllabus Bachelor Law of Obligations),* Leiden: Leiden Law School 2012b.

Leiden Law School 2012c

Leiden Law School, *Tentamen Goederenrecht 8 maart 2012 (Exam Property Law 8 March 2012),* Leiden: Leiden Law School 2012c.

Leiden Law School 2012d

Leiden Law School, *Tentamen Inleiding burgerlijk recht 31 mei 2012 (Exam Introduction to Civil Law 31 May 2012),* Leiden: Leiden Law School 2012d.

Leiden Law School 2012e

Leiden Law School, *Werkboek burgerlijk procesrecht (Exercise Book Civil Procedure Law),* Leiden: Leiden Law School 2012e.

Leiden Law School 2012f

Leiden Law School, *Werkboek goederenrecht (Exercise Book Property Law),* Leiden: Leiden Law School 2012f.

Leiden Law School 2012g

Leiden Law School, *Werkboek inleiding burgerlijk recht (Exercise Book Introduction to Civil Law)* Leiden: Leiden Law School 2012g.

Leiden Law School 2012h
Leiden Law School, *Werkboek mastervak burgerlijk procesrecht (Exercise Book Master Course Civil Procedure Law),* Leiden: Leiden Law School 2012h.
Leiden Law School 2012i
Leiden Law School, *Werkboek verbintenissenrecht (Exercise Book Law of Obligations),* Leiden: Leiden Law School 2012i.
Leon 1850a
D. Leon, *De regtspraak van den Hoogen Raad, van 1 October 1838 tot 1 September 1850, gebragt op de artikelen der staats- en burgerlijke wetten, besluiten en verordeningen, Deel 1 (Cases of the Supreme Court, from 1 October 1838 till 1 September 1850, Brought under the Articles of Constitutional and Civil Statutes, Decisions and Ordinances, Volume 1),* The Hague: Belinfante 1850a.
Leon 1850b
D. Leon, *De regtspraak van den Hoogen Raad, van 1 October 1838 tot 1 September 1850, gebragt op de artikelen der staats- en burgerlijke wetten, besluiten en verordeningen, Deel 2 (Cases of the Supreme Court, from 1 October 1838 till 1 September 1850, Brought under the Articles of Constitutional and Civil Statutes, Decisions and Ordinances, Volume 2),* The Hague: Belinfante 1850b.
Li 2011
J. Li, 'Zhidaoxing Anli Falu Xiaoli de Gefang Guandian (Various Views on the Force of Guiding Cases)', *Fazhi Ribao (Legal Daily),* 2011.
Li & Meng 2002
j. Li & H. Meng, 'Tianji Fayuan Jiang Shishi "Panli Zhidao Zhidu" (Tianjin Court is Going to Implement Precedent Guidance System)', http://news.xinhuanet.com/newscenter/2002-08/30/content_544991.htm.
Li 2010
L. Li, 'Corruption in China's Courts', in: R. Peerenboom (ed.), *Judicial Independence in China, Lessons for Global Rule of Law Promotion,* Cambridge: Cambridge University Press 2010, p. 196-220.
Li 2009a

S. Li, 'Anli Zhidao Zhidu de Lingyitiao Silu (An Alternative Perspective on the Case Guidance System)', *Legal Science Monthly* 2009a, p. 59-77.
Li 2009b
S. Li, 'Goujian Anli Zhidao Zhidu zhi Shijian yu Sikao (Practices to Create a Case Guidance System and Reflections upon such Practices)', in: D. Shen (ed.), *Zhongguo Tese Anli Zhidao Zhidu Yanjiu (Research on the Case Guidance System with Chinese Characteristics),* Beijing: Renmin Fayuan Chubanshe (Court Press) 2009b, p. 85-93.
Li & Pan 2006
Z. Li & H. Pan, 'Lun Woguo Chengwenfa de Buzu Ji Yingdui Celue (On the Limitations of Legislation in China and Possible Solutions)', *Wuhan Keji Xueyuan Xuebao (Journal of Wuhan Science and Technology College)* 2006, p. 85-87.
Liang 1991
Z. Liang, 'Yingguo Panlifa (Precedent System in England)', *Falu Kexue (Law Science)* 1991, p. 10-21.
Liebman 2011a
B.L. Liebman, 'A Populist Threat to China's Courts?', in: M.Y.K. Woo & M.E. Gallagher (eds.), *Chinese Justice, Civil Dispute Resolution in Contemporary China,* Cambridge: Cambridge University Press 2011a, p. 269-313.
Liebman 2011b
B.L. Liebman, 'A Return to Populist Legality? Historical Legacies and Legal Reform', in: S. Heilmann & E.J. Perry (eds.), *Mao's Invisible Hand,* Cambridge: Harvard University Press 2011b, p. 165-200.
Lin 2009
Y. Lin, 'Meiguo Fayuan Ruhe Zunxun Xianli (How do US Courts Follow Precedents)', *Zhongwai Faxue (Peking University Law Journal)* 2009, p. 951-962.
Lindenbergh 2008a
S.D. Lindenbergh, 'Abstractie bij overlijdensschade HR 11 juli 2008, RvdW 2008, 724 (Abstraction in Case of Death Damages HR 11 July 2008, RvdW 2008, 724)', *Maandblad voor vermogensrecht* 2008a, p. 235-239.
Lindenbergh 2008b

S.D. Lindenbergh, 'Moord en doodslag in het aansprakelijkheidsrecht (Murder and Manslaughter in Tort Law)', *Ars Aequi* 2008b, p. 598-599.

Lindenbergh 2008c

S.D. Lindenbergh, 'Olie op het vuur (Oil on the Fire)', *Ars Aequi* 2008c, p. 358-361.

Lindenbergh 2008d

S.D. Lindenbergh, 'Vaststelling van letselschade, Veel aandacht voor een fictieve toekomst, weinig voor daadwerkelijke financiële zekerheid (Settling Damages for Bodily Injuries, Much Attention for a Fictitious Future, Little for Real Financial Certainty)', *Maandblad voor vermogensrecht* 2008d, p. 118-124.

Lindenbergh & Van der Zalm 2009

S.D. Lindenbergh & I. Van der Zalm, 'Vergoeding ter zake van verzorging en huishoudelijke hulp bij letsel en overlijden (Compensation of Nursing and Domestic Help Costs in Bodily Injury and Death Cases)', *Maandblad voor vermogensrecht* 2009, p. 146-151.

Lindenbergh & Van Maanen 2011

S.D. Lindenbergh & G.E. Van Maanen, *EVRM en privaatrecht: is alles van waarde weerloos? (ECHR and the Private Law: is Everything of Value Helpless),* Deventer: Kluwer 2011.

Lindo 1993

C.M.T. Lindo, 'De engelbewaarders van de Nederlandse Jurisprudentie (The Guardian Angels of the Netherlands Cases)', *Nederlandsch Juristenblad* 1993, p. 1297-1303.

Lipstein 1946

D.K. Lipstein, 'The Doctrine of Precedent in Continental Law with Special Reference to French and German Law', *Journal of Comparative Legislation and International Law* 1946, p. 34-44.

Liu 2007a

P. Liu, 'Jiejian, Ronghe yu Zhongguo Panli Zhidu Goujian (Learning, Convergence and Construction of China's Case Law System)', http://www.cnki.net.

Liu 2009

Y. Liu, 'Zhidaoxing Anli de Tuixuan yu Fabu Chengxu Yanjiu (On the Selection and Publication of Guiding Cases)', in: D. Shen (ed.), *Zhongguo Tese Anli Zhidao Zhidu Yanjiu (Research on the Case*

Guidance System with Chinese Characteristics), Beijing: Renmin Fayuan Chubanshe (Court Press) 2009, p. 105-113.

Liu 2006

Z. Liu, 'Women Weishenme Yao Shixing Anli Zhidao Zhidu (Why Should We Implement the Case Guidance System)', *Falu Shiyong (Application of Law)* 2006, p. 5-8.

Liu 2007b

Z. Liu, 'Ying Yunxu Yong Anli Duanan (Judges Should be Allowed to Decide Cases According to Precedents)', *Minzhu yu Fazhi (Democracy and Legal System)* 2007b, p. 32-33.

Liu & Xu 2006

Z. Liu & J. Xu, 'Anli Zhidao Zhidu de Lilun Jichu (Theoretical Foundations of the Case Guidance System)', *Faxue Yanjiu (Chinese Journal of Law)* 2006, p. 16-29.

Loussouarn 1958

Y. Loussouarn, 'The Relative Importance of Legislation, Custom, Doctrine, and Precedent in French Law', *Louisiana Law Review* 1958, p. 235-270.

Lü 2010

L. Lü, 'Lun Yingmei Panlifa Zhong Leibi Falu Tuili de Shiyong (On the Application of Analogous Reasoning in the Common Law Precedent System)', http://www.cnki.net.

Lu 2011

Y. Lu, 'Anli Zhidao Zhidu Lilun yu Shijian Yantaohui Zhaokai (Seminar on Theory and Practice of the Case Guidance System)', http://law.nju.edu.cn/Print.asp?ArticleID=2011322174646297.

Lubbers 2008

A.O. Lubbers, ''Spoedcursus' arresten lezen en analyseren (''Crash Course'' in Reading and Analysing Cases)', *Ars Aequi* 2008, p. 163-166.

Lund 1997

A.P. Lund, 'The Binding Force of Precedent', in: D.N. MacCormick & R.S. Summers (eds.), *Interpreting Precedents, a Comparative Study,* Dartmouth: Ashgate 1997, p. 461-479.

Lundmark 2003

T. Lundmark, '''Soft'' stare decisis: the common law doctrine retooled for Europe', in: R. Schulze & U. Self (eds.), *Richterrecht und Rechtsfortbildung in der Europäischen Rechtsgemeinschaft,* Tubingen: Mohr 2003, p. 161-168.

Ma & Cha 2011
F. Ma & B. Cha, 'Difang Fayuan Tuixing Anli Zhidao Zhidu de Biyaoxing Ji Lujing Xuanze (the necessity and Possible Ways for Local Courts to Establish the Case Guidance System)', *Guanghua Faxue* 2011, p. 59-71.
MacCormick & Summers 1997a
D.N. MacCormick & R.S. Summers, 'Further General Reflections and Conclusions', in: D.N. MacCormick & R.S. Summers (eds.), *Interpreting Precedents, A Comparative Study,* Dartmouth: Ashgate 1997a, p. 531-550.
MacCormick & Summers 1997b
D.N. MacCormick & R.S. Summers (eds.), *Interpreting Precedents, a Comparative Study*, Dartmouth: Ashgate 1997b.
MacCormick & Summers 1997c
D.N. MacCormick & R.S. Summers, 'Introduction', in: D.N. MacCormick & R.S. Summers (eds.), *Interpreting Precedents, a Comparative Study,* Dartmouth: Ashgate 1997c, p. 1-15.
Markesinis 1994
B.S. Markesinis, 'Learning from Europe and Learning in Europe', in: B.S. Markesinis (ed.), *The Gradual Convergence,* Oxford: Clarendon Press 1994, p. 1-32.
Markman 2003
S. Markman, 'Precedent: Tension Between Continuity in the Law and the Perpetuation of Wrong Decisions', *Texas Review of Law & Politics* 2003, p. 283-287.
Martens 2000
S.K. Martens, 'De grenzen van de rechtsvormende taak van de rechter (The Boundaries of the Lawmaking Task of the Judge)', *Nederlandsch Juristenblad* 2000, p. 747-758.
Mattei & Pes 2008
U. Mattei & L.G. Pes, 'Civil Law and Common Law: Toward Convergence?', in: K.E. Whittington, R.D. Kelemen & G.A. Caldeira (eds.), *The Oxford Handbook of Law and Politics,* Oxford: Oxford University Press 2008, p. 267-280.
Matthijssen 2000
L. Matthijssen, *Jurisprudentiedatabanken, Een internationaal vergelijkende studie naar de publicatie van rechterlijke uitspraken met behulp van informatietechnologie (Case Law Databases, An International Comparative Study on the Publication of Court*

Judgments by Means of Information Technology), Deventer: Kluwer 2000.
McLeod 2011
I. McLeod, *Legal Method,* Basingstoke: Palgrave Macmillan Limited 2011.
Meijers 1951
E.M. Meijers, 'Case Law and Codified Systems of Private Law', *Journal of Comparative Legislation and International Law* 1951, p. 8-18.
Meng 2004
F. Meng, 'Putong Faxi de Panli Zhidu, Yige Yuan yu Liu de Jiedu (Precedent System in Common Law, An Understanding of Its Source and Flowing)', http://www.cnki.net.
Mensonides 1988
H. Mensonides, 'Interview in het kader van het 150-jarig bestaan van de Hoge Raad met raadsheer mr. H.L.J. Roelvink (Interview with Master H.L.J. Roelvink, Judge of the Supreme Court on the Occasion of 150th Anniversary of the Supreme Court)', in: M. Beerepoot, M. Draaisma & B. Duynstee (eds.), *Hoge Raad 150 jaar (Supreme Court 150 Years),* Nijmegen: Landelijk overleg juridische faculteitsbladen 1988, p. 10-14.
Merryman 1974
J.H. Merryman, 'The Italian Legal Style III: Interpretation', in: J. Dainow (ed.), *The Role of Judicial Decisions and Doctrine in Civil Law and in Mixed Jurisdictions,* Baton Rouge: Louisiana State University Press 1974, p. 163-201.
Ministerie van Binnenlandse Zaken (Ministry of Internal Affairs) 1997
Ministerie van Binnenlandse Zaken (Ministry of Internal Affairs), *Naar toegankelijkheid van overheidsinformatie: beleidskader voor het vergroten van de toegankelijkheid van overheidsinformatie met informatie- en communicatietechnologie (Towards Accessibility of Governement Information: Policy Framework for Broadening the Accessibility of Government Information by Information and Communication Technology),* The Hague: Ministerie van Binnenlandse Zaken 1997.
Mommers, Zwenne & Schermer 2010
L. Mommers, G. Zwenne & B. Schermer, 'Het best bewaarde geheim van de raadkamer, Over de ontoegankelijkheid van de

rechtspraak (The Best Kept Secret of the Judge's Chamber, On the Inaccessibility of Court Judgments)', *Nederlandsch Juristenblad* 2010, p. 2072-2078.
Montesquieu 2001
Montesquieu, *De l'esprit des lois,* Kitchener: Batoche Books 2001.
Mou 2014
L. Mou, 'Lun Zhidaoxing Anli de Xiaoli (On the Force of guiding cases)', http://www.aisixiang.com/data/73953.html.
Nederpel 1985
M.C. Nederpel, 'Rechtsbronnen (Sources of Law)', in: H. Franken (ed.), *Inleiden tot de rechtswetenschap (Introduction to the Legal Science),* Arnhem: Gouda Quint 1985, p. 97-122.
Nelson 2011
C. Nelson, 'Stare decisis and Demonstrably Erroneous Precedents', *Virginia Law Review* 2011, p. 1-84.
Nieuwenhuis 2000
J.H. Nieuwenhuis, 'De kunst van het zaklopen, Rechtsvorming door de cassatierechter (The Art of the Sack Race, Lawmaking by the Cassation Court)', *Nederlandsch Juristenblad* 2000, p. 687-689.
Nieuwenhuis 2010
J.H. Nieuwenhuis, 'Eenzame hoogte: het DES-arrest (Lonely Hight: The DES Case)', *Ars Aequi* 2010, p. 417-419.
Nieuwenhuis 2013
J.H. Nieuwenhuis, *Hoofdstukken vermogensrecht (Chapters The Law of Property),* Deventer: Kluwer 2013.
Nieuwenhuis, Stolker & Valk 2011
J.H. Nieuwenhuis, C.J.J.M. Stolker & W.L. Valk, *Burgerlijk Wetboek: de tekst van de boeken 1, 2, 3, 4, 5, 6, 7, 8, 10 van het BW en International Convention for the unification of certain rules of law relating to bills of lading, voorzien van commentaar (The Civil Code: the Text of the Books 1, 2, 3, 4, 5, 6, 7, 8, 9, 10 of the Civil Code and the International Convention for the unification of certain rules of law relating to bills of lading, Supplemented with Comments),* Deventer: Kluwer 2011.
Noordam 2008
A.J. Noordam, *WPSN en goede trouw (Personal Debt Repayment Act and Good Faith),* Deventer: Kluwer 2008.
Noorlander & Paijmans 2011

C.W. Noorlander & B.M. Paijmans, ''Educational Malpractice' als relatief nieuw fenomeen binnen het Nederlandse aansprakelijkheidsrecht ("Educational Malpractice" as a Relatively Recent Phenomenon in the Dutch Tort Law)', *Nederlands tijdschrift voor burgerlijk recht* 2011, no. 32.

Oderkerk 1999
A.E. Oderkerk, *De preliminaire fase van het rechtsvergelijkend onderzoek (The Preliminary Phase of Comparative Legal Research),* Nijmegen: Ars Aequi Libri 1999.

Oderkerk 2001
A.E. Oderkerk, 'The Importance of Context: Selecting Legal Systems in Comparative Legal Research', *Netherlands International Law Review* 2001, p. 293-318.

Oldenhuis 2010
F.T. Oldenhuis, 'De Hangmatzaak (The Hammock Case)', *Nederlands juristenblad* 2010, p. 2456-2460.

Oldenhuis 2011
F.T. Oldenhuis, 'Hoge Raad zet in Wilniszaak rem op te ruim risicoaansprakelijkheid (Supreme Court Limits Strict Liability in Wilnis Case)', *Nederlands juristenblad* 2011, p. 668-672.

Opstelten 2012
I.W. Opstelten, 'Kamerstukken II 2010/11, 32 612, nr. 3 (Explanatory Notes on the Act of Preliminary Rulings by the Supreme Court)', https://zoek.officielebekendmakingen.nl/dossier/32612/kst-32612-3?resultIndex=2&sorttype=1&sortorder=8.

Opzoomer 1865
C.W. Opzoomer, *Het burgerlijke wetboek verklaard door mr. C. W. Opzoomer (The Civil Code Explained by Master C.W. Opzoomer),* Amsterdam: J.H. Gebhard & Comp 1865.

Owsia 1991
P. Owsia, 'Sources of Law under English, French, Islamic and Iranian Law: A Comparative Review', *Arab Law Quarterly* 1991, p. 33-67.

Pan 1998
R. Pan, 'Dalu Faxi de Sifa Panli Ji Qishi (Judicial Precedents in Civil Law Systems and Inspiration)', *Shandong Faxue* 1998, p. 52-54.

Phillippart 2010

R.C.A.M. Phillippart, 'Toegankelijkheid van rechtspraak, Reactie op 'Het best bewaarde geheim van de raadkamer' (Accessibility of Court Judgments, Reaction to "The Best Kept Secret of the Judge's Chamber)', *Nederlandsch Juristenblad* 2010, p. 2356.

Pitlo 1968

A. Pitlo, *Het systeem van het Nederlandse privaatrecht (The System of the Dutch Private Law),* Haarlem: H.D. Tjeenk Willink & Zoon 1968.

Polak 1953

J.M. Polak, *Theorie en praktijk der rechtsvinding (Theory and Practice of Judicial Decision-Making),* Zwolle: W.E.J. Tjeenk Willink 1953.

Pound 1908

R. Pound, 'Common Law and Legislation', *Harvard Law Review* 1908, p. 383-407.

Qin 2007

W. Qin, 'Lun Woguo Anli Zhidao Zhidu de Goujian he Shiyong Fangfa (On the Creation and Operation of the Case Guidance System)', in: H. Ge (ed.), *Falu Fangfa yu Falu Siwei (Legal Method and Legal Thinking),* Beijing: Falu Chubanshe (Law Press) 2007, p. 205-221.

Raad van State 2013

Raad van State, 'Jaarverslag Raad van State (Annual Report Council of State)', http://jaarverslag.raadvanstate.nl/download-of-bestel/cDU509_Download-of-bestel-het-jaarverslag.aspx.

Raad voor de Rechtspraak (Council for the Judiciary) 2003

Raad voor de Rechtspraak (Council for the Judiciary), 'Jaarverslag van de rechtspraak 2002 (Annual Report of the Judiciary 2002)', http://www.rechtspraak.nl/Organisatie/Publicaties-En-Brochures/Documents/jaarverslag 2002.pdf.

Raad voor de Rechtspraak (Council for the Judiciary) 2004

Raad voor de Rechtspraak (Council for the Judiciary), 'Jaarverslag van de rechtspraak 2003 (Annual Report of the Judiciary 2003)', http://www.rechtspraak.nl/Organisatie/Publicaties-En-Brochures/Documents/jaarverslag 2003.pdf.

Raad voor de Rechtspraak (Council for the Judiciary) 2006

Raad voor de Rechtspraak (Council for the Judiciary), 'Jaarverslag van de rechtspraak 2005 (Annual Report of the Judiciary 2005)',

http://www.rechtspraak.nl/Organisatie/Publicaties-En-Brochures/Documents/jaarverslag 2005.pdf.
Raad voor de Rechtspraak (Council for the Judiciary) 2007
Raad voor de Rechtspraak (Council for the Judiciary), 'Anonimiseringsrichtlijnen (Anonymization Guidelines)', http://www.rechtspraak.nl/Uitspraken-en-Registers/uitspraken/Anonimiseringsrichtlijnen/Pages/default.aspx.
Raad voor de Rechtspraak (Council for the Judiciary) 2009
Raad voor de Rechtspraak (Council for the Judiciary), 'Jaarverslag van de rechtspraak 2008 (Annual Report of the Judiciary 2008)', http://www.rechtspraak.nl/Organisatie/Publicaties-En-Brochures/Documents/jaarverslag 2008.pdf.
Raad voor de Rechtspraak (Council for the Judiciary) 2011
Raad voor de Rechtspraak (Council for the Judiciary), 'Jaarverslag van de rechtspraak 2010 (Annual Report of the Judiciary 2010)', http://www.rechtspraak.nl/Organisatie/Publicaties-En-Brochures/Documents/2010 Jaarverslag Rechtspraak%5B1%5D.pdf.
Raad voor de Rechtspraak (Council for the Judiciary) 2012
Raad voor de Rechtspraak (Council for the Judiciary), 'European Case Law Identifier vervangt Landelijk Jurisprudentienummer (European Case Law Identifier Replaces National Case Law Number)', http://www.rechtspraak.nl/Actualiteiten/Nieuws/Pages/European-Case-Law-Identifier-vervangt-Landelijk-Jurisprudentie-Nummer.aspx.
Raad voor de rechtspraak (Council for the Judiciary) e.a. 2012
Raad voor de rechtspraak (Council for the Judiciary) e.a., 'Besluit selectiecriteria uitsprakendatabank Rechtspraak.nl (Resolution Selection Criteria Judgments Database Rechtspraak.nl)', http://www.rechtspraak.nl/Uitspraken-en-Registers/uitspraken/Selectiecriteria/Pages/default.aspx.
Rao & Yan 2004
A. Rao & Y. Yan, 'Panlifa de Linghun, Dui "Zunxun Xianli" Yuanze de Zai Renshi (The Soul of the Precedent System, Stare Decisis Revisited)', *Guangxi Shehui Kexue (Guangxi Social Sciences)* 2004, p. 93-95.
Rao & Liao 2009

L. Rao & Y. Liao, 'Guanyu Shixing Anli Zhidao Zhidu de Diaoyan Baogao (Research Report on the Implementation of the Case Guidance System)', in: D. Shen (ed.), *Zhongguo Tese Anli Zhidao Zhidu Yanjiu (A Study of the Case Guidance System with Chinese Characteristics),* Beijing: Court Press (Renmin Fayuan Chubanshe) 2009, p. 114-122.
Ras 1988
H.E. Ras, 'De Burgerlijke kamer (inclusief de Antilliaanse cassatieregeling) [The Civil Panel (Including Cassation for the Netherlands Antilles]', in: J. Van Soest (ed.), *De Hoge Raad der Nederlanden 1838-1988, Een portret (The Supreme Court of the Netherlands 1838-1988, A Sketch),* Zwolle: W.E.J. Tjeenk Willink 1988, p. 73-82.
Remmelink e.a. 1988
J. Remmelink e.a., *NJ 1913-1988, Annotatoren kijken terug (NJ 1913-1988, Annotators Look Back),* Zwolle: Tjeenk Willink 1988.
Research Department of the Higher People's Court of Shanghai 2009
Research Department of the Higher People's Court of Shanghai, 'Guifan yu Shifan Bingzhong, Duoji Wangluo Hudong, Shanghai Fayuan Goujian Anli Zhidao Zhidu de Shijian yu Sikao (Equal Emphasis on Regulation and Demonstration, Intraction between Multilevel Networks, Experiments by Shanghai Courts to create a Case Guidance System and Reflections upon these Experiments)', in: D. Shen (ed.), *Zhongguo Tese Anli Zhidao Zhidu Yanjiu (A Study of the Case Guidance System with Chinese Characteristics),* Beijing: Court Press (Renmin Fayuan Chubanshe) 2009, p. 60-71.
Research Department of the Supreme People's Court 2007
Research Department of the Supreme People's Court (ed.), *Shenpan Qianyan Wenti Yanjiu (Research on Adjudication Frontier Issues),* Beijing: Renmin Fayuan Chubanshe (Court Press) 2007.
Research Group of the Editor's Office of People's Court Daily 2007
Research Group of the Editor's Office of People's Court Daily, 'Anli Zhidao Zhidu de Diaoyan Baogao (Research Report on the Case Guidance System)', in: Research Department of the Supreme People's Court (ed.), *Shenpan Qianyan Wenti Yanjiu (Research on Adjudication Frontier Issues),* Beijing: Court Press (Renmin Fayuan Chubanshe) 2007, p. 465.

Research Group of the Higher People's Court of Beijing 2007
Research Group of the Higher People's Court of Beijing, 'Guanyu Wanshan Anli Zhidao Zhidu de Diaoyan Baogao (Research Report on the Perfection of the Case Guidance System)', in: Research Department of the Supreme People's Court (ed.), *Shenpan Qianyan Wenti Yanjiu (Research on Adjudication Frontier Issues),* Beijing: Renmin Fayuan Chubanshe (Court Press) 2007, p. 344-368.
Rijpkema 2001
P. Rijpkema, *Rechtersrecht, Over de rechtsvormende rol van de rechter in een democratische rechtsstaat (Judge-made Law, On the Lawmaking role of the Judge in a Democratic Constitutional State),* The Hague: Boom Juridische uitgevers 2001.
Roelofs 2008
L.C. Roelofs, 'Het schademoment als uitgangspunt voor hypothetische en 'onderbroken' causaliteit (The Damage Moment as Starting Point for Hypothetical and "Broken" Causality)', *Nederlands tijdschrift voor burgerlijk recht* 2008, p. Nr 48.
Rudden 1974
B. Rudden, 'Courts and Codes in England, France and Soviet Russia', *Tulane Law Review* 1974, p. 1010-1028.
Rutten-Roos 1970
A. Rutten-Roos, 'Ouders, Kinderen en wettelijke aansprakelijkheid', *Weekblad voor Privaatrecht, Notaris-ambt en Registratie* 1970, p. 101-107.
Schaefer 1967
W.V. Schaefer, 'The Control of "sunbursts": techniques of Prospective Overruling', *New York University Law Review* 1967,
Schlossels 2012
R.J.N. Schlossels, 'De noot van de toekomst, De toekomst van de noot? (Case Annotations of the Future, The Future of Case Annotations?)', *Ars Aequi* 2012, p. 230-233.
Schlossels & Zijlstra 2010
R.J.N. Schlossels & S. Zijlstra, *Bestuursrecht in de sociale rechtsstaat (Administrative Law in the Social Constitutional State),* Deventer: Kluwer 2010.
Scholten 1931
P. Scholten, *Mr. C. Asser's Handleiding tot de beoefening van het Nederlandsch Burgerlijk Recht, Algemeen Deel (Mr. C. Asser's*

Guidebook to the Practice of Dutch Civil Law, The General Part), Zwolle: W.E.J. Tjeenk Willink 1931.
Scholten 1934
P. Scholten, *Mr. C. Asser's Handleiding tot de beoefening van het Nederlandsch Burgerlijk Recht, Algemeen Deel (Mr. C. Asser's Guidebook to the Practice of Dutch Civil Law, The General Part),* Zwolle: W.E.J. Tjeenk Willink 1934.
Schoordijk 1988
H.C.F. Schoordijk, 'Hoe vat(te) de Burgerlijke Kamer van de Hoge Raad zijn rechtsvormende taak op? (How does/did the Civil Chamber of the Supreme Court of the Netherlands Conceive its Lawmaking Task?)', in: B. Baardman (ed.), *De plaats van de Hoge Raad in het huidige staatsbestel (The Place of the Supreme Court in the Current Constitutional System of the Netherlands),* Zwolle: W.E.J. Tjeenk Willink 1988, p. 3-63.
Schuijt 2004
G.A.I. Schuijt, '[De voetballer] en [de prinses] ([The Football Player] and [the Princes]) ', *Nederlandsch Juristenblad* 2004, p. 18-19.
Schutgens 2009
R.J.B. Schutgens, 'Onrechtmatige wetgeving (Unlawful Legislation)', *Ars Aequi* 2009, p. 850-854.
Scott 1999
G.K. Scott, 'Judge-Made Law: Constitutional Duties & Obligations Under the Separation of Powers Doctrine', *Depaul Law Review* 1999, p. 511-517.
Seawright & Gerring 2008
J. Seawright & J. Gerring, 'Case Selection Techniques in Case Study Research: A Menu of Qualitative and Quantitative Options', *Political Research Quarterly* 2008, p. 294-308.
Shen 2009a
D. Shen, 'Yi Qiuzhen Wushi he Gaige Chuangxin Jingshen Tansuo Jianli Zhongguo Tese Anli Zhidao Zhidu (Exploring a Case Guidance System with Chinese Characteristics in the Spirit of Seeking Truth and Carrying Out Innovative Reform)', in: D. Shen (ed.), *Zhongguo Tese Anli Zhidao Zhidu Yanjiu (Research on the Case Guidance System with Chinese Characteristics),* Beijing: Renmin Fayuan Chubanshe (Court Press) 2009a, p. 3-7.
Shen 2009b

D. Shen (ed.), *Zhongguo Tese Anli Zhidao Zhidu Yanjiu (Research on the Case Guidance System with Chinese Characteristics)*, Beijing: Renmin Fayuan Chubanshe (Court Press) 2009b.
Shen 2004
F. Shen, 'Shilun Panli Ye Yingdang Chengwei Woguo de Falu Yuanyuan (Cases Should Also Become a Source of Law in China)', in: S. Wu (ed.), *Panli Zhidu Yanjiu (Research on Case Law Systems),* Beijing: Remin Fayuan Chubanshe (Court Press) 2004, p. 18-23.
Shen 2000
H. Shen, 'Academic Freedom and Academic Duty in Chinese Universities', in: OECD (ed.), *Current Issues in Chinese Higher Education,* Paris: OECD Publications 2000, p. 21-36.
Shen, Liu & Fan 2009
Z. Shen, L. Liu & L. Fan, 'Zhongji Renmin Fayuan Fahui Anli Zhidao Zuoyong de Tansuo yu Sikao (Experiments by Middle People's Courts to explore the use of the Case Guidance System and Reflections upon such Experiments)', in: D. Shen (ed.), *Zhongguo Tese Anli Zhidao Zhidu Yanjiu (Research on the Case Guidance System with Chinese Characteristics),* Beijing: Renmin Fayuan Chubanshe (Court Press) 2009, p. 94-104.
Silving 1966
H. Silving, '"Stare decisis" in the Civil and in the Common Law', *Revista juridica de la Universidad de Puerto Rico* 1966, p. 194-242.
Smits 2000
J.M. Smits, 'Rechterlijk overgangsrecht: op zoek naar consistentie (Judge-made Transitional Privisions in Law: in search for consistency)', in: I. Brand (ed.), *Tijd en onzekerheid (Time and Uncertainty),* Deventer: Gouda Quint 2000, p. 11-26.
Smits 2012
J.M. Smits, 'The Netherlands', in: J.M. Smits (ed.), *Elgar Encyclopedia of Comparative Law,* Cheltenham: Edward Elgar 2012, p. 620-624.
Snijders 1977
H.J. Snijders, 'Afschaffing van de rechterlijke omgangsregeling na echtscheiding? (Abolishing the Judicial Visitation Rules after Divorce?)', *Nederlandsch Juristenblad* 1977, p. 525-531.
Snijders 1978

H.J. Snijders, *Rechtsvinding door de burgerlijke rechter, Een kwantitatief rechtspraakonderzoek bij de Hoge Raad en de Gerechtshoven (Adjudication by Civil Judges, a Qualitative Research in Cases decided by the Supreme Court and the Courts of Appeal)* Deventer: Kluwer 1978.

Snijders 1988

H.J. Snijders, 'Hoge Raad, Goede Raad, Enige beschouwingen bij de literatuur rond het 150 jarig jubileum van de Hoge Raad (Supreme Court, Good Court, Brief Review of the Literature on the Occasion of the 150th Anniversary of the Supreme Court of the Netherlands)', *Nederlandsch Juristenblad* 1988,

Snijders 2003

H.J. Snijders, 'Annoteren, een summum van rechtswetenschappelijk presteren? (Case annotation, A Summit of Legal Scientific Achievement?)', *Nederlands tijdschrift voor burgerlijk recht* 2003, p. 173.

Snijders 2007

H.J. Snijders, 'Uitleg van rechterlijke uitspraken (Interpretation of Court Judgments)', *WPNR* 2007, p. 431-444.

Song 2009

F. Song, 'Renmin Fayuan Anlixuan Di 26 Ji Shuping (Book Review Selection of Cases Decided by People's Courts Volume 26)', http://www.lawbook.com.cn/lw/lw_view.asp?no=9837.

Spier 2010a

J. Spier, 'Conclusie 09/01675 (Advisory Opinion 09/01675)', http://uitspraken.rechtspraak.nl/inziendocument?id=ECLI:NL:PHR:2010:BM6095&keyword=BM6095.

Spier 2010b

J. Spier, 'Conclusie 09/03735 (Advisory Opinion 09/03735)', http://uitspraken.rechtspraak.nl/inziendocument?id=ECLI:NL:PHR:2010:BN6236&keyword=bn6236.

Spier e.a. 2012

J. Spier e.a., *Verbintenissen uit de wet en schadevergoeding (Obligations Based on Enacted Laws and Damage Compensation),* Deventer: Kluwer 2012.

Stanford Law School China Guiding Cases Project 2013

Stanford Law School China Guiding Cases Project, 'China's Guiding Cases System: Evolution, Impact and Prospects', http://cgc.law.stanford.edu/.

Stockmann & Gallagher 2011
D. Stockmann & M.E. Gallagher, 'Remote Control: How the Media Sustain Authoritarian Rule in China', *Comparative Political Studies* 2011, p. 436-467.
Stone 1959
J. Stone, 'The Ratio of Ratio Decidendi', *Modern Law Review* 1959, p. 597-620.
Struycken & Haazen 1993
T. Struycken & O.A. Haazen, 'De binding aan precedenten (Binding by Precedents)', in: H.G. Schermers, T.L. Bellekom & P.T.C. Van Kampen (eds.), *De rol van de rechter in de moderne westerse samenleving (The Role of the Judge in Modern Western Society),* Leiden: Mordenate College 1993, p. 91-150.
Su & Li 2009
Z. Su & X. Li, 'Lun Sifa Tongyi Yu Anli Zhidao Zhidu de Wanshan (On the perfection of Judicial Unity and the Case Guidance System)', *Zhongguo Sifa (Justice of China)* 2009, p. 12-16.
Suijling 1918
J.P. Suijling, *Inleiding tot het burgerlijk recht (Introduction to the Civil Law),* Haarlem: De Erven F. Bohn 1918.
Suijling 1927
J.P. Suijling, *Inleiding tot het burgerlijk recht (Introduction to the Civil Law),* Haarlem: De Erven F. Bohn 1927.
Sun 2011
Y. Sun, 'Zhongguo Falu Jiaoyu Luanxiang (Chaos in China's Legal Education)', http://www.legaldaily.cn/zmbm/content/2011-07/19/content_2800818.htm?node=20351.
Supreme People's Court of the People's Republic of China 2005
Supreme People's Court of the People's Republic of China, 'Renmin Fayuan Di'erge Wunian Gaige Gangyao (Second Five-Year Reform Outline of the People's Courts)', http://www.chinalawinfo.com.
Supreme People's Court of the People's Republic of China 2009
Supreme People's Court of the People's Republic of China, 'Zuigao Renmin Fayuan Guanyu Sifa Gongkai de Liuxiang Guiding (Supreme People's Court's Six Rules to Promote Transparancy in the Judiciary System)', http://oldfyb2009.chinacourt.org/public/detail.php?id=134636.
Supreme People’s Court of the People’s Republic of China 1993

Supreme People's Court of the People's Republic of China, 'Zuigao Renmin Fayuan Shenpan Weiyuanhui Gongzuo Guize (Working Rules of the Adjudication Committee of the Supreme People's Court)', http://www.law-lib.com/law/law_view.asp?id=9800.

Supreme People's Court of the People's Republic of China 2007
Supreme People's Court of the People's Republic of China, 'Zuigao Renmin Fayuan Guanyu Sifa Jieshi Gongzuo de Guiding (Provisions of the Supreme People's Court on the Work of Judicial Interpretation)', http://news.xinhuanet.com/legal/2007-03/23/content_5885460.htm.

Supreme People's Court of the People's Republic of China 2010a
Supreme People's Court of the People's Republic of China, 'Renmin Fayuan Liangxing Zhidao Yijiang (Opinions on Sentencing Guidance for People's Courts)', http://china.findlaw.cn/lawyers/article/d46240.html.

Supreme People's Court of the People's Republic of China 2010b
Supreme People's Court of the People's Republic of China, 'Zuigao Renmin Fayuan Guanyu Anli Zhidao Gongzuo de Guiding (Provisions of the Supreme People's Court Concerning Work on Guiding Cases)', http://vip.chinalawinfo.com/newlaw2002/slc/slc.asp?db=chl&gid=143870.

Supreme People's Court of the People's Republic of China 2010c
Supreme People's Court of the People's Republic of China, 'Zuigao Renmin Fayuan Guanyu Gaige he Wanshan Renmin Fayuan Shepan Weiyuanhui Zhidu de Shishi Yijian (Opinions of the Supreme People's Court on the Reform and Improvment of the Insitution of Adjudication Committee)', http://www.court.gov.cn/qwfb/sfw j/yj/201003/t20100331_3604.htm.

Supreme People's Court of the People's Republic of China 2013
Supreme People's Court of the People's Republic of China, 'Zuigao Renmin Fayuan Guanyu Renmin Fayuan zai Hulianwang Gongbu Caipan Wenshu de Guiding (Supreme People's Court's Privisions on Online Publication of judgments by People's Courts)', http://www.chinacourt.org/la w/detail/2013/11/id/147242.shtml.

Supreme People's Court of the People's Republic of China 2014

Supreme People's Court of the People's Republic of China, 'Zuigao Renmin Fayuan Gongzuo Baogao (Annual Report of the Supreme People's Court)', http://news.xinhuanet.com/politics/2014-03/17/c_119797489.htm.

Tan & Chen 2014

D. Tan & Y. Chen, 'Guizhou Gaoyuan Sheli Anli Zhidao Gongzuo Zhuanjia Weiyuanhui (Higher People's Court of Guizhou Province Sets Up Case Guidance Expert Committee)', *Renmin Fayuanbao (People's Court Daily),* 2014.

Taruffo 1997

M. Taruffo, 'Institutional Factors Influencing Precedents', in: D.N. MacCormick & R.S. Summers (eds.), *Interpreting Precedents, a Comparative Study,* Dartmouth: Ashgate 1997, p. 437-460.

Taruffo 2007

M. Taruffo, 'Precedents in Italy', in: E. Hondius (ed.), *Precedent and the Law,* Brussels: Bruylant 2007, p. 177-188.

Teixeira de Mattos 1885

A. Teixeira de Mattos, *Handleiding tot het Burgerlijk Wetbook door Mr. A. De Pinto, Tweede gedeelte (Guide to the Civil Code by Master A. de Pinto, Second Part),* Zwolle: W.E.J. Tjeenk Willink 1885.

Telders 1938

B.M. Telders, 'Het B.W. en de rechtsrpaak van 1838 tot heden, in het bizonder de standaardarresten van den Hoogen Raad (Arrest de Reglement) [The Civil Code and the Adjudication from 1838 till Present, in Particular the Standard Cases Decided by the Supreme Court (Arret de Reglement)]', in: P. Scholten & E.M. Meijers (eds.), *Gedenkboek burgerlijk wetboek 1838-1938 (Commemorative Volume Civil Code 1838-1938),* Zwolle: W.E.J. Tjeenk Willink 1938, p. 197-209.

Tjong Tjin Tai 2005

T.F.E. Tjong Tjin Tai, 'Toerekening van kennis en zorgvuldigheidsnorm (Attribution of Knowledge and the Norm of Care)', *Bedrijfsjuridische berichten* 2005, p. Nr. 70.

Tjong Tjin Tai 2011

T.F.E. Tjong Tjin Tai, "The centre cannot hold': aansprakelijkheid voor moderne collectieven ("The Centre Cannot Hold": Liability for Modern Collectives)', *Nederlands tijdschrift voor burgerlijk recht,* 2011.

Tran 2009
T.L. Tran, 'Damages for Non–conforming Goods under Vienna Convention, A Comparison with Vietnamese Law', http://privat.bahnhof.se/wb250067/buongiorno/vietnam/documents/theses/Tran Thuy Linh.doc.
Troper & Grzegorczyk 1997
M. Troper & C. Grzegorczyk, 'Precedent in France', in: D.N. MacCormick & R.S. Summers (eds.), *Interpreting Precedents, a Comparative Study,* Dartmouth: Ashgate 1997, p. 103-140.
Van Apeldoorn 1939
L.J. Van Apeldoorn, *Inleiding tot de studie van het Nederlandsche recht (Introduction to the Study of the Dutch Law),* Zwolle: W.E.J. Tjeenk Willink 1939.
Van Arkel 1994
E.A. Van Arkel, 'Jurisprudentie en uitgever (Case Law and Publishers)', in: J.M. Van Dunné & R.J.P. Kottenhagen (eds.), *Symposium Toegankelijkheid van Rechtspraak (Symposium Accessibility of Court Judgments),* Arnhem: Gouda Quint 1994, p. 81-89.
Van Caenegem 1987
R.C. Van Caenegem, *Judges, Legislators and Professors,* Cambridge: Cambridge University Press 1987.
Van Dam 2010
C.C. Van Dam, 'Aansprakelijkheid voor falend toezicht in tijden van financiële cholera (Liability for Failing Supervision in Times of Financial Cholera)', *Nederlands tijdschrift voor burgerlijk recht* 2010, p. Nr. 30.
Van den Berg 1994
P.G.J. Van den Berg, 'Toegankelijkheid van rechtspraak, Verslag van een symposium te Rotterdam op 14 april 1994 (Accessibility of Judgments, Report on a Symposium in Rotterdam on 14 April 1994)', *Nederlandsch Juristenblad* 1994, p. 960-962.
Van Den Honert 1942
J. Van Den Honert, *Verzameling van arresten van den Hoogen Raad der Nederlanden (Collection of Judgments of the Supreme Court of the Netherlands),* Amsterdam: C.G. Sulpke en Gebroeders Diederichs 1942.
Van der Hoek 2010

F. Van der Hoek, 'Huidige opzet van rechtspraak.nl zo slecht nog niet, Reactie op 'Het best bewaarde geheim van de raadkamer' (Current Set-up of rechtspraak.nl is Not That Bad, Reaction to "The Best Kept Secret of the Judge's Chamber")', *Nederlandsch Juristenblad* 2010, p. 2357.
Van Dunné 1994
J.M. Van Dunné, 'Toegankelijkheid van rechtspraak, Een inleiding (Accessibility of Court Judgments, An Introduction)', in: J.M. Van Dunné & R.J.P. Kottenhagen (eds.), *Symposium Toegankelijkheid van Rechtspraak (Symposium Accessibility of Court Judgments),* Arnhem: Gouda Quint 1994, p. 1-12.
Van Hall 1851
J. Van Hall, *Handleiding tot de beoefening van het burgerlijk regt in Nederland (Guidebook to the Practice of Civil Law in the Netherlands),* Amsterdam: Johannes Muller 1851.
Van Hattum 2012
W.F. Van Hattum, *Non Bis in Idem, De ontwikkeling van een beginsel (Non Bis in Idem, The Development of a Principle),* Nijmegen: Wolf Legal Publishers 2012.
Van Holk 1963
L.E. Van Holk, '50 jaar juridische documentatie (50 Years of Legal Dcumentation)', *Nederlandsch Juristenblad* 1963, p. 641-648.
Van Maanen 2007
G.E. Van Maanen, 'De taak van de rechtswetenschap en de plaats van de Hoge Raad (The Task of the Legal Science and the Place of the Supreme Court)', *Nederlands tijdschrift voor burgerlijk recht* 2007, p. Nr 27.
Van Maanen 2009
G.E. Van Maanen, 'Lindenbaum/Cohen (Lindenbaum vs Cohen)', *Ars Aequi* 2009, p. 778-780.
Van Opijnen 2006a
M. Van Opijnen, 'A Public Index of case Law References - The End of Multiple and Complex Citations', http://ssrn.com/abstract=2046297.
Van Opijnen 2006b
M. Van Opijnen, 'Uitspraken op Rechtspraak.nl, Een representatief beeld? (Cases on Rechtspraak.nl, A Representative Picture?)', *Trema* 2006b, p. 14-22.
Van Opijnen 2011a

M. Van Opijnen, 'Jurisprudentiestatistiek, Over de publicatie, annotatie en citatie van rechterlijke uitspraken (Case Law Statistics, On the Publication, Annotation and Citation of Court Judgments)', *Nederlandsch Juristenblad* 2011a, p. 2142-2150.

Van Opijnen 2011b

M. Van Opijnen, 'Selectie en publicatie van rechterlijke uitspraken in rechtsvergelijkend perspectief (Selection and Publication of Court Judgments from the Perspective of Comparative Law)', *Trema* 2011b, p. 176-183.

Van Opijnen 2014

M. Van Opijnen, *Op en in het web, Hoe de toegangkelijkheid van rechterlijke uitspraken kan worden verbeterd (On and In the Web, How Can the Accessibility to Court Judgments Be Improved),* The Hague: Boom Juridische Uitgevers 2014.

Van Rooij 2004

B. Van Rooij, 'Falu de Weidu, Cong Kongjian Shang Jiedu Falu Shibai (The Dimension of Law, Legal Failure from the Perspective of Spatial Interpretation)', *Sixiang Zhanxian* 2004, p. 109-116.

Van Rooij 2006

B. Van Rooij, *Regulating Land and Pollution in China, Lawmaking, Compliance and Enforcement; Theory and Cases,* Leiden: Leiden University Press 2006.

Van Vleuten & Perk 1839

C.J. Van Vleuten & C.H. Perk, *Het regt in Nederland, Regtsgeleerd tijdschrift (The Law in the Netherlands, Legal Journal),* Amsterdam: S. De Grebber 1839.

Van Vugt 2005

D. Van Vugt, *Rechter en wetgever: partners in the business of law? (Judge and Legislature: Partners in the Business of Law?),* Rotterdam: Rotterdam University 2005.

Veegens 1971

D.J. Veegens, *Cassatie in burgerlijke zaken (Cassation in Civil Cases),* Zwolle: W.E.J. Tjeenk Willink 1971.

Verburg 2009

G.J.M. Verburg, *Vaststelling van smartengeld (Assessing damages for Pain and Suffering),* Deventer: Kluwer 2009.

Verburg 1975

M.P.J. Verburg, 'Stellingen (Propositions)', *Nederlandsch Juristenblad* 1975, p. 507-508.

Vogenauer 2006
S. Vogenauer, 'Sources of Law and Legal Method in Comparative Law', in: M. Reimann & R. Zimmermann (eds.), *The Oxford Handbook of Comparative Law,* Oxford: 2006, p. 870-898.
Voskuil 1980
C.C.A. Voskuil, *Verzameling, ordening en publicatie van rechterlijke uitspraken, Enige aspecten van het administratieve beheer en het toegankelijk maken van rechtspraak bij de rechterlijke colleges (Collecting, Structuring and Publication of Court Judgments, Several Aspects of the Administration of Judgments and the Practice of Making Judgments accesible in Courts),* The Hague: 1980.
Vranken 1988
J.B.M. Vranken, 'Een voorwaardelijk precedentenstelsel in Nederland? (A Conditional Precedent System in the Netherlands?)', *Nederlandsch Juristenblad* 1988, p. 1161-1163.
Vranken 1995
J.B.M. Vranken, *Mr. C. Asser's Handleiding tot de beoefening van het Nederlands burgerlijk recht, Algemeen Deel (Mr. C. Asser's Guidebook to the Exercise of Dutch Civil Law, General Part),* Zwolle: W.E.J. Tjeenk Willink 1995.
Vranken 2000
J.B.M. Vranken, 'Toeval of beleid? Over rechtsvorming door de hoogste rechters (Coincidence or Policy? On the Making of Law by the Highest Judges)', *Nederlandsch Juristenblad* 2000, p. 1-5.
Vranken 2005
J.B.M. Vranken, *Mr. C. Asser's Handleiding tot de beoefening van het Nederlands burgerlijk recht, Algemeen Deel, Een vervolg (Mr. C. Asser's Guidebook to the Exercise of Dutch Civil Law, General Part, A Sequel),* Zwolle: W.E.J. Tjeenk Willink 2005.
Wang 2006
C. Wang, 'Law-making functions of the Chinese courts: Judicial activism in a country of rapid social changes', *Frontiers of Law in China* 2006, p. 524-549.
Wang 2012a
D. Wang, 'Lun Woguo Xueshu Ziyou de Xianfa Jichu (On the Constitutional Foundation of Academic Freedom in China)', *Zhongguo Faxue (China Legal Science)* 2012a, p. 5-23.
Wang & Gong 2013

H. Wang & L. Gong, 'Liuming Faxuejia Luxin Zuigao Fayuan (Six Legal Scholars Receiving New Appointments in Supreme People's Court)', *Guangming Ribao (Guangming Daily),* 2013.
Wang 2004a
L. Wang, 'Lun Zhongguo Panli Zhidu de Chuangjian (On the Creation of China's Case Law System)', in: S. Wu (ed.), *Panli Zhidu Yanjiu (Research on Case Law System),* Beijing: Court Press (Renmin Fayuan Chubanshe) 2004a, p. 549-575.
Wang 2009
L. Wang, 'Yuan Anli Zhidao Zhidu Zhongjie "Tongan bu Tongpan" (May the Case Guidance System Cure the Problem of Like Cases Being Decided Differently)', *Dongfang Zaobao (Dongfang Daily),* 2009.
Wang 2012b
L. Wang, 'Chengwenfa Chuantong Zhong de Chuangxin, Zenme Kan Anli Zhidao Zhidu (Innovation in a Tradition of Codification, How to Understand the Case Guidance System)', http://www.chinacourt.org/article/detail/2012/02/id/473206.shtml.
Wang 2004b
Y. Wang, 'Panli Bijiao Yanjue (Comparative Study on Precedents)', in: S. Wu (ed.), *Panli Zhidu Yanjiu (Research on Case Law Systems),* Beijing: Remin Fayuan Chubanshe (Court Press) 2004b, p. 54-62.
Wang 2005
Z. Wang, 'Case Precedent in Qing China: Rethinking Traditional Case Law', *Columbia Journal of Asian Law* 2005, p. 323-344.
Weatherley 2006
R. Weatherley, *Politics in China since 1949, Legitimizing Authoritarian Rule,* New York: Routledge 2006.
Wegerif 2011
D.N.R. Wegerif, 'Aansprakelijkheid voor een dijkbeheerder (Liability for a Dike Administrator)', *Nederlands tijdschrift voor burgerlijk recht* 2011, p. nr. 34.
Wessels 2006
B. Wessels, 'Toerekening van kennis van een adviseur aan de cliënt, deel I (Attribution of Knowledge of an Advisor to the Client, Part I)', *Weekblad voor Privaatrecht, Notaris-ambt en Registratie* 2006,
Wiarda 1972

G.J. Wiarda, *Drie Typen van rechtsvinding (Three Types of Law-Finding),* Zwolle: Tjeenk Willink 1972.
Wu 2004
S. Wu (ed.), *Panli Zhidu Yanjiu (Research on Case Law Systems),* Beijing: Remin Fayuan Chubanshe (Court Press) 2004.
Wu 2011a
Y. Wu, 'Anli Zhidao Zhidu Neng Zou Duoyuan?(How Far can the Case Guidance System Go?)', *Jiangsu Daxue Xuebao (Jiangsu University Journal)* 2011a, p. 32-37.
Wu 2011b
Y. Wu, 'Jinfang Anli Zhidao Zhidu Keneng de "Pingjing" (Watch Out for the Possible "Bottleneck" of the Case Guidance System)', *Faxue (Legal Science)* 2011b, p. 45-53.
Wu 2010
Z. Wu, 'Shilun Panli Zuowei Minfa Diyitao Zhi Xiguanfa (The Precedent Refers as the Custom of Taiwan's Civil Code Art. 1)', *NTU Law Journal* 2010, p. 227-299.
Xie 2014
E. Xie, 'Goujian Zhongguo de Sifa Panli Zhidu (Constructing China's Judicial Precedent System)', http://paper.people.com.cn/rmlt/html/2014-01/15/contnt_1389767.htm.
Xu 2012
A. Xu, 'Qi Mo Jishou Dalu Faxi Chuantong de Yingxiang (The Reception of the Civil Law Tradition in China at the End of the Qing Dynasty)', http://article.chinalawinfo.com/article_print.asp?articleid=68012.
Xu 2004
C. Xu, 'Ying Jianli You Zhongguo Tese de Panli Zhidu (A Precedent System with Chinese Characteristics Should be Established)', in: S. Wu (ed.), *Panli Zhidu Yanjiu (Research on Case Law Systems),* Beijing: Remin Fayuan Chubanshe (Court Press) 2004, p. 3-5.
Xu 2009
X. Xu, 'Maixiang Sifa Tongyi de Anli Zhidao Zhidu (A Case Guidance System that Marches Towards Uniform Administration of Justice)', *Xuexi yu Tansuo (Study & Exploration)* 2009, p. 157-164.
Yan 2009

Q. Yan, 'Guanyu Jianli Juyou Zhongguo Tese de Anli Zhidao Zhidu de Sikao (Reflections on the Creation of a Case Guidance System with Chinese Characteristics)', in: D. Shen (ed.), *Zhongguo Tese Anli Zhidao Zhidu Yanjiu (A Study of the Case Guidance System with Chinese Characteristics),* Beijing: Renmin Fayuan Chubanshe (Court Press) 2009, p. 139-145.
Yiannopoulos 1974
A.N. Yiannopoulos, 'Jurisprudence and Doctrine as Sources of Law in Louisiana and in France', in: J. Dainow (ed.), *The Role of Judicial Decisioins and Doctrine in Civil Law and in Mixed Jurisdictions,* Baton Rouge: Louisiana State University Press 1974, p. 69-90.
Yuan 2013
D. Yuan, 'Zuigaofa Gongbu Disipi Shiliuge Zhidaoxing Anli, Jiang Chu Shishi Xize Jiejue Shiyong Nan (The Supreme People's Court Releases the Fourth Batch of Guiding Cases and Will Release Implementation Details Document)', http://www.legaldaily.com.cn/xwzx/content/2013-11/14/content_5033403.htm?node=53628.
Yuan 2014
G. Yuan, 'Zhidao Anli: Guize Cuangzhi Zhidu (Guiding Cases: A Norm-Creating Institution)', http://www.pkulawrev.com/?p=841.
Yuan 2009
X. Yuan, 'Woguo Anli Zhidao Zhidu de Shijian Yunzuo ji qi Pingxi, yi Zuigao Renmin Fayuan Gongbao Zhong de Zhishi Chanquan Anli wei Duixiang (Evaluation of the Operation of China's Case Guidance System, a Study of the Intellectual Property Cases Published in the Supreme People's Courts Gazette)', *Fashang Yanjiu (Studies in Business and Law)* 2009, p. 102-109.
Yuan 2012
Y. Yuan, 'Zunxun Xianli yu Anli Zhidao Zhidu de Bijiao Yanjiu (A Comparative Study on Stare Decisis and the Case Guidance System)', http://www.cnki.net.
Zeng 2004
Q. Zeng, 'Duibi Liangda Faxi Kan Woguo Queli Panli Zhidu de Biyaoxing (On the Necessity for China to Establish a Precedent System Based on Comparison with the Two Major Legal Families)', in: S. Wu (ed.), *Panli Zhidu Yanjiu (Research on Case Law Systems),* Beijing: Court Press 2004, p. 63-67.
Zevenbergen 1925

W. Zevenbergen, *Formeele Encyclopaedie der Rechtswetenschap (Formal General Introduction to the Legal Science),* The Hague: Befinfante 1925.
Zhang 2009
D. Zhang, 'Jianli Anli Zhidao Zhidu de Shizheng Baogao (Empirical Report on the Creation of a Case Guidance System)', in: D. Shen (ed.), *Zhongguo Tese Anli Zhidao Zhidu Yanjiu (A Study of the Case Guidance System with Chinese Characteristics),* Beijing: Court Press (Renmin Fayuan Chubanshe) 2009, p. 123-138.
Zhang & Zhu 2007
H. Zhang & M. Zhu, 'Panjue Wenshu Wangshang Gongkai Wenti Yuanjiu (Online Publication of Court Judgments)', *Jinlin Falu Pinglun (Jinlin Law Review)* 2007, p. 66-71.
Zhang 2002a
Q. Zhang, 'Panlifa de Bijiao Yanjiu (A Comparative Study on Case Law)', *Bijiaofa Yanjiu (Comparative Law Research)* 2002a, p. 79-94.
Zhang 2002b
Q. Zhang, '"Panlifa“ Zhiyi (Oppugning "Case Law")', *Bijiaofa Yanjiu (Comparative Law Research)* 2002b, p. 109-113.
Zhang 2004
Q. Zhang, 'Jianli Zhongguo Xianli Zhidu de Yiyi yu Lujing, Jianda "Panlifa" Zhiyi (The Significance and Approach to Establish a Precedent System in China, A Response to Oppugning "Case Law")', *Fazhi yu Shehui Fazhan (Law and Social Development)* 2004, p. 98-114.
Zhang 2008a
T. Zhang, 'Deguo Minshi Panli Zhidu Kaocha, Jianlun Woguo Minshi Panli Zhidu de Jianshe (A Study of Germany's Civil Precedent System, And the Construction of China's Civil Precedent System)', http://www.cnki.net.
Zhang 2011
X. Zhang, 'Yonghao Yonghuo Zhidaoxing Anli, Nuli Shixian Sifa gongzheng, Zuigao Renmin Fayuan Yuanjiushi Fuzeren Jiu Anli Zhidao Zhidu Da Jizhe Wen (Using Guiding Cases Well to Achieve Justice in Adjudication, Chief of the Research Department of the Supreme People’s Court Answers Questions Raised by Reporter)', *Renmin Fayuanbao (People's Court Daily),* 2011.
Zhang 2008b

Z. Zhang, 'Lun Sifa Gaige Zhong de Zhuti Shige Wenti , Yi Xianli Panjue Zhidu Weili (On the Proper Qualifications of the Initiators of Judicial Reforms, Using the Precedent Judgment System as an Example)', *Renmin Fayuan Bao (People's Court Daily),* 2008b.

Zhao 2009

L. Zhao, '"Tongan Tongpan" Shi Yige Shenhua? (Is "Like Cases Being Treated Alike" a Fairy Tale?)', *Nanfang Zhoumo (Southern Weekly),* 2009.

Zhao & Liu 2004

W. Zhao & P. Liu, 'Guanyu jianli Panli Zhidu de jidian Sikao (Several Thoughts on Establishing a Precedent System)', in: *Panli Zhidu Yanjiu (Research on Case Law Systems),* Beijing: Court Press 2004, p. 533-539.

Zhong 1989

J. Zhong, 'Putongfa Zunxun Xianli Yuanze de Xingcheng yu Fazhan (The Forming and Development of Stare Decisis in Common Law)', *Bijiaofa Yanjiu (Comparative Law Research)* 1989, p. 30-34.

Zhou 2011

B. Zhou, 'Sanwei Dafaguan Changtan Zhongguo Tese Anli Zhidao Zhidu (Three Senior Judges Discussing the Case Guidance System with Chinese Characteristics)', *Fazhi Ribao (Legal Daily),* 2011.

Zhou 2004

D. Zhou, 'Zhongguo Anli Zhidu de Lishi yu Fazhan (History and Evolution of China's Case System)', *Journal of Law Application* 2004, p. 2-8.

Zhou 2009

W. Zhou, 'Tongguo Anli Jieshi Falu: Zuigao Renmin Fayuan Anli Zhidao Zhidu de Fazhan (Interpretation of Law through Cases: Development of the Case Guiding System of the Supreme People's Court)', *Dangdai Faxue (Contemporary Law Review)* 2009, p. 139-146.

Zhu 2008

J. Zhu, 'Goujian Anli Zhidao Zhidu de Jige Juti Wenti, Jiyu Xiaoli Dingwei de Shijiao (Several Concrete Issues on the Creation of the Case Guidance System, from the Perspective of the Effect of Guiding Cases)', *Fazhi Yanjiu (Study of the Rule of Law)* 2008, p. 35-39.

Zhu 2010

X. Zhu, 'Woguo Buying Yinru Zunxun Xianli Yuanze (Stare Decisis should not be introduced into the Chinese Legal System)', http://www.hicourt.gov.cn/theory/artilce_list.asp?id=5558&l_class=3.

Zonderland 1974

P. Zonderland, *Methode van het privaatrecht (Method of the Private Law),* Amsterdam: Agon Elsevier 1974.

Zong 2009

Y. Zong, 'Cong "Linshixing Qiangjian" Kan Panjueshu Shuoli ("Temporary Rape" and Legal Reasoning in Court Judgments)', *Jiancha Ribao (Procuratorial Daily),* 2009.

Zuo 2004

T. Zuo, 'Shilun Panli Zai Woguo Falu Yuanyuan Zhongde Diwei (On the Status of Cases as a Source of Law in China)', in: S. Wu (ed.), *Panli Zhidu Yanjiu (Research on Case Law Systems),* Beijing: Remin Fayuan Chubanshe (Court Press) 2004, p. 98-100.

Zweigert & Kötz 1998

K. Zweigert & H. Kötz, *Introduction to Comparative Law,* Oxford: Clarendon Press 1998.

For Product Safety Concerns and Information please contact our EU representative GPSR@taylorandfrancis.com
Taylor & Francis Verlag GmbH, Kaufingerstraße 24, 80331 München, Germany

www.ingramcontent.com/pod-product-compliance
Ingram Content Group UK Ltd.
Pitfield, Milton Keynes, MK11 3LW, UK
UKHW020022200926
475702UK00014B/2010

* 9 7 8 9 0 5 6 2 9 7 5 9 6 *